Monographs in Theoretical Computer Science
An EATCS Series

T0224162

For further volumes:
http://www.springer.com/series/776

Ferdinando Cicalese

Fault-Tolerant Search Algorithms

Reliable Computation with Unreliable Information

Ferdinando Cicalese
Dipartimento di Informatica
Università degli Studi di Salerno
Fisciano
Italy

Series Editors

Monika Henzinger
University of Vienna
Vienna, Austria

Juraj Hromkovič
ETH Zentrum
Swiss Federal Institute of Technology
Zürich, Switzerland

Mogens Nielsen
Aarhus University
Aarhus, Denmark

Grzegorz Rozenberg
Leiden Institute of Advanced
  Computer Science
University of Leiden
Leiden, The Netherlands

Arto Salomaa
Turku Centre of Computer Science
Turku, Finland

ISSN 1431-2654
ISBN 978-3-662-51871-7   ISBN 978-3-642-17327-1 (eBook)
DOI 10.1007/978-3-642-17327-1
Springer Heidelberg New York Dordrecht London

To Zsuzsa, Réka, and Noémi

Preface

The wisest of the wise may err.

Aeschylus, Fragments

The study of the effect that errors may have on computation started at the very beginning of the history of computer science. It dates back to the early 1950s, to the research by von Neumann[1] and Moore-Shannon[2] on the design of reliable Boolean networks built with low-reliability components. Since then the study of fault-tolerant computing has evolved into a broad discipline, one that encompasses all aspects of reliable computer design: from the identification of failure dynamics in integrated circuits to the design of robust software.

The design of reliable computers is much harder than the design of other complex human-made objects. Citing the IEEE Spectrum,[3]

> [...] Information-processing errors can occur through a failure lasting a billionth of a second in one of the hundreds of thousands of digital components that switch billions of times a day.

In fact, it seems rather hopeless to attain high reliability in computer design by the so-called fault-avoidance techniques, that is, by only relying upon high-quality thoroughly tested components. Owing to the intrinsic complexity of modern computers, it is more sensible to focus on software robustness for the detection and/or correction of errors which will invariably occur as information is being stored, transferred, and manipulated. This is typically achieved by introducing some redundancy (in the information) to improve the reliability of the computational systems, as already suggested in the seminal papers by von Neumann and Moore-Shannon.

---

[1] *Automata Studies*, Princeton University Press (1956).

[2] J. Franklin Inst. (1956).

[3] *IEEE Spectrum*. Oct. 81, p. 41.

One more reason to prefer fault-tolerance to fault-avoidance techniques is given by the error statistics in the electronic systems. Typically, failure occurrence in electronic components follows the so-called *bathtub* curve. This means that a large failure rate is more likely for a short initial period known as the burn-in period. After this, components may experience a small failure rate for the rest of their operational life. Therefore a small probability of component failure exists during the useful life. It seems natural to look at error-correcting and error-detecting coding techniques as the most promising means to provide low-cost error control in computation.

The original scope of the theory of error-correcting codes was the design of reliable communication systems. It is clear that the problem of reliable computation differs significantly from the problem of reliable communication: for example, communication error-control schemes usually assume perfectly reliable computing and processing at the transmitter and receiver ends. They put fewer severe restraints on computation time for error correction and obey different statistics for error occurrence than ruling computer systems. Nevertheless, the fundamental principles of communication coding theory also are essential to the understanding and design of error control for reliable computation. Winograd and Cowan[4] pointed out that (subject to some assumptions) Shannon's noisy-channel coding theorem may be extended to include noisy computation. Thus, computation of logical functions in the presence of unreliable modules may be thought of as analogous to communication over a noisy channel of a certain capacity.

In this book we shall be mainly concerned with fault tolerance in the context of algorithmic search theory. Problems of search, with their wide applicability, allow us to show fault-tolerant techniques as they apply to many different contexts. Moreover, search theory is one of the classical fields in the science of the computation.

As with fault-tolerant techniques, the necessity of efficient search procedures arose very early in computer science. One can say that the theory of searching starts with the first computers.

In the early 1950s, while the first fault-tolerant techniques were being devised, the new availability of larger and larger random-access memories eventually led to the recognition that *searching* was an interesting problem in its own right. All of a sudden memory space was not anymore a problem of scarcity but rather because of the lack of efficient techniques for making the best use of it. Almost instantaneously, *searching* became a flourishing field of research. The first surveys on search problems had already been published in 1956.[5]

Since these pioneering works, searching has been a very active field of investigation. As a matter of fact, search procedures can constitute the most time-consuming parts of software, and the substitution of a good search method for a bad one then brings a substantial improvement. The entire third volume of Donald Knuth's celebrated series *The Art of Computer Programming* is focused on search and

---

[4] *Reliable Computation in the Presence of Noise* (1963).
[5] See [29, 96, 170].

sorting algorithms. In the introduction of this volume, Knuth makes the following claim:

> Indeed, I believe that virtually every important aspect of programming arises somewhere in the context of sorting and searching.

Whether every scientific problem can be reduced to a search problem may be a matter of philosophical debate. Nonetheless, it is undeniable that many problems of practical importance can be reduced to searching.

The structure of a typical search problem appears more often than one would expect, in surprisingly diverse scenarios. A search problem can be the task of: (1) identifying objects within a set via a series of tests (identification); (2) learning the structure of a given function via sampling (learning); (3) determining the most concise way of representing a given piece of information so that recovery is uniquely achievable (encoding); (4) distinguishing patterns on the basis of exact or approximate examples (classification). Depending on the application at hand, any one of the above may be the most appropriate or convenient problem formulation. However, a unified perspective has the advantage that it allows for cross-fertilization of ideas and methodologies.

Our motivation for studying fault-tolerant computation in the context of search is twofold: From a more analytical point of view, there exists a large class of combinatorial problems of practical importance which can be studied in a unified way under the common concept of *search*. Moreover, from a more application-oriented perspective, *search problems* in their many different facets lie at the heart of managing large data sets, one of today's major IT challenges. Current computer applications handle data sets that are not only larger than ever before but also include highly complex objects. To tame the data deluge, it is crucial to develop the capacity for appropriately organizing, storing, and, most importantly, *searching* through such a mass of data.

In our excursus on fault-tolerant search algorithms, we shall see that many methodologies originally thought of and developed in the context of search problems were proved useful, in some cases even rediscovered, in areas that might appear far from searching. To disclose such connections and bridge these gaps among connected fields of research will be another aim of this book.

The book is self-contained and assumes no special knowledge beyond a standard undergraduate background in basic algorithmics, complexity, combinatorics, and probability theory. All necessary concepts are introduced and all the results are proved before they are used, even when one could assume them known. There are a very limited number of exceptions, where we decided to either omit a detailed involved proof or delay its presentation with respect to its use, because we preferred to focus on the broad picture without risking to distract the reader from the main train of thoughts. Even in these cases, all necessary pointers are always provided. The bibliographic notes refer the reader to appropriate sources of information for closing any gap of knowledge necessary for a complete understanding of the proof.

Each chapter is concluded by a set of exercises of varying difficulty. In general, these exercises are meant to present problems which should allow the reader to deepen his/her understanding of the material covered in a chapter. Some of these exercises are variants, extensions, or particular cases of proofs or algorithms presented in the text. Some exercises are also used to cover important complementary results which should have been but eventually were not included due to logistic constraints.

At the end of each chapter a brief historical account of some fundamental publications has been included, describing the origins of the main results. The bibliography at the end of the book includes most of the key articles in the field and references to other books and survey papers on the subject.

Salerno/Verona, Italy   Ferdinando Cicalese
September 2012

Acknowledgments

The core of this monograph is a revised and extended version of part of my doctoral thesis, submitted at the University of Salerno and written under the supervision of Daniele Mundici and Ugo Vaccaro. First and foremost I ought to thank Daniele and Ugo, who taught me how to look for answers without preventing me from questioning them. After them I also learnt how to enjoy science seriously. Most of the material contained in the following pages is the result of hours of pleasant discussions with them.

I would like to thank Martin Aigner, Gyula Katona, and Andrzej Pelc for their useful suggestions and comments, which also helped to improve some of the results I obtained in the field of combinatorial search and which are now chapters of this book.

I thank the Alexander von Humboldt Foundation for having supported my research in Germany from 2004 to 2009. I spent those years at AG Genominformatik at Bielefeld University, where I found a wonderful research environment. It is there that the seeds of this book were first planted. Thanks to all members of my group on combinatorial search for bioinformatics: Christian Heup, José Quitzau, Julia Mixtaki, Martin Milanič, Michael Kaltenbach, Travis Gagie, Qin Xin, Zsuzsanna Lipták.

During the years spent at Bielefeld University, I also had the fortune of collaborating with Rudolf Ahlswede. It is sad for me that Rudi will not be able to see this book. A special thanks goes to him: wherever he is, no combinatorial search should exist without Rudi's challenging questions.

Many parts of the material of the book appeared in publications coauthored with Rudolf Ahlswede, Peter Damaschke, Christian Deppe, Luisa Gargano, Daniele Mundici, and Ugo Vaccaro, whom I thank once more. The chapter on group testing is partially based on the work done with José Quitzau which also appeared in preliminary form in his Ph.D. thesis.

Mentioning all those who have accompanied me on this adventure with search and fault-tolerance would require more than a chapter of this book. No fault-tolerant tool would prevent me from forgetting some important names.

I want to thank my little daughters Réka and Noémi. They might and should not realize how much this book owes to them—including delaying its writing—and how important their questions are, notwithstanding my faulty answers.

Thanks to Zsuzsa, who makes all possible!

Contents

Chapter 1
Prologue: What This Book Is About

For hateful in my eyes, even as the gates of Hades
is that man that hideth one thing in his mind and sayeth another.

Homer, Iliad IX. 312 313

The typical structure of a search problem is defined by a set of objects $\mathcal{U}$, a family of tests $\mathcal{T}$ which can be used to acquire information on the elements of $\mathcal{U}$; a set of rules $\mathcal{R}$ about the way the tests can be chosen or combined; and some performance measure $\mathcal{M}$. The goal is to provide a strategy to select tests from $\mathcal{T}$ according to the given rules $\mathcal{R}$, in order to guarantee the correct identification of some initially unknown object in $\mathcal{U}$, and optimize the given performance measure (e.g., worst case or average number of queries, time or space complexity, etc.).

According to the application at hand, such a model can also represent the process of learning the structure of a given function via sampling; or determining the most concise way of representing a given piece of information; or classifying patterns on the basis of exact or approximate examples.

This book considers search problems in which tests can be erroneous and/or provide only partially the information expected from performing them. The book is divided into two parts. In the first part, we introduce the basic concepts and techniques and show their applications for several variants of the basic model. In the second part we will deal with more involved models and more advanced topics.

1.1 Part I: The Basic Model

We shall start by looking at one paradigmatic model for fault-tolerant search: the so-called Ulam-Rényi problem. This can be summarized as follows. How many questions do we need in order to determine an unknown element x taken from a finite set $\mathcal{U}$ by only asking subset questions when up to a finite number of answers

F. Cicalese, *Fault-Tolerant Search Algorithms*, Monographs in Theoretical Computer Science. An EATCS Series, DOI 10.1007/978-3-642-17327-1_1,
© Springer-Verlag Berlin Heidelberg 2013

can be lies, i.e., untrue. By a subset question we mean one like: does x belong to the set A (for some $A \subseteq \mathcal{U}$)?

Most of the first part of this book will be devoted to analyzing variants of this simple model, which will allow us to describe the fundamental combinatorial and algorithmic issues in the design of fault-tolerant search procedures.

The Ulam-Rényi problem models a situation of processing and sending information that can be altered by some kind of "noise". The Questioner's aim is to find the most efficient way of recovering information in spite of possible distortions. One may assume that messages/data get altered with a given (small) probability. Such a probabilistic setting was studied by Rényi. If the probability of error is very small, one may alternatively model the situation assuming that there exists a fixed value e, such that no more than e errors will occur during the entire transmission/computation. This justifies interest in the version of the game with a fixed bound on the number of errors.

Non-interactive fault-tolerant search strategies assuming at most e errors are equivalent to e-error correcting codes. Therefore, optimal Questioner's strategies in this version of the game yield the shortest e-error correcting block codes. Finding such codes is considered to be the main problem of coding theory. We shall discuss more deeply this correspondence between error-correcting encoding and searching with unreliable tests in Chap. 3.

In fact, independently of Ulam and Rényi, Berlekamp had considered the problem of evaluating the size of a shortest, though successful, fault-tolerant search strategy in the context of block coding for the binary symmetric channel with noiseless, delayless feedback.

A complete treatment of the research field of fault-tolerant search, even if restricted to the Ulam-Rényi model, would be beyond the scope of a single book, due to the vast literature and the wealth of different variations of the basic model depicted above. Nevertheless, in the first part of this book, we shall do our best to cover all the basic material on this topic, with particular focus on those results that cross boundaries of different fields of computer science.

1.1.1 Adaptive vs. Non-adaptive Search

Probably among the first issues to consider when dealing with a search problem is the one of adaptiveness. In the classical formulation of the Ulam-Rényi game, one assumes that the search is carried out in a fully adaptive manner, i.e., the ith question is asked knowing the answer to the previous $(i - 1)$ questions. However, in many practical situations it is desirable to have search strategies with a small degree of adaptiveness, that is, search strategies in which all the questions (or at least many of them) can be prepared in advance, and asked at once. This is the case, for example, when Questioner and Responder are to communicate over a slow channel. Also, in medical applications, where preparation of the tests usually means rearrangement of the laboratory, it is preferred to have search strategies using at most two stages of tests, and hence using adaptiveness only once. Complete elimination of the adaptiveness, that is, a fully non-adaptive search strategy, turns out to be a main issue in coding theory and in many cases has proved impossible.

In fact, non-adaptive *perfect*[1] codes have been the Holy Grail of 30 years of research on error-correcting codes. Since the discovery of Hamming codes and subsequently of the Golay codes, the question about the existence and the construction of perfect codes for an arbitrary number of possible errors has been a leading one in combinatorial coding theory. Unfortunately, a breakthrough has eventually come from the non-existence theorems of Tietäväinen[2] and Zinoviev-Leontiev,[3] to the effect that, with the only exception of the Golay codes, no perfect non-adaptive search strategy can exist when the number of allowed lies is greater than 1.

Two decades later, a celebrated result of Spencer proved that perfect strategies are in fact asymptotically attainable for every fixed number of possible errors but at the expense of the maximum degree of adaptiveness. Under the hypothesis of full adaptiveness and for a small number of errors, algorithmic perfect search strategies have been provided for arbitrary large search spaces. The actual amount of interaction necessary to keep the search perfect is not known yet.

We shall consider "the curse of adaptiveness" in Chap. 3. We shall describe several cases in which the full adaptiveness is not a necessary feature of perfect search strategies when the number of errors is big and the searcher cannot exploit symmetries of the model. In some cases it will be possible to show that *the least possible amount of adaptiveness is enough to allow the strategy to be perfect, whatever the number of allowed errors.*

1.1.2 Q-ary Search with Lies

A natural generalization of the Ulam-Rényi game is obtained by allowing questions with q-many possible answers. Non-binary search with lies arises, for instance, in the particular framework of finding a defective coin with unreliable weighting. This problem is equivalent to a ternary search with additional constraints.

In Chap. 5, we shall consider the problem of fault-tolerant search under different variants on the type of questions allowed, e.g., bit queries, alphabetic search, interval search, and multi-interval search. We shall then discuss the trade-off between the optimal strategy size and the complexity of query description, which is a critical issue when one is finally happy with the combinatorics and tries to implement it in algorithms.

---

[1] This concept will be precisely formalized later.
[2] SIAM J. Appl. Math. 24 (1973).
[3] Probl. Contr. Inform. Theory 2 (1973).

1.1.3   Half-Lies, Erasures and Other Types of Errors

Most of the error-correcting coding techniques are developed under the assumption of symmetric errors. The errors in magnetic tapes and some of the random access memories can be considered as symmetric errors. This means that, assuming a binary representation of the information, the corruption of a 0 into a 1 and of a 1 into a 0 are both possible. On the other hand, the failures in the memory cells of some of the LSI single-transistor cell memories and metal-nitride-oxide semiconductor (MNOS) memories are most likely caused by leakage of charge. Therefore, if the presence of charge in a cell is represented by 1 and the absence of charge by 0, the errors in these types of memories can be modeled as $(1 \mapsto 0)$-type asymmetric errors. This is because the charge cannot be created except by a rewrite process; hence $(0 \mapsto 1)$-type errors in the memory cells are almost impossible.

Another typical case where the assumption of asymmetry on the types of possible errors is preferable to the classical assumption of symmetrical errors is in optical communication systems, where photons may fail to be detected $(1 \rightarrow 0)$, but the creation of spurious photons $(0 \rightarrow 1)$ is impossible.

In Chap. 4 we shall analyze how these different types of error models change the combinatorics and complexity of the Ulam-Rényi problem.

1.1.4   Heuristics

A complete solution of a given search problem, i.e., the determination of the optimal solution for all instances, can have a very complex description. In the context of our Ulam-Rényi model, an example is given by the formulations of the exact, best possible (minimum-length) strategies given by Pelc, Guzicki, and Deppe for an arbitrary size of the search space, and for one, two and three lies, respectively. These results do not seem to give hope for a closed-form formula describing this length in the general case. This is due to the necessity to list all the particular cases or classes of particular cases.

Such a situation has left space for research aiming at constructing efficient algorithms which are based on some easy-to-describe heuristics, and whose performance can be proved to be close to that of the optimal algorithm.

We shall describe some heuristic-based algorithms to solve problems of searching in the presence of errors, while trying to highlight the main ideas and techniques.

1.2   Part II: More Models and Applications

In the second part of the book we shall broaden our perspective and part from the basic model given by the Ulam-Rényi game. We shall look at different abstractions of unreliability.

1.2.1 Erasure Errors, Delays and Time-outs

In Chap. 6 we analyze the case of the so-called erasure-errors. Here, an error is no longer understood as a mendacious answer, but rather, as a lost or refused answer.

The erasure of an answer may also be thought of as the effect of (software or hardware) devices whose task is to clear spurious bits from the communication channel that the Questioner and the Responder are using to exchange information. Altogether, we assume the existence of a *time-out* parameter d, which represents the maximum time the Receiver (the Questioner) is to wait before the sent bit (an answer) reaches him. After the deadline of d time units has expired, an undelivered bit is automatically destroyed (as a *time-out* bit) in order to prevent desynchronization of the communication channel.

We will present a general correspondence between the problem of finding the fastest broadcasting protocol over a point-to-point network and the problem of devising the shortest search strategy in a finite set by using only comparison questions.

1.2.2 Group Testing

In Chap. 7, we shall switch to the more general search paradigm, known as group testing, where more than one element has to be identified in the search space, and a question is answered positively if at least one of the elements searched for is indicated in the query. We shall be mainly concerned with variants of group testing in the context of computational biology applications. In this framework, we shall analyze the effect of errors together with limitations on the test structure. We shall also touch upon the notion of inhibitory errors, i.e., errors due to the presence in the search space of elements which prevent a test from disclosing information about the items searched for.

1.2.3 Memory Faults and Resilient Search

In Chap. 8, we shall discuss the effect of random memory faults on search algorithms. In contrast with the case of the Ulam-Rényi game, here repeating the same question does not help since repeatedly probing a corrupted location keeps on resulting in a wrong value. We shall study the maximum number of memory faults that can be tolerated by an algorithm which reports the correct answer without significantly diverging in terms of performance with respect to the optimal algorithm in the absence of faults.

1.2.4   A Model of Learning

Finally, in Chap. 9 we shall discuss the interplay between fault-tolerant search and a model of computational learning. Starting with a classical result of Rényi, we will look at learning in a noisy environment as a search problem. We shall show how prediction with expert advice can be recast in a "gambling" variant of the Ulam-Rényi game and provide an optimal solution for both problems. In the reverse direction, from learning to search, we shall show how a Bayesian learning approach can be used to find optimal solutions in the search model proposed by Rényi.

1.3   Bibliographic Notes

The first comprehensive surveys of search theory can be considered [184] and [174]. For a recent and more combinatorial-oriented account, see also [6] and [4].

Besides the papers by von Neumann [207], Moore-Shannon [149, 150] and Winograd [210], cited in the Preface, more results in the field of fault-tolerant circuits can be found in [179].

The problem of searching in the presence of errors seems to appear for the first time in a paper of Rényi [183] published in 1961, where the authors describes the following game: "Two players are playing the game, let us call them A and B. A thinks of something and B must guess it. B can ask questions which can be answered by *yes* or *no* and he must find out what A had thought from the answers. [. . .] it is better to suppose that a given percentage of the answers are wrong (because A misunderstands the questions or does not know certain facts)". Here the model seems to assume random errors, while in later publications, e.g., [182], Rényi himself reformulated the problem, speaking of a fixed number of lies. In 1969 the game of the 20 Questions with lies, later introduced by Ulam, was implicitly used by Berlekamp [22] to study error-correcting codes for the symmetric channel with feedback. After these seminal papers, to the best of our knowledge the first paper presenting results for the Ulam-Rényi problem is due to Rivest et al. [185]. A survey of the literature in the area is [160].

Problems of searching with lies had been also studied by Yaglom and Yaglom [213], who considered the following one: Determine which city, among A, B, C, you are in by asking yes/no questions to the people around. The only available information you have is that inhabitants of A always speak the truth; inhabitants of B always lie, and inhabitants of C alternate between one lie and one correct answer (but the nature of the first answer is not known). The same problem is also analyzed by Picard [174].

Part I
The Ulam-Rényi Game and Its Variants

Chapter 2
Fault-Tolerant Search à la Ulam-Rényi

Are you sitting comfortably? Then I'll begin.

J. S. Lang, Listen with Mother

2.1 Introduction

The problem of efficient search for an unknown element in a finite set S can be reformulated as a game between two players—one deciding the questions to be asked, and the other deciding the answering strategy that makes as hard as possible the first player's task.

In his autobiography *Adventures of a Mathematician,*[1] Stanisław Ulam raised the following question:

> Someone thinks of a number between one and one million (which is just less than 2^{20}). Another person is allowed to ask up to twenty questions, to each of which the first person is supposed to answer only yes or no. Obviously the number can be guessed by asking first: Is the number in the first half-million? and then again reduce the reservoir of numbers in the next question by one-half, and so on. Finally the number is obtained in less than $\log_2(1,000,000)$. Now suppose one were allowed to lie once or twice, then how many questions would one need to get the right answer? One clearly needs more than n questions for guessing one of the 2^n objects because one does not know when the lie was told. This problem is not solved in general.

The very same problem was also considered by Alfréd Rényi in his half-fictitious book *A Diary on Information Theory*[2]

> ...I made up the following version, which I called "Bar-kochba with lies". Assume that the number of questions which can be asked to figure out the "something" being thought of is fixed and the one who answers is allowed to lie a certain number of times. The questioner,

---

[1]p. 281, Scribner's, New York (1976).

[2]Gondolat, Budapest (1976).

F. Cicalese, *Fault-Tolerant Search Algorithms*, Monographs in Theoretical Computer Science. An EATCS Series, DOI 10.1007/978-3-642-17327-1_2,
© Springer-Verlag Berlin Heidelberg 2013

of course, doesn't know which answer is true and which is not. Moreover the one answering is not required to lie as many times as is allowed.

For example, when only two things can be thought of and only one lie is allowed, then 3 questions are needed ... If there are four things to choose from and one lie is allowed, then five questions are needed. If two or more lies are allowed, then the calculation of the minimum number of questions is quite complicated ... It does seem to be a very profound problem ...

In the model depicted by Ulam and Rényi, which we shall call the Ulam-Rényi problem, it is also assumed that the player who gives the answers is not fully reliable, or, more pictorially speaking, she is a liar.

Following a consolidated tradition in the area, we shall call the two players Paul (the Questioner) and Carole (the Responder).[3] Our basic problem of fault-tolerant search is then formulated as follows.

2.1.1   The Binary Ulam-Rényi Game

Carole and Paul fix a finite set $S = \{0, 1, \ldots, M - 1\}$, called the *search space*, and an integer $e \geq 0$; Carole chooses a number x in S and Paul must guess x by asking questions of the form "does x belong to T?" where T is an arbitrary subset of S. Carole's only possible answers are *yes* or *no*. Then what is the minimum number $N(M, e)$ of questions that Paul has to ask in order to infallibly determine the number x, assuming that Carole can lie at most e times?

For the case $e = 0$, classical binary search yields $N(M, 0) = \lceil \log_2 M \rceil$, the smallest integer not smaller than $\log_2 M$. When lies are allowed to Carole, the situation is slightly more complicated. Suppose Paul's first question is T. In the classical case $e = 0$, if Carole's answer is "*yes*" (resp. "*no*"), Paul will discard all of $S \setminus T$ (resp. T) and reduce his search space from S to T (resp. $S \setminus T$). In contrast, if $e > 0$, then Paul's strategy must be more flexible. In particular, a number can be discarded by Paul if and only if it falsifies more than e of Carole's answers. All the numbers which are not consistent with e or less of Carole's answers are still possible solutions, because Carole could have chosen one of them and decided to lie as much as the rule of the game allows her.

Thus, when $e > 0$ and Paul's question is T, Carole's answer has the following effect on Paul's *state of knowledge*, i.e., on Paul's subsequent assumptions on the set of possible solutions.

- Carole's answer is "*yes*". Then Paul's search shall continue not only over those elements of the set T which falsify up to e answers, but also over those elements in the complementary set $S \setminus T$ which happened to falsify up to $e - 1$ answers

---

[3]See notes at the end of this chapter for some explanation about these names.

before the last question T was asked (since now they still falsify up to e of the answers so far).

- Carole's answer is "*no*". Then the search shall continue over those elements of the set $S \setminus T$ which falsify up to e answers, as well as over those elements of T which falsified up to $e - 1$ answers before the last question was asked (and now falsify up to e of the given answers).

It is clear that for any number $x \in S$, Paul has to take note of the number of Carole's answers falsified by x, until x happens to falsify more than e answers, and Paul can safely assume that it is not Carole's secret number.

Assume t questions have been answered. For each $j = 0, \ldots, e$, let L_j^t denote the set of elements of S falsifying exactly j answers. Thus, before the first question is asked, we can write $L_0^0 = \{0, 1, \ldots, M - 1\}$, $L_1^0 = \cdots = L_e^0 = \emptyset$. Let T denote the $(t+1)$th question. Suppose the answer is "*yes*" (resp., "*no*"). Then we can write for each $j = 1, \ldots, e$,

$$
\begin{cases}
L_0^{t+1} = L_0^t \cap T & \text{(resp., } L_0^t \setminus T\text{);} \\
L_j^{t+1} = (L_j^t \cap T) \cup (L_{j-1}^t \setminus T) & \text{(resp., } (L_j^t \setminus T) \cup (L_{j-1}^t \cap T)\text{).}
\end{cases}
\tag{2.1}
$$

At any stage t of the game, we say that $(L_0^t, L_1^t, \ldots, L_e^t)$ is Paul's *state* (of knowledge). Let $x_i = |L_i^t|$ for each $i = 0, 1, \ldots, e$. Then the state $\sigma = (L_0^t, L_1^t, \ldots, L_e^t)$ is said to be of *type* $(x_0, x_1, \ldots, x_e)$.

We shall be mainly concerned with the problem of minimizing the *number* of questions rather than explicitly formulating these questions as subsets of S.[4] Then, we can focus on the cardinalities x_i rather than on the sets L_i^t, and by abusing terminology, we call *state* also the $(e + 1)$-tuple of integers $(x_0, \ldots, x_e)$.

Definition 2.1. A *final state* is a state $(x_0, x_1, \ldots, x_e)$ such that $\sum_{j=0}^{e} x_j \leq 1$.

Final states correspond to ending game conditions. Indeed, $\sum_{j=0}^{e} x_j = 1$ means that only one number in S is consistent with Carole's answers (but for at most e lies), so it must be the secret number. On the other hand, the condition $\sum_{j=0}^{e} x_j = 0$ means that no number in S is consistent with Carole's answers, even when assuming that up to e of these answers are lies. In other words, this means that Carole has not been following the rule of the game[5] and now Paul can realize it, so the game ends.

In the setting where sets are replaced by their cardinalities, a *question* T is completely specified once we know the number t_j of elements in L_j^t quoted by T. Thus a question T shall be denoted by $[t_0, \ldots, t_e]$, where $t_j = |T \cap L_j^t|$.

Suppose that Paul's state is $(x_0, \ldots, x_e)$, and the question $\delta = [a_0, \ldots, a_e]$ is asked. If Carole's answer is "yes" (resp., "no"), then the resulting state $(x_0', \ldots, x_e')$ is given by

---

[4]We shall consider later this issue and the problem it raises in terms of the complexity of representing the strategies.

[5]More precisely, either she did not choose any number and answered randomly in order to fool Paul, or she chose a number but she lied more than e times.

$$\begin{cases} x'_0 = a_0 & (\text{resp., } x'_0 = x_0 - a_0) \\ x'_j = a_j + (x_{j-1} - a_{j-1}) \text{ (resp., } x'_j = x_j - a_j + a_{j-1}) \ j = 1, \ldots, e. \end{cases} \quad (2.2)$$

Given a state $\sigma = (x_0, \ldots, x_e)$ and a question δ, the two possible answers to δ determine two more informative states σ^{yes} and σ^{no}. Paul will then adaptively ask the next question and, depending on Carole's answers, he will be left in one of the four possible states $\sigma^{yes,yes}, \sigma^{yes,no}, \sigma^{no,yes}, \sigma^{no,no}$. Proceeding inductively, Paul can build a labelled binary tree $\mathcal{T}$, rooted at σ, as follows: Any node v is mapped to a question T_v. The two edges stemming from v are labelled *yes* and *no* (the possible answers given by Carole). The nodes which these edges are incident to are labelled by the states resulting from the corresponding answer of Carole to T_v. We say that $\mathcal{T}$ is Paul's *strategy*. We say that the state σ has a *winning strategy of size t* if there exists a binary tree $\mathcal{T}$ of height t, rooted at σ, whose leaves are final states.

Definition 2.2. A *winning n-state* is a state $\sigma = (x_0, x_1, \ldots, x_e)$ such that there exists a winning strategy of size n for it. We say that $(x_0, x_1, \ldots, x_e)$ is a *borderline winning n-state* if it is a winning n-state but not a winning $(n-1)$-state.

Definition 2.3. Let $\sigma = (x_0, \ldots, x_e)$ be a state such that x_i is even for each $i = 0, \ldots, e$. Then, the question $\delta = [\frac{x_0}{2}, \frac{x_1}{2}, \ldots, \frac{x_e}{2}]$ is called an *even splitting question* for σ.

If σ has also odd components, by abuse of terminology, the $(e + 1)$-tuple of rationals, $\delta = [\frac{x_0}{2}, \frac{x_1}{2}, \ldots, \frac{x_e}{2}]$, shall be called a *pseudo* even splitting question. Note that in this case the two n-tuples of rationals resulting from Carole's answer to δ via (2.2) need no longer be states, because their components may be non-integral. However, the dynamic laws given by (2.2) can still be applied without problems.

Definition 2.4. Let $\sigma = (x_0, \ldots, x_e)$ and $\sigma' = (y_0, \ldots, y_e)$ be two states such that $\sum_{j=0}^{k} x_j \geq \sum_{j=0}^{k} y_j$ holds for each $k = 0, \ldots, e$. Then, we say that σ' is a *substate* of σ, and we write $\sigma' \preceq \sigma$.

2.2   The Volume Bound

The following theorem provides a lower bound on the size of winning strategies.

Theorem 2.1 (Volume Bound). *If $\sigma = (\hat{x}_0, \hat{x}_1, \ldots, \hat{x}_e)$ is a winning n-state then*

$$\sum_{i=0}^{e} \hat{x}_i \sum_{j=0}^{e-i} \binom{n}{j} \leq 2^n.$$

Proof. By hypothesis there exists a strategy $\mathcal{T}$ of size n rooted in σ whose leaves are states $(x'_0, \ldots, x'_e)$ with $\sum_{j=0}^{e} x'_j \leq 1$. Let us relax for the moment the requirement that states be n-tuples of integers. Replacing all questions in $\mathcal{T}$

by *pseudo* even splitting questions, and formally applying the dynamical rules (2.2), we will still get a tree rooted in σ, of height equal to n, whose leaves are vectors $(y'_0, \ldots, y'_e)$ (possibly with rational, non-integral components) and such that $\sum_{j=0}^{q} y'_j \leq 1$. A simple inductive argument works based on the fact that for any state and any question the sum of the components of one of the resulting states is not smaller than the sum of the components of the resulting state when the question asked is an even splitting.

Thus, the question to be asked in state $(x_0, \ldots, x_e)$ will be given by $[\frac{x_0}{2}, \ldots, \frac{x_e}{2}]$.

Let us use the notation $a = \frac{1}{2}$. By repeated application of (2.2), the ith component $x_i^{(j)}$ of the vector $(x_0^{(j)}, \ldots, x_e^{(j)})$ obtained from $(\hat{x}_0, \hat{x}_1, \ldots, \hat{x}_e)$ after j questions is given by

$$\begin{cases} x_0^{(j)} = ax_0^{(j-1)}, & x_0^{(0)} = \hat{x}_0 \\ x_i^{(j)} = ax_i^{(j-1)} + (1-a)x_{i-1}^{(j-1)}, & x_i^{(0)} = \hat{x}_i \quad 1 \leq i \leq e. \end{cases} \tag{2.3}$$

All vectors $(x_0^{(n)}, \ldots, x_e^{(n)})$ obtained after n *pseudo* even splitting questions have the following property:

$$\sum_{i=0}^{e} x_i^{(n)} \leq 1. \tag{2.4}$$

For all $i = 0, \ldots, e$, let $F_i(t) = \sum_{j \geq 0} x_i^{(j)} t^j$ denote the *generating function* of the sequence $x_i^{(0)}, x_i^{(1)}, x_i^{(2)}, \ldots$. Stated otherwise, $F_i(t) = \sum_{j \geq 0} x_i^{(j)} t^j$. From (2.3) we get:

$$F_0(t) = at F_0(t) + \hat{x}_0$$
$$F_i(t) = at F_i(t) + (1-a)t F_{i-1}(t) + \hat{x}_i \qquad 1 \leq i \leq e,$$

or equivalently,

$$F_0(t) = \frac{\hat{x}_0}{1 - at}$$
$$F_i(t) = (1-at)^{-1} ((1-a)t F_{i-1}(t) + \hat{x}_i) \qquad 1 \leq i \leq e.$$

It follows that

$$F_i(t) = \sum_{j=0}^{i} (1-a)^j \frac{t^j \hat{x}_{i-j}}{(1-at)^{j+1}} = \sum_{j=0}^{i} \sum_{n \geq 0} \binom{n}{j} (1-a)^j a^{n-j} \hat{x}_{i-j} t^n \tag{2.5}$$

for all $0 \leq i \leq e$. Condition (2.4) now becomes

$$[t^n] \left(\sum_{i=0}^{e} F_i(t) \right) \leq 1, \tag{2.6}$$

where $[t^n] f(t)$ denotes the coefficient of the nth power of t in the power series expansion of $f(t)$. Recalling that $a = \frac{1}{2}$, from (2.5) we see that inequality (2.6) can be reformulated as

$$\sum_{i=0}^{e} \sum_{j=0}^{i} \binom{n}{j} \hat{x}_{i-j} \leq 2^n.$$

To complete the proof it is sufficient to write

$$\sum_{i=0}^{e} \sum_{j=0}^{i} \binom{n}{j} \hat{x}_{i-j} = \sum_{i=0}^{e} \hat{x}_i \sum_{j=0}^{e-i} \binom{n}{j}.$$

The above theorem motivates the following definition.

Definition 2.5. The *nth volume*, $V_n(x_0, \ldots, x_e)$, of a state $(x_0, \ldots, x_e)$ is defined by

$$V_n(x_0, x_1, \ldots, x_e) = \sum_{i=0}^{e} x_i \sum_{j=0}^{e-i} \binom{n}{j}.$$

The nth volume of a state $\sigma = (x_0, \ldots, x_e) = (|L_0|, \ldots, |L_e|)$ counts the number of answering strategies available to Carole when the state of the game is σ and n questions are still to be asked.

One can conveniently allow Carole to use a malicious answering strategy. Thus, for instance, x need not be chosen once and for all at the beginning of the game, but can be suitably changed—provided that the new choice comply with the number e of allowed lies—so as to make Paul's task as hard as possible.

For each one of the x_i many elements of L_i, Carole can still lie up to $e - i$ times. If she decides to lie precisely j times ($j = 0, \ldots, e - i$), she can still choose where to lie, in $\binom{n}{j}$ ways. One then easily sees that, given the state $(x_0, \ldots, x_e)$, the overall number of ways for Carole to answer coincides with $V_n(x_0, \ldots, x_e)$.

Intuitively, the Volume Bound says that a winning strategy of Paul's must be large enough to accommodate the number of possible answering strategies of Carole's. It does not restrict the structure of such a winning strategy.

Trivially, if a state $\sigma = (x_0, x_1, \ldots, x_e)$ fails to satisfy the condition

$$V_n(x_0, x_1, \ldots, x_e) \leq 2^n, \tag{2.7}$$

then as an immediate consequence of Theorem 2.1, σ cannot be a winning n-state. Instead of saying that a state σ satisfies condition (2.7) we shall henceforth say that σ *satisfies the Volume Bound for n questions.*

Definition 2.6. The *character* of a state $\sigma = (x_0, \ldots, x_e)$ is the smallest integer n such that σ satisfies the Volume Bound for n questions; in symbols,

$$\mathrm{ch}(x_0, x_1, \ldots, x_e) = \min\{n \mid V_n(x_0, x_1, \ldots, x_e) \le 2^n\}.$$

A strategy $\mathscr{S}$ of size q for a state σ is said to be *perfect* if $\mathscr{S}$ is winning for σ and $q = \mathrm{ch}(\sigma)$.

A perfect strategy $\mathscr{S}$ which uses the least possible number of questions, as given by the Volume Bound, is an *optimal* winning strategy, in the sense that it cannot be superseded by a shorter winning strategy. On the other hand, we will see several non-perfect optimal winning strategies.

For all integers $M \ge 0$ and $e \ge 0$, let us define

$$N_{\min}(M, e) = \min \left\{ n \mid M \sum_{j=0}^{e} \binom{n}{j} \le 2^n \right\}. \tag{2.8}$$

Then by Theorem 2.1 we immediately have the following lower bound on the size of the shortest winning strategy for the Ulam-Rényi game with e lies over a search space of cardinality M :

$$N(M, e) \ge N_{\min}(M, e).$$

Lemma 2.1. *Let σ and σ' be two states, with σ a substate of σ'. Then the following conditions hold:*

(a) *for all integers $i \ge 0$, $V_i(\sigma) \le V_i(\sigma')$;*
(b) $\mathrm{ch}(\sigma) \le \mathrm{ch}(\sigma')$;
(c) *if σ' is a winning k-state then so is σ.*

Proof. Conditions (a) and (b) are immediate consequences of the definitions.

Condition (c) follows from a simple restriction of the winning strategy for σ' to the state σ. In order to simplify the proof we resort to thinking of states as vectors of subsets of the search space. Modulo some renaming of the elements, we can assume that the two states $\sigma = (L_0, \ldots, L_e)$ and $\sigma' = (L'_0, \ldots, L'_e)$ satisfy $\bigcup_{j=0}^{k} L_j \subseteq \bigcup_{j=0}^{k} L'_j$ for each $k = 0, \ldots, e$. Then, the winning strategy of size k for σ' is also a winning strategy of size k for σ. In fact, in the dynamics induced by a sequence of questions and answers an element x moves rightward through the components of the state σ at the same pace as it does in σ'. Therefore, if as a result of a sequence of questions and answers σ' is emptied of all but at most one element, so is σ.

The proof of the following *conservation law* amounts to a straightforward verification:

Theorem 2.2. *For any state* $\sigma = (x_0, \ldots, x_e)$ *and question* δ, *let us denote by* σ^{yes} *and* σ^{no} *the two states resulting from* σ *after Carole's answer to* δ. *Then for all integers* $n \geq 0$ *we have*

$$V_{n-1}(\sigma^{yes}) + V_{n-1}(\sigma^{no}) = V_n(\sigma).$$

Corollary 2.1. *Suppose* $\sigma' = (y_0, \ldots, y_e)$ *is the state resulting from* $\sigma = (x_0, \ldots, x_e)$ *after an even splitting question. It follows that*

(a) *If* σ *satisfies the Volume Bound for n questions, then* σ' *satisfies the Volume Bound for* $n - 1$ *questions.*
(b) $\mathrm{ch}(\sigma') = \mathrm{ch}(\sigma) - 1$.

Proof. From Theorem 2.2 we get $2V_{n-1}(y_0, \ldots, y_e) = V_n(x_0, \ldots, x_e)$. By hypothesis, $V_n(x_0, \ldots, x_e) \leq q^n$, whence $V_{n-1}(y_0, \ldots, y_e) = \frac{1}{2}V_n(x_0, \ldots, x_e) \leq 2^{n-1}$, which settles (a). Condition (b) immediately follows from (a), by definition of character.

For later purposes we record the following easy result.

Lemma 2.2. *Let* $\sigma = (A_0, A_1, \ldots, A_e)$, *with* $\bigcup_{j=0}^{e} A_j = \{x, y\}$. *Let* i, j *be such that* $x \in A_i$ *and* $y \in A_j$. *Then* σ *is a borderline winning* $(2e - (i + j) + 1)$-*state.*

Proof. Let T be the question "Is x_{Carole} equal to x?". Let Paul ask $2e - (i + j) + 1$ times the question T. According to whether Carole gives $e - j + 1$ positive answers or $e - i + 1$ negative answers, Paul can safely conclude that the secret number is x or y respectively. For otherwise, Carole has lied more than she was allowed to.

We now prove that, conversely, $2e - (i + j) + 1$ questions are necessary for Paul to always find the secret number. Indeed, we have

$$V_{2e-i-j}(\sigma) = \sum_{k=0}^{e-i} \binom{2e-i-j}{k} + \sum_{k=0}^{e-j} \binom{2e-i-j}{k}$$

$$= \sum_{k=0}^{e-i} \binom{2e-i-j}{k} + \sum_{k=e-i}^{2e-i-j} \binom{2e-i-j}{k}$$

$$= \sum_{k=0}^{2e-i-j} \binom{2e-i-j}{k} + \binom{2e-i-j}{e-i} > 2^{2e-i-j}.$$

Then the desired result is a direct consequence of Theorem 2.1.

The following theorem yields a lower bound on the size of the smallest winning strategy in a game with $e + 1$ lies, given the size of the smallest winning strategy in a game with e lies.

Theorem 2.3 (Translation Bound). *Let* $\sigma = (x_0, \ldots, x_{e-1}, x_e)$ *with* $\sum_{j=0}^{e} x_j \geq 3$. *If* σ *is a winning m-state and* $\tau = (0, x_0, \ldots, x_{e-1})$ *is a borderline winning n-state* $(n > 0)$, *then* $m \geq n + 3$.

Proof. The proof is by induction on n.

Induction Base. τ is a winning 1-state. The only possibility is $\tau = (0, 0, \ldots, 0, 2)$. Thus $\sigma = (0, 0, \ldots, 0, 2, x_e)$, with $x_e \geq 1$. Therefore, $V_3(\sigma) = x_e + 8 \geq 2^3$ for all $x_e \geq 1$, and by Theorem 2.1 σ cannot be a winning 3-state. This settles the case $n = 1$.

Induction Hypothesis. If σ is a winning m'-state and τ is a borderline winning ℓ-state for some $1 \leq \ell \leq n - 1$, then $i \geq \ell + 3$.

Induction Step. Let τ be a borderline n-state with $n > 1$. Suppose (*absurdum hypothesis*) that there exists a winning strategy of size $n + 2$ for σ. Let $\delta = [a_0, a_1, \ldots, a_e]$ be the first question in such a strategy. Define the question $\delta' = (0, a_0, \ldots, a_{e-1})$.

Denote by $\sigma^{yes} = (x_0^{yes}, \ldots, x_e^{yes})$ and $\sigma^{no} = (x_0^{no}, \ldots, x_e^{no})$ the two possible states resulting from Carole's answer to the question δ when Paul's state of knowledge is σ. Similarly, denote by τ^{yes} and τ^{no}, the two possible states resulting from Carole's answer to the question δ' when Paul's state of knowledge is τ. It is not hard to verify that $\tau^{yes} = (0, x_0^{yes}, \ldots, x_{e-1}^{yes})$ and $\tau^{no} = (0, x_0^{no}, \ldots, x_{e-1}^{no})$.

By hypothesis, both σ^{yes} and σ^{no} are winning $(n + 1)$-states.

Suppose that $\sum_{j=0}^{e} x_j^{yes} \geq 3$ and $\sum_{j=0}^{e} x_j^{no} \geq 3$. Then, by induction hypothesis, τ^{yes} and τ^{no} are winning $(n-2)$-states, contradicting the hypothesis that no winning strategy of size $n - 1$ exists for τ.

Conversely, suppose that $\sum_{j=0}^{e} x_j^{yes} \leq 2$. Thus, by hypothesis, we have $\sum_{j=0}^{e} x_j \geq 3$. Moreover, either $\sum_{j=0}^{e-1} x_j^{yes} \geq 2$ or $\sum_{j=0}^{e-1} x_j^{no} \geq 2$, for otherwise τ^{yes} and τ^{no} are final states contradicting the hypothesis that τ is not a winning 1-state.

Therefore, we get $\sum_{j=0}^{e} x_j^{no} \geq 3$, which, in turn, implies that $\sigma^{yes} = (0, \ldots, 1, 0, \ldots, 1)$, i.e., τ^{yes} is a final state. Again, by induction hypothesis, τ^{no} is a winning $(n-2)$-state and we reach the contradiction that τ is a winning $(n-1)$-state.

The proof is complete. $\qquad\blacksquare$

2.3 Borderline States Satisfying the Volume Bound with Equality

From the previous sections we know that the states satisfying the volume bound with equality are in some sense maximal with respect to the property of being possibly winning. Such states are somehow the most difficult ones. We also know that a substate of a state σ can be solved by using the winning strategy for σ. Suppose now that we have a list of borderline states of "full" volume for which we know the perfect winning strategy. If our list is complete, in the sense that every state that is

Table 2.1 States exactly attaining the volume bound

$\sigma_{i,j}$	$s_{.,1}$	$s_{.,2}$	$s_{.,3}$	$s_{.,4}$	$s_{.,5}$	$s_{.,6}$	$s_{.,7}$	$s_{.,8}$
$\sigma_{1,\cdot}$	$\overset{2}{4}$	$\overset{5}{8}$	$\overset{8}{36}$	$\overset{11}{152}$	$\overset{14}{644}$	$\overset{17}{2728}$	$\overset{20}{11556}$	$\cdots$
$\sigma_{2,\cdot}$	$\overset{1}{2}$	$\overset{4}{6}$	$\overset{7}{22}$	$\overset{10}{94}$	$\overset{13}{398}$	$\overset{16}{1686}$	$\overset{19}{7142}$	$\cdots$
$\sigma_{3,\cdot}$	$\overset{0}{1}$	$\overset{3}{4}$	$\overset{6}{14}$	$\overset{9}{58}$	$\overset{12}{246}$	$\overset{15}{1042}$	$\overset{18}{4414}$	$\cdots$
$\sigma_{4,\cdot}$	$\overset{0}{1}$	$\overset{2}{1}$	$\overset{5}{10}$	$\overset{8}{36}$	$\overset{11}{152}$	$\overset{14}{644}$	$\overset{17}{2728}$	$\cdots$
$\sigma_{5,\cdot}$	$\overset{0}{1}$	$\overset{0}{0}$	$\overset{4}{5}$	$\overset{7}{24}$	$\overset{10}{94}$	$\overset{13}{398}$	$\overset{16}{1686}$	$\cdots$
$\vdots$	$\vdots$	$\vdots$	$\vdots$	$\vdots$	$\vdots$	$\vdots$	$\vdots$	$\ddots$

not listed is a substate of one in the list with the same character, then we are done. Our list basically provides us with all the strategies we need for solving an arbitrary instance of the Ulam-Rényi problem.

While the existence of such a "universal" list might be hard to believe, the above idea can be constructively followed to accommodate several interesting and non-finite cases. In particular, we shall show its implementation in the proof of Theorem 2.4.

For any number of lies, Table 2.1 displays an infinite sequence of states admitting a *perfect* winning strategy. Moreover, any such state σ is *maximal*, in the sense that $V_n(\sigma) = 2^n$, where $n = \text{ch}(\sigma)$.

Let $s_{i,j}$ be the (i, j) entry of Table 2.1, occurring in row i and column j. Let $\sigma_{i,j}$ denote the state $(s_{i,1}, s_{i,2}, \ldots, s_{i,j})$. Thus $\sigma_{i,j}$ is a state in the game with $j - 1$ lies. To signify that $\sigma_{i,j}$ is a winning n-state we place the integer n above the entry $s_{i,m}$ in the table.

Table 2.1 is constructed as follows: First of all, $s_{i,1} = 1$ and $s_{i,2} = 0$ for all $i = 5, 6, \ldots$. For each $i = 1, 2, 3, 4, \ldots$, the value $s_{i,1}$ is the largest possible cardinality n of a search space where Paul can successfully search by using $\lceil \log_2 n \rceil$ questions in the game with no lies. The values of $s_{i,2}$ are chosen so as to ensure that the state $(s_{i,1}, s_{i,2})$ is a winning n-state, with $n = \text{ch}(s_{i,1}, s_{i,2})$, and there exists a question δ reducing $\sigma_{i,2}$ to $\sigma_{i+1,2}$ for all $i = 1, 2, 3, 4, \ldots$.

The remaining columns of Table 2.1 ($j \geq 3$) are given by the following recurrence:

$$\begin{cases} \text{for } i \geq 3, \ s_{i,j} = s_{i-1,j-1} + s_{i-2,j-1} \\ \text{for } i = 2, \ s_{2,j} = s_{3,j} + s_{1,j-1} \\ \text{for } i = 1, \ s_{1,j} = s_{2,j} + s_{3,j}. \end{cases} \tag{2.9}$$

Lemma 2.3. *With reference to Table 2.1 we have:*

(a) *For each $i = 1, 2$ and for all $j = 1, 2, \ldots$, there exists a question δ for the state $\sigma_{i,j}$ such that the two states resulting from $\sigma_{i,j}$ coincide with $\sigma_{i+1,j}$.*

(b) *For all $i \geq 3$ and $j = 1, 2, \ldots$, there exists a question δ for the state $\sigma_{i,j}$ such that the two resulting states coincide with $\sigma_{i+1,j}$ and $\sigma_{i-2,j-1}$, respectively.*

(c) *For each $j = 1, 2, \ldots$, and $i \leq 2j$, the state $\sigma_{i,j}$ is a borderline winning $(3j - i)$-state.*

(d) *For all $i = 1, 2, \ldots$, and $j \geq i$, with the exceptions of $s_{1,1}$, $s_{1,2}$, and $s_{2,2}$, the integer $s_{i,j}$ coincides with*

$$\left\lfloor 2(2 + \sqrt{5})^j \left(\frac{\sqrt{5} - 1}{2} \right)^{i+2} + \frac{1}{2} \right\rfloor.$$

(e) *For all $i = 1, 2, \ldots$, and all integers $j \geq \max\{3, i\}$, the state $\sigma_{i,j}$ satisfies the recurrence law*

$$s_{ij} = \left\lfloor s_{i,j-1} (2 + \sqrt{5}) + \frac{1}{2} \right\rfloor.$$

Proof. (d) and (e) are easily proved by using standard techniques for solving recurrences. We now focus on the proof of (a), (b), and (c).

(a) Let $\sigma = \sigma_{i,j}$ and δ be an even splitting question, i.e., $\delta = [s_{i,1}/2, s_{i,2}/2, \ldots, s_{i,j}/2]$. Let σ^{yes} and σ^{no} be the two resulting states. We shall prove that $\sigma^{yes} = \sigma^{no} = \sigma_{i+1,j}$.

Let $\sigma^{yes} = \sigma^{no} = (r_1, \ldots, r_j)$. By definition of $s_{i,k}$, we get

$$r_k = s_{i,k}/2 + s_{i,k-1}/2 = \begin{cases} s_{2,k}/2 + s_{3,k}/2 + s_{2,k}/2 - s_{3,k}/2 = s_{2,k} & i = 1, \\ s_{3,k}/2 + s_{1,k-1}/2 + s_{3,k}/2 - s_{1,k-1}/2 = s_{3,k} & i = 2. \end{cases}$$

(b) Let $\sigma = \sigma_{i,j}$. Let $\delta = [r_1, \ldots, r_j]$, be defined by

$$r_k = \begin{cases} 0 & \text{for } k = 1, \\ s_{i-2,k-1} - s_{i,k-1} + r_{k-1} & \text{for } k = 2, \ldots, j. \end{cases}$$

Let $\sigma^{yes} = (u_0, u_1, \ldots, u_{j-1})$ and $\sigma^{no} = (z_1, z_2, \ldots, z_j)$. Thus, recalling (2.2), we have $u_0 = 0$, and for $k = 1, 2, \ldots, j - 1$ it holds that $u_k = r_{k+1} + s_{i,k} - r_k = s_{i-2,k} - s_{i,k} + r_k + s_{i,k} - r_k = s_{i-2,k}$ Hence $\sigma^{yes} = (0, s_{i-2,1}, s_{i-2,2}, \ldots, s_{i-2,j-1}) = \sigma_{i-2,j-1}.$[6]

On the other hand, we have $z_1 = s_{i,1} - r_1 = 1 = s_{i+1,1}$, and for $k = 2, 3, \ldots, j$ it holds that $z_k = s_{i,k} - r_k + r_{k-1} = s_{i,k} - s_{i-2,k-1} + s_{i,k-1} - r_{k-1} + r_{k-1} = s_{i-1,k-1} + s_{i,k-1} = s_{i+1,k}$. Hence $\sigma^{no} = \sigma_{i+1,j}$, as desired.

(c) By induction on j. The claim is easily true for $j = 1, 2$. Let $j \geq 3$ and $i \leq 2j$. Then by (a) and (b) there exists a question such that the two resulting states are either both equal to $\sigma_{i+1,j}$, or are respectively $\sigma^{yes} = \sigma_{i-2,j-1}$ and $\sigma^{no} =$

---

[6]Note that any state $(s_0, s_1, \ldots, s_j)$ in the game with j lies is the same as the state $(0, s_0, s_1, \ldots, s_j)$ in the game with $j + 1$ lies.

Table 2.2 Other states exactly attaining the volume bound

$\tau_{i,j}$	$u_{.,1}$	$u_{.,2}$	$u_{.,3}$	$u_{.,4}$	$u_{.,5}$	$u_{.,6}$
$\tau_{1,.}$	$\overset{3}{8}$	$\overset{7}{64}$	$\overset{11}{744}$	$\overset{15}{8512}$	$\overset{19}{97416}$	$\ldots$
$\tau_{2,.}$	$\overset{2}{4}$	$\overset{6}{36}$	$\overset{10}{404}$	$\overset{14}{4628}$	$\overset{18}{52964}$	$\ldots$
$\tau_{3,.}$	$\overset{1}{2}$	$\overset{5}{20}$	$\overset{9}{220}$	$\overset{13}{2516}$	$\overset{17}{28796}$	$\ldots$
$\tau_{4,.}$	$\overset{0}{1}$	$\overset{4}{11}$	$\overset{8}{120}$	$\overset{12}{1368}$	$\overset{16}{15656}$	$\ldots$
$\tau_{5,.}$	$\overset{0}{1}$	$\overset{3}{4}$	$\overset{7}{67}$	$\overset{11}{744}$	$\overset{15}{8512}$	$\ldots$
$\tau_{6,.}$	$\overset{0}{1}$	$\overset{2}{1}$	$\overset{6}{35}$	$\overset{10}{407}$	$\overset{14}{4628}$	$\ldots$
$\tau_{7,.}$	$\overset{0}{1}$	$\overset{0}{0}$	$\overset{5}{16}$	$\overset{9}{222}$	$\overset{13}{2519}$	$\ldots$
$\vdots$	$\vdots$	$\vdots$	$\vdots$	$\vdots$	$\vdots$	$\vdots$	$\ddots$

$\sigma_{i+1,j}$. Suppose that $\sigma^{yes} = \sigma^{no} = \sigma_{i+1,j}$; hence, a fortiori, $i \le 2$. Then we have the desired result by induction, since by hypothesis $j \ge 3$; hence $i - 1 \le 2j$. Indeed, $\sigma_{i-1,j}$ is a winning $(3j - i - 1)$-state and a fortiori we have the desired result for $\sigma_{i,j}$.

Conversely, let $\sigma^{yes} = \sigma_{i-2,j-1}$ and $\sigma^{no} = \sigma_{i+1,j}$. Again, the desired result will follow from both σ^{yes} and σ^{no} being winning $(3j - i - 1)$-states.

Indeed, σ^{yes} is a winning $(3j - i - 1)$-state by induction. On the other hand, if $i + 1 \le 2j$ then again an inductive argument shows that σ^{no} is a winning $(3j - i - 1)$-state. Finally, if $i + 1 \ge 2j + 1$, then σ^{no} is a final state; hence it is also a winning $(3j - i - 1)$-state. The proof is complete.

As a matter of fact, Table 2.1 is a special case of the following more general construction. Let $t = 3, 4, 5, \ldots$, and for all positive integers i and j define recursively the quantity $a_{i,j}$ as follows:

$$a_{i,1} = 2^{\max\{t-i,0\}}, \tag{2.10}$$

$$a_{i,2} = \max\{0, 2^{2t-i} - 2^{\max\{t-1,0\}}(2t - i + 1)\}, \tag{2.11}$$

$$a_{i,j} = \begin{cases} \sum_{k=i+1}^{t} a_{k,j} + \sum_{k=1}^{i} -1 a_{k,j-1} & i = 1, 2, \ldots, t - 1 \\ \sum_{k=1}^{t-1} a_{i-k,j-1} & i \ge t. \end{cases} \quad \text{for } j \ge 3. \tag{2.12}$$

The interesting property is that any state $\alpha_{i,j} = (a_{i,1}, \ldots, a_{i,j})$ is a winning $(tj - i)$-state, with $ch(\alpha_{i,j}) = tj - i$, and $V_{(tj-i)}(\alpha_{i,j}) = 2^{(tj-i)}$. In other words, any state in the table has a perfect winning strategy and is *maximal* in the previously defined terms.

Another useful characteristic of such a table is that the increase in the number of necessary and sufficient questions when translating from the state $\alpha_{i,j}$ to $\alpha_{i,j+1}$ is equal to t.

Table 2.1 is the one obtained in the particular case $t = 3$. For later, we also precisely list the table obtained in the case $t = 4$, which coincides with Table 2.2.

2.4 The Solution of the 20 Question Game with Lies

We shall now use the original instance of the problem given by Ulam ($M = 2^{20}$) to show how the tables introduced in the previous section can help analyzing Paul's strategies and constructing optimal once. Recall that $N(M, e)$ denotes the size of the shortest winning strategy for the Ulam-Rényi game over a search space of cardinality M when up to e answers may be mendacious. We shall prove the following.

Theorem 2.4. *The values of* $N(2^{20}, e)$ *are given by the following table:*

e	0	1	2	3	4	5	6	7	8	9	...	e	...
$N(2^{20}, e)$	20	25	29	33	37	40	43	46	50	53	...	$3e + 26$	...

For all $e \geq 8$, *we have* $N(2^{20}, e) = 3e + 26$.

Proof. Starting from the initial state $\sigma_e^{(0)} = (2^{20}, \underbrace{0, \ldots, 0}_{e \text{ zeros}})$, and asking 20 even splitting questions, Paul will be in a sequence of states $\sigma_e^{(1)}, \ldots, \sigma_e^{(20)}$, where

$$\sigma_e^{(i)} = \left(2^{20-i}, i\,2^{20-i}, \binom{i}{2}2^{20-i}, \ldots, \binom{i}{j}2^{20-i}, \ldots, \binom{i}{e}2^{20-i}\right)$$

for each $i = 1, \ldots, 20$. In particular, after these initial 20 questions are answered, and independently of Carole's answers, Paul's state is given by

$$\chi_e = \left(1, 20, \binom{20}{2}, \ldots, \binom{20}{j}, \ldots, \binom{20}{e}\right). \tag{2.13}$$

Clearly, there exists no even splitting question for Paul in such a state. As we shall see, all he has to do is to reduce the state (2.13) to a substate of some state in Table 2.1.

We shall argue by cases:

Case 1. $e \geq 8$.

Then, by direct inspection, $\text{ch}(\sigma_8^{(0)}) = 50$. By the Translation Bound and Corollary 2.1, for all $e \geq 8$ no winning strategy exists for χ_e using $< 6 + 3e$ questions. Thus we have only to prove that a winning strategy of size $6 + 3e$ exists.

We now use *quasi* even splitting questions in the next six questions. For any state $\sigma = (x_0, x_1, \ldots, x_e)$ the question $\delta = [\lceil \frac{x_0}{2} \rceil, \lceil \frac{x_1}{2} \rceil, \ldots, \lceil \frac{x_e}{2} \rceil]$ is said to be quasi-even splitting. A quasi-even splitting corresponds to an even splitting in the particular case when all the components of the state σ are even.

As a result, the 64 states obtained after these six quasi-even splitting questions will be substates of

$$\sigma^{\sharp} = (1, 1, 5, 41, 233, 1028, 3597, 10278, 24411, 48821, \ldots).$$

Let us display the winning $3e$-state $\sigma_{3,e+1}$ in Table 2.1 as follows:

$$\sigma_{3,e+1} = (1, 4, 14, 58, 246, 1042, 4414, 18698, \ldots).$$

In light of Lemma 2.1, it is sufficient to prove that $\sigma^{\sharp}$ is a substate of $\sigma_{3,e+1}$ for all $e \geq 8$. For $e = 8$ the claim follows by direct inspection. Proceeding by induction, and letting a_i be the ith component of $\sigma^{\sharp}$, we have $a_i \leq s_{3,i}$ for all $i = 1, 2, \ldots, 9$. It is not hard to see that for all $i \geq 10$,

$$a_i < \left\lfloor a_{i-1}(2 + \sqrt{5}) + \frac{1}{2} \right\rfloor.$$

Since each component of $\sigma^{\sharp}$ grows at a smaller rate than its corresponding component in $\sigma_{3,e+1}$, we conclude that

$$a_i < \left\lfloor a_{i-1}(2 + \sqrt{5}) + \frac{1}{2} \right\rfloor \leq \left\lfloor s_{i-1}(2 + \sqrt{5}) + \frac{1}{2} \right\rfloor = s_i,$$

thus settling the present case.

Case 2. $e \leq 7$.

The cases $e = 1, e = 2, e = 3$ and $e = 4$ are settled arguing as for Case 1 in the light of Table 2.2. More precisely, it is easily checked that for each $e = 1, 2, 3, 4$, the state χ_e is a substate of $\tau_{3,e+1}$ in Table 2.2, which is a winning $(4e + 1)$-state. Thus we immediately have the desired result that $\sigma_e^{(0)}$ is a winning $(4e + 21)$-state. The cases $e = 5, 6, 7$ will be settled using ad hoc strategies, based on ideas described in Sect. 2.6.

The proof is complete.

Remark. Ulam's instance $M = 10^6$ can now be settled without much effort. In the exceptional case $e = 4$, we have $\mathrm{ch}(10^6, 0, 0, 0, 0) = 36$ and $\mathrm{ch}(2^{20}, 0, 0, 0, 0) = 37$. As a matter of fact, there exists a *perfect* strategy for the state $(10^6, 0, 0, 0, 0)$, whence $N(10^6, 4) = 36$. For the remaining values of e one has $N(10^6, e) = N(2^{20}, e)$, because $\mathrm{ch}(10^6, 0, \ldots, 0) = \mathrm{ch}(2^{20}, 0, \ldots, 0)$ and by Lemma 2.1 any winning strategy for $(2^{20}, 0, \ldots, 0)$ trivially yields a winning strategy for $(10^6, 0, \ldots, 0)$.

2.5 Asymptotics for the Ulam-Rényi Problem

In the previous section we presented a family of searching strategies for the original Ulam instance. The common idea underlying these strategies is summarized in the following steps:

1. Use even splitting questions for the first 20 questions.
2. Use quasi-even splitting questions until the resulting state of knowledge σ is a substate of some $\alpha_{i,j}$ and $\text{ch}(\alpha_{i,j}) = \text{ch}(\sigma)$.
3. According to Lemma 2.1, transform the perfect strategy for $\alpha_{i,j}$ into a perfect strategy for σ.

The basic ingredient is a question that splits the volume of the current state as evenly as possible. Indeed, this is exactly what happens, when even splitting questions are used. Moreover, the possibility to define questions which exactly split the volume is one of the main features of the states $\alpha_{i,j}$ in Tables 2.1 and 2.2.

It is natural to wonder whether such a strategy exists for all possible states. Unfortunately, this is not the case. Consider, for example, the state $\sigma = (5, 0)$. We have $\text{ch}(\sigma) = 5$, and $V_5(\sigma) = 30 \leq 2^5$. The question that best splits the volume of σ is $[2, 0]$ (or, equivalently the symmetric question $[3, 0]$). Now if Carole answers "*no*", the resulting state is $\sigma^{no} = (3, 2)$, and we have $V_2(\sigma^{no}) = 17 > 2^4$, so it is no longer possible to finish the search within four more questions. We conclude that five questions, although necessary, are not sufficient to guess an unknown number in a set of cardinality 5 when one of the answers is a lie.

Unlike the cases considered in the previous section, quasi-even splitting questions are not always effective. So it is generally a hard task to find the best question for a given state. Equivalently, no general rule exists to determine the length of the shortest searching strategy for arbitrary cardinality of the search space and number of lies.

Nonetheless, for any fixed number of lies, e, we can provide asymptotic conditions on the states of knowledge which allow a perfect winning strategy.

Theorem 2.5. *There exist constants K_e and Q_e (depending on e) having the following property: for all integers $n \geq Q_e$, if a state $(x_0, \ldots, x_e)$ satisfies $V_n(x_0, \ldots, x_e) \leq 2^n$ and $x_e \geq K_e n^e$, then the state is n-winning.*

Proof (Sketch). [7] Let $\sigma = (x_0, x_1, \ldots, x_e)$, with $\text{ch}(\sigma) = n$. For $i = 0, 1, \ldots, e - 1$, let a_i be chosen as $\lfloor \frac{x_i}{2} \rfloor$ or $\lceil \frac{x_i}{2} \rceil$ on an alternate basis. Then define a_e as the integer minimizing the quantity $\Delta = (2a_e - x_e) + \sum_{j=0}^{e-1}(x_i - 2a_i)\binom{n-1}{e-j}$. Let $\delta_\sigma = [a_0, a_1, \ldots, a_e]$.

The standing hypothesis on x_e guarantees the possibility of balanced volume splitting. In fact, because of the large number of elements whose weight in the volume is 1, Paul can use them to cope with the possible

---

[7]In Chap. 4, we provide a stronger result, of which this is a special case.

unbalance due to the use of quasi-even splitting. Thus, Paul can effectively[8] make use of the above rule in defining his questions until the resulting state is of the form $\sigma' = (0, \ldots, 0, 1, 0, \ldots, 0, x_e)$. This is a substate of $(0, \ldots, 0, 1, 0, \ldots, 0, 2^{\mathrm{ch}(\sigma')} - \sum_{j=0}^{e} \binom{\mathrm{ch}(\sigma')}{j})$, which is evenly splitted by the question of type $\delta' = [0, \ldots, 0, 1, 0, \ldots, 0, 2^{\mathrm{ch}(\sigma')-1} - \sum_{j=0}^{e} \binom{\mathrm{ch}(\sigma')-1}{j}]$.

By recursively applying questions of type δ', Paul *perfectly* gets through to the end.

This theorem has an immediate consequence on the existence of perfect strategies for specific instances of the game: Let us fix two integers $e, m \geq 0$. Let S be a search space of cardinality $M = 2^m$. Then, up to finitely many exceptional m's, there exists a *perfect* winning strategy for Paul. Stated differently, Paul can win the game over S with e lies using n questions, with n being the smallest integer satisfying the Volume Bound. Trivially, no such winning strategy can use less than n questions.

In fact, for all sufficiently large m, starting from the initial state $\sigma = (2^m, 0, \ldots, 0)$ with $ch(\sigma) = n$, after the first m even splitting questions, the resulting state is $\sigma' = (1, m, \binom{m}{2}, \ldots, \binom{m}{e})$ with $ch(\sigma') = n - m$, which satisfy the hypothesis of Theorem 2.5, since it can be shown that $\binom{m}{e} \sim m^e \gg (n-m)^e$.

2.6 Heuristics for the Ulam-Rényi Problem

Despite its far-reaching generality, the asymptotic result of Theorem 2.5 does not provide the ultimate solution to the Ulam-Rényi problem. Of practical interest is also the question of generating the winning strategy for any small instance. Optimal algorithms are known to find the exact solution of the Ulam-Rényi problem over an arbitrary search space when the number of allowed lies is small. For the general case of an arbitrary number of lies, only heuristic-based algorithms have been proposed. In this section we shall present two such heuristics.

Algorithm 1

Let $\sigma = (x_0, x_1, \ldots, x_e)$, with $ch(\sigma) = n$. Define $\delta = [a_0, a_1, \ldots, a_e]$ by recursively choosing $a_i \in \{0, 1, \ldots, x_i\}$ in order to minimize $\left| \sum_{j=0}^{i} \binom{n-1}{e-j}(x_j - 2a_j) \right|$, i.e.,

$$a_i = \operatorname*{argmin}_{0 \leq a_i \leq x_i} \left| \sum_{j=0}^{i} \binom{n-1}{e-j}(x_j - 2a_j) \right| \qquad i = 0, 1, \ldots, e.$$

---

[8]Here, we mean that on a state σ, Paul's questions δ_σ will result in two states σ^{yes} and σ^{no}, such that $\mathrm{ch}(\sigma^{yes}), \mathrm{ch}(\sigma^{no}) \leq \mathrm{ch}(\sigma) - 1$.

This rule slightly refines the strategy depicted in Theorem 2.5 by a component-wise balancing of the resulting states' volume.

This heuristic has one main drawback: it does not take into account the translation bound. In fact, the second heuristic we present is based on this observation and tries to take into account both the volume and the translation bound.

Algorithm 2

Let $\sigma = (x_0, x_1, \ldots, x_e)$. We will denote by $\Theta(\sigma)$ the state $(0, x_0, x_1, \ldots, x_{e-1})$. This state is obtained by shifting the components of σ one place to the right. This is also equivalent to *translating* σ into the corresponding state for the game with $e - 1$ lies. For any $i = 1, 2, \ldots, e$, we define $\Theta^i(\sigma) = \Theta(\Theta^{i-1}(\sigma))$, with $\Theta^0(\sigma) = \sigma$.

Let the function $\mathscr{G} : \mathbf{N}^{e+1} \mapsto \mathbf{N}$ be recursively defined by

$$\mathscr{G}(x_0, \ldots, x_e) = \begin{cases} \mathrm{ch}(x_0, \ldots, x_e) & \text{if } \sum_{i=0}^{e} x_i \leq 2; \\ \max\{\mathscr{G}(0, x_0, \ldots, x_{e-1}) + 3, \ \mathrm{ch}(x_0, \ldots, x_e)\} & \text{otherwise.} \end{cases}$$
(2.14)

Further, with any state $\sigma = (x_0, \ldots, x_e)$ we associate the vector $\Gamma(\sigma) = (\gamma_0, \gamma_1, \ldots, \gamma_e)$ defined by

$$\gamma_i = \max\left\{\mathscr{G}(\Theta^{e-i}(\sigma)), \mathscr{G}(\sigma) - 3(e - i)\right\} \qquad \text{for } i = 0, 1, \ldots, e. \quad (2.15)$$

An immediate property of the vector $\Gamma(\sigma)$ is given by the following lemma.

Lemma 2.4. *Let $\sigma = (x_0, x_1, \ldots, x_e)$ and $\Gamma(\sigma) = (\gamma_0, \gamma_1, \ldots, \gamma_e)$ be defined as in formulae (2.14) and (2.15) above. Let $j = \min\{i \mid \sum_{k=0}^{i} x_k \geq 3\}$. Then, for any $i \geq j$ we have*

$$\gamma_i = \gamma_e - 3(e - i).$$

Proof. By definition we have $\gamma_e = \mathscr{G}(\sigma)$. Hence, for $i = 0, 1, \ldots, e$ we also have $\gamma_i = \max\{\mathscr{G}(\Theta^{e-i}(\sigma)), \gamma_e - 3(e - i)\}$. Then we only need to prove $\gamma_e - 3(e - i) \geq \mathscr{G}(\Theta^{e-i}(\sigma))$, or, equivalently $\gamma_e \geq \mathscr{G}(\Theta^{e-i}(\sigma)) + 3(e - i)$, for all $i \geq j$.

Indeed, by hypothesis we have $\sum_{k=0}^{i} x_k \geq 3$, for all $i \geq j$. Then (2.14) yields

$$\gamma_e = \mathscr{G}(\sigma) \geq \mathscr{G}(\Theta^1(\sigma)) + 3 \geq \mathscr{G}(\Theta^2(\sigma)) + 6 \geq \cdots \geq \mathscr{G}(\Theta^{e-i}(\sigma)) + 3(e - i),$$

which gives the desired result.

Intuitively, γ_e yields a lower bound for the length of the shortest winning strategy for σ, considering both Volume and Translation Bound. In addition, γ_{e-i} stands for an upper bound on the length of the shortest winning strategy for $\Theta^i(\sigma)$ provided that there exists a winning strategy for σ with γ_e questions. This is proved by the following corollary.

Corollary 2.2. *Let* $\sigma = (x_0, x_1, \ldots, x_e)$ *be a state. Let* $(\gamma_0, \gamma_1, \ldots, \gamma_e) = \Gamma(\sigma)$.

(a) If there exists a winning strategy for σ with q questions, then $q \geq \gamma_e$;

(b) If $q = \gamma_e$, then for all $i = 1, \ldots, e$, there exists a winning strategy for $\Theta^i(\sigma) = (0, \ldots, 0, x_0, \ldots, x_{e-i})$ with γ_{e-i} questions.

The following lemma states that in most cases the optimal winning strategy for σ (with respect to the lower bound γ_e) implicitly behaves like an optimal winning strategy for the states $\Theta^i(\sigma)$ (with respect to the upper bound γ_{e-i}).

Lemma 2.5. *Let* $\sigma = (x_0, x_1, \ldots, x_e)$ *be a state. Let* $(\gamma_0, \gamma_1, \ldots, \gamma_e) = \Gamma(\sigma)$. *Let Σ be a winning strategy for σ using exactly γ_e questions. Moreover, let $\delta = [a_0, a_1, \ldots, a_e]$ be the first question in the winning strategy Σ and σ^{yes} and σ^{no} be the resulting states from a positive and a negative answer to δ, respectively. Then, for all $i = 1, \ldots, e$ such that $\sum_{j=0}^{e-i} x_j \geq 3$, we have*

$$V_{\gamma_{e-i}-1}(\Theta^i(\sigma^{yes})) \leq 2^{\gamma_{e-i}-1} \text{ and } V_{\gamma_{e-i}-1}(\Theta^i(\sigma^{no})) \leq 2^{\gamma_{e-i}-1}.$$

Proof. By $\sum_{j=0}^{e-i} x_j \geq 3$, Lemma 2.4 yields $\gamma_e = \gamma_{e-i} + 3i$. Suppose by contradiction that for some $i \in \{1, \ldots, e\}$ it holds that $V_{\gamma_{e-i}-1}(\Theta^i(\sigma^{yes})) > 2^{\gamma_{e-i}-1}$. Then, setting $(\gamma_0', \gamma_1', \ldots, \gamma_e') = \Gamma(\sigma^{yes})$, we have $\gamma_{e-i}' \geq \gamma_{e-i}$. Let $\sigma^{yes} = (y_0, \ldots, y_e)$ as in (2.2). Thus $\sum_{j=0}^{e-i+1} y_j \geq 3$ and we have $\gamma_e' \geq \gamma_{e-i}' + 3i \geq \gamma_{e-i} + 3i = \gamma_e$. Therefore, at least γ_e questions are necessary to reach a final state from σ^{yes}. Since $\gamma_e - 1$ questions are left in Σ, it cannot be a winning strategy.

Symmetrically, we have the proof for the condition on $\Theta^i(\sigma^{no})$.

The above Lemma 2.5 and Corollary 2.2 formalize the intuition behind our heuristic. By Corollary 2.2, given a state $\sigma = (x_0, \ldots, x_e)$ and the corresponding $(e + 1)$-tuple $(\gamma_0, \ldots, \gamma_e) = \Gamma(\sigma)$, the first question $\delta = [a_0, \ldots, a_e]$ in any optimal winning strategy (i.e., one which uses *exactly* γ_e questions) must satisfy the following property:

for $i = 0, \ldots, e$, $\sigma_i^{yes} = (0, \ldots, 0, y_0, \ldots, y_i)$ and $\sigma_i^{no} = (0, \ldots, 0, n_0, \ldots, n_i)$, the two states resulting from the state $(0, \ldots, 0, x_0, \ldots, x_i)$ on question $\delta_i = (0, \ldots, 0, a_0, \ldots, a_i)$ must be both winning $(\gamma_i - 1)$-states; y_j and n_j are computed according to (2.2).

Thus Paul would seem to be well advised to define the component a_i for any $i = 0, \ldots, e$ such that the quantities $V_{\gamma_i-1}(\sigma_i^{yes})$ and $V_{\gamma_i-1}(\sigma_i^{no})$ are as nearly equal as possible.

Unfortunately, this is not sufficient, since the choice of a_i affects the states σ_{i+j}^{yes} and σ_{i+j}^{no} for $j = 1, \ldots, e - i$.

Let us define for any $i = 0, \ldots, e - 1$ and $j = 1, \ldots, e - i$ the *pseudo states*

$$\alpha_{i,j} = (0, \ldots, 0, y_0, \ldots, y_i, \underbrace{x_i - a_i, 0, \ldots, 0}_{j-1}) \quad \beta_{i,j} = (0, \ldots, 0, n_0, \ldots, n_i, \underbrace{a_i, 0, \ldots, 0}_{j-1}).$$

Such states record what is already known about the states σ_{i+j}^{yes} and σ_{i+j}^{no} as soon as the component a_i has been chosen but the components $a_{i+1}, \ldots, a_{i+j}$ have not been chosen yet.

The strategy also tries to take care of the states σ_{i+j}^{yes} and σ_{i+j}^{no} while deciding the component a_i by requiring that $V_{\gamma_{i+j}-1}(\alpha_{i,j}) \leq 2^{\gamma_{i+j}-1}$ and $V_{\gamma_{i+j}-1}(\beta_{i,j}) \leq 2^{\gamma_{i+j}-1}$.

This is the best we can do if we decide to choose the components of the question step by step, without allowing backtracking.

We then define a_i as the integer $x \in \{0, 1, \ldots, x_i\}$ such that for the question $\delta_i = (0, \ldots, 0, a_0, a_1, \ldots, a_{i-1}, x)$ the difference

$$|V_{\gamma_i-1}(\sigma_i^{yes}) - V_{\gamma_i-1}(\sigma_i^{no})|$$

is minimum and for any $j = 1, \ldots, e - i$ it holds that

$$V_{\gamma_{i+j}-1}(\alpha_{i,j}) \leq 2^{\gamma_{i+j}-1} \qquad \text{and} \qquad V_{\gamma_{i+j}-1}(\beta_{i,j}) \leq 2^{\gamma_{i+j}-1}.$$

Such a strategy corresponds to the one which first aims at being a winning strategy for the state $\Theta^{e-i}(\sigma) = (0, \ldots, 0, x_0, \ldots, x_i)$, for $i = 0, \ldots, e - 1$ with γ_i questions.

Notice that this condition need not hold in general, since Lemma 2.5 only constrains the states $\Theta^{e-i}(\sigma)$ that satisfy $\sum_{j=0}^{i} x_j \geq 3$. However, the heuristic still yields optimal results in many different cases.

2.6.1 Experimental Validation of the Heuristics

Algorithm 2 was experimentally proved to provide optimal strategies for the Ulam-Rényi game over a search space of cardinality 2^m with e lies, for each $m = 1, \ldots, 16$ and each $e = 1, \ldots, 9$.

The lengths of the corresponding strategies are summarized in Table 2.3. When tested over the same sample of instances, Algorithm 1 does not give *optimal* results for the cases

$$(m, e) \in \{(8, 5), (8, 6), \ldots, (8, 9), (11, 6), (11, 7), (11, 8), (11, 9), (14, 7), (14, 8), (14, 9)\}.$$

Nonetheless, it is much simpler to implement, and in all the above cases it provides solutions which differ by at most two questions.

We close this section by mentioning a result obtained by combining the theoretical techniques of the previous sections and the heuristics. It is known that for $e \geq 6$ and a search space of cardinality $M = 2^{14}$ the optimal solution requires exactly $3e + 17$ questions. The proof of this fact relies on the solution of the case $M = 2^{14}$ and $e = 14$ given by Algorithm 2 and the general technique of Sect. 2.4 to extend this result to arbitrary value of $e \geq 6$.

Table 2.3 Optimal solution (minimum number of queries) for $|S| = 2^m$ and e lies

	m															
	1	2	3	4	5	6	7	8	9	10	11	12	13	14	15	16
e																
1	3	5	6	7	9	10	11	12	13	14	15	17	18	19	20	21
2	5	8	9	10	12	13	14	15	17	18	19	20	21	22	24	25
3	7	11	12	13	15	16	17	18	20	21	22	23	25	26	27	28
4	9	14	15	16	18	19	20	21	23	24	25	27	28	29	30	32
5	11	17	18	19	21	22	23	24	26	27	28	30	31	32	34	35
6	13	20	21	22	24	25	26	27	29	30	31	33	34	35	37	38
7	15	23	24	25	27	28	29	30	32	33	34	36	37	38	40	41
8	17	26	27	28	30	31	32	33	35	36	37	39	40	41	43	44
9	19	29	30	31	33	34	35	36	38	39	40	42	43	44	46	47

The exact value of $N(2^m, e)$ for $m = 1, 2, \ldots, 16$ and $e = 1, \ldots, 9$

2.7 Bibliographic Notes

The specific names Paul and Carole were not randomly chosen. The initials P and C refer to Pusher-Chooser games investigated by Spencer in [196]. Paul may be considered the great questioner Paul Erdős. Carole may be thought of as her anagram: Oracle!

The Volume Bound was first proved by Berlekamp [22]. Subsequently, Rivest et al. [185] re-proved it for the continuous case. Pelc [162] also gave his own proof of this bound. We included here a novel, induction-free proof, originally presented in [58], for the more general case of q-ary search. An alternative proof of Volume Bound can be found in [5].

Different proofs of Theorem 2.3 and Lemma 2.2 can be found in [22], where they first appeared. Berlekamp's nth Volume of a state is also defined as the nth weight, or, more simply, the weight of a state, in most of the later papers on the topic of the Ulam-Rényi problem.

For $e = 1, 2, 3$, the exact value of $N(2^{20}, e)$ was computed in the papers [83, 157, 162]. In the same papers the reader can find the exact value of $N(2^m, e)$ for all integers $m \geq 0$, for the cases $e = 1$, $e = 2$, $e = 3$, respectively. For $e = 1, 2, 3$, evaluation of $N(M, e)$ for all integers $M \geq 1$ can be found in [89, 115, 162], respectively. Hill et al. [119–121] were the first to give complete solutions for the Ulam-Rényi problem over a search space of cardinalities 2^{20} and 10^6. More precisely, with respect to the presentation given in this chapter, they settled the case $e = 5$ in the light of Berlekamp's Tables (Figs. 9 and 11 of [22]). The use of infinite tables of winning states was started by Berlekamp [22]. As a matter of fact, Tables 2.1 and 2.2 first appeared in [22], together with a more general description also given in this chapter. We have partially deviated from Berlekamp's original presentation, and preferred to give our own construction, principally based on the simplification and correction given in [121] (see also [119, 120]).

For the details on Theorem 2.5, refer to [198]. Algorithm 1 is presented in [138], while Algorithm 2 was originally presented in [52].

2.8 Exercises

1. Show that there is no strategy matching the volume bound for the Ulam-Rényi game with 2 lies over a search space of size 4. In particular, this means that no winning strategy can exist using at most 7 questions.
2. Show that for any variant of the Ulam-Rényi game with e lies there exists a strategy using $(2e + 1)N^*(M)$ questions, where $N^*(M)$ denotes the minimum number of questions sufficient to win the game for Paul when Carole is not allowed to lie.
3. Is the Volume Bound still valid for the variant of the game where Carole is allowed to answer *sincerely* at most e times?
4. Consider the Ulam-Rényi game with one lie. Suppose that, after having chosen the secret number, Carole answers each question insincerely with probability $1/2$, as long as she still has the possibility to lie.

   What is the expected number of questions Paul needs as a function of the search space size n. What about the case of $e > 1$ lies?
5. Describe what is in general the best answering strategy for Carole. What is the space and time complexity of such a strategy?
6. In a variant of the Ulam-Rényi game, Carole wants to finish the game as soon as possible and Paul wants to continue as long as possible. What is the minimum length (in terms of number of questions) of such a game, if the number of objects is 4 and Carole is allowed to lie at most twice?
7. Consider the Ulam-Rényi game with 1 lie over a search space of cardinality 10^6. Assume that the only questions allowed are of the form "Is x in Q?", where $|Q| \leq 20$. What is now the minimum number of questions that Paul has to ask in order to identify Carole's secret number?
8. With reference to the model in the previous exercise, assume now that the search space has cardinality q^m and each question cannot be of cardinality larger than m. Provide upper and lower bounds on the size of a minimum size strategy for Paul as a function of m.
9. Professor Quick has thought of the following alternative heuristics for solving any instance of the Ulam-Rényi game where the search space cardinality is of the form 2^m: Ask m even splitting questions and let σ be the resulting state. Find the most appropriate values of t, i, j, such that the state $(a_{i1}, \ldots a_{ij})$ from the table defined in (2.10)–(2.12) is the "closest" superstate of σ. Then, use Lemma 2.1 to complete the strategy.

   Try to analyze this strategy by providing un upper bound on how many more questions are needed with respect to the character of the original state. Try to estimate the complexity of the resulting algorithm.

Chapter 3
Adaptive vs. Non-adaptive Search

A liar should have a good memory

Quintilian, *Institutes of Oratory*

3.1 Coding in a Channel with Noiseless Feedback

Led by Schalkwijk and Kailath, Berlekamp proposed the following model for information transmission over a noisy channel equipped with a noiseless and delayless feedback channel of large capacity: Suppose the source must send a message μ from a set $\mathcal{M}$ of M many possible messages. Assume that the channel can only deliver bits, and that up to e of the bits can be distorted during transmission. In order to communicate the message to the receiver, the source sends a certain number n of bits over the noisy channel. In contrast with traditional e-error correcting codes, these n bits may adaptively depend on the information received by the source via the feedback channel.

As an equivalent formulation, one may suppose that, after the source has chosen the message μ, the receiver chooses a subset Q_1 of $\mathcal{M}$, and then asks the following *yes-no* question over the noiseless feedback channel:

Is your message μ an element of Q_1?

The source's answer (one bit) is then sent to the receiver via the noisy channel. The receiver gets a (possibly distorted) answer, and then adaptively asks the next question Q_2. *At each step t adaptively asks the question $Q_t \subseteq \mathcal{M}$ knowing the answers to the preceding questions.*

Since the receiver's questions range over all possible subsets of a space of cardinality M, one might be led to think that any such question requires M bits to be sent over the noiseless channel. It turns out, however, that *only one feedback bit suffices for each bit transmitted by the source.* This is so because we can safely assume a cooperative model, where the source knows the receiver's search strategy

F. Cicalese, *Fault-Tolerant Search Algorithms*, Monographs in Theoretical Computer Science. An EATCS Series, DOI 10.1007/978-3-642-17327-1_3,
© Springer-Verlag Berlin Heidelberg 2013

(question selection). Thus, in particular, the first question Q_1 is known to the source: the first bit $A_1^* \in \{0, 1\} = \{no, yes\}$ transmitted via the noisy channel is the answer to this question. This bit is received as A_1 where $A_1 = 1 - A_1^*$ or $A_1 = A_1^*$ according to whether distortion occurs or not during its transmission.

Proceeding inductively, let Q_{i+1} be the $(i + 1)$th question, A_{i+1}^* be the answer as transmitted from the source-end of the noisy channel, and A_{i+1} be the (possibly noisy) answer delivered at the receiver end by the noisy channel, as obtained by the receiver. Since question Q_{t+1} depends only on the previous answers $A_1, \ldots, A_t$, for the source to know question Q_{t+1} it is sufficient for it to know the bits $A_1, \ldots, A_t$. By safely sending these bits over the feedback noiseless channel, the receiver allows the source to know question Q_{t+1}.

For any given M and e, one can naturally consider the problem of minimizing the number n of feedback bits—precisely as in the Ulam-Rényi game. As we shall see, any encoding scheme for Berlekamp's binary symmetric channel with noiseless feedback is essentially the same thing as a winning strategy for the Ulam-Rényi game. In particular, any winning strategy with a minimum number of questions amounts to a shortest error-correcting code for this sort of channel—and vice versa.

3.2 No Feedback Equals Error-Correcting Codes

Let us suppose that the feedback channel is not available. Then the problem is to send a message μ using the minimum number of bits in such a way that the receiver can recover μ even if up to e of these bits may be distorted during transmission.

This is precisely the main issue of the theory of (binary) error-correcting codes: Here, source and receiver agree on fixing an injective map $c : \mathcal{M} \mapsto \{0, 1\}^n$. To transmit a message $\mu \in \mathcal{M}$, the source sends $\mathbf{x} = c(\mu)$ over the noisy channel. The original n-tuple of bits $\mathbf{x}$ is received as $\mathbf{x}'$ after transmission over the noisy channel, and in general $\mathbf{x}' \neq \mathbf{x}$, because of distortion. Given the maximum number e of bits that can be distorted, a careful choice of the map c should allow the receiver to compute $\mathbf{x}$ from $\mathbf{x}'$ and then, by inverting c, to recover the original message μ.

Under this representation, one can safely regard the range of c as a set of possible sequences of answers to suitably chosen yes-no questions in a Ulam-Rényi game with e lies. More precisely, let

$$\mathcal{Q}_i = \{\mu \in \mathcal{M} \mid \text{the } i\text{th bit of } c(\mu) \text{ is } 1\}.$$

From the viewpoint of the source end, computing $c(\mu)$ is the same as answering the questions "Does the message μ belong to the set $\mathcal{Q}_i$?", for $i = 1, 2, \ldots, n$.

On the other hand, suppose $\mathcal{Q}_i \subseteq \mathcal{M}$ $(i = 1, 2, \ldots, n)$ is an n-tuple of (predetermined, non-adaptive) questions having the following property: even if up to e of the answers may be erroneous, from the n answers to the $\mathcal{Q}_i$ the secret number can always be guessed. Let the map $c : \mathcal{M} \mapsto \{0, 1\}^n$ transform each message $\mu \in \mathcal{M}$ into the n-tuple of bits $x_1, x_2, \ldots, x_n$, given by $x_i = 1$ or $x_i = 0$ according to whether $\mu \in \mathcal{Q}_i$ or $\mu \notin \mathcal{Q}_i$, respectively.

Then one can naturally say that the range $c(\mathcal{M})$ of c is the encoding of the set $\mathcal{M}$ of messages. Thus, a code is the same as the range of such a map c. Finding shortest codes amounts to finding shortest questioning strategies. In contrast with the original Ulam-Rényi game, here the receiver cannot adaptively ask his $(t+1)$th question in the light of the previous t answers: all questions must be known in advance to the source, before any bit is sent.

3.3 Elements of the Theory of Error-Correcting Codes

Since shortest error-correcting codes are the same as solutions of the non-adaptive case of the Ulam-Rényi problem, for later use we shall collect here all necessary background material from the theory of error-correcting codes. It is convenient to relax the assumption that the channel can deliver only binary digits (corresponding to the assumption that only *yes-no* answers are allowed).

For arbitrary integers $q \geq 2$ and $n > 0$ let $\mathbf{x}, \mathbf{y} \in \{0, 1, \ldots, q - 1\}^n$. Then the *Hamming distance* $d_H(\mathbf{x}, \mathbf{y})$ is defined by

$$d_H(\mathbf{x}, \mathbf{y}) = |\{i \in \{1, \ldots, n\} \mid x_i \neq y_i\}|,$$

where, as above, $|A|$ denotes the number of elements of A.

The *Hamming sphere* $\mathcal{B}_r(\mathbf{x})$ *with radius r and center $\mathbf{x}$* is the set of elements of $\{0, 1, \ldots, q - 1\}^n$ whose Hamming distance from $\mathbf{x}$ is $\leq r$; in symbols,

$$\mathcal{B}_r(\mathbf{x}) = \{\mathbf{y} \in \{0, 1, \ldots, q - 1\}^n \mid d_H(\mathbf{x}, \mathbf{y}) \leq r\}.$$

For each $\mathbf{x} \in \{0, 1, \ldots, q - 1\}^n$ we have

$$|\mathcal{B}_r(\mathbf{x})| = \sum_{i=0}^{r} \binom{n}{i} (q - 1)^i. \tag{3.1}$$

The *Hamming weight* $w_H(\mathbf{x})$ is the number of non-zero digits of $\mathbf{x}$.

When q is clear from the context, by a code we shall mean a q-ary code in the following sense:

Definition 3.1. A *(q-ary) code $\mathcal{C}$ of length n* is a subset of $\{0, 1, \ldots, q-1\}^n$. When $q = 2$ we will call $\mathcal{C}$ a *binary* code. Its elements are called *codewords*. The set $\{0, 1, \ldots, q - 1\}$ is called the *alphabet* of the code $\mathcal{C}$. The *minimum distance* of $\mathcal{C}$ is given by

$$\delta(\mathcal{C}) = \min\{d_H(\mathbf{x}, \mathbf{y}) \mid \mathbf{x}, \mathbf{y} \in \mathcal{C}, \mathbf{x} \neq \mathbf{y}\}.$$

We say that $\mathscr{C}$ is an (n, M, d) *code* if $\mathscr{C}$ has length n, $|\mathscr{C}| = M$ and $\delta(\mathscr{C}) = d$. The *minimum weight* of $\mathscr{C}$ is the minimum of the Hamming weights of its codewords; in symbols, $\mu(\mathscr{C}) = \min\{w_H(\mathbf{x}) \mid \mathbf{x} \in \mathscr{C}\}$.

Let $\mathscr{C}_1$ and $\mathscr{C}_2$ be two codes of length n. The *minimum distance between $\mathscr{C}_1$ and $\mathscr{C}_2$* is defined by

$$\Delta(\mathscr{C}_1, \mathscr{C}_2) = \min\{d_H(\mathbf{x}, \mathbf{y}) \mid \mathbf{x} \in \mathscr{C}_1, \mathbf{y} \in \mathscr{C}_2\}.$$

By definition, the empty set $\emptyset$ is an $(n, 0, d)$ q-ary code for all integers $n, d \geq 0$ and $q \geq 2$. Further, for any code $\mathscr{C}$ and integer $d \geq 0$, we have the inequality $\Delta(\emptyset, \mathscr{C}) \geq d$. Similarly, the code consisting of the single codeword $\underbrace{0 \cdots 0}_{n \text{ times}}$ is an $(n, 1, d)$ q-ary code for all integers $d \geq 0$ and $q \geq 2$.

Let $\mathscr{C}$ be a q-ary code and $\mathbf{x}$ be a codeword of $\mathscr{C}$. Suppose we send $\mathbf{x}$ over a noisy channel. Under the assumption that at most e of the digits of $\mathbf{x}$ may be distorted, the received word $\mathbf{y} \in \{0, 1, \ldots, q-1\}^n$ trivially belongs to the Hamming sphere $\mathscr{B}_e(\mathbf{x})$.

If the Hamming spheres of radius e surrounding the codewords of $\mathscr{C}$ are pairwise disjoint, then for all received $\mathbf{y}$ there must exist exactly one $\mathbf{x}$ such that $\mathbf{y} \in \mathscr{B}_e(\mathbf{x})$. Thus at the receiving end it is safe to decode $\mathbf{y}$ as $\mathbf{x}$. Indeed, for any $\mathbf{z} \in \mathscr{C}$ such that $\mathbf{z} \neq \mathbf{x}$, we have $d_H(\mathbf{z}, \mathbf{y}) \geq e + 1$.

Therefore, any (n, M, d) code $\mathscr{C}$ is capable of correcting e errors if and only if $d \geq 2e + 1$; when this is the case we say that $\mathscr{C}$ is an e *error-correcting code*.

Thus for an e error-correcting code $\mathscr{C}$, the Hamming spheres of radius e centered in the codewords of $\mathscr{C}$ must be pairwise disjoint. Since their union does not exceed the set $\{0, 1, \ldots, q - 1\}^n$, we immediately have:

Theorem 3.1 (Hamming or Sphere Packing Bound). *Let $\mathscr{C}$ be an q-ary code of length n and cardinality $|\mathscr{C}| = M$. If $\mathscr{C}$ is an e error-correcting code, then*

$$M \sum_{j=0}^{e} \binom{n}{j}(q - 1)^j \leq q^n. \tag{3.2}$$

Definition 3.2. A q-ary (n, M, d)-code $\mathscr{C}$ with minimum distance $d = 2e + 1$ is called *perfect* if for each $\mathbf{x} \in \{0, 1, \ldots, q - 1\}^n$ there exists exactly one $\mathbf{y} \in \mathscr{C}$ such that $d_H(\mathbf{x}, \mathbf{y}) \leq e$.

Perfect e error-correcting codes are the most peculiar example of perfect non-adaptive winning strategies for the Ulam-Rényi game. More generally, perfect strategies for the non-adaptive Ulam-Rényi game over a search space of cardinality M are the same as e error-correcting codes that minimize n with respect to the bound in Theorem 3.1. These codes shall be our main concern in the rest of this section. As of today, however, up to finitely many exceptional values of e and M, the best *known* codes are far from matching the lower bound provided in (3.2).

3.3.1 Linear and Hamming Codes

The alphabet of every code $\mathscr{C}$ considered in this subsection shall be assumed to coincide with a finite field F_q, where $q = p^r$, the integer p is prime and $r \geq 1$. We let F_q^n denote the n-dimensional vector space over F_q. Thus every code $\mathscr{C}$ of length n satisfies $\mathscr{C} \subseteq F_q^n$.

Recall Definition 3.1:

Definition 3.3. A *linear code* $\mathscr{C}$ of length n is a linear subspace of F_q^n. If $\mathscr{C}$ is m-dimensional then $\mathscr{C}$ is called an $[n, m]$ code. We say for short that $\mathscr{C}$ is an $[n, m, d]$ *code* if $\mathscr{C}$ is an m-dimensional linear code of length n and minimum distance d.

By an $[n, m, d]$ *code* we mean an (n, q^m, d)-code whose codewords form a vector subspace of the vector space F_q^n.

Every linear code is specified by a pair of matrices whose effect is to simplify the encoding and decoding steps of the transmission protocol.

Definition 3.4. A *generator matrix* G for an $[n, m]$ code $\mathscr{C}$ is an $m \times n$ matrix whose rows yield a basis of $\mathscr{C}$.

A *parity check matrix* H of an $[n, m]$ code $\mathscr{C}$ is an $(n - m) \times n$ matrix such that, for all $\mathbf{x} \in C$, we have $H \mathbf{x}^T = \mathbf{0}$.

Let G be a generator matrix of an $[n, m]$ code $\mathscr{C}$. If G is in the form[1] $[I_m \mid A]$, where I_m is the identity $(m \times m)$-matrix, then the matrix $H = [-A^T \mid I_{n-m}]$ is a parity check matrix for $\mathscr{C}$.

Remark. It is not hard to prove that for any $[n, m, d]$ code $\mathscr{C}$ with parity check matrix H, the minimum distance d of $\mathscr{C}$ is equal to the minimum number of linearly dependent columns of H. One can now get a procedure to determine the minimum distance of a linear code, as well as its error-correcting capability.

Let us identify, without loss of generality, the source messages with q-ary vectors of length m, i.e., with vectors in $S = \{0, 1, \ldots, q - 1\}^m$; it follows that, for each $\mathbf{u} \in S$, its corresponding codeword is given by $\mathbf{x} = \mathbf{u} \cdot G$. The map $\mathbf{u} \mapsto \mathbf{x}$ is easily computable. Hence, if a linear code is available the encoding procedure becomes very efficient.

We shall now discuss the decoding procedure.

Definition 3.5. If $\mathscr{C}$ is a linear code with parity check matrix H, then for each $\mathbf{x} \in F_k^q$ we call $H \mathbf{x}^T$ the *syndrome* of $\mathbf{x}$.

By definition, codewords are characterized as having syndrome $\mathbf{0}$.

---

[1]Given an $(m \times n_1)$ matrix A_1 and an $(m \times n_2)$ matrix A_2, we shall denote by $[A_1 \mid A_2]$ the $(m \times (n_1 + n_2))$ matrix whose first n_1 columns are those of A_1 and the remaining ones are those of A_2, in the same order.

Let $\mathbf{x} \in \mathscr{C}$ be the transmitted codeword and $\mathbf{y} \in \{0, 1, \ldots, q-1\}^n$ be the received word. Then $\mathbf{e} = \mathbf{y} - \mathbf{x}$ is the error pattern. On the other hand, at the receiver end, the syndrome of the received word $\mathbf{y}$ is simply given by

$$H \, \mathbf{y}^T = H \, (\mathbf{x} + \mathbf{e})^T = H \, \mathbf{e}^T.$$

Since, by hypothesis, at most e errors have occurred, $w_H(\mathbf{e}) \le e$.

We now note that for any two vectors $\mathbf{e}_1, \mathbf{e}_2 \in \{0, 1, \ldots, q-1\}^n$ of Hamming weight $\le e$, we have $d_H(\mathbf{e}_1, \mathbf{e}_2) \le 2e$, whence $H \, \mathbf{e}_1^T \ne H \, \mathbf{e}_2^T$. Thus, any syndrome corresponds to a unique error pattern.

Assuming that the number of errors is $\le e$, the decoder must simply compute the syndrome of the received word $\mathbf{y}$. As we have seen, this amounts to recovering the error pattern $\mathbf{e}$, from which the decoder can easily obtain the original codeword $\mathbf{x} = \mathbf{y} - \mathbf{e}$. For the decoder it is then sufficient to use a look-up table (syndrome to error pattern) with q^{n-m} entries. This results in a significant improvement with respect to the general case of a code with no structure—where, using a table with q^n entries, one associates with every received vector $\mathbf{x} \in F_q^n$ its corresponding codeword $\mathbf{x}$. In practice, more sophisticated and space-saving techniques are available.

Definition 3.6. For all integers $m \ge 1$, let $n = \frac{q^m-1}{q-1}$, where q is a prime power. An $[n, n-m]$ code over F_q is called a *Hamming code* if the columns of its parity check matrix are pairwise linearly independent vectors (over F_q). Stated differently, these columns yield a maximal set of pairwise linearly independent vectors.

Remark. The columns of the parity check matrix of a *binary* Hamming code ($q = 2$) precisely exhaust the set of non-zero vectors of F_2^m. Since the minimum number of linearly dependent columns in the parity matrix of a Hamming code is 3, the minimum distance of a Hamming code is equal to 3. Hence, Hamming codes are one error-correcting codes. Further, we have the following.

Theorem 3.2. *Hamming codes are perfect one error-correcting codes.*

Corollary 3.1. *For each $m = 1, 2, 3, \ldots,$*

$$N(2^m, 1) = N_{\min}(2^m, 1) = \min\{n = 0, 1, 2, \ldots \mid 2^n \ge 2^m(n + 1)\}.$$

3.3.2 MDS Codes and the Reed-Solomon Codes

One of the most fascinating notions in coding theory is that of MDS code. In order to introduce such a class of codes, we will start by proving the following easy result, generally known as the Singleton Bound.

Theorem 3.3 (Singleton Bound). *For all integers $q \ge 2$ and $n, d \ge 0$, if there exists an (n, M, d) q-ary code $\mathscr{C}$, then*

$$M \leq q^{n-d+1}.$$

Proof. By contradiction, assume that $M > q^{n-d+1}$; then there must exist two distinct codewords $\mathbf{x}, \mathbf{y} \in \mathscr{C}$ and $n - d + 1$ indices $1 \leq i_1 \leq i_2 \leq \cdots \leq i_{n-d+1} \leq n$ such that

$$x_{i_j} = y_{i_j} \qquad \text{for all } j = 1, 2, \ldots, n - d + 1.$$

This implies that $d_H(\mathbf{x}, \mathbf{y}) \leq n - (n - d + 1) = d - 1$, contradicting the hypothesis that $\delta(\mathscr{C}) = d$.

If an (n, M, d) q-ary code satisfies the above bound with equality, i.e., $M = q^{n-d+1}$, then it is called a *Maximum Distance Separable (MDS) code*. "Maximum distance" accounts for the fact that such a code $\mathscr{C}$ has the maximum possible distance $\delta(\mathscr{C})$ for the given size M and the given length n. "Separable" refers to the fact that the codewords of $\mathscr{C}$ can be separated into message symbols and check symbols. In fact, for any fixed set of $k = n - d + 1$ positions, the projection of the codewords of $\mathscr{C}$ over such positions coincides with $\{0, 1, \ldots, q - 1\}^k$.

The following lemma gives a useful combinatorial characterization of the codewords in an MDS code.

Lemma 3.1. *For q a prime power, the number of codewords of Hamming weight w in an $(n, q^k, d = n - k + 1)$ MDS q-ary code is*

$$A_w = \binom{n}{w}(q - 1)\sum_{j=0}^{w-d}(-1)^j\binom{w - 1}{j}q^{w-d-j}.$$

The problem of finding the longest possible MDS code for a given dimension $k = n - d + 1$ is related to a great variety of combinatorial problems. Exercises 6, 7, and 8 will analyze one such relationships with Latin Squares.

The Reed-Solomon Codes. One of the most important and well-studied families of MDS codes are the Reed-Solomon (RS) codes. An $(n, k + 1)$-RS code, with $k < n$ and $q \geq n$ is defined as follows: Fix n distinct elements $\alpha_1, \ldots, \alpha_n$, in the finite field F_q, which exist due to the assumption $q \geq n$. Each source message is uniquely associated with a polynomial over F_q of degree at most k. Therefore, the source message space is identified with F_q^{k+1}, by viewing a source message $\mathbf{u} = (u_0, \ldots, u_k)$ as the polynomial $p_{\mathbf{u}} = u_0 + u_1 x + u_2 x^2 + \cdots + u_k x^k$.

The encoding of $\mathbf{u}$ is obtained by evaluating the corresponding polynomial $p_{\mathbf{u}}$ in the n field elements $\alpha_1, \ldots, \alpha_n$, that is, by the encoding rule

$$\mathbf{u} \mapsto (p_{\mathbf{u}}(\alpha_1), p_{\mathbf{u}}(\alpha_2), \ldots, p_{\mathbf{u}}(\alpha_n)).$$

Since any pair of distinct polynomials of degree at most k coincide in at most k points, it follows that the Hamming distance of the code is at least $n - k$. Therefore, an (n, k+1)-RS code is an $(n, q^{k+1}, n - k)$ code, and, hence, it is an MDS code.

Due to their strong algebraic structure and the resulting encoding-decoding characteristics, Reed-Solomon codes have found applications both in many theoretical studies and in a wide range of "real-world" applications, like satellite and wireless communication, compact disc players, and high-speed modems such ADSL.

3.3.3 Bounds on Codes

As we have seen above, the non-adaptive Ulam-Rényi problem with e lies over a search space of cardinality M amounts to finding a shortest *binary e-error-correcting* code with M many codewords. Thus the non-adaptive Ulam-Rényi problem is an equivalent reformulation of the following main issue in combinatorial coding theory: *evaluate the maximum number $A(n, d)$ of codewords in a binary code of length n and minimum distance d.*

We shall now recall some of the principal known bounds on $A(n, d)$.

Surprisingly enough, the best known lower bound on $A(n, d)$ is just the most trivial one:

Theorem 3.4 (Gilbert Bound). *For all integers $q \geq 2$, $n \geq 1$, $1 \leq d \leq n$, there exists a q-ary (n, M, d)-code $\mathscr{C}$ with*

$$M \geq \frac{q^n}{\sum_{j=0}^{d-1} \binom{n}{j}(q-1)^j},$$

whence

$$A(n, d) \geq \frac{2^n}{\sum_{j=0}^{d-1} \binom{n}{j}}.$$

Proof. Starting with any arbitrary $\mathbf{x} \in \{0, 1, \ldots, q-1\}^n$, one routinely keeps adding codewords lying at a distance at least d from all previously added codewords. The process stops and the desired $\mathscr{C}$ is obtained when, for each $\mathbf{z} \in \{0, 1, \ldots, q-1\}^n$, there is at least one $\mathbf{x} \in \mathscr{C}$ such that $\mathbf{y} \in \mathscr{B}_{d-1}(\mathbf{x})$. Thus the Hamming spheres of radius $d-1$ surrounding the codewords of $\mathscr{C}$ cover the whole space $\{0, 1, \ldots, q-1\}^n$, whence

$$|\mathscr{C}| \sum_{j=0}^{d-1} \binom{n}{j}(q-1)^j \geq q^n,$$

as required to complete the proof.

Table 3.1 Bounds on the rate of the best binary codes for large n

$\frac{d}{n}$	Gilbert-Varshamov lower bound	Sphere Packing-Hamming upper bound	McEliece et al. upper bound
0	1	1	1
0.1	0.531	0.714	0.693
0.2	0.278	0.531	0.461
0.3	0.119	0.390	0.250
0.4	0.029	0.278	0.081
0.5	0	0.189	0

By definition, for all integers n and d, the *rate* of the largest binary code of length n and minimum distance d is given by

$$R(n,d) = \frac{1}{n} \log_2 A(n,d).$$

Most of the known upper bounds on $A(n,d)$ are expressed in terms of $R(n,d)$ as a function of d/n. The following theorem gives an upper bound on the largest size of a binary code of length n and minimum distance d for all sufficiently large n. The theorem is due to McEliece-Rodemich-Rumsey-Welch [148].

Theorem 3.5 (McEliece, Rodemich, Rumsey, Welch). *For all sufficiently large n and for $0 \leq d/n \leq 1/2$, we have*

$$R(n,d) \leq \min_{0 \leq u \leq 1-2d/n} \left\{ 1 + h(u^2) - h\left(u^2 + 2\frac{du}{n} + \frac{2d}{n}\right) \right\},$$

where $h(x) = \mathcal{H}(\frac{1}{2} - \frac{1}{2}\sqrt{1-x})$ and $\mathcal{H}(x)$ denotes the binary entropy function $\mathcal{H}(x) = -x \log_2 x - (1-x) \log_2(1-x)$.

In Table 3.1, we list as a function of d/n the rates of the largest binary codes allowed by the Gilbert, Hamming, and McEliece et al. bounds, respectively.

Evidently, there still exists a significant gap between the best known asymptotic lower and upper bounds on the size of the largest binary codes.

Moreover, the largest binary code of length n and minimum distance d as given by the McEliece et al. bound is far from matching the Hamming bound. Equivalently, in our terminology, the best known non-adaptive searching strategies for the Ulam-Rényi game over a search space of cardinality M and e lies are far from being *perfect*.

In particular, when there exists an integer n such that $M \sum_{j=0}^{e} \binom{n}{j} = 2^n$, we have the following stronger negative result:

Theorem 3.6 (Tietäväinen-Zinoviev-Leontiev Theorem). *For each integer $e > 1$ no non-trivial perfect e-error-correcting code exists except the $[23, 12, 7]$ binary Golay code and the ternary $[11, 6, 5]$ Golay code.*[2]

As an interesting example, let $M = 2^{78}$ and $e = 2$. Then for $n = 90$

$$M \left(\binom{n}{2} + n + 1 \right) = 2^n.$$

By the Tietäväinen Theorem no non-adaptive *perfect* strategy exists for solving the Ulam-Rényi problem with the above parameters. On the other hand, as we shall see in the next section, least adaptive and a fortiori fully adaptive perfect strategies do exist.

3.4   Fault-Tolerant q-ary Search and Minimum Feedback

> *I know a trick worth two of that*
>
> W. Shakespeare, *Henry IV*

Let us consider the case $M = 2^m$, and let the search space S coincide now with the set of m-bit integers, $S = \{0, 1, \ldots, 2^m - 1\}$. By Theorem 2.1, at least $N_{\min}(2^m, e)$ questions are *necessary* to find the secret number $x_* \in S$ in the adaptive and, a fortiori, in the non-adaptive Ulam-Rényi game with e lies.

In the fully adaptive case, Theorem 2.5 (see also the remark following it) shows that $N_{\min}(2^m, e)$ questions are always sufficient, up to finitely many exceptional m's. Optimal searching strategies have been explicitly given, respectively for the cases $e = 1$, $e = 2$ and $e = 3$. Altogether, *fully adaptive* fault-tolerant search can be performed in a very satisfactory manner.

In many practical situations, however, it is desirable to have searching strategies with small degree of adaptiveness—that is, strategies in which most questions are predetermined, and can be asked in parallel. This is the case, e.g., when the questioner and the responder are far away from each other and can interact only on a slow channel.

Minimum feedback is also desirable in all situations when the mere process of formulating the queries is so costly that the questioner finds it more convenient to prepare them in advance. For instance, in certain applications of computational molecular biology, preferably, two-stage searching strategies are used, where the search is adapted only once.

---

[2]Golay codes were introduced by Golay in [113] (see Chap. 20 of [145] for more details).

In the case where no errors or lies are possible, an optimal, fully non-adaptive searching strategy—as powerful as the best adaptive one—exists with $\lceil \log_2 |S| \rceil$ questions simply amounts to asking $\lceil \log_2 |S| \rceil$ queries about the occurrences of the bit 1 in the binary expansion of the unknown number $x_* \in S$.

For $e > 0$, in the fully non-adaptive case, finding a perfect strategy (i.e., a winning strategy of size $N_{\min}(2^m, e)$) amounts to finding an e-error correcting code of length $N_{\min}(2^m, e)$ with 2^m codewords. By Theorem 3.2, Hamming codes yield perfect non-adaptive searching strategies (i.e., one-round strategies) with the smallest possible number $N_{\min}(2^m, 1)$ of questions, for the particular case $e = 1$.

However, for $e \geq 2$, fully non-adaptive searching strategies with exactly $N_{\min}(2^m, e)$ questions—or equivalently, e error-correcting codes with 2^m codewords of length $N_{\min}(2^m, e)$—are rare objects.

A natural question to ask is then: *what happens if a small amount of adaptiveness is allowed to the questioner?*

In this section we shall show that for each e, and for all sufficiently large m, there exist searching strategies using *exactly* the theoretical minimum number $N_{\min}(2^m, e)$ of questions in which questions can be submitted in *only two* rounds. Specifically, for the questioner to infallibly guess the responder's secret number $x_* \in S$ it is *sufficient* to ask a first batch of m non-adaptive questions, and then, only depending on the m-tuple of answers, ask a second mini-batch of $s = O(e \log(m))$ non-adaptive questions.

These strategies are *perfect*, in that $m + s$ coincides with $N_{\min}(2^m, e)$, the number of questions that are a priori *necessary* to accommodate all possible answering strategies if up to e lies are allowed in the answers.

Since the questioner can adapt the strategy only once, we have indeed e fault-tolerant search strategies with *minimum* (non-zero) adaptiveness and the least possible number of tests.

This result will be presented in terms of the natural generalization of the Ulam-Rényi game obtained by assuming that Paul asks questions allowing Carole to choose from among q many possible alternative answers. One is then concerned with *fault-tolerant q-ary search*.[3] The classical Ulam-Rényi problem is clearly the same as q-ary search with lies and $q = 2$.

We shall introduce q-ary search and then prove that for any $q \geq 2$ and $e \geq 0$ and up to finitely many exceptional sizes of the search space, in the q-ary Ulam-Rényi game with e lies there exists a search strategy using at most one additional question with respect to the theoretical minimum number of questions needed, i.e.,

$$N_{\min}^{[q]}(M, e) \leq N^{[q]}(M, e) \leq N_{\min}^{[q]}(M, e) + 1,$$

where $N_{\min}^{[q]}(M, e)$ denotes the minimum integer n such that n, M, e satisfy the Hamming Bound for q-ary codes (3.2) and $N^{[q]}(M, e)$ denotes the size of the

---

[3]This e-fault-tolerant q-ary search corresponds to e error-correcting encoding for the q-ary symmetric channel with noiseless, delay-less feedback.

shortest winning strategy for the Ulam-Rényi game with q-ary search and e lies over the search space $\{0, 1 \ldots, M - 1\}$. We will see that this result holds under the stronger hypothesis that adaptiveness is used only once. In particular, the lower bound is always achievable when $M = q^m$, up to finitely many exceptional m's.

We will also give exact results for small instances. In doing so, we will analyze general tools that can be used for dealing with practical instances of the problem.

3.4.1 Fault-Tolerant q-ary search

In the Ulam-Rényi game with q-ary search, Paul and Carole first fix two integers $q \geq 2$ and $M \geq 1$. The search space S is identified with the set $\{0, 1, \ldots, M - 1\}$. The definition of *state* and *final state* are the same as in Sect. 2.1. Typically, a q-ary *question* **T** has the form

Which one of the sets $T_0, T_1, \ldots, T_{q-1}$ does x_* belong to?,

where $\mathbf{T} = (T_0, T_1, \ldots, T_{q-1})$ is a q-tuple of (possibly empty) pairwise disjoint subsets of S whose union is S, and x_* stands for the number secretly chosen by Carole. Whenever Paul's state of knowledge $\sigma = (A_0, A_1, A_2, \ldots, A_e)$ is clear from the context, it will be tacitly assumed that a question actually partitions only the set $A_0 \cup A_1 \cup \cdots \cup A_e$ of surviving elements in σ. For the sake of definiteness, the remaining elements of S can be safely attached to T_{q-1}.

Carole's answer is an integer $i \in \{0, 1, \ldots, q - 1\}$ telling Paul that x_* belongs to T_i. Generalizing (2.1), if Paul is in state $\sigma = (A_0, A_1, \ldots, A_e)$ and Carole's answer is equal to i, then Paul's state becomes

$$\sigma^i = (A_0 \cap T_i, \ (A_0 \setminus T_i) \cup (A_1 \cap T_i), \ \cdots, \ (A_{e-1} \setminus T_i) \cup (A_e \cap T_i)). \quad (3.3)$$

In analogy with what we do for the binary case, a q-ary question corresponding to the partition $(T_0, \ldots, T_{q-1})$ will be denoted by

$$[(a_{00}, \ldots, a_{0e}) : \cdots : (a_{q-10}, \ldots, a_{q-1e})],$$

where $a_{ij} = |T_i \cap A_j|$, meaning that the set T_i contains a_{ij} elements from A_j. If it holds that $a_{ij} = a_{i'j}$ for any $i \neq i'$ we say that the question is *even splitting*.

We will often use the shorthand notation $[(a_0, \ldots, a_e) : (q - 1) \cdot (b_0, \ldots, b_e)]$ to mean that the last $(q - 1)$ components (the $(e + 1)$-tuples) of the question are identical, i.e., they refer to subsets of S whose intersections with A_j have the same size, for any j.

Let $(x_0, \ldots, x_e)$ be the current state and $\mathbf{T} = [(a_{00}, \ldots, a_{0e}) : \cdots : (a_{q-10}, \ldots, a_{qe})]$ be the question asked by Paul. If Carole's answer is "i" for some $i \in \{0, \ldots, q-1\}$, then, according to the rules in (3.3), the resulting new state is $\sigma^i = (x'_0, \ldots, x'_e)$, where

$$\begin{cases} x_0' = a_{i0} \\ x_j' = a_{ij} + \sum_{\substack{k=1 \\ k \neq i}}^{q} a_{k\,j-1} = a_{ij} + (x_{j-1} - a_{i\,j-1})\,j = 1, \ldots, e. \end{cases} \tag{3.4}$$

The definition of *winning q-ary strategies* in terms of a labeled q-ary tree is the natural generalization of that given in Sect. 2.1.

For every integer $q \geq 2$ and state σ of type $(x_0, x_1, \ldots, x_e)$, the *(q-ary) nth volume of σ* is defined by

$$V_n^{[q]}(\sigma) = \sum_{i=0}^{e} a_i \sum_{j=0}^{e-i} (q-1)^j \binom{n}{j}. \tag{3.5}$$

This generalizes Definition 2.5. Accordingly, Theorems 2.1 and 2.2 have the following q-ary generalization.

Proposition 3.1. *Let σ be an arbitrary state and $\mathbf{T}$ be a question. Define $\mathrm{ch}^{[q]}(\sigma) = \min\{n = 0, 1, 2, \ldots \mid V_n^{[q]}(\sigma) \leq q^n\}$. Let σ^i be as in (3.3) and (3.4).*

(a) For every integer $n \geq 1$ we have

$$V_n^{[q]}(\sigma) = \sum_{i=0}^{q-1} V_{n-1}^{[q]}(\sigma^i).$$

(b) If σ has a winning q-ary strategy with n questions then $n \geq \mathrm{ch}^{[q]}(\sigma)$.

(c) Let $\tau = (y_0, \ldots, y_e)$ be a state such that $\sum_{j=0}^{k} y_j \leq \sum_{j=0}^{k} x_j$ for each $k = 0, \ldots, e$. For any winning strategy of size n for σ there exists a winning strategy of size n for the state τ.

As an immediate corollary of the above proposition we have

$$N^{[q]}(M, e) \geq N_{\min}^{[q]}(M, e) = \mathrm{ch}^{[q]}(M, 0, \ldots, 0)$$

for all $M \geq 1$ and $e \geq 0$.

Generalizing Definition 2.6 by a *perfect q-ary strategy for σ* we now mean a winning strategy for σ only requiring $\mathrm{ch}^{[q]}(\sigma)$ questions. We say that a strategy $\mathscr{S}$ for a state σ of type $(q^m, 0, \ldots, 0)$ is *canonical* iff $\mathscr{S}$ is winning for σ and consists of two batches of non-adaptive questions, where the questions in the first batch ask for the q-ary digits of x_*, and the second batch depends only on the m-tuple of Carole's answers to these questions.

3.4.2   *Perfect Strategies and Least Adaptiveness:* $M = q^m$

To guess the secret number x_* in $N_{\min}^{[q]}(q^m, e) = \mathrm{ch}^{[q]}(q^m, 0, \ldots, 0)$ questions, Paul adopts a canonical strategy $\mathscr{S}$ as follows: He first non-adaptively asks for the q-ary expansion of x_*—thus using m questions. After receiving Carole's answers, Paul fixes a q-ary encoding of the surviving candidates, and then non-adaptively asks Carole for the updated encoding of x_*. With finitely many exceptions m, the success of Paul's search is guaranteed by Theorem 3.7 below, which in turns relies on a multitude of results in the theory of error-correcting codes.

By definition, the *first batch of questions* of $\mathscr{S}$ is given by:

For each $i = 1, 2, \ldots, m$, let $\mathbf{D}_i = (D_{i,0}, \ldots, D_{i,q-1})$ denote the question "Which is the ith digit in the q-ary expansion of x_*?" Thus a number $y \in S$ belongs to $D_{i,j}$ iff the ith digit of its q-ary expansion $\mathbf{y} = y_1 \cdots y_m$ is equal to j.

Let $b_i \in \{0, 1, \ldots, q - 1\}$ be Carole's answer to question $\mathbf{D}_i$. Let the string $\mathbf{b}$ of q-ary digits be defined by $\mathbf{b} = b_1 \cdots b_m$. Repeated application of (3.3), beginning with the initial state $\sigma = (S, \emptyset, \ldots, \emptyset)$, shows that Paul's state of knowledge as an effect of Carole's answers is an e-tuple $\sigma^{\mathbf{b}} = (A_0, \ldots, A_e)$, where $A_i = \{y \in S \mid d_H(\mathbf{y}, \mathbf{b}) = i\}$, for each $i = 0, \ldots, e$.

Thus the state $\sigma^{\mathbf{b}}$ has type $(1, m(q-1), \ldots, \binom{m}{e}(q-1)^e)$. Moreover, repeated application of Proposition 3.1(i) yields $\mathrm{ch}^{[q]}(\sigma^{\mathbf{b}}) = \mathrm{ch}^{[q]}(q^m, 0, \ldots, 0) - m$.

The Non-adaptive Second Batch of Questions

For each m-tuple $\mathbf{b} \in \{0, 1, \ldots, q - 1\}^m$ given by Carole's answers, we shall construct a non-adaptive q-ary strategy with $\mathrm{ch}^{[q]}(1, m(q-1), \ldots, \binom{m}{e}(q-1)^e)$ questions, and show that the strategy is winning for the state $\sigma^{\mathbf{b}}$.

For this purpose, let us consider the values of $\mathrm{ch}^{[q]}(1, m(q-1), \ldots, \binom{m}{e}(q-1)^e)$ for $m \geq 1$.

Definition 3.7. Let $q \geq 2$ and $n \geq 3$ be arbitrary integers. The *q-ary critical index* $m_n^{[q]}$ is the largest integer $m \geq 0$ such that $\mathrm{ch}^{[q]}(1, m(q-1), \ldots, \binom{m}{e}(q-1)^e) = n$.

Lemma 3.2. *Let $q \geq 2$, $e \geq 1$ and $n \geq 2e$ be arbitrary integers. Then*

$$\left\lfloor \frac{\sqrt[e]{e! q^{\frac{n}{e}}}}{(q-1)} \right\rfloor - n - e \leq m_{n,e}^{[q]} < \left\lfloor \frac{\sqrt[e]{e! q^{\frac{n}{e}}}}{q-1} \right\rfloor + e. \qquad (3.6)$$

Proof. By definition, $m_{n,e}^{[q]} = \max\left\{ m \mid V_n^{[q]}\left(1, m(q-1), \ldots, \binom{m}{e}(q-1)^e\right) \leq q^n \right\}$.

The right inequality in (3.2) is a direct consequence of the inequality $V_n^{[q]}(\sigma) > q^n$, where $\sigma = \left(1, m^*(q-1), \dots, \binom{m^*}{e}(q-1)^e\right)$ and $m^* = \left\lfloor \frac{\sqrt[e]{e!q^{\frac{n}{e}}}}{q-1} \right\rfloor + e$; in fact

$$V_n^{[q]}(\sigma) > V_n^{[q]}\left(0, \dots, 0, \binom{m^*}{e}(q-1)^e\right)$$

$$= \binom{m^*}{e}(q-1)^e = (q-1)^e \frac{m^*(m^*-1)\cdots(m^*-e+1)}{e!}$$

$$\geq (q-1)^e \frac{\left(\frac{\sqrt[e]{e!q^{\frac{n}{e}}}}{q-1}\right)^e}{e!} = q^n.$$

Let $\tilde{m} = \left\lfloor \frac{\sqrt[e]{e!q^{\frac{n}{e}}}}{(q-1)} \right\rfloor - n - e$. In order to prove the left inequality, we need to show that

$$V_{n+\tilde{m}}^{[q]}\left(q^{\tilde{m}}, 0, \dots, 0\right) \leq q^{n+\tilde{m}},$$

which is equivalent to proving

$$\sum_{j=0}^{e} \binom{\tilde{m}+n}{j}(q-1)^j \leq q^n.$$

We have

$$\sum_{j=0}^{e} \binom{\tilde{m}+n}{j}(q-1)^j \leq (q-1)^e \sum_{j=0}^{e} \binom{\tilde{m}+n}{j}$$

$$\leq (q-1)^e \binom{\tilde{m}+n+e}{e}$$

$$= (q-1)^e \frac{(\tilde{m}+n+e)(\tilde{m}+n+e-1)\cdots(\tilde{m}+n+1)}{e!}$$

$$\leq (q-1)^e \frac{(\tilde{m}+n+e)^e}{e!}$$

$$\leq \frac{(q-1)^e}{e!}\left(\frac{\sqrt[e]{e!q^{\frac{n}{e}}}}{q-1} - n - e + n + e\right)^e = q^n,$$

which completes the proof.

The second batch of questions is obtainable from the following lemma, which formally states the correspondence between non-adaptive winning strategies and certain special codes.

Lemma 3.3. *Fix integers $a_0, a_1, \ldots, a_e \geq 0$, $q \geq 2$ and $n \geq \mathrm{ch}^{[q]}(a_0, a_1, \ldots, a_e)$. Let $\sigma = (A_0, A_1, \ldots, A_e)$ be a state of type $(a_0, a_1, \ldots, a_e)$. Then there exists a non-adaptive winning q-ary strategy for σ with n questions if and only if for all $i = 0, 1, 2, \ldots, e - 1$ there are integers $d_i \geq 2(e - i) + 1$, together with an e-tuple of q-ary codes $\Gamma = \{\mathscr{C}_0, \mathscr{C}_1, \mathscr{C}_2, \ldots, \mathscr{C}_{e-1}\}$, such that each $\mathscr{C}_i$ is an (n, a_i, d_i) code and $\Delta(\mathscr{C}_i, \mathscr{C}_j) \geq 2e - (i + j) + 1$, (for all $0 \leq i < j \leq e - 1$).*

Proof. We first prove the implication *strategy* $\Rightarrow$ *codes*. Let $\sigma = (A_0, A_1, \ldots, A_e)$ be a state of type $(a_0, a_1, \ldots, a_e)$ having a non-adaptive winning strategy $\mathscr{S}$ with n questions $\mathbf{T}_j = \{T_{j0}, T_{j1}, \ldots, T_{jq-1}\}$, $j = 1, 2, \ldots, n$ and $n \geq \mathrm{ch}(\sigma)$. Let the map

$$z \in A_0 \cup A_1 \cup A_2 \cup \cdots \cup A_e \mapsto \mathbf{z}^{\mathscr{S}} \in \{0, 1, \ldots, q - 1\}^n$$

send each $z \in A_0 \cup A_1 \cup A_2 \cup \cdots \cup A_e$ into the n-tuple of digits $\mathbf{z}^{\mathscr{S}} = z_1^{\mathscr{S}} \cdots z_n^{\mathscr{S}}$ arising from the sequence of "true" answers to the questions "Which set among $T_{j0}, T_{j1}, \ldots, T_{jq-1}$ does z belong to?", $j = 1, 2, \ldots, n$. More precisely, for each $j = 1, \ldots, n$, $z_j^{\mathscr{S}} = i$ iff $z \in T_{ji}$. Let $\mathscr{C} \subseteq \{0, 1, \ldots, q - 1\}^n$ be the range of the map $z \mapsto \mathbf{z}^{\mathscr{S}}$. We shall first prove that, for every $i = 0, \ldots, e - 1$ there exists an integer $d_i \geq 2(e - i) + 1$ such that the set $\mathscr{C}_i = \{\mathbf{y}^{\mathscr{S}} \in \mathscr{C} \mid y \in A_i\}$ is an (n, a_i, d_i) code.

Since $\mathscr{S}$ is winning, the map $z \mapsto \mathbf{z}^{\mathscr{S}}$ is one-to-one, whence, in particular, $|\mathscr{C}_i| = a_i$ for any $i = 0, 1, 2, \ldots, e - 1$. Moreover, by definition, the $\mathscr{C}_i$'s are subsets of $\{0, 1, \ldots, q - 1\}^n$.

Claim 1. Fix integers $0 \leq i \leq j \leq e$ and $x, y \in S$ and define $\tau = (B_0, B_1, \ldots, B_e)$ such that $\cup_{j=0}^e B_j = \{x, y\}$ and $x \in B_i$ and $y \in B_j$. Then, for each $n \leq 2e - (i + j)$, the state τ is not a winning n-state.

We prove the statement by contradiction. Suppose that there exists a strategy $\mathscr{S}$ with $2e - (i + j)$ questions which is winning for τ. Assume first that for each question $\mathbf{T} = \{T_0, T_1, \ldots, T_{q-1}\}$ in $\mathscr{S}$ it holds that $x \in T_0$, $y \in T_1$. Suppose now that $x_* = x$, and Carole answers "0" to the first $e - j$ questions and answers "1" to the following $e - i$ questions. Therefore, by (3.3), the resulting state after Carole's answers is $\tau' = (0, 0, \ldots, \{x, y\})$, contradicting the hypothesis that $\mathscr{S}$ is winning.

On the other hand, suppose there exists a question $\mathbf{T} = \{T_0, T_1, \ldots, T_{q-1}\}$ such that for some $i = 0, 1, \ldots, q - 1$, it holds that $\{x, y\} \subseteq T_i$; then, by assuming again that Carole answers exactly $e - j$ times by pointing at the set containing x and for the remaining $e - i$ times she indicates the set containing y, we have that the resulting state is a *superstate* of τ'. This, again, contradicts the hypothesis and complete the proof.

Claim 2. For any $0 \leq i \leq j \leq e - 1$ and for each $y \in A_i$ and $h \in A_j$ we have the inequality $d_H(\mathbf{y}^{\mathscr{S}}, \mathbf{h}^{\mathscr{S}}) \geq 2e - (i + j) + 1$.

For otherwise (absurdum hypothesis), let $y \in A_i, h \in A_j$ be a counterexample, and $d_H(\mathbf{y}^{\mathscr{S}}, \mathbf{h}^{\mathscr{S}}) \leq 2e - (i + j)$. Writing $\mathbf{y}^{\mathscr{S}} = y_1^{\mathscr{S}} \ldots y_n^{\mathscr{S}}$ and $\mathbf{h}^{\mathscr{S}} = h_1^{\mathscr{S}} \ldots h_n^{\mathscr{S}}$, there is no loss of generality in assuming $h_k^{\mathscr{S}} = y_k^{\mathscr{S}}$, for all $k = 1, \ldots, n - (2e - (i + j))$. Suppose that the answer to question T_k is "i" where $i = h_k^{\mathscr{S}}$. Then the state resulting from these answers has the form $\sigma'' = (A_0'', A_1'', A_2'', \ldots, A_e'')$, where $y \in A_i''$ and $h \in A_i''$. Then σ'' is a substate of the state τ in the previous claim, which together with Proposition 3.1 (iii) proves that $2e - (i + j)$ additional questions will not suffice to find the unknown number. This contradicts the assumption that $\mathscr{S}$ is a winning strategy.

In conclusion, for all $i = 0, 1, \ldots, e - 1$, $\mathscr{C}_i$ is an (n, a_i, d_i) code with $d_i \geq 2(e - i) + 1$, and for all $j = 0, \ldots, i - 1, i + 1, \ldots, e - 1$ we have the desired inequality $\Delta(\mathscr{C}_i, \mathscr{C}_j) \geq 2e - (i + j) + 1$.

Now we prove the converse implication: *strategy $\Leftarrow$ codes.*

Let $\Gamma = (\mathscr{C}_0, \mathscr{C}_1, \mathscr{C}_2, \ldots, \mathscr{C}_{e-1})$ be an e-tuple of codes satisfying the hypothesis. The *Hamming sphere $\mathscr{B}_r(\mathbf{x})$ with radius r and center $\mathbf{x}$* is the set of elements of $\{0, 1, \ldots, q - 1\}^n$ whose Hamming distance from $\mathbf{x}$ is at most r; in symbols,

$$\mathscr{B}_r(\mathbf{x}) = \{\mathbf{y} \in \{0, 1, \ldots, q - 1\}^n \mid d_H(\mathbf{x}, \mathbf{y}) \leq r\}.$$

Notice that for any $\mathbf{x} \in \{0, 1, \ldots, q - 1\}^n$, and $r \geq 0$, we have $|\mathscr{B}_r(\mathbf{x})| = \sum_{i=0}^{r} \binom{n}{i}(q - 1)^i$.

Let

$$\mathscr{H} = \bigcup_{i=0}^{e-1} \bigcup_{\mathbf{x} \in \mathscr{C}_i} \mathscr{B}_{e-i}(\mathbf{x}).$$

By hypothesis, for any $i, j \in \{0, 1, \ldots, e - 1\}$ and $\mathbf{x} \in \mathscr{C}_i, \mathbf{y} \in \mathscr{C}_j$ we have $d_H(\mathbf{x}, \mathbf{y}) \geq 2e - (i + j) + 1$. It follows that the Hamming spheres $\mathscr{B}_{e-i}(\mathbf{x}), B_{e-j}(\mathbf{y})$ are pairwise disjoint and hence

$$|\mathscr{H}| = \sum_{i=0}^{e-1} a_i \sum_{j=0}^{e-i} \binom{n}{j}(q - 1)^j. \tag{3.7}$$

Let $\mathscr{D} = \{0, 1, \ldots, q - 1\}^n \setminus \mathscr{H}$. Since $n \geq \mathrm{ch}^{[q]}(a_0, a_1, a_2, \ldots, a_e)$, by definition of character we have $q^n \geq \sum_{i=0}^{e} a_i \sum_{j=0}^{e-i} \binom{n}{j}(q - 1)^j$. From (3.7) it follows that

$$|\mathscr{D}| = q^n - \sum_{i=0}^{e-1} a_i \sum_{j=0}^{e-i} \binom{n}{j}(q - 1)^j \geq a_e. \tag{3.8}$$

Let $\sigma = (A_0, A_1, A_2, \ldots, A_e)$ be an arbitrary state of type $(a_0, a_1, a_2, \ldots, a_e)$. Let us now fix, once and for all, $e + 1$ one-one maps $f_i: A_i \to \mathscr{C}_i$ for $i = 0, 1, \ldots, e-1$, and $f_e: A_e \to \mathscr{D}$. The existence of the map f_i, for all $i = 0, 1, \ldots, e$, is ensured by our assumptions about Γ, together with (3.8).

Let the map $f: A_0 \cup A_1 \cup A_2 \cup \cdots \cup A_e \to \{0, 1, \ldots, q-1\}^n$ be defined by cases as follows:

$$f(y) = \begin{cases} f_0(y), \, y \in A_0 \\ f_1(y), \, y \in A_1 \\ \vdots \\ f_e(y), \, y \in A_e \end{cases} \tag{3.9}$$

Note that f is one-one. For each $y \in A_0 \cup A_1 \cup A_2 \cup \cdots \cup A_e$ and $j = 1, \ldots, n$ let $f(y)_j$ be the jth digit of the n-tuple $f(y) \in \{0, 1, \ldots, q-1\}^n$. We can now exhibit the questions $\mathbf{T}_j = (T_{j0}, T_{j1}, \ldots, T_{jq-1})$, $j = 1, 2, \ldots, n$, of our search strategies:

For each $j = 1, \ldots, n$ let the set $T_{ji} \subseteq S$ be defined by $T_{ji} = \{z \in \bigcup_{k=0}^e A_k \mid f(z)_j = i\}$. Intuitively, $\mathbf{T}_j$ asks "What is the jth digit in the q-ary expansion of $f(x_*)$?"

The answers to questions $\mathbf{T}_1, \ldots, \mathbf{T}_n$ determine an n-tuple of digits $\mathbf{b} = b_1 \cdots b_n$. We shall show that the sequence $\mathbf{T}_1, \ldots, \mathbf{T}_n$ yields an optimal non-adaptive winning strategy for σ. Let $\sigma_1 = \sigma^{b_1}$, $\sigma_2 = \sigma_1^{b_2}, \ldots, \sigma_n = \sigma_{n-1}^{b_n}$. Arguing by cases we shall show that $\sigma_n = (A_0^*, A_1^*, \ldots, A_e^*)$ is a final state.

By (3.3), for all $i = 0, 1, \ldots, e$, any $z \in A_{e-i}$ that falsifies $> i$ answers does not survive in σ_n—in the sense that $z \notin A_0^* \cup A_1^* \cup \cdots \cup A_e^*$.

Case 1. $\mathbf{b} \notin \bigcup_{i=0}^e \bigcup_{y \in A_i} \mathscr{B}_{e-i}(f(y))$.

For all $i = 0, 1, \ldots, e$ and for each $y \in A_i$ we must have $y \notin A_0^* \cup A_1^* \cup \cdots \cup A_e^*$. Indeed, the assumption $\mathbf{b} \notin \mathscr{B}_{e-i}(f(y))$ implies $d_H(f(y), \mathbf{b}) > e - i$, whence y falsifies $> e - i$ of the answers to $\mathbf{T}_1, \ldots, \mathbf{T}_n$, and y does not survive in σ_n. We have proved that $A_0^* \cup A_1^* \cup \cdots \cup A_e^*$ is empty, and σ_n is a final state.

Case 2. $\mathbf{b} \in \mathscr{B}_{e-i}(f(y))$ for some $i \in \{0, 1, \ldots, e\}$ and $y \in A_i$.

Then $y \in A_0^* \cup A_1^* \cup \cdots \cup A_e^*$, because $d_H(f(y), \mathbf{b}) \le e - i$, whence y falsifies $\le e - i$ answers. Our assumptions about Γ ensure that, for all $j = 0, 1, \ldots, e$ and for all $y' \in A_j$ and $y \ne y'$, we have $\mathbf{b} \notin \mathscr{B}_{e-j}(f(y'))$. Thus, $d_H(f(y'), \mathbf{b}) > e - j$ and y' falsifies $> e - j$ of the answers to $\mathbf{T}_1, \ldots, \mathbf{T}_n$, whence y' does not survive in σ_n. This shows that for any $y' \ne y$, we have $y' \notin A_0^* \cup A_1^* \cup \cdots \cup A_e^*$. Therefore, $A_0^* \cup A_1^* \cup \cdots \cup A_e^*$ only contains the element y, and σ_n is a final state.

According to this result, the second batch of non-adaptive questions will be given by the family of codes provided in the following lemma.

Lemma 3.4. *For any fixed integers $k \ge 0$ and $e \ge 1$ and for all sufficiently large integers n, there exists an e-tuple of q-ary codes $\Gamma = (\mathscr{C}_0, \mathscr{C}_1, \ldots, \mathscr{C}_{e-1})$ together with integers $d_i \ge 2(e - i) + 1$ $(i = 0, 1, \ldots, e - 1)$ such that*

(a) Each $\mathscr{C}_i$ is an $(n + k, \binom{m_{n,e}^{[q]}-k}{i}(q-1)^i q^k, d_i)$ code;

(b) $\Delta(\mathscr{C}_i, \mathscr{C}_j) \geq 2e - (i + j) + 1$ (whenever $0 \leq i < j \leq e - 1$).

Proof. Let $n' = n - e^2 + k$. First we prove the existence of an $(n', \binom{m_{n,e}^{[q]}-k}{e-1})$ $(q-1)^{e-1}q^k, 2e + 1)$ code. From Lemma 3.2, together with the trivial inequality $e! \leq \frac{(e+1)^e}{2^e}$, it follows that, for all sufficiently large n

$$\binom{m_{n,e}^{[q]}}{e-1}(q-1)^{e-1}q^k < (m_{n,e}^{[q]})^{e-1}(q-1)^{e-1}q^k$$

$$< (\frac{\sqrt[e]{e!}\, q^{\frac{n}{e}}}{q-1} + e)^{e-1}(q-1)^{e-1}q^k$$

$$\leq (\frac{e\, q^{\frac{n}{e}}}{q-1})^{e-1}(q-1)^{e-1}q^k$$

$$\leq e^{e-1}q^{n-\frac{n}{e}+k}$$

$$= e^{e-1}\frac{q^{n-e^2}}{q^{\frac{n}{e}-e^2-k}}$$

$$\leq \frac{q^{n-e^2+k}}{\sum_{j=0}^{2e}\binom{n-e^2+k}{j}(q-1)^j},$$

since $\sum_{j=0}^{2e}\binom{n-e^2+k}{j}(q-1)^j$ is polynomial in n.

The existence of the desired $(n', \binom{m_{n,e}^{[q]}-k}{e-1}(q-1)^{e-1}q^k, 2e + 1)$ code now follows from Theorem 3.4. We have proved that, for all sufficiently large n, there exists an $(n - e^2 + k, \binom{m_{n,e}^{[q]}-k}{e-1}(q-1)^{e-1}q^k, 2e + 1)$ code $\mathscr{C}'$. For each $i = 0, 1, \ldots, e-1$ let the e^2-tuple $\mathbf{a}_i$ be defined by

$$\mathbf{a}_i = \underbrace{00\ldots0}_{ie}\underbrace{11\ldots1}_{e}\underbrace{00\ldots0}_{e^2-(i+1)e}.$$

Furthermore, let $\mathscr{C}_i''$ be the code obtained by appending the suffix $\mathbf{a}_i$ to the codewords of $\mathscr{C}'$; in symbols,

$$\mathscr{C}_i'' = \mathscr{C}' \otimes \mathbf{a}_i.$$

Trivially, $\mathscr{C}_i''$ is an $(n + k, \binom{m_{n,e}^{[q]}-k}{e-1}(q-1)^{e-1}q^k, 2e + 1)$ code for all $i = 0, 1, \ldots, e-1$. Furthermore, we have $\Delta(\mathscr{C}_i'', \mathscr{C}_j'') = 2e \geq 2e - (i + j) + 1$ whenever $0 \leq i < j \leq e - 1$. For each $i = 0, 1, \ldots, e-1$, pick a subcode $\mathscr{C}_i \subseteq \mathscr{C}_i''$ with $|\mathscr{C}_i| = \binom{m_{n,e}^{[q]}-k}{i}(q-1)^i q^k$. Then the new e-tuple of codes $\Gamma = (\mathscr{C}_0, \mathscr{C}_1, \ldots, \mathscr{C}_{e-1})$ satisfies both conditions (a) and (b), and the proof is complete.

The following summarizes the main results of this section, showing the existence of minimum adaptiveness perfect search strategies for the Ulam-Rényi game with q-ary questions and e errors when the search space has cardinality q^m for some sufficiently large integer m.

Theorem 3.7. *Fix an integer $e \geq 0$. Then for all sufficiently large integers m there exists a perfect winning strategy $\mathscr{S}$ for the Ulam-Rényi game with q-ary questions and e lies over the search space of cardinality q^m, which uses adaptiveness only once. More precisely, $\mathscr{S}$ has exactly size $N^{[q]}_{\min}(q^m, e)$. Therefore,*

$$N^{[q]}(q^m, e) = N^{[q]}_{\min}(q^m, e).$$

Proof. Skipping the trivialities, assume $e \geq 1$. We know that there exists a batch of m non-adaptive questions which leads Paul from the initial state to some state σ_m of type $(1, m(q-1), \ldots, \binom{m}{e}(q-1)^e)$. We have that $\mathrm{ch}^{[q]}(\sigma_m) = N^{[q]}_{\min}(q^m, e) - m$. Therefore, to complete the proof it is enough to show that there exists a non-adaptive winning strategy $\mathscr{S}$ for σ_m such that the number of questions in $\mathscr{S}$ coincides with Berlekamp's lower bound $\mathrm{ch}^{[q]}(\sigma) = N^{[q]}_{\min}(q^m, e) - m$.

Let $n = \mathrm{ch}^{[q]}(\sigma_m)$ and $k = 0$. By definition, $n \to \infty$ as $m \to \infty$. Lemmas 3.4 and 3.3 yield a non-adaptive winning strategy with n questions for any state of type $(1, m^{[q]}_{n,e}(q-1), \binom{m^{[q]}_{n,e}}{2}(q-1)^2, \ldots, \binom{m^{[q]}_{n,e}}{e}(q-1)^e)$. By Definition 3.7, $m \leq m^{[q]}_{n,e}$, and a fortiori, for all sufficiently large m, a non-adaptive winning strategy with n questions exists for any state of type $(1, m(q-1), \ldots, \binom{m}{e}(q-1)^e)$. The proof is complete.

Shrinking the First Batch of Questions

In view of the last result, let us now return to Berlekamp's model in Sect. 3.1, and focus on the *asymmetric* nature of the communication between the questioner and responder: The forward questioner-to-responder channel is *noiseless*, while the feedback channel is *noisy*. In the cooperative model, where questioner and responder have agreed on the searching strategy, and lies are replaced by distortions, the result of the previous section shows that error-correcting transmission can be achieved via the following protocol, where $m = \lfloor \log M \rfloor$:

(a) Send m bits over the noisy responder-to-questioner channel,
(b) Over the noiseless feedback channel, send to the responder the m-tuple of bits, as actually received by the questioner,
(c) Finally send to the questioner a final tip of $N^{[q]}_{\min}(M, e) - m$ bits over the noisy channel.

Since in many concrete situations the noiseless feedback channel is much more costly than the forward noisy channel, one can reasonably consider the problem of minimizing the number of feedback bits to be sent during stage (c). The following problem is especially interesting for us:

To what extent can one decrease the number of bits sent over the noiseless channel, while still keeping to a minimum both the total number of questions and the number of non-adaptive batches of questions?

As we will see, for every fixed integer $k \geq 1$ one can always reduce from m to $m - k$ the number of questions in the first batch (and similarly reduce the number of feedback bits over the noiseless channel) for all suitably large m.

Fix an integer $k \geq 1$ and let m be a sufficiently large integer. Suppose that the first batch of questions only consists of the first $m - k$ queries of Sect. 3.4.2. Then a direct computation shows that the resulting state $\sigma_k = (A_0, A_1, \ldots, A_e)$ is of type

$$\left(q^k, q^k (m - k)(q - 1), q^k \binom{m - k}{2}(q - 1)^2, \ldots, q^k \binom{m - k}{e}(q - 1)^e \right),$$

and $\mathrm{ch}^{[q]}(\sigma_k) = N_{\min}^{[q]}(q^m, e) - m + k$. For the desired perfect two-round strategy, we must exhibit, for the state σ_k, a non-adaptive winning strategy with $N_{\min}^{[q]}(q^m, e) - m + k$ questions. For this purpose, we can use again Lemma 3.4 with the appropriate k.

The following corollary implies the existence of minimum adaptiveness perfect searching strategies with a first batch of $m - k$, rather than m, questions.

Corollary 3.2. *Fix two integers $e \geq 0$, and $k \geq 0$. Then for all sufficiently large integers m and for every state σ_k of type $(q^k, (m-k)q^k(q-1), \ldots, \binom{m-k}{e}q^k(q-1)^e)$ there exists a non-adaptive winning strategy $\mathscr{S}$ such that the number of questions in $\mathscr{S}$ coincides with Berlekamp's lower bound $\mathrm{ch}^{[q]}(\sigma_k) = N_{\min}^{[q]}(q^m, e) - m + k$.*

Proof. We can safely assume $e, k \geq 1$. Let $n = \mathrm{ch}^{[q]}(\sigma_k)$. By definition, $n \to \infty$ as $m \to \infty$. Lemmas 3.4 and 3.3 yield a non-adaptive winning strategy with n questions for any state of type $(q^k, q^k(m_{n,e} - k)(q - 1), q^k \binom{m_{n,e}-k}{2}$ $(q - 1)^2, \ldots, q^k \binom{m_{n,e}-k}{e}(q - 1)^e)$. By Definition 3.7, $m \leq m_{n,e}^{[q]}$, whence a fortiori, for all sufficiently large m, a non-adaptive winning strategy with n questions exists for any state of type $(q^k, q^k(m - k)(q - 1), q^k \binom{m-k}{2}(q - 1)^2, \ldots, q^k \binom{m-k}{e}(q - 1)^e)$.

3.4.3 Arbitrary Cardinality of the Search Space: Least Adaptive Quasi-perfect Strategies

The last two results can be extended to the case of search space of arbitrary cardinality M, not necessarily being a power of q. For the moment, we shall have to trade generality for optimality. In particular, we shall lose our *perfectness* and we shall be able to guarantee the minimum adaptiveness for a strategy that uses at most one question more than the minimum possible as given by the Hamming Bound.

More About Perfect Minimally Adaptive Strategies

The following lemma extends the result of the previous section. It implies that for any $e \geq 1$ there are infinitely many values of M (besides $M = q^m$) for which perfect and minimally adaptive search strategies exist.

Lemma 3.5. *Fix $q \geq 2$, $e \geq 0$. Then, for all sufficiently large n, and*

$$\sigma = \left((q+1)q^{m_{n,e}^{[q]}-1}, 0, \ldots, 0\right).$$

there exists a perfect strategy for σ using $ch(\sigma) = (m_{n,e}^{[q]} + n + 1)$ questions, asked in two non-adaptive batches.

Proof. First we prove that $ch^{[q]}(\sigma) \geq m_{n,e}^{[q]} + n + 1$. By definition of *character*, it is enough to show that the $(n + m_{n,e}^{[q]})$th q-ary volume of σ exceeds $q^{n+m_{n,e}^{[q]}}$, that is,

$$V_{n+m_{n,e}^{[q]}}^{[q]}(\sigma) > q^{n+m_{n,e}^{[q]}}.$$

For $i = 0, 1, \ldots, m_{n,e}^{[q]} - 1$, let $\sigma_i = (a_{i\,0}, a_{i\,1}, \ldots, a_{i\,e})$, where

$$a_{i\,j} = (q+1)q^{m_{n,e}^{[q]}-1-i}\binom{i}{j}(q-1)^j.$$

For $i = 0, 1, \ldots, m_{n,e}^{[q]} - 2$, the state σ_{i+1} coincides with the one produced by asking an even splitting question in the state σ_i. Hence, by Proposition 3.1 (a) we have

$$V_{n+m_{n,e}^{[q]}-i}^{[q]}(\sigma_i) = q\, V_{n+m_{n,e}^{[q]}-i-1}^{[q]}(\sigma_{i+1}).$$

Let us now consider the state $\sigma' = (a'_0, a'_1, \ldots, a'_e)$, with $a'_i = (q+1)\binom{m_{n,e}^{[q]}-1}{i}(q-1)^i$ for $i = 0, \ldots, e$. It holds that

$$V_{n+1}^{[q]}(\sigma') = \sum_{j=0}^{e}(q+1)\binom{m_{n,e}^{[q]}-1}{j}(q-1)^j \sum_{i=0}^{e-j}\binom{n+1}{i}(q-1)^i$$

$$\geq \sum_{j=0}^{e}(q+1)\binom{m_{n,e}^{[q]}-1}{j}(q-1)^j\binom{n+1}{e-j}(q-1)^{e-j}$$

$$= (q+1)(q-1)^e \sum_{j=0}^{e}\binom{m_{n,e}^{[q]}-1}{j}\binom{n+1}{e-j}$$

$$= (q+1)(q-1)^e \binom{m_{n,e}^{[q]} + n}{e}$$

$$\geq \frac{(q+1)(q-1)^e}{e!} (m_{n,e}^{[q]} + n - e)^e$$

$$> \frac{(q+1)(q-1)^e}{e!} \left(\frac{\sqrt[e]{e!} q^{\frac{n}{e}}}{(q-1)} - 2e - 1 \right)^e$$

$$> \frac{q(1+\frac{1}{q})(q-1)^e}{e!} \left(\frac{1}{1+\frac{1}{q}} \frac{\sqrt[e]{e!} q^{\frac{n}{e}}}{(q-1)} \right)^e$$

$$= q^{n+1}.$$

Thus we have the desired result

$$V_{n+m_{n,e}^{[q]}}^{[q]} (\sigma) = V_{n+m_{n,e}^{[q]}}^{[q]} (\sigma_0) = q^{m_{n,e}^{[q]}-1} V_{n+1}^{[q]} \left(\sigma_{m_{n,e}^{[q]}-1} \right) = q^{m_{n,e}^{[q]}-1} V_{n+1}^{[q]} (\sigma')$$

$$> q^{m_{n,e}^{[q]}-1+n+1} = q^{m_{n,e}^{[q]}+n}.$$

It remains to prove that there exists a q-ary winning strategy of length $n+m_{n,e}^{[q]}+1$ for the state σ.

In fact, we already implicitly proved that there exists a non-adaptive sequence of $m_{n,e}^{[q]} - 1$ questions (the even splitting questions mentioned above) with which, starting in the state σ, Paul ends up into the state σ'. In particular, these questions can be asked non-adaptively as follows:

For each $j = 1, 2, \ldots, m_{n,e}^{[q]} - 1$, let $\mathcal{D}_j = (D_{j0}, D_{j1}, \ldots, D_{jq-1})$ denote the question "What is the jth (q-ary) least significant digit of x_*?" Thus, a number $y \in S$ belongs to D_{ji} iff the rightmost jth symbol y_j of its q-ary expansion $\mathbf{y} = y_1 \cdots y_m$ is equal to i.

Therefore, in order to complete the proof it is enough to show that there exists a winning strategy for the state σ' with $n+2$ questions. Such a strategy is immediately obtained by Lemmas 3.4 (setting $k = 2$ and using the fact that $q + 1 < q^2$ for any $q \geq 2$) and 3.3. In fact, such a strategy is a non-adaptive one. This concludes the proof.

We shall also need the following technical results.

Proposition 3.2. *Let* $k \geq 4e^2$; *then it holds that*

$$\sum_{j=0}^{e-1} \left(\binom{k}{j} + \binom{k+1}{j} \right) (q-1)^j \leq \sum_{j=0}^{e} \binom{k}{j} (q-1)^j.$$

Proof. For $k \geq 4e^2$ we have $k^2 + 3k + 2 \geq ke^2 + 2ke + 3e$. It follows that

$$\binom{k}{e} \geq e\binom{k+1}{e-1} \geq \sum_{j=0}^{e-1}\binom{k+1}{j}.$$

With this we get the desired result

$$\sum_{j=0}^{e-1}\left(\binom{k}{j} + \binom{k+1}{j}\right)(q-1)^j \leq \sum_{j=0}^{e}\binom{k}{j}(q-1)^j.$$

Lemma 3.6. *Let $N_{\min}^{[q]}(q^m, e) \geq 4e^2$; then it holds that*

$$N_{\min}^{[q]}(q^m, e) + 1 \leq N_{\min}^{[q]}(q^{m+1}, e) \leq N_{\min}^{[q]}(q^m, e) + 2.$$

Proof. Let $k = N_{\min}^{[q]}(q^m, e)$. By definition it holds that

$$q^m \sum_{j=0}^{e}\binom{k}{j}(q-1)^j \leq q^k \qquad \text{and} \qquad q^m \sum_{j=0}^{e}\binom{k-1}{j}(q-1)^j > q^{k-1}.$$

$$\tag{3.10}$$

From the right inequality in (3.10) we have

$$q^{m+1}\sum_{j=0}^{e}\binom{k}{j}(q-1)^j q^{m+1}\sum_{j=0}^{e}\binom{k-1}{j}(q-1)^j > q^k,$$

yielding, by Proposition 3.1, $N_{\min}^{[q]}(q^{m+1}, e) \geq k + 1$. Hence,

$$N_{\min}^{[q]}(q^m, e) + 1 \leq N_{\min}^{[q]}(q^{m+1}, e). \tag{3.11}$$

From the left inequality in (3.10) we get

$$q^{m+1}\sum_{j=0}^{e}\binom{k}{j}(q-1)^j \leq q^{k+1}.$$

Thus, using Property 3.2,

$$\sum_{j=0}^{e} \binom{k+2}{j} (q-1)^j = \sum_{j=0}^{e} \left(\binom{k}{j-1} + \binom{k}{j} + \binom{k+1}{j-1} \right) (q-1)^j$$

$$= \sum_{j=0}^{e} \binom{k}{j} (q-1)^j + \sum_{j=0}^{e-1} \left(\binom{k}{j} + \binom{k+1}{j} \right) (q-1)^j$$

$$\leq q^{(k+1)-(m+1)} + \sum_{j=0}^{e} \binom{k}{j} (q-1)^j$$

Hence,

$$q^{m+1} \sum_{j=0}^{e} \binom{k+2}{j} (q-1)^j \leq q^{k+1} + q^{m+1} \sum_{j=0}^{e} \binom{k}{j} (q-1)^j \leq q^{k+2}.$$

yielding $N_{\min}^{[q]}(q^{m+1}, e) \leq k + 2$.

Quasi-perfect Strategies: The Main Theorem

We are now ready to prove that for any $e \geq 1$ and up to finitely many exceptional M, search strategies with at most $N_{\min}^{[q]}(M, e) + 1$ questions always exist which use adaptiveness only once.

Theorem 3.8. *For any fixed $e \geq 0$ and $q \geq 2$ and for all sufficiently large M it holds that*

$$N_{\min}^{[q]}(M, e) \leq N^{[q]}(M, e) \leq N_{\min}^{[q]}(M, e) + 1.$$

Proof. Let $m = \lfloor \log_q M \rfloor$. Thus,

$$N^{[q]}(q^m, e) \leq N^{[q]}(M, e) \leq N^{[q]}(q^{m+1}, e).$$

Fix the smallest integer n such that $m \leq m_{n,e}^{[q]}$. Hence, by definition and Theorem 3.7 we have

$$N_{\min}^{[q]}(q^m, e) = m + n = N^{[q]}(q^m, e).$$

We shall now argue by cases.

Case 1. $m < m_{n,e}^{[q]}$. Hence, $m + 1 \leq m_{n,e}^{[q]}$. Definition 3.7 and Theorem 3.7 yield

$$N_{\min}^{[q]}(q^{m+1}, e) = m + 1 + n = N^{[q]}(q^{m+1}, e).$$

Thus, we have the desired result

$$N^{[q]}(M, e) \leq N^{[q]}(q^{m+1}, e) = N^{[q]}(q^m, e) + 1 = N_{\min}^{[q]}(q^m, e) + 1 \leq N^{[q]}(M, e) + 1.$$

Case 2. $m = m_{n,e}^{[q]}$. Thus, $m + 1 > m_{n,e}^{[q]}$, and by definition we have

$$N_{\min}^{[q]}(q^{m+1}, e) \geq m + 1 + n + 1 = m + n + 2.$$

On the other hand, by Lemma 3.6 we have

$$N_{\min}^{[q]}(q^{m+1}, e) \leq N_{\min}^{[q]}(q^m, e) + 2 = m + n + 2.$$

Hence, $N_{\min}^{[q]}(q^{m+1}, e) = n + m + 2$. Moreover, by Theorem 3.7, we also have that $N^{[q]}(q^{m+1}, e) = m + n + 2$.

Recalling that $m = m_{n,e}^{[q]}$, Lemma 3.5 yields

$$N^{[q]}((q + 1)q^{m-1}, e) = m + n + 1 = N_{\min}^{[q]}((q + 1)q^{m-1}, e).$$

We have the following two subcases, both leading to the desired result.

Subcase 1. $q^m \leq M \leq (q + 1)q^{m-1}$. Thus,

$$N^{[q]}(M, e) \leq N(q + 1)q^{m-1} = m + n + 1 = N_{\min}^{[q]}(q^m, e) + 1 \leq N_{\min}^{[q]}(M, e) + 1.$$

Subcase 2. $(q + 1)q^{m-1} < M < q^{m+1}$. Thus,

$$N^{[q]}(M, e) \leq N^{[q]}(q^{m+1}, e) = m + n + 2 = N_{\min}^{[q]}((q + 1)q^{m-1}, e) + 1 \leq N_{\min}^{[q]}(M, e) + 1.$$

The proof is complete.

3.5 Some Finite Exact Results for the q-ary Adaptive Ulam-Rényi game

In this section we return to the fully adaptive version of the game and show some results providing exact estimates on the size of the optimal strategies for special instances. These results are interesting because they are based on a new recursive definition of borderline states for the q-ary variant of the game. Before presenting a new table of maximal borderline states we show a q-ary generalization of the translation bound (Theorem 2.3).

The following theorem yields a lower bound on the size of the smallest winning strategy in a game with e lies in terms of the size of the smallest winning strategy in a game with $e - 1$ lies.

Theorem 3.9. *If $(x_0, \ldots, x_{e-1}, x_e)$ is a winning m-state and $(0, x_0, \ldots, x_{e-1})$ is a borderline winning n-state then $m \geq n + 2$.*

Proof. If $(x_0, \ldots, x_{e-1}, x_e)$ is a winning m-state then it admits a winning strategy $\mathscr{S}$ of size m. Starting in the state $(x_0, \ldots, x_e)$, after asking the first $n - 1$ questions of $\mathscr{S}$, there exists at least one resulting state, say $\tau = (y_0, \ldots, y_e)$, such that $\sum_{i=0}^{e-1} y_i \geq 2$. Indeed were this not the case, the state $(0, x_0, \ldots, x_{e-1})$ would be a winning $(n - 1)$-state, contradicting the hypothesis. Notice that the state $\sigma = (s_0, \ldots, s_e) = (0, \ldots, 0, 2, 0)$ is a borderline winning 3-state and $\sum_{j=0}^{k} s_j \leq \sum_{j=0}^{k} y_j$ for any $k = 0, \ldots, e$. Then, by Proposition 3.1 (c) any winning strategy for τ has size at least 3; therefore, the winning strategy $\mathscr{S}$ for $(x_0, \ldots, x_e)$ has size at least $(n - 1) + 3$. Therefore, we conclude that $m \geq n - 1 + 3 = n + 2$.

Note that this is a weaker result than the one in Theorem 2.3 for the binary case. In fact, under the same hypothesis of Theorem 3.9 above, and up to finitely many exceptions, in the binary case it holds that $m \geq n + 3$.

An Infinite Sequence of Winning States for q-ary Search

Table 3.2 shows an infinite sequence of winning states for the q-ary Ulam-Rényi problem. The table is built by generalizing ideas presented in Sect. 2.4. Thus, the states included in such a table are particular cases of states allowing perfect strategies, since they are maximal with respect to their volume. Indeed, they give us the basic ingredients to prove the main results of this section.

Let $s_{i,j}$ be the (i, j) entry of Table 3.2, with $s_{1,1}$ the leftmost upper corner entry, and let $\sigma_{i,m}$ denote the state $(s_{i,1}, s_{i,2}, \ldots, s_{i,m})$. Then the number, say n, above the entry $s_{i,m}$ indicates that $\sigma_{i,m}$ is a winning n-state.

Table 3.2 is constructed as follows. The first two columns set the initial conditions, and are defined in order to have winning states satisfy the volume bound with equality for the cases $e = 0$ and $e = 1$, respectively. The sequences of 1's and 0's from third row on continue endlessly.

The state $\sigma_{2,2}$ is the first state to be defined as the non-trivial winning 2-state satisfying exactly the volume bound. Indeed, from $\sigma_{2,2} = (1, (q-1)^2)$, the question $[(1, 0) : (q - 1) \cdot (0, q - 1)]$ yields the two possible states $(1, 0)$ and $(0, q)$, which are winning 0- and 1-states respectively. Finally, the state $\sigma_{1,2}$ is the one which yields $\sigma_{2,2}$, after an even splitting question.

The rest of Table 3.2 (which has to be thought of as continuing infinitely) is completed by means of the following rules: For $j \geq 3$

$$\begin{cases} \text{for } i \geq 2, \ s_{i,j} = (q-1)s_{i-1,j-1} \\ \text{for } i = 1, \ s_{1,j} = (q-1)^2 s_{1,j-1} \end{cases} \tag{3.12}$$

Lemma 3.7. *Any state in Table 3.2 has a perfect strategy.*

Proof. Trivially, the states $\sigma_{i,m}$ with $i > m$ are final states. For $i \leq m$, let us consider the state $\sigma_{i,m}$ which satisfies the volume bound with equality for n questions, where $n = 2m - i$. We show that there exists a question which leads to new states satisfying exactly the volume bound for $n - 1$ questions.

Let $i = 1$. For any m, the state $\sigma_{1,m}$ satisfies exactly the volume bound for $n = 2m - 1$. We show that, by using an even splitting question, we get the state $\sigma_{2,m}$, which satisfies exactly the volume bound for $n' = 2m - 2 = n - 1$ questions. We prove the claim for any component $s_{1,j}$. The claim is obviously true for $j = 1, 2$ by the way we have defined $\sigma_{1,2}$. Then, for any $j \geq 3$, the jth component of the state resulting from $\sigma_{1,m}$, by using an even splitting question is $\frac{1}{q}s_{1,j} + \frac{q-1}{q}s_{1,j-1}$. Moreover, from (3.12), we have $\frac{1}{q}s_{1,j} + \frac{q-1}{q}s_{1,j-1} = \frac{(q-1)^2}{q}s_{1,j-1} + \frac{q-1}{q}s_{1,j-1} = (q-1)s_{1,j-1} = s_{2,j}$.

For all $i \geq 2$, we shall show that there exists a question **T** such that the two states resulting from $\sigma_{i,m}$, upon asking **T**, are $\sigma_{i+1,m}$ and $\sigma_{i-1,m-1}$ (actually the latter state is $(0, \sigma_{i-1,m-1}) = (0, s_{i-1,1}, \ldots, s_{i-1,m-1})$; recall that the leftmost zeroes in the vector notation used for the states are meaningless, i.e., the state $\sigma_{i-1,m-1}$ is equivalent to the state $(0, \sigma_{i-1,m-1}) = (0, s_{i-1,1}, \ldots, s_{i-1,m-1})$).

Let us define $\mathbf{T} = [(a_1, a_2, \ldots, a_m) : (q-1) \cdot (b_1, b_2, \ldots b_m)]$ where for any i, a_i and b_i are recursively defined as follows:

$$a_1 = s_{i+1,1}, \quad a_j = s_{i+1,j} - (q-1)b_{j-1} \quad \text{for } j = 2, 3, \ldots, m,$$
$$b_1 = 0, \quad b_j = s_{i-1,j-1} - (q-2)b_{j-1} - a_{j-1} \quad \text{for } j = 2, 3, \ldots, m.$$

It is apparent that the possible states resulting from such a question, are either $\sigma_{i+1,m}$ or $\sigma_{i-1,m-1}$. It remains to prove that **T** is a feasible question, i.e., it defines a partition of $\sigma_{i,m}$.

We prove it, inductively, by showing that $s_{i,k} = a_k + (q-1)b_k$, for any k. This is trivially true for $k = 1$. Suppose that it holds for $k = j < m$; then, for $k = j + 1$ we get:

$$a_{j+1} + (q-1)b_{j+1} = s_{i+1,j+1} - (q-1)b_j + (q-1)s_{i-1,j} - (q-2)(q-1)b_j$$
$$- (q-1)a_j$$
$$= s_{i+1,j+1} - (q-1)[(q-1)b_j + a_j] + (q-1)s_{i-1,j}$$
$$= (q-1)s_{i,j} - (q-1)s_{i,j} + (q-1)s_{i-1,j}$$
$$= s_{i,j+1}$$

Table 3.2 Perfect states for q-ary search with lies

$\sigma_{i,j}$	$s_{.,1}$	$s_{.,2}$	$s_{.,3}$	$s_{.,4}$	$\cdots$
$\sigma_{1,.}$	q	$q^3 - 3q^2 + 2q$	$q^5 - 5q^4 + 9q^3 - 7q^2 + 2q$	$q^7 - 7q^6 + 20q^5 - 30q^4 + 25q^3 - 11q^2 + 2q$	$\vdots$
$\sigma_{2,.}$	1	$(q-1)^2$	$q^4 - 4q^3 + 5q^2 - 2q$	$q^6 - 6q^5 + 14q^4 - 16q^3 + 9q^2 - 2q$	$\vdots$
$\sigma_{3,.}$	1	0	$(q-1)^3$	$q^5 - 5q^4 + 9q^3 - 7q^2 + 2q$	$\vdots$
$\sigma_{4,.}$	1	0	0	$(q-1)^4$	$\vdots$
$\cdots$	$\cdots$	$\cdots$	$\cdots$	$\cdots$	$\ddots$

This proves that for any state in the table, satisfying the volume bound with equality for n questions, there exists a question that leads to a new state which satisfies, exactly, the volume bound for $n - 1$ questions. By iterating exactly n times, we eventually reach a final state. The total number of questions asked is then exactly equal to the character of the state considered, i.e., n. We have indeed proved that any state in Table 3.2 has a perfect strategy.

Coping with Many Lies When $M = q^m$

Now we are ready to give some exact estimate of $N^{[q]}(M, e)$, for $e \geq 3$, and $M = q^m$. More precisely, we shall prove that:

- if $m \leq q - 1$ then $N^{[q]}(q^m, e) = m + 2e$;
- if $q \leq m \leq \min\{q(q - 2), 2(q - 1)\}$ then $N^{[q]}(q^m, e) = (m + 1) + 2e$.

We start by giving lower bounds for $N^{[q]}(q^m, e)$.

Lemma 3.8. *Let $q > 1$. For any non-negative integer r let $f(r, q) = \sum_{j=0}^{r} q^j - (r + 1)$. Then, $f(r, q) < m \leq f(r + 1, q)$, if and only if $\mathrm{ch}^{[q]}(q^m, 0) = (m + 2) + r$.*

Proof. The proof is by induction on r.
For $r = 0$, the desired result follows from solving the system of inequalities:

$$\begin{cases} V_{m+2}^{[q]}(q^m, 0) \leq q^{m+2}, \\ V_{m+1}^{[q]}(q^m, 0) > q^{m+1} \end{cases}$$

which is equivalent to

$$\begin{cases} q^2 - (m + 2)q + (i + 1) \geq 0, \\ qm > m \end{cases}$$

Let the lemma be true for any $r \leq k - 1$. Then $f(k - 1, q) < m \leq f(k, q)$ iff $\mathrm{ch}^{[q]}(q^m, 0) = m + 2 + k - 1 = m + 1 + k$, which gives that for $m > f(k, q)$ we have $V_{(m+1)+k}^{[q]}(q^m, 0) > q^{(m+1)+k}$. Moreover, we have $V_{(m+1)+(k+1)}^{[q]}(q^m, 0) \leq q^{(m+1)+(k+1)}$ if and only if $[(m + 2) + k](q - 1) + 1 \leq q^{k+2}$; equivalently,

$$q^{k+2} - [(m + 2) + k]q + [(m + 1) + k] \geq 0,$$

which for $q \geq 1$ has solution

$$m \leq q^{k+1} + q^k + \cdots + q - (k + 1) = f(k + 1, q).$$

Therefore, we have proved that for $f(k, q) < m \leq f(k + 1, q)$ it holds that $\mathrm{ch}^{[q]}(q^m, 0) = (m + 2) + k$, i.e., the statement holds also when $r = k$, which concludes the proof.

Corollary 3.3. *Let $q \geq 2$ and $f(r, q)$ be defined as in Lemma 3.8. If $f(r, q) < m \leq f(r + 1, q)$ then $N^{[q]}(q^m, e) \geq m + r + 2e$.*

Proof. When $e = 1$, the conclusion follows straightforwardly from Lemma 3.8 and Proposition 3.1. By using Theorem 3.9 we have the desired result for $e > 1$. ∎

Now we can prove the main results of this section.

Theorem 3.10. *If $M = q^m$ and $m \leq q - 1$ then $N^{[q]}(M, e) = m + 2e$.*

Proof. From Corollary 3.3, by setting $r = 0$, we get $N^{[q]}(q^m, e) \geq i + 2e$. We prove that the converse is also true, i.e., $N^{[q]}(q^m, e) \leq m + 2e$. If we consider again the case $e = 1$ after asking m even splitting questions, the resulting state is $(1, m(q - 1))$. Moreover, when $m \leq q - 1$, the state $(1, m(q - 1))$ is a substate of $(1, (q - 1)^2) = \sigma_{2,2}$, which is a winning 2-state, from Table 3.2. In the case $e > 1$, after m even splitting questions the resulting state is

$$\left(1, \binom{m}{1}(q - 1), \binom{m}{2}(q - 1)^2, \binom{m}{3}(q - 1)^3, \ldots \right),$$

whose components grow at rate less than $\frac{m}{2}(q - 1)$. Since the components of the state $\sigma_{2,e+1}$ in Table 3.2 grow at rate not less than $(q - 1)^2$, in the case $m \leq q - 1$ and for any number of lies, the state we get after m even splitting questions is always a substate of $\sigma_{2,e+1}$, which is a winning $2e$-state. This concludes the proof. ∎

Theorem 3.11. *If $M = q^m$ and $q \leq m \leq \min\{q(q - 2), 2(q - 1)\}$ then $N^{[q]}(M, e) = (m + 1) + 2e$.*

Proof. From Corollary 3.3, by setting $r = 1$, we get $N^{[q]}(M, e) \geq (m + 1) + 2e$ when $m \leq q^2 + q - 2$, which satisfies the hypothesis of the theorem since $\min\{q(q - 2), 2(q - 1)\} \leq q^2 + q - 2$.

We now prove that $N^{[q]}(M, e) \leq (m + 1) + 2e$. Indeed, the state $(q^m, 0, \ldots, 0)$ after m even splitting questions reduces to

$$\tau = \left(1, m(q - 1), \binom{m}{2}(q - 1)^2, \ldots, \binom{m}{e}(q - 1)^e \right).$$

By comparing this state with state $\sigma_{1,e+1}$, in Table 3.2 we note that for the second component, $m(q - 1)$, we have

$$m(q - 1) \leq q(q - 1)(q - 2) \text{ iff } m \leq q(q - 2). \tag{3.13}$$

Furthermore, the components of $\sigma_{1,e+1}$ grow at rate $r_1 = (q - 1)^2$, while the components of τ grow at rate not greater than $r_2 = \frac{m}{2}(q - 1)$.

Since $r_1 \geq r_2$ whenever $m \leq 2(q - 1)$, considering (3.13) it follows that $m \leq \min\{q(q - 2), 2(q - 1)\}$ implies that τ is a substate of $\sigma_{1,e+1}$, which is a winning $(2e + 1)$-state. Thus $N^{[q]}(M, e) = (m + 1) + 2e$. ∎

As a corollary we obtain the following results when the cardinality of the solution space, M, is not restricted to being a power of q.

Corollary 3.4. *For any non-negative integers M and e and any $q \geq 2$, we have*

(i) *if $\lceil \log_q M \rceil \leq q - 1$ then $N^{[q]}(M, e) = \lceil \log_q M \rceil + 2e$.*
(ii) *if $q - 1 < \lceil \log_q M \rceil \leq \min\{q(q-2), 2(q-1)\}$ then $\lceil \log_q M \rceil + 2e \leq N^{[q]}(M, e) \leq \lceil \log_q M \rceil + 1 + 2e$.*

Proof. (i) Let $m = \lceil \log_q M \rceil$; then, by Theorem 3.9 we get $N^{[q]}(M, e) \geq m + 2e$. Moreover, $(M, 0, 0)$ is a substate of $(q^m, 0, 0)$, and $m \leq q - 1$; then, by Theorem 3.10 we obtain $N^{[q]}(M, e) \leq m + 2e$, which concludes the proof of (i).

(ii) Let $m = \lceil \log_q M \rceil$; then, $q^{m-1} < M \leq q^m$, with $q - 1 < m \leq \min\{q(q-2), 2(q-1)\}$. Then, in view of the monotonicity of $N^{[q]}(M, e)$ with respect to M, by Theorem 3.11 we have the conclusion.

3.6   Bibliographic Notes

Coding Theory can be thought of as beginning in the late 1940s with the work of Golay [113], Hamming [116] and Shannon [190, 191]. Although it has its origins in an engineering problem, the subject has developed by using more and more sophisticated mathematical techniques. We presented just the material necessary for understanding the following chapters. For more complete treatment of coding theory, the reader is referred to, e.g., [145] [205] [23]. More on the origin of error-correcting coding theory can be found in [200]. It seems that Hamming was irritated by the fact that his computer kept on stopping when it detected an error. He correctly decided that if it could detect errors, it should be able to locate them and then get on with the job!

MDS codes were for the first time considered in Singleton's seminal paper [194], where a connection between orthogonal Latin Squares and MDS codes was also mentioned (see Exercises 6, 7, 8). See also Chap. 11 of [145] for more. The problem of finding two orthogonal Latin Squares of order q was considered by Euler, who claimed it impossible for the case $q = 2, 6$ and all $q \equiv 2 \pmod 4$. This statement was known as Euler's conjecture for 177 years, until it was suddenly and completely disproved by Bose et al. [34]. More on Latin Squares and Orthogonal Latin Squares can be found in [206].

The RS codes were introduced by Irvin S. Reed and Gustav Solomon in 1960 [181]. Fast decoding procedures with running time $O(n^2)$ or even better are well-known based on the Berlekamp and Massey algorithm [145]. For a detailed account of several applications of RS codes refer to [209] and [195].

Theorem 3.6 was independently proved by Tietäväinen [201] and Zinoviev-Leontiev [215]. Theorem 3.5 first appeared in [148] and is the most celebrated result obtained by a technique originally presented by Delsarte [88] for obtaining upper bounds on codes. For up-to-date tables of the largest known codes refer to N.J. Sloane's Web page.

Error-correcting transmission in the presence of a feedback channel was also considered by Shannon [192] and Dobrushin [93]. Here we followed Berlekamp's description, for which we refer the interested reader to [22] (and references therein).

The monographs [6] and [94] also discuss the power of adaptive and non-adaptive searching strategies and their possible uses in different contexts. In particular, for application of two-stage strategies in the special context of computational molecular biology, see [134].

The study of the perfect non-adaptive winning strategy for one lie, as given by Hamming codes [116], has been further deepened by Pelc [166]. In [166] it is shown that adaptiveness in this case is irrelevant even under the stronger assumption that repetition of the same question is forbidden.

The first to consider non-binary search with lies was Pelc [165], in the context of detecting counterfeit coins with unreliable weightings. This is in fact a q-ary search in the particular case $q = 3$. For the general case $q \geq 2$, the problem of q-ary search with $e = 1$ lies was considered by Malinowski [146] and Aigner [5], who independently evaluated the size of the shortest searching strategy for a search space of arbitrary cardinality $M \geq 1$. A general asymptotic solution of the Ulam-Rény game with q-ary questions was given by Muthukrishnan [156], who generalized Spencer's results for the binary case. More precisely, Muthukrishnan [156] proved that, for each $e \geq 1$ and for all sufficiently large m, Paul can infallibly guess an unknown number in a search space of cardinality $M = q^m$, using q-ary questions with e lies—by asking the theoretical minimum number of questions. Stated differently, we have that for all integers $q \geq 2$, $e \geq 1$ and for all sufficiently large m, $N^{[q]}(q^m, e) = N_{\min}^{[q]}(q^m, e)$.

An alternative formulation of Lemma 3.4 has been considered and proved in [216]. In this paper, in disguised form, the problem of finding non-adaptive perfect strategies for an arbitrarily chosen state in the Ulam-Rényi game is considered and partially solved.

3.7 Exercises

1. Provide an inductive proof of the q-ary variant of the volume bound.
2. Show that there exists an $n \geq 1$ and states σ in the q-ary problem ($q > 2$) that satisfy the volume bound for n questions without having a winning strategy of size n.

3. Prove or disprove the existence of a $q \geq 2$ and a state $\sigma = (x_0, \ldots, x_e)$ such that in the Ulam-Rényi problem with q-ary search $ch(\sigma) = ch(\sigma') + 1$ where $\sigma' = (x_0, \ldots, x_{e-1})$.

4. Show that the translation bound (i.e., the difference of three questions at least) does not hold in general in the case of q-ary search, for $q \geq 3$.

5. Prove the following bounds on the critical index for the particular case $e = 2$. Let $n \geq 3$ be an arbitrary integer. Then for all $q \geq 2$ we have

$$
\left\lfloor \frac{\sqrt{2}\, q^{\frac{n}{2}}}{q-1} \right\rfloor - n - 1 \leq m_n^{[q]} \leq \left\lfloor \frac{\sqrt{2}\, q^{\frac{n}{2}}}{q-1} \right\rfloor - n + 1.
$$

6. A *Latin Square* of order n is an $n \times n$ matrix such that every row and every column of it is a permutation of $\{1, 2, \ldots, n\}$. Two Latin Squares A and B of order n are said to be *orthogonal* when for each ordered pair $(x, y) \in \{1, 2, \ldots, n\}^2$ there is a unique pair of indices i, j such that the (i, j) entries of A and B are x and y, respectively.
   Show that an $(n, q^2, d = r + 1)$ q-ary code (with $n = r + 2$) is equivalent to a set of r pairwise orthogonal Latin Squares of order q.

7. Bose et al. proved the following: For each $q = 3, 4, 5, 7, 8, \ldots$, there exists a pair of orthogonal Latin Squares of order q. Moreover, for $q = 2, 6$ there does not exist any pair of orthogonal Latin Squares of order n.
   Using these results, prove that for any integer $q \geq 3$ there exists a $(4, q^2, 3)$ q-ary code *if and only if* $q \neq 6$.

8. Show that for any $k \geq 1$, $r \geq 1$, $q \geq 2$ such that $k + r \leq q - 1$, there exists an (n, q^k, d) code with $n = k + r$ and $d = r + 1$.

9. Show that for each $m = 1, 2, 3, \ldots$, it holds that $N^{[2]}(2^m, 1) = N_{\min}^{[2]}(2^m, 1)$, i.e., the size of the shortest possible strategy satisfies with equality the Volume Bound.
   What does an optimal strategy look like?

Chapter 4
Weighted Errors over a General Channel

Questions are never indiscreet. Answers sometimes are.

O. Wilde, *An Ideal Husband*

4.1 Introduction

In this chapter, we will analyze a variant of the Ulam-Rényi problem with q-ary questions where we assume that Carole's lies are constrained to patterns agreed upon in advance and known to Paul. This is the case, e.g., when in the classical *yes-no* question game one stipulates that Carole can only lie if the correct answer to Paul's question is *yes*, while she must answer sincerely whenever the correct answer to Paul's question is *no*. This particular variant of the game is also known as the half-lie game.

More generally, we will allow different types of errors to have different weights and understand the parameter e as a bound on the total weight of Carole's answers. The resulting new model generalizes all the variants seen so far. Under this more general setting we will show a strong, and somehow surprising, result, namely that for any choice of the error weights and any constant bound on the (total weight of the) errors, asymptotically, every possible instance of the problem is solvable by a *perfect* strategy that uses adaptiveness only once.

4.2 Two-Batch Search with Weighted Lies

A function $\Gamma : \mathcal{Q} \times \mathcal{Q} \to \mathbb{N}_0 = \{0, 1, 2, \ldots\}$ is given such that $\Gamma(i, i) = 0$ for each i and $\Gamma(i, j) > 0$ for each $i \neq j$. We shall also refer to Γ as "channel", a name suggested by the information-theoretical model of the problem. Γ is used to assign weights to Carole's answers. These weights, together with a parameter $e \geq 0$, are given and bound the number of Carole's lies.

F. Cicalese, *Fault-Tolerant Search Algorithms*, Monographs in Theoretical Computer Science. An EATCS Series, DOI 10.1007/978-3-642-17327-1__4, © Springer-Verlag Berlin Heidelberg 2013

If Carole answers j to a question whose correct answer is i, then this answer has *individual weight* $\Gamma(i, j)$. Every correct answer has weight 0. The total weight of Carole's answers at the end of the game is not allowed to be larger than the given parameter e. The lie bound e is known to both players.

We use w to denote the weight of the *cheapest* possible lie allowed to Carole, that is, $w = w^\Gamma = \min\{\Gamma(i, j) : i \neq j\}$.

We also define the set F of all possible sequences of $\lfloor e/w \rfloor$ lies, with total weight not larger than e. Note that these are the longest allowed sequences of lies. Intuitively, these are the sequences of lies on which Carole has the largest number of possible alternatives. It turns out that, asymptotically, only the number of such sequences counts, regardless of the actual structure of the channel.

Formally, $F = F^\Gamma$ is the set of all $\lfloor e/w \rfloor$-tuples $((a_1, b_1), \cdots, (a_{\lfloor e/w \rfloor}, b_{\lfloor e/w \rfloor}))$ of ordered pairs from $\mathcal{Q} \times \mathcal{Q}$ such that for each $j = 1, \ldots, \lfloor e/w \rfloor$ it holds that $a_j \neq b_j$ and $\sum_{j=1}^{\lfloor e/w \rfloor} \Gamma(a_j, b_j) \leq e$.

In this chapter we shall attack the problem from a different perspective. For any choice of q, e, Γ, and n we shall focus on the largest possible $M = M(q, e, \Gamma, n)$ for which it is possible to find an unknown number $x \in \mathcal{U}$ with n q-ary questions and maximum lie cost e.

As in the previous chapter, at any stage of the game, when questions $\mathbf{T}_1, \ldots, \mathbf{T}_t$ have been asked and answers $\mathbf{B}^t = b_1, \ldots, b_t$ have been received (with $b_i \in \mathcal{Q}$), Paul's *state* of knowledge is represented by an $(e + 1)$-tuple $\sigma = (A_0, A_1, A_2, \ldots, A_e)$ of pairwise disjoint subsets of $\mathcal{U}$, where for each $i = 0, 1, 2, \ldots, e$ A_i is the set of elements of $\mathcal{U}$ which could possibly coincide with x, supposing that the sum of the individual weights of Carole's answers $b_1, \ldots, b_t$ equals i. In particular, the *initial* state σ_0 is given by $(\mathcal{U}, \emptyset, \emptyset, \ldots, \emptyset)$. Let $k = b_t$ and assume Paul is in state $\sigma_{t-1} = (B_0, \ldots, B_e)$. Then, Paul's new state $\sigma_t = \sigma_{t-1}^k = (C_0^k, \ldots, C_e^k)$ resulting from Carole's answer k to question $\mathbf{T}_t$ is given by

$$C_i^k = \bigcup_{\{j \in \mathcal{Q} :: \Gamma(j,k) \leq i\}} \left(B_{i-\Gamma(j,k)} \cap T_j\right). \tag{4.1}$$

Carole's answers $b_1, \ldots, b_t$ determine a sequence of states $\sigma_0 = \sigma$, $\sigma_1 = \sigma_0^{b_1}$, $\sigma_2 = \sigma_1^{b_2}$, $\ldots$, $\sigma_t = \sigma_{t-1}^{b_t}$.

A state $(A_0, A_1, A_2, \ldots, A_e)$ is *final* iff the set $A_0 \cup A_1 \cup A_2 \cup \cdots \cup A_e$ has at most one element.

A *strategy* $\mathscr{S}$ with n questions is a q-ary tree of depth n, where each node v is mapped into a question $\mathbf{T}_v$, and the q edges $\eta_0, \eta_1, \ldots, \eta_{q-1}$ generated by v are labelled $0, 1, \ldots, q - 1$, which represent Carole's possible answers to $\mathbf{T}_v$. Let $\eta = \eta_1, \ldots, \eta_n$ be a path in $\mathscr{S}$ from the root to a leaf, with respective labels $b_1, \ldots, b_n$, generating nodes $v_1, \ldots, v_n$ and associated questions $\mathbf{T}_{v_1}, \ldots, \mathbf{T}_{v_n}$. We say that strategy $\mathscr{S}$ is *winning* for σ iff for every path η the state σ^η is final. A strategy is said to be *nonadaptive* if all nodes at the same depth of the tree are mapped into the same question.

The main result of this chapter is summarized in the following.

Theorem 4.1. *Asymptotically with n, we have*

$$M(q, e, \Gamma, n) = q^{n + \lfloor e/w \rfloor} / |F| \binom{n}{\lfloor e/w \rfloor} + o(1).$$

Moreover, we provide optimal search strategies consisting of two batches of non-adaptive questions.

The following result is a well-known application of Chernoff's bound.

Lemma 4.1. *Let $X_1, \ldots, X_n$ be independent 0-1 random variables. Let $X = \sum_{i=1}^{n} X_i$ and $\mu = \mathbf{E}[X]$. For $0 < \delta < 1$,*

$$Pr(|X - \mu| > \delta\mu) \le 2e^{-\mu\delta^2/3}.$$

Definition 4.1. Let n and $q > 1$ be integers. A sequence $\mathbf{s} = s_1, \ldots, s_n$ from $\mathcal{Q}^n$ is called *regular* if there exists a number $\sqrt{n} \ll r \ll n$ such that for each $a \in \mathcal{Q}$ the number of occurrences of a in $\mathbf{s}$, denoted by $\#_\mathbf{s}(a)$, satisfies $|\#_\mathbf{s}(a) - n/q| \le r$.

We say that $\mathbf{s}$ is *P-wise regular* if, dividing $\mathbf{s}$ into P parts as evenly as possible (up to rounding), each part contains at least $\frac{n}{qP}(1 - \frac{1}{P})$ occurrences of each element in $\mathcal{Q}$.

We will use the following two technical results. The first is an easy consequence of Lemma 4.1. The second, whose proof is due to Dumitriu and Spencer, shows that it is enough to consider numbers of the type $\lfloor (1-\delta)aq^m \rfloor$, where $a \in (q^T, q^{T+1}] \cap \mathbb{N}$, with T being an integer depending only on δ and q.

Lemma 4.2. *For any integer $q > 1$ and real $\delta > 0$, there exists n_0 such that for all integers $n \ge n_0$ the number of sequences in $\mathcal{Q}^n$ that are not regular is bounded from above by δq^n.*

Proof. Fix an integer $c \in \mathcal{Q}$. Let X_i be the random variable that takes value 1 if the ith value in the sequence is c, and $Pr(X_i = 1) = 1/q$. Then, the number of sequences that are not regular, because the number of occurrences of c does not respect the required bound, can be computed as $q^n \times Pr(|\sum_{i=1}^{n} X_i - n/q| > r)$.

Thus, the desired result directly follows from Lemma 4.1. ∎

Lemma 4.3. *Given $q, g, k, \delta \in (0, 1)$ and given any $0 < \alpha < \alpha' < q^{\lfloor e/w \rfloor}/g$, there exists $T \in \mathbb{N}$ and $n_0 \in \mathbb{N}$ such that for any $n \ge n_0$, and any $M \le \alpha \frac{q^n}{\binom{n}{\lfloor e/w \rfloor}}$, there exists $a \in (q^T, q^{T+1}] \cap \mathbb{N}$, and a nonnegative integer m such that*

$$M \le (1 - \delta)aq^m < \alpha' \frac{q^n}{\binom{n}{\lfloor e/w \rfloor}}. \tag{4.2}$$

Proof. Fix T such that $\alpha'\left(1 - \frac{1}{q^{T+1}}\right) > \alpha$. For the sake of easing the notation let us set $D = \frac{q^n}{(1-\delta)\binom{n}{\lfloor e/w \rfloor}}$. Fix n_0 such that $\alpha'D > q^T$ for all $n \ge n_0$. Now, let $a \in [q^T, q^{T+1}) \cap \mathbb{N}$ and m be such that $aq^m < \alpha' D \le (a+1)q^m$, which exist since the intervals $(aq^m, (a+1)q^m]$ have union (q^T, ∞).

The desired upper bound on $(1-\delta)aq^m$ follows from the upper bound on aq^m. Furthermore, from the lower bound

$$aq^m = \left(1 - \frac{1}{a+1}\right)(a+1)q^m \ge \left(1 - \frac{1}{q^t + 1}\right)\alpha' D > \alpha D,$$

we have $M \le \alpha(1-\delta)D \le (1-\delta)aq^m$.

4.3 The Lower Bound: The Winning Strategy

In this section we will prove the following lower bound on $M(q, e, \Gamma, n)$.

Theorem 4.2. *Let* $M \le \alpha \dfrac{q^n}{\binom{n}{\lfloor e/w \rfloor}}$ *for some* $\alpha < \dfrac{q^{\lfloor e/w \rfloor}}{|F|}$. *Then, Paul has a strategy of size n to determine Carole's secret number in the Ulam-Rényi game over the channel Γ with total weight e, over a search space of cardinality M. Moreover, Paul's questions can be asked in two batches of non-adaptive questions.*

Let $M \le \alpha \dfrac{q^n}{\binom{n}{\lfloor e/w \rfloor}}$ for some $\alpha < \dfrac{q^{\lfloor e/w \rfloor}}{|F|}$. There exist α' and δ such that

$$\frac{q^{\lfloor e/w \rfloor}}{|F|} > \alpha' > \alpha \quad \text{and} \quad \frac{\alpha'}{1-\delta} < \frac{q^n}{\binom{n}{\lfloor e/w \rfloor}}. \tag{4.3}$$

Moreover, by Lemma 4.3, there exist m and a such that

$$M \le aq^m < \frac{\alpha'}{1-\delta}\frac{q^n}{\binom{n}{\lfloor e/w \rfloor}}. \tag{4.4}$$

Note that $n \to \infty$ implies $m \to \infty$. By Lemma 4.2 there exist at least $(1-\delta)q^m$ regular sequences in the space $\mathscr{Q}^m$. By Lemma 4.3 there are at most $aq^m(1-\delta)$ elements in the search space $\mathscr{U}$. Therefore, Paul can define an injective function f that maps elements of the search space $\mathscr{U}$ to pairs $(i, \mathbf{w})$ such that $i \in \{1, 2, \ldots, a\}$ and $\mathbf{w}$ is a regular sequence in $\mathscr{Q}^m$.

4.3.1 The First Batch of Questions

Let x^* be the element chosen by Carole, and $f(x^*) = (i^*, \mathbf{w}^*)$, according to the function fixed by Paul. Paul asks a first batch of m questions, where the ith question is "What is the ith component of $\mathbf{w}^*$?"

Let $\mathbf{w}'$ be the sequence of Carole's answers. We can immediately observe that for each $i \in \mathcal{Q}$ the number of occurrences of i in $\mathbf{w}'$ is at most $m/q + r + \lfloor e/w \rfloor$.

For each $j = 0, 1, \ldots, \lfloor e/w \rfloor$ and $k = 0, 1, 2, \ldots, j$, let $F_k^{(j)}$ denote the set of possible sequences of k lies $(a_1, b_1), \ldots, (a_k, b_k)$ with total weight $\left(\sum_{\ell=1}^{k} \Gamma(a_\ell, b\ell) \right) \in \{jw, jw + 1, \ldots, j(w + 1) - 1\} \cap \{0, 1, \ldots, e\}$.

Proposition 4.1. *Let* $\sigma = (A_0, \ldots, A_e)$ *be the state resulting from Carole's answers to Paul's first batch of questions. For* $j = 0, 1, \ldots, \lfloor e/w \rfloor - 1$ *we have*

$$(i) \quad \frac{1}{a} \sum_{i=0}^{w-1} |A_{jw+i}| \leq \sum_{k=0}^{j} \frac{|F_k^{(j)}|}{k!} \left(\frac{m}{q} + r + \left\lfloor \frac{e}{w} \right\rfloor \right)^k$$

$$(ii) \quad \frac{1}{a} \sum_{i=\lfloor e/w \rfloor w}^{e} |A_i| \leq \sum_{k=0}^{\lfloor e/w \rfloor} \frac{|F_k^{(\lfloor e/w \rfloor)}|}{k!} \left(\frac{m}{q} + r + \left\lfloor \frac{e}{w} \right\rfloor \right)^k.$$

Proof. For (i) we count the number of distinct sequences of correct answers that can have led Carole to answer the way she did.

First we notice that in a sequence of Carole's answers with total weight between jw and $j(w + 1) - 1$ there can be at most j lies.

Given $0 \leq k \leq j$, there are $|F_k^{(j)}|$ possible sequences of k lies $(a_1, b_1), \ldots, (a_k, b_k)$ of total weight between jw and $j(w + 1) - 1$. Each position a_i can be chosen in at most $(\frac{m}{q} + r + \lfloor \frac{e}{w} \rfloor)$ ways, due to the regularity property and the maximum possible number of deviations from regularity given by the allowed maximum number of wrong answers.

This gives us at most $|F_k^{(j)}|(\frac{m}{q} + r + \lfloor \frac{e}{w} \rfloor)^k$ mendacious sequences. Finally, we notice that each distinct sequence appears in this counting once for each possible permutation of the positions for the a_i's. Hence, we divide by a $k!$ factor.

Summing over all possible k's we obtain the desired result.

The same argument can be used to prove (ii). In this case we need to set $j = \lfloor e/w \rfloor$ and we only take into consideration lie patterns and sequences of answers with total weight not exceeding e, which might be smaller than $(j + 1)w - 1$.

An immediate consequence of this proposition is the following Gilbert-like bound.

Lemma 4.4. *There exists an n_0 such that for all $n \geq n_0$ we have the inequality*

$$q^{n-m} \geq \left(\sum_{j=0}^{w \lfloor e/w \rfloor - 1} |A_j| \right) \left(\sum_{i=0}^{2\lfloor e/w \rfloor} \binom{n - m}{i} q^i \right) + \sum_{j=w \lfloor e/w \rfloor}^{e} |A_j|,$$

where $\sigma = (A_0, \ldots, A_e)$ *is the state resulting from Carole's answers to Paul's first batch of questions.*

Proof. By the above assumption, via (4.4), we have that $m = O(q^{(n-m)/\lfloor e/w \rfloor})$.

By Proposition 4.1, asymptotically with n (hence also with m) it holds that the sum of the cardinalities of the sets $A_1, \ldots, A_{w\lfloor e/w \rfloor - 1}$ is bounded by

$$O\left(m^{\lfloor e/w \rfloor - 1}\right) = O\left(q^{(n-m)\frac{\lfloor e/w \rfloor - 1}{\lfloor e/w \rfloor}}\right) = o(q^{n-m}) = q^{n-m}(1 - \Omega(1)).$$

Moreover, observing that the factor $\sum_{i=0}^{2\lfloor e/w \rfloor} \binom{n-m}{i} q^i$ accompanying $|A_j|$ is polynomial in $n - m$, we can have it absorbed in the above calculation.

With regard to the sets $A_{\lfloor e/w \rfloor}, \ldots, A_e$ we need to be just a little bit more careful. By Proposition 4.1, the sum of the cardinalities of these sets is bounded by $O(|F|/q^{\lfloor e/w \rfloor} \frac{n^{\lfloor e/w \rfloor}}{\lfloor e/w \rfloor!})$, which is bounded by $O(q^{n-m-\lfloor e/w \rfloor} |F|/\alpha') = q^{n-m}(1 - \Omega(1))$ (by Lemma 4.3).

This result will be the key to prove that, starting from the position reached after the first m questions, Paul can encode the remaining candidates in order to successfully finish the game. We have the following.

Theorem 4.3. *Let $\sigma = (A_0, \ldots, A_e)$ be the state resulting from Carole's answers to Paul's first batch of questions. Then, starting from σ, there exists a non-adaptive winning strategy of size $n - m$ over the channel Γ with total weight e.*

Proof. As a consequence of the previous lemma, there exists a mapping θ sending elements of $\bigcup_{i=0}^{w\lfloor e/w \rfloor - 1} A_i$ one-to-one onto a set $\mathscr{C}_1 \subseteq \mathscr{Q}^{n-m}$ and elements of $\bigcup_{j=w\lfloor e/w \rfloor}^{e} A_j$ one-to-one onto a set $\mathscr{C}_2 \subseteq \mathscr{Q}^{n-m}$ in such a way that

(a) for all $\mathbf{x}_1, \mathbf{x}_2 \in \mathscr{C}_1$, $d_H(\mathbf{x}_1, \mathbf{x}_2) \geq 2 \lfloor e/w \rfloor + 1$,
(b) for all $\mathbf{x}_1 \in \mathscr{C}_1, \mathbf{x}_2 \in \mathscr{C}_2$, $d_H(\mathbf{x}_1, \mathbf{x}_2) \geq \lfloor e/w \rfloor + 1$,

where $d_H(\cdot, \cdot)$ is the Hamming distance between q-ary sequences.

The following simple algorithm accomplishes the above task. Start with $\mathscr{C}_1 = \mathscr{C}_2 = \mathscr{A} = \emptyset$. (1) Pick up an arbitrary element $\mathbf{x} \in \mathscr{Q}^{n-m} \setminus \mathscr{A}$ and add it to $\mathscr{C}_1$. (2) Add to $\mathscr{A}$ the set $\{\mathbf{y} \in \mathscr{Q}^{n-m} \setminus \mathscr{A} \mid d_H(\mathbf{x}, \mathbf{y}) \leq 2\lfloor e/w \rfloor\}$. Repeat (1) and (2) until $\mathscr{C}_1$ reaches the desired cardinality. Finally, pick up $|\bigcup_{j=w\lfloor e/w \rfloor}^{e} A_j|$ elements from $\mathscr{Q}^{n-m} \setminus \mathscr{A}$ and put them in $\mathscr{C}_2$.

Lemma 4.4 guarantees that one can extend $\mathscr{C}_1$ up to the desired cardinality and be left with enough elements in $\mathscr{Q}^{n-m} \setminus \mathscr{A}$ to accommodate the desired set $\mathscr{C}_2$.

By construction, it is also clear that $\mathscr{C}_1$ and $\mathscr{C}_2$ satisfy the desired distance constraints.

4.3.2   The Second Batch of Questions

Paul arbitrarily fixes the map θ. Then, he asks Carole "What is the jth component of the element of $\mathscr{Q}^{n-m}$ onto which the secret number x is mapped by θ?", for $j = 1, 2, \ldots, n - m$.

The constraints on the Hamming distance between any two sequences of length $(n-m)$ in $\mathscr{C}_1$ and $\mathscr{C}_2$ ensure that Paul, independently of Carole's lies, will be able to identify x as the number $a \in \bigcup_{i=1}^{e} A_j$ of minimum Hamming distance from the sequence of length $(n-m)$ defined by the answers of Carole.

Notice that, due to the constraints on the lie weight, Carole in this second batch cannot lie at all if the secret number is one of the elements in $\bigcup_{j=w\lfloor e/w \rfloor}^{e} A_j$. Alternatively, she cannot lie more than $\lfloor e/w \rfloor$ times if the secret number is one of the elements in $\bigcup_{i=0}^{w\lfloor e/w \rfloor - 1} A_i$.

Therefore, if $x \in \bigcup_{j=w\lfloor e/w \rfloor}^{e} A_j$, the sequence of her answers will be exactly one of the sequences in $\mathscr{C}_2$. Hence, Paul by inverting θ will correctly identify the secret number.

Conversely, if $x \in \bigcup_{i=0}^{w\lfloor e/w \rfloor - 1} A_i$ the sequence of Carole's answers will not differ from $\theta(x)$ in more than $\lfloor e/w \rfloor$ places. For any $y \in \bigcup_{i=0}^{e} A_i$, $y \neq x$, we have $d_H(\theta(y), \theta(x)) \geq 2e+1$. Thus, $\theta(y)$ differs from the sequence of Carole's answers in more than e places, whence, by choosing the a such that $\theta(a)$ has minimum distance from the sequence of length $(n-m)$ of Carole's answers, Paul correctly identifies x.

4.4 The Upper Bound

We now show that the strategy provided in the previous section is (asymptotically) best possible in the sense that there is a matching upper bound on $M(q, e, \Gamma, n)$, the largest integer M such that Paul has a strategy of size n to determine Carole's secret number in the Ulam-Rényi game over the channel Γ with total weight e, over a search space of cardinality M.

Definition 4.2. For $x \in \mathscr{U}$ and $0 \leq i \leq e$, an (i, x)-path in the strategy of Paul is a root to leaf path π s.t. the state $\sigma^\pi = (A_0, \ldots, A_e)$ satisfies $|A_i| = \{x\}$ and $A_j = \emptyset$ for all $j \neq i$. For any $x \in \mathscr{U}$ the $(0, x)$-path is also referred to as the *sincere* path for x, since it describes a play in which Carole's secret number is x and she always answers sincerely.

We define the x-bush as the set of all (i, x)-paths, for any $i = 0, 1, \ldots, e$.

Let $\mathscr{S}$ be a winning strategy for Paul with n questions. Fix an element x of the search space. Let $\eta = \eta_1, \ldots, \eta_n$ be the corresponding $(0, x)$-path in $\mathscr{S}$, with respective labels $b_1, \ldots, b_n$ generating nodes $v_1, \ldots, v_n$ and associated questions $\mathbf{T}_{v_1}, \ldots, \mathbf{T}_{v_n}$. For each $i = 1, 2, \ldots, n$ and each $j \in \mathscr{Q} \setminus \{b_i\}$, let $\mathscr{T}_{i,j}$ be the subtree of $\mathscr{S}$ rooted at the node reached by the path $\eta_1, \ldots, \eta_{i-1}, \eta_i'$ with η_i' being the edge stemming from v_i that is labeled $j \neq b_i$. For each $i = 1, 2, \ldots, n$ and for each $j \neq b_i$ such that $\Gamma(b_i, j) \leq e$, there must exist a $(\Gamma(b_i, j), x)$-path in $\mathscr{S}$ that coincides with η in the first $i - 1$ components and whose ith component is j. In fact, this is the (only) path that coincides with the outcome of the game, when Carole chooses the number x and decides to lie (only) at the ith question by answering j instead of b_i.

Let $\pi = \pi_1, \ldots, \pi_n$ be such a path. Let $c_1, \ldots, c_n$ be the label of the edges in π and $v'_1, \ldots, v'_n$ be the generating nodes. By definition, π coincides with η in the first $i - 1$ positions. Let us now concentrate on the remaining part of π. We can now repeat the argument used for η. In fact, for each $k = i + 1, i + 2, \ldots, n$ and each $\ell \neq c_k$ such that $\Gamma(b_i, j) + \Gamma(c_k, \ell) \leq e$, the strategy $\mathscr{S}$ must include a $(\Gamma(b_i, j) + \Gamma(c_k, \ell), x)$-path that coincides with π in its first k components and whose kth edge is labeled ℓ. Of course, now one can repeat the same consideration on such a path to claim the necessity of some (t, x)-path with $\Gamma(b_i, j) + \Gamma(b_k, \ell) \leq t \leq e$, and so on.

In order to turn the above observation into a practical way to count the paths in the x-bush for some number x, we need to consider the structure of the paths involved. In fact, by knowing the labels on the edges of the sincere path one can count the number of necessary paths to accommodate Carole's possible strategies that are based on just one lie, the so called 1-lie-paths. Then, once these paths have been given, on the basis of their structure one could count the number of paths necessary to accommodate Carole's possible strategies that are based on just two lies, the so called 2-lie-paths, and so on.

This gives us a way to obtain an upper bound on the size of the search space where Paul can successfully search with a strategy with n questions. In fact, Paul has to accommodate M bushes (one for each number in the search space) in a tree with q^n paths. This is only possible if he can accurately choose the sincere paths so that there is space for the 1-lie-paths. Then he can fix the paths for the 1-lie-paths strategies of Carole in order to have space for the paths necessary to accommodate the resulting possible strategies of Carole including two lies. This must be possible for all answering strategies of Carole using lies of total weight $\leq e$. In other words, repeating the above way of counting the new strategies, necessarily available to Carole, must always result in having space in the q^n paths in Paul's strategy.

Conversely, Paul has no way to define a winning strategy of size n if there is no way for him to choose the sincere paths and the 1-lie-paths, and so on, in such a way that the *necessarily* resulting paths are in total at most q^n.

The key to our upper bound will be to prove that, for all sufficiently large n, in a strategy of size n, almost all bushes include $\binom{n}{\lfloor e/w \rfloor} \frac{|F|}{q^{\lfloor e/w \rfloor}} + o(1)$ paths. In fact, the number of bushes that might violate this bound is negligible.

In the following we shall identify a path by its associated sequence of labels. We shall need one more definition.

Definition 4.3. A bush is called *regular* if for all the paths it consists of the sequence of labels along each path from a P-wise regular sequence in $\mathscr{Q}^n$. By identifying paths with their sequence of labels, we shall also call such paths P-wise regular paths.

We will now bound the number of bushes that Paul can pack in a tree/strategy of size n. The main observation is that, asymptotically with n, bushes are almost all regular. Thus, paths represent plays in which Carole has a lot of freedom in choosing the position for her lies. In turn, this gives us the possibility to bound the size of a bush from below and hence the number of such bushes that can be contained in a tree with q^n leaves. We start with the following.

Lemma 4.5. *For each $\epsilon > 0$ there exists n_0, such that for all $n \geq n_0$ the size of a regular bush in a winning strategy for Paul with n questions is at least*

$$\binom{n}{\lfloor \frac{e}{w} \rfloor} \left(\frac{q^{\lfloor \frac{e}{w} \rfloor}}{|F|} + \frac{\epsilon}{2} \right)^{-1}.$$

Proof. Let P be a large integer. Let us think of each path in Paul's strategy as divided into P parts, almost evenly. We know that in each of such parts, each label occurs at least $\frac{n}{qP}(1 - \frac{1}{P})$ times. Assume that Carole accepts to follow the additional rule[1]: for each $j = 1, 2, \ldots, P$, the sequence of answers to the questions from the (jn/P)th one to the $((j+1)n/P - 1)$th one will contain at most one wrong answer.

Let x be given and let us count the total number of (i, x)-paths, with $i \in \{w \lfloor e/w \rfloor, \ldots, e\}$. These are all and only the paths followed by the game when Carole uses exactly $\lfloor e/w \rfloor$ lies. There are $|F|$ possible sequences of $\lfloor e/w \rfloor$ lies, such that the total lie weight is not larger than e. According to the deal above, Carole can choose the parts in which she will answer incorrectly in $\binom{P}{\lfloor e/w \rfloor}$ ways. Finally, in each of these parts she can place the lie in at least $\frac{n}{qP}(1 - \frac{1}{P})$ ways, due to the number of occurrences of each label in each Pth fraction of a P-wise regular path. Summarizing, there are at least

$$\binom{P}{\lfloor e/w \rfloor} |F| \left(\frac{n}{qP}(1 - \frac{1}{P}) \right)^{\lfloor e/w \rfloor}$$

paths in the x-bush. For each ϵ there is a large P such that

$$\binom{P}{\lfloor e/w \rfloor} |F| (\frac{n}{qP}(1 - \frac{1}{P}))^{\lfloor e/w \rfloor} > \binom{n}{\lfloor \frac{e}{w} \rfloor} (\frac{q^{\lfloor \frac{e}{w} \rfloor}}{|F|} + \frac{\epsilon}{2})^{-1},$$

which completes the proof.

We are now ready to prove the upper bound.

Theorem 4.4. *For all $\epsilon > 0$ there exists an integer n_0 such that for all integers $n > n_0$, if Paul has a strategy of size n to determine a number $x \in \mathcal{U}$ in the q-ary Rényi-Berlekamp-Ulam game with lies with total weight e over the channel Γ, then*

$$M \leq \left(\frac{q^{\lfloor \frac{e}{w} \rfloor}}{|F|} + \epsilon \right) \frac{q^n}{\binom{n}{\lfloor \frac{e}{w} \rfloor}}.$$

---

[1] Notice that, by this rule, we are making life harder for Carole, and we are actually strengthening our claim.

Proof. By the previous lemma, it follows that Paul can have at most

$$\frac{q^n}{\binom{n}{\lfloor e/w \rfloor}} \left(\frac{q^{\lfloor e/w \rfloor}}{|F|} + \frac{\epsilon}{2} \right)$$

regular bushes in his strategy.

On the other hand, he cannot have room for more than $\frac{q^n}{\binom{n}{\lfloor e/w \rfloor}} \frac{\epsilon}{2}$ non-regular bushes, since there are at most so many paths that are not P-wise regular. In fact, by using for P-wise regular sequences Lemma 4.1 in a way analogous to its use in Lemma 4.2, one can easily bound from above the number of sequences that are not P-wise regular by $q^{n(1-c)}$ for some constant c only depending on P and q. Moreover, for any constant c and for any $\epsilon > 0$ we have $q^{n(1-c)} \leq \frac{q^n}{\binom{n}{\lfloor e/w \rfloor}} \frac{\epsilon}{2}$ for all sufficiently large n.

Summing up, we have that Paul's strategy (tree) cannot contain all bushes if $M > \frac{q^n}{\binom{n}{\lfloor e/w \rfloor}} \left(\frac{q^{\lfloor e/w \rfloor}}{|F|} + \epsilon \right)$. The proof is now complete.

The proof of Theorem 4.1 now follows directly from Theorems 4.2 and 4.4.

4.5   Other Noise Models: Unidirectional Errors

Another well-studied model of information distortion is given by the so-called unidirectional errors. Let us first assume that the channel is completely symmetric and all lies have weight 1. We say that the game is on unidirectional errors if at the beginning of the game Carole has also to decide the direction of all her lies. More precisely, if she chooses *increasing* (*decreasing*) lies, she agrees to the following: she decides that when the correct answer to a question is i, she only chooses the lies among the j's such that $j > i$ ($j < i$). This information is kept secret to Paul. In other words, we can think of Carole and Paul stipulating that the game can be played over two different channels, one that only includes errors of the type $i \rightarrow j$ ($j > i$) and another that only includes errors of the type $i \rightarrow j$ ($j < i$). At the beginning, Carole can choose the channel she prefers to use, but then she will only use that one. Her choice is secret to Paul. We expect this assumption to restrict the number of possible lie patterns that Carole can use. Having tighter bounds for such situations is important in those applications where engineering constraints may allow us to assume that errors in the same transmission block only occur in one direction.

By using arguments analogous to the one employed in the previous section, and assuming the parameter e fixed in advance, one can prove the following very general result.

Theorem 4.5. *Let $\Gamma_1, \Gamma_2, \ldots, \Gamma_t$ be channels. For $j = 1, \ldots, t$, let $w_j = w^{\Gamma_j}$. Let $\tilde{w} = \min_{j=1}^{t} w_j$ and $\tilde{e} = \lfloor e/\tilde{w} \rfloor$. Let $G_i = G^{\Gamma_i}$ be defined as*

$$
G_i = \{((a_1, b_1), \cdots, (a_{\tilde{e}}, b_{\tilde{e}})) : a_j \neq b_j \ \forall j, \sum_{j=1}^{\tilde{e}} \Gamma_i(a_j, b_j) \leq e\}.
$$

Let $M(n)$ be the largest size of a search space where Paul can find a secret number in the variant of the game where Carole is allowed to choose the Γ_i she wants to play with, and keep it a secret from Paul.
Then, for all sufficiently large n, we have

$$
M(n) = \frac{q^{n+\tilde{e}}}{\binom{n}{\tilde{e}}} \left| \bigcup_{i : w_i = \tilde{w}} G_i \right|^{-1} + o(1).
$$

The strategy can be implemented in two batches.

4.6 Bibliographic Notes

In [185] the binary game with asymmetric error was introduced. With the notation used in this chapter, the model of [185] coincides with the case $\Gamma = \begin{pmatrix} 0 & e+1 \\ 1 & 0 \end{pmatrix}$.

For the same type of errors, but for the special case of only one error, i.e., $e = 1$, an exact estimate of $M(2, 1, \Gamma, n)$ was given in [55], for n sufficiently large. In the same paper were introduced some of the tools which subsequently led to the solution of the most general version of the problem: a probabilistic analysis and a new version of the conservation of the volume. More generally, games with $q \geq 2$ and $\Gamma(i, j) \in \{1, e+1\}$ for all $i \neq j$ were considered in [97] and for them $M(q, e, \Gamma, n)$ was determined asymptotically with precision $o(1)$ as n goes to infinity.

Concerning strategies with little adaptiveness, it was shown in [54, 61] that two-batch strategies can be as powerful as the fully adaptive ones for $\Gamma = \begin{pmatrix} 0 & e+1 \\ 1 & 0 \end{pmatrix}$. Subsequently, in [98] the results of [97] were also obtained with two-batch strategies.

The special case where the channel satisfies $|\{(j, k) : \Gamma(j, k) = w, j \in \mathcal{Q}\}| = d$ for all $k \in \mathcal{Q}$ and the cardinality of the search space is a power of q, i.e., $M = q^m$, was analyzed in [56], where upper and lower bounds were given. However, the lower bound of [56] only holds if w is a divisor of e, and in this case the bounds are tight. This result was later generalized in [2] to the case of arbitrary search space dimension M and channel Γ. Finally, the more general result presented in this chapter first appeared in [3].

4.7   Exercises

1. Consider the channel $\Gamma = \begin{pmatrix} 0 & e+1 \\ 1 & 0 \end{pmatrix}$, i.e., the case where only negative answers can be lies and any yes answer can be safely assumed to be sincere.

   Construct an optimal strategy for the case $e = 1$ and $M = 2^{20}$.

2. The model considered in the previous exercise is usually referred to as the *half-lie* or *half-liar* game. Is it correct to say that in the half-lie game answering yes to a question is the same as answering no to the complementary questions?

3. Consider the ternary ($q = 3$) generalization of the *half-lie* game defined by the channel $\Gamma(i, j) = e + 1$ for $i < j$ and $\Gamma(i, j) = 1$ for $i > j$.

   For $e = 1, 2$ and restricted to instances with $M = q^m$, provide an upper and a lower bound for the size of a shortest strategy for Paul.

4. Provide a proof of Theorem 4.5 for the case when the only lies allowed to Carole is to answer $j \leq i$ whenever the correct answer is i and this is known to Paul.

5. What is a good definition of the volume of a state (see Definition 2.5) in the game with weighted lies considered in this chapter?

6. Carole chooses a number from the set $S = \{0, 1, \ldots, 31\}$. Pauls asks yes/no questions. The rule is that Paul wins either if he determines Carole's number or if he can prove that Carole has lied at least once.

   Assuming that Carole is allowed to lie at most $e = 2$ times, what is the minimum number of adaptive questions Paul has to ask? What is the minimum number of questions if they have to be asked non-adaptively?

Chapter 5
Variations on a Theme of Ulam and Rényi: More Types of Questions and Lies

This is the sublime and refined point of felicity,
called, the possession of being well deceived;
the serene peaceful state of being a fool among knaves.

J. Swift, *A Tale of a Tub*

In the search model investigated in the previous chapters, questions are allowed to be arbitrary subsets of the search space. Such an assumption implies an "expensive" representation of both the strategies and the states of the game: For a game over a search space of cardinality $M = 2^m$, one needs M bits for describing each query and each component of the state. In this chapter, we will analyze the query complexity of strategies for the Ulam-Rényi game using only interval and comparison questions, which admit a much more concise representation, and, hence, are more space conscious, so to say. For example, a comparison question, over a search space of cardinality $M = 2^m$, can be described with $O(m)$ bits. We will also discuss an even simpler type of question, namely bit questions, whose representation requires $\log m$ bits.

The above variants study how much the strategy is affected under different constraints on the expressive power of Paul. In this chapter, we shall also study variants of the game in which Carole is provided with more freedom in lying, i.e., alternative ways of bounding lies are used.

5.1 Comparison-Based Search: The Multiple-Interval Queries

We have seen in the previous chapters that by allowing subset queries, the information-theoretic lower bound (aka the Volume Bound) can almost always be achieved. Here we focus on the problem of simplifying the representation of

F. Cicalese, *Fault-Tolerant Search Algorithms*, Monographs in Theoretical
Computer Science. An EATCS Series, DOI 10.1007/978-3-642-17327-1_5,
© Springer-Verlag Berlin Heidelberg 2013

the questions. The subset questions have a very expensive representation, which affects both the formulation of the queries and the updating of the states, which is also necessary for the questioner to formulate the next question. Comparison and interval questions have also been considered in the literature. We shall show that optimal strategies can be implemented by using questions that are expressible as the union of a constant (dependent on e) number of intervals. In addition one can analogously bound the size of the representation of the states of the game.

The basic strategies seen in the previous chapters require $\log M + O(e \log \log M)$ queries, each of which is an arbitrary subset of the search space, hence it might require $\Theta(M)$ bits to be represented. In total, such a strategy uses $O(M \log M)$ bits.

In the strategies we shall present in the next section, each query can be represented by $O(e^2)$ intervals, therefore $O(e^2 \log M)$ bits suffice for the description of each question. The questioner only needs to send to the responder the sequence of intervals' boundaries. This means that the total number of bits the questioner and the responder exchange reduces to $O(e^2 \log^2 M)$.

The Ulam-Rényi Game with Multi-interval Questions. In this variant of the game, the players fix an additional parameter k which determines the maximum number of intervals in a question. A question is any subset of the search space which is expressible as the union of at most k intervals. More formally, the set of allowed questions is the family of sets: $\mathcal{T} = \{\cup_{i=1}^{k}\{a_i, a_i + 1, \ldots, b_i\} \mid 1 \leq a_1 \leq b_1 \leq a_2 \leq b_2 \leq \cdots \leq a_k \leq b_k \leq M\}$. Such questions will be referred to as k-interval queries.

The problem we deal with in this chapter is to find shortest strategies only using k-interval queries. A related problem is to ask for which values of k there exist optimal strategies for the basic Ulam-Rényi game which are only based on k-interval queries.

5.2   Query Optimal Multi-interval Search with $k = O(e^2)$

It will be convenient to represent the search problem by a different game involving moving chips on a board. A *chip* is one of the numbers in the search space. In particular, there are $M = 2^m$ chips, which are marked by the numbers in the search space $\{0, 1, \ldots, 2^m - 1\}$. When a chip i is in position j it means that if i is the number chosen by Carole, then Carole has so far lied j times. Initially all chips are in position 0. For each $i = 0, 1, \ldots, e$ the set of chips in position i is referred to as the ith *pile*. As a convention, we assume that the piles are placed from left to right in order of increasing index, i.e., with the 0th pile as the leftmost one and the eth pile as the rightmost one.

The game starts with all the 2^m chips placed in the 0th pile. In each round Paul selects a set S of chips, corresponding to asking the question whether the secret number is in S. In particular, we shall restrict S to be the union of (at most) k

intervals, for some fixed integer k. Then, either Carole moves the chips in S one position forward (to the right), or she moves the chips in the complement of S one position forward. We can imagine that there is a gate at position e and that a chip is eliminated from the board as soon as it reaches past the gate. Paul's aim is to reach the situation in which only one chip is left on the board. Carole's aim is to keep on the board as many chips as possible for as long as possible. A nice feature of this chip game perspective is that it captures more evidently the adversarial nature of Carole. Here, it is clear that she need not have any particular chip in mind. Rather, she merely tries to prevent Paul from eliminating $M - 1$ chips.

We need some more definitions. A *pack* is a maximal interval of chips in a pile which is disjoint from the remaining set of chips in the same pile. For each $j = 0, \ldots, e$, we denote by p_j the number of packs in the jth pile. By a round of the game we understand the sequence of moves comprising a question and its corresponding answer. For $t = 0, 1, 2, \ldots$ we denote by p_j^t the number of packs in the jth pile at the end of the tth round, i.e., after Carole has answered the tth query. In general, for every pile attribute that may vary in time, the subscript will denote the pile, and the superscript the iteration/round.

For $j = 0, \ldots, e$ we let x_j^t denote the number of chips in the jth pile after t rounds, and $C^t = \sum_{j=0}^{e} x_j^t$, be the total number of chips on the board after t rounds. We also define $P^t = \sum_{j=0}^{e} p_j^t$ as the total number of packs on the board at the end of the tth round.

Following the notation used for the Ulam-Rényi game, we say that $\sigma^t = (x_0^t, \ldots, x_e^t)$ is the state (of the game) after t rounds, and, in particular, the state $\sigma^0 = (2^m, 0, \ldots, 0)$ is the initial state. Recall also that, $ch(x_0^t, \ldots, x_e^t) = \min\{q \mid V_q(x_0^t, \ldots, x_e^t) \leq 2^q\}$ is the character of the state $(x_0^t, \ldots, x_e^t)$, with $V_q(\sigma^t) = \sum_{j=0}^{e} x_j^t \sum_{\ell=0}^{e-j} \binom{q}{\ell}$ being the volume of the state $\sigma^t = (x_0^t, \ldots, x_e^t)$. We also recall that by the Volume Bound, when the current state is σ, Paul cannot win the game in less than $ch(\sigma)$ rounds. Hence, starting with $\sigma^0 = (2^m, 0, \ldots, 0)$, Paul needs at least $N_{\min}(2^m, e) = ch(2^m, 0, \ldots, 0)$ rounds to finish the game.

For $t \geq 1$, let S^t denote the tth question asked by Paul. We denote by s_j^t the number of chips in the tth question taken from the jth pile.

In order to finish his quest in $N_{\min}(2^m, e)$ rounds, Paul has to guarantee that each question asked induces a strict decrease of the character of the state of the game. The following lemma provides a sufficient condition on Paul's question for attaining the above character decrease.

Lemma 5.1. *Let σ be the current state, with $q = ch(\sigma)$. Let S be Paul's question. If $|V_{q-1}(\sigma_{yes}) - V_{q-1}(\sigma_{no})| \leq 1$ then it holds that $ch(\sigma_{yes}) \leq q-1$ and $ch(\sigma_{yes}) \leq q-1$.*

Proof. Assume, w.l.o.g., that $V_{q-1}(\sigma_{yes}) \geq V_{q-1}(\sigma_{no})$. Then, from the hypothesis, it follows that $V_{q-1}(\sigma_{no}) \geq V_{q-1}(\sigma_{yes}) - 1$. By definition of character we have

$$2^q \geq V_q(\sigma) = V_{q-1}(\sigma_{yes}) - V_{q-1}(\sigma_{no}) \geq 2V_{q-1}(\sigma_{yes}) - 1,$$

hence, $V_{q-1}(\sigma_{no}) \leq V_{q-1}(\sigma_{yes}) \leq 2^{q-1} + 1/2$, which together with the integrality of the volume, implies that for both σ_{yes} and σ_{no} the $(q-1)$th volume is not larger than 2^{q-1}, hence their character is not larger than $q-1$, as desired.

A question which satisfies the hypothesis of Lemma 5.1 will be called *balanced*.

Paul's aim will be to ask balanced k-interval-queries, i.e., such that for each $t = 1, \ldots, q$, the quantity

$$\Delta_{q-t}(\sigma^{t-1}, S^t) = |V_{q-t}(\sigma_{yes}^{t-1}) - V_{q-t}(\sigma_{no}^{t-1})| = \left| \sum_{j=0}^{e} (2s_j^t - x_j^{t-1}) \binom{q-t}{e-j} \right|$$

is not larger than 1. By Lemma 5.1, this will guarantee the optimality of the strategy in terms of number of questions asked. We will show that this can be achieved with k-interval-query satisfying $k = O(e^2)$. Moreover, we will also show that the total number of packs in each intermediate state encountered will be $O(e^2)$.

Splitting Evenly the Packs in a Pile. Let us now fix $t \geq 0$ and focus on the $(t+1)$th round of the game. For some $j \in \{0, 1, \ldots, e\}$ let $\chi_1 \ldots, \chi_{p_j}$ be the packs in the jth pile, in non-decreasing order of size. Let us denote by $\mathscr{X}_j$ the family of packs in the jth pile, and recall that x_j^t denotes the total number of chips in the jth pile at this stage of the game.

We will show how to choose the chips from this pile to be included in the next question, in order to fulfill two requirements: (1) to have a balanced question; and (2) to avoid that the number of packs in each pile grows above a given threshold.

Let us create from $\mathscr{X}_j - \{\chi_{p_j}\}$ two new families of packs $\mathscr{X}_j^+, \mathscr{X}_j^-$ where $\mathscr{X}_j^+ = \{\chi_1, \chi_3, \ldots, \chi_{2\lfloor n/2 \rfloor + 1}\}$ contains the packs with an odd index and $\mathscr{X}_j^+ = \{\chi_2, \chi_4, \ldots, \chi_{2\lceil n/2 \rceil - 2}\}$ contains the packs with an even index. Finally we split the pack χ_{p_j} into two parts and include one part into $\mathscr{X}_j^+$ and the other into $\mathscr{X}_j^-$ so that the total number of chips in the two new families differs by at most 1. The following easy proposition shows that the above splitting is always possible.

Proposition 5.1. *For every sequence $\{z_1, z_2, \ldots, z_n\}$ of non-negative integers such that $z_i \leq z_j$ for any $i < j$, there are two non-negative integers a and b such that $z_n = a + b$ and*

$$\left| \left(a + \sum_{k=0}^{\lfloor \frac{n}{2} \rfloor - 1} z_{2k+1} \right) - \left(b + \sum_{k=1}^{\lceil \frac{n}{2} \rceil - 1} z_{2k} \right) \right| \leq 1$$

Proof. Assume first that n is an even number. Let $A = \sum_{k=0}^{\lfloor \frac{n}{2} \rfloor - 1} z_{2k+1} = z_1 + z_3 + \cdots + z_{n-1}$ and $B = \sum_{k=1}^{\lceil \frac{n}{2} \rceil - 1} z_{2k} = z_2 + z_4 + \cdots + z_{n-2}$. We have

$$B \leq A \leq B + z_n,$$

which implies that $z_n = A - B + \alpha$ for some integer $\alpha > 0$. Then, the desired result easily follows by setting $b = A - B + \lfloor \frac{\alpha}{2} \rfloor$. In fact, we have $a = \lceil \frac{\alpha}{2} \rceil$ and $B + b = B + A - B + \lfloor \frac{\alpha}{2} \rfloor \geq A + \lceil \frac{\alpha}{2} \rceil - 1 = A + a - 1$.

Alternatively, when n is an odd number, we have $A = \sum_{k=0}^{\lfloor \frac{n}{2} \rfloor - 1} z_{2k+1} = z_1 + z_3 + \cdots + z_{n-2}$ and $B = \sum_{k=1}^{\lceil \frac{n}{2} \rceil - 1} z_{2k} = z_2 + z_4 + \cdots + z_{n-1}$. In this case, we have

$$A \leq B \leq A + z_n,$$

which implies that $z_n = B - A + \alpha$ for some integer $\alpha > 0$. Then, the desired result easily follows by setting $a = B - A + \lfloor \frac{\alpha}{2} \rfloor$. In fact, we have $b = \lceil \frac{\alpha}{2} \rceil$ and $A + a = A + B - A + \lfloor \frac{\alpha}{2} \rfloor \geq B + \lceil \frac{\alpha}{2} \rceil - 1 = B + b - 1$.

Therefore, for each $j = 0, 1, \ldots, e - 1$, the jth pile, $\mathcal{X}_j$, can be split into two sub-piles $\mathcal{X}_j^+, \mathcal{X}_j^-$, in such a way that the resulting sub-piles' cardinalities differ by at most one chip. Moreover, each sub-pile contains at most $\lceil (p_j + 1)/2 \rceil$ packs, where p_j is the number of packs in $\mathcal{X}_j$. We will assume, w.l.o.g., that $\mathcal{X}_j^+$ includes a total number of coins which is not smaller than the total number of coins in $\mathcal{X}_j^-$. The next query S^{t+1} is determined according to the following procedure which is a variant of the strategy used to prove Theorem 2.5.

For each $j = 0, 1, \ldots, e - 1$, in order to decide which one of $\mathcal{X}_j^-$ and $\mathcal{X}_j^+$ will be put into S^{t+1} we use the following alternating rule: Let $0 \leq j_1 < j_2 < \cdots < j_t \leq e - 1$ be the indices for which $\mathcal{X}_{j_i}^-$ and $\mathcal{X}_{j_i}^+$ differ in the number of chips they contain.[1] Then, we put in S^{t+1} the piles: $\mathcal{X}_{j_1}^-, \mathcal{X}_{j_2}^+, \mathcal{X}_{j_3}^-, \ldots$ alternating between the one with fewer and the one with more chips, starting with the one with fewer chips. For each $j \notin \{j_1, \ldots, j_t\}$, we (arbitrarily) choose to put X_j^+ into S^{t+1}.

Notice that for each $j = 0, 1, \ldots, e - 1$, we have that from the jth pile we add into S^{t+1} at most $\lceil (p_j + 1)/2 \rceil$ packs and s_j^{t+1} chips with $\lfloor x_j^t/2 \rfloor \leq s_j^{t+1} \leq \lceil x_j^t/2 \rceil$; moreover, for each $j \notin \{j_1, \ldots, j_t\}$ we have $s_j^{t+1} = x_j^t/2$.

We have to take special care when deciding which parts of the eth pile should contribute to S^{t+1}.

For $j = 0, 1, \ldots, e - 1$, let $\tilde{\mathcal{X}}_j$ be the part of $\mathcal{X}_j$ which has been included into S^{t+1} according to the above rule, then we have that $s_j^{t+1} = |\tilde{\mathcal{X}}_j|$ is the number of chips it includes. We define

$$imbalance(S^{t+1}) = \sum_{j=0}^{e-1} \binom{q-1}{e-j} (2s_j^{t+1} - x_j^t),$$

where $q = ch(\sigma^t)$.

---

[1] And they differ by exactly one, as noticed before.

Notice that $imbalance(S^{t+1})$ is the contribution of the chips already put in S^{t+1} (i.e., coming from the piles $0, 1, \ldots, e-1$) to the volume-difference between the two possible states of the game arising from Carole's answer.

Paul's aim now is to choose the chips from the eth pile which will be added to S^{t+1}, in order to rebalance such differences. If he can achieve this, the resulting S^{t+1} will correspond to a balanced question which according to Lemma 5.1 will guarantee the optimality of the strategy in the present round.

Because of the way Paul has selected from the first e piles, the packs already put in S^{t+1}, we have that for each $j = 0, 1, \ldots, e-1$, $(2s_j^{t+1} - x_j^t) \in \{-1, 1\}$ and in particular for $j^* = \min\{j = 0, \ldots, e-1 \mid 2s_j^{t+1} - x_j^t \neq 0\}$, we have $(2s_j^{t+1} - x_j^t) = -1$. Therefore, the alternating rule guarantees

$$0 \geq imbalance(S^{t+1}) \geq -\binom{q-1}{e}. \tag{5.1}$$

Let $\mathscr{X}_e = \{\chi_1, \ldots, \chi_{p_e}\}$, with $\chi_{p_e} = [u, w]$ being the largest pack in the eth pile. Assume that $w - u + 1 \geq |imbalance(S^{t+1})|$. This assumption will be shown to hold in Theorem 5.1.

We first remove from χ_{p_e} the first $|imbalance(S^{t+1})|$ chips, i.e., the chips in the interval $\iota = [u, u + imbalance(S^{t+1}) - 1]$. These chips will be used to balance the choice made so far. We will say that these chips are used for *rebalancing*. Let $\chi'_{p_e} = [u + imbalance(S), w]$,[2] be the remaining chips from χ_{p_e}.

Let $\mathscr{X}'_e = \mathscr{X}_e \setminus \{\chi_{p_e}\} \cup \{\chi'_{p_e}\}$. Split $\mathscr{X}'_e$ into two subfamilies $\mathscr{X}_e^+$ and $\mathscr{X}_e^-$ following the procedure described before for splitting the other piles. Assume, w.l.o.g., that $\mathscr{X}_e^+$ contains a pack $\iota' = [u + imbalance(S^{t+1}), w']$. We set $\tilde{\mathscr{X}}_e = \mathscr{X}_e^+ \setminus \iota' \cup [u, w']$ and we add it to S^{t+1}. Since $\mathscr{X}_e^+$ contains at most $\lceil (p_e + 1)/2 \rceil$ packs, we have that also $\tilde{\mathscr{X}}_e$ contributes to S^{t+1} with at most $\lceil (p_e + 1)/2 \rceil$ packs.

In words, in the case of the eth pile, we first reserve as many chips as necessary from the largest pack to rebalance the choices already made with the other piles and then split the remaining packs as we did for all the other piles. In this process, we take care to merge the rebalancing chips with one of the packs generated in the splitting of the pile, so that the overall number of packs added to S^t remains bounded by $\lceil (p_e + 1)/2 \rceil$.

Before stating the main result of this section, we need some technical results.

Lemma 5.2. *For any $t \geq 0$, and for each $j = 0, \ldots, e$, in the tth round, the jth pile contains at most $2j + 1$ packs.*

Proof. The proof is by induction on the number of rounds.

The statement is clearly true for the initial state, where the only non-empty pile is the 0th pile, which contains exactly one pack.

---

[2] If $w < u + imbalance(S)$ we take $\chi'_{p_e} = \emptyset$.

Assume that the statement is true after t rounds, for some $t \geq 0$, i.e., $p_j^t \leq 2j+1$, for each $j = 0, \ldots, e$. For each $j = 0, \ldots, e$, from the jth pile, the splitting operation used for choosing the set S^{t+1}, creates two new piles each containing at most $\lceil (p_j^t + 1)/2 \rceil$ packs, which, because of the induction hypothesis, is bounded by $j + 1$. Therefore, after the $(t + 1)$th answer, in the jth pile there will be at most $(j + 1)$ packs, coming from the splitting of the jth pile, plus j packs, coming from the splitting of the $(j - 1)$th pile, i.e., at most $2j + 1$ packs. This concludes the induction step and the proof of the lemma.

The following claim provides a useful asymptotic estimate of the character of the initial state.

Proposition 5.2. *For any $e \geq 0$ and for all sufficiently large m, it holds that $q = N_{\min}(2^m, e) = ch(\sigma^0)$ satisfies the following inequalities.*

$$m + e \log m - e \log e \leq q \leq m + e(1 + \log m) + \log(e + 1). \qquad (5.2)$$

Proof. For the right inequality, setting $q' = m + e \log m + (e + 1) \log(e + 1)$, it follows that

$$2^{q'} \geq 2^m \cdot m^e \cdot (e + 1)2^e = 2^m (e + 1)(2m)^e \geq 2^m (e + 1) \binom{q'}{e} \geq 2^m \sum_{j=0}^{e} \binom{q'}{j},$$

implying $q' \geq ch(2^m, 0, \ldots, 0) = q$.

Conversely, for the left inequality, we notice that, setting $q'' = m + e \log m - e \log e$, we have

$$2^{q'' - m} = (m/e)^e \leq \binom{q''}{e} \leq \sum_{j=0}^{e} \binom{q''}{j},$$

whence $q'' \leq ch(2^m, 0, \ldots, 0) = q$. The proof of the claim is complete.

As a consequence of Proposition 5.2, we can use the asymptotic estimate $q \sim m + e \log m + O(e \log e)$. In the following, for simplifying the notation we will disregard floors and ceilings.

Lemma 5.3. *For $t = m, m + 1, \ldots, m + (e - \frac{1}{4}) \log m$, let $\chi_{p_e}^t$ be the largest pack in the eth pile after t rounds in a game where Paul plays each round using the strategy above, starting from the initial state $\sigma^0 = (2^m, 0, \ldots, 0)$. Then, for all sufficiently large m, we have $|\chi_{p_e}^t| \geq \binom{q-t-1}{e}$, where $q = N_{\min}(2^m, e)$.*

In addition, for $t = m + (e - \frac{1}{4}) \log m$ we have that in σ^t the first e piles contain in total at most 1 chip.

Proof. Recall that S^{t+1} denotes Paul's $(t + 1)$th question. It is not hard to see that for each $t = 0, \ldots, m - 1$, after t rounds, the cardinalities of the piles in the state

σ^t are even and Paul's strategy guarantees $x_j^{t+1} = \frac{x_{j-1}^t}{2} + \frac{x_j^t}{2}$, yielding $x_j^{t+1} = 2^{m-t-1}\binom{t+1}{j}$, for each $j = 0, \ldots, e$. In particular, after m rounds, the resulting state is

$$\sigma^m = \left(1, m, \binom{m}{2}, \ldots, \binom{m}{j}, \ldots, \binom{m}{e}\right), \tag{5.3}$$

and we have $ch(\sigma^m) = q - m$.

In general, Paul's strategy guarantees that for each $t \geq 0$, in the $t + 1$th round, with state σ^t, whose piles have cardinalities $(x_0^t, \ldots, x_e^t)$, at least $x_{e-1}^t/2$ chips are moved from the $(e-1)$th pile to the eth pile. Moreover, since at most $\binom{q-t-1}{e}$ of the chips in the eth pile are used for the rebalancing, it follows that at least $(x_e^t - \binom{q-t-1}{e})/2$ chips from the eth pile remain in the eth pile. More precisely, we have

$$x_e^{t+1} \geq \frac{x_{e-1}^t}{2} + \frac{x_e^t - \binom{q-t-1}{e}}{2} - 1.$$

Therefore, recalling (5.3), for $t = m, m + 1 \ldots, m + (e - \frac{1}{4}) \log m - 1$, we can bound, for all large m,

$$x_e^t \geq \frac{\binom{t}{e}}{2^{t-m}} - (t - m)\frac{\binom{q-m-1}{e}}{2}.$$

Therefore, for each $t = m, \ldots, m + (e - \frac{1}{4}) \log m$, we can estimate the size of $\chi_{p_e}^t$, the largest pack in the eth pile on the board after the tth round, by an average argument and using $q - m - 1 \ll m$ which follows from Proposition 5.2.

Since, by Lemma 5.2, the eth pile does not contain more than $2e + 1$ pack, we have that (asymptotically with m)

$$|\chi_{p_e}^t| \geq \frac{x_e^t}{2e + 1} \geq \frac{\frac{(t/e)^e}{2^{(e-1/4)\log m}} - (q - m)^{e+1}}{(2e + 1)} \geq \frac{\frac{m^{1/4}}{e^e} - (2e \log m)^{e+1}}{(2e + 1)}$$

$$\geq (2e \log m)^e \geq \binom{q - t}{e},$$

which proves the first statement of the lemma.

In order to prove the second statement, we first observe that for $j = 0, \ldots, e - 1$, the number of chips in the jth pile satisfies

$$x_j^{t+1} \leq \frac{x_{j-1}^t}{2} + \frac{x_j^t}{2} + 1 \leq \frac{\binom{t+1}{j}}{2^{t+1-m}} + O(1).$$

Therefore, for $t = m + (e - \frac{1}{2})\log m, \ldots m + (e - \frac{1}{4})\log m$, we have that for each $j = 0, \ldots, e - 1$,

$$x_j^t \leq \frac{\binom{t}{j}}{2^{t-m}} + O(1) \leq \frac{(m + e\log m)^j}{2^{(e-\frac{1}{2})\log m}} + O(1) \leq \frac{m^{e-1}(1 + o(1))}{m^{e-\frac{1}{2}}},$$

from which it follows that already at the beginning of this phase of the game—when $t = m + (e - \frac{1}{2})\log m$—there is a bounded number of chips in the first e piles. Now, we use the fact that when we choose the chips to put into the question, from the first $e - 1$ piles, we do it using the alternating strategy. As a result, as long as there is more than one chip in the first e piles, in each round, at least one chip gets moved from its pile, say the jth one, into the next one, namely the $(j+1)$th one. Therefore, since we start with a bounded number of chips and we have $\Theta(1/4 \log m)$ rounds in this phase, at the end of the phase we are left with at most one non-empty pile among the first $e - 1$. Recall that we are arguing asymptotically with m.

The following proposition provides an end-game strategy.

Proposition 5.3. *Let* $\sigma = (x_0, \ldots, x_e)$ *be a state such that* $x_e > 0$ *and* $\sum_{j=0}^{e-1} x_j \leq 1$. *Let* $ch(\sigma) = q$. *Let* P *be the total number of packs in the state* σ. *Then, starting in state* σ *Paul can discover Carole's secret number asking exactly* q *many 1-interval-queries. Moreover, during the whole process, the total number of packs does not increase, i.e., remains not larger than* P.

Proof. We prove the proposition by induction on q, the character of the state. If $q = 1$, the only possibility is $\sum_{j=0}^{e-1} x_j = 0$ and $x_e = 2$. Then, a question containing exactly one of the elements in the eth pile is enough to conclude the search.

Now assume that $q > 1$ and that the statement holds for any state with the same structure and character $\leq q - 1$.

If $\sum_{j=0}^{e-1} x_j = 0$ then the solution is provided by the classical binary search in the eth pile which can be clearly implemented using 1-interval-queries. Notice also that the number of intervals needed to represent the new state is never more than the number of intervals needed to represent σ.

Assume now that $\sum_{j=0}^{e-1} x_j = 0$ and let i be the index such that $x_i = 1$. Let c be the only element in the ith pile.

The critical observation is that $\alpha = \sum_{j=0}^{e-i} \binom{q-1}{j} \leq 2^{q-1}$. This directly follows from the assumption on the character of σ implying $\sum_{j=0}^{e-i} \binom{q}{j} \leq 2^q$, hence $e - i < q$.

Since the character of σ is q, we have $\sum_{j=0}^{e-i} \binom{q}{j} \leq V_q(\sigma) \leq 2^q$, hence $e - i < q$, and $\alpha = \sum_{j=0}^{e-i} \binom{q-1}{j} \leq 2^{q-1}$.

In addition, we have $\sum_{j=0}^{e-i} \binom{q-1}{j} + x_e > 2^{q-1}$.

Choose S to be the largest interval including c and $2^{q-1} - \alpha$ other elements from the eth pile. The above observation guarantees the existence of such an interval. The possible states arising from such a question satisfy $V_{q-1}(\sigma_{yes}) = 2^{q-1}$ and are $V_{q-1}(\sigma_{no}) = V_q(\sigma) - V_{q-1}(\sigma_{yes}) \leq 2^q - 2^{q-1}$. Hence, both states have character not larger than $q-1$. It is also not hard to say that they both have a structure satisfying the hypothesis of the proposition. Therefore, Paul can continue his strategy by induction hypothesis.

Notice that also in this case the number of intervals necessary to represent the state is not larger than the initial one.

The previous lemma implies that the eth pile always contains a pack which is large enough to implement the *rebalance*. This leads to the following result.

Theorem 5.1. *For any $e \geq 1$ and for all sufficiently large m in the game played over the search space $\{0, \ldots, 2^m - 1\}$ with e lies, there exists a strategy for Paul which is perfect—i.e., with at most $N_{\min}(2^m, e)$ questions—and uses only multi-interval questions with at most $\frac{e^2+3e+2}{2}$ intervals. Moreover, each intermediate state can be represented by $(e + 1)^2$ intervals.*

Proof. We need to show that the strategy we have described is feasible and that it will lead to a final state in the minimum possible number of rounds, $N_{\min}(2^m, e)$.

Let $q = N_{\min}(2^m, e)$. We split the analysis into two parts: Phase 1: the first $m + (e - \frac{1}{4})\log m$ rounds; Phase 2: the last $q - m - (e - \frac{1}{4})\log m$ rounds.

Let us first consider Phase 1. We first show that Paul's strategy is feasible throughout the whole phase by using an inductive argument.

The critical point in Paul's strategy is the existence of a pack in the eth pile which allows rebalancing. This is trivially true in the first m rounds where no rebalancing actually takes place. In fact, it is not hard to see that for each $t = 0, \ldots, m$, after t rounds, the state cardinalities of the piles in the state σ^t satisfy $x_j^t = 2^{m-t}\binom{t}{j}$, for each $j = 0, \ldots, e$. Therefore, for each $t = 1, \ldots, m - 1$, we have that each component of the state after t rounds is even and we have $imbalance(S^{t+1}) = 0$. Hence, in this phase Paul does not actually need any rebalancing. After m rounds, the cardinality of the piles in the resulting state σ^m satisfy $x_j^m = \binom{m}{j}$, for each $j = 0, 1, \ldots, e$; and we have $ch(\sigma^m) = q - m$.

Assume now that, for some $m < t < m+(e-\frac{1}{4})\log m$, the strategy is feasible up to the tth round. Let χ_{p_e} denote the pack of largest size in the eth pile after t rounds. Lemma 5.3 together with (5.1) implies that $|\chi_{p_e}| \geq -imbalance(S)$. Therefore, we can complete the $(t + 1)$th round as well. This completes our inductive argument and shows the feasibility of the strategy.

Let σ' be the state at the end of Phase 1. We have that $ch(\sigma') = q - m - (e - \frac{1}{4})\log m$. This follows from Lemma 5.1 because for each $t = 1, \ldots, m + (e - \frac{1}{4})\log m$, the question S^t asked by Paul guarantees that $|V_{q-t}(\sigma_{yes}^t) - V_{q-t}(\sigma_{no}^t)| \leq 1$.

From Lemma 5.3 it also follows that at the end of Phase 1 there is at most one chip in the first e piles. Therefore, by Proposition 5.3, we have that $ch(\sigma') = q - m - (e - \frac{1}{4})\log m$ additional 1-interval-queries are sufficient for reaching a final state.

Therefore, in total, Paul reaches a final state after asking exactly $q = N_{\min}(2^m, e)$ queries, as desired.

Finally, by Lemma 5.2, for each $j = 0, 1, \ldots, e$, the number of packs in the jth pile is at most $2j + 1$. Therefore, the total number of packs on the board is never greater than

$$\sum_{j=0}^{e}(2j + 1) = (e + 1)^2$$

and the amount of packs in each question is bounded by

$$\sum_{j=0}^{e}(p_j + 1)/2 \le \sum_{j=0}^{e}(j + 1) = \binom{e + 1}{2} + e + 1 = \frac{e^2 + 3e + 2}{2},$$

i.e., the strategy only uses multi-interval questions with the desired number of intervals.

5.2.1   The Case of Two Lies: A Canonical Representation of States and 2-Interval Queries

Mundici and Trombetta were the first to consider multi-interval questions. They focussed on queries of the form "does x satisfy either condition $a \le x \le b$ or $c \le x \le d$?", which they call *bicomparisons*. Clearly, bicomparisons are the same as 2-interval-queries.

For the particular case $e = 2$, Mundici and Trombetta proved that for all $m \ge 1$ and $m \ne 2$, an unknown m-bit number can always be found by asking $N_{\min}(2^m, 2)$ bicomparison questions. Therefore, despite the limitations in Paul's expressive power imposed by restriction to 2-interval-queries, for $e = 2$, the shortest search strategy has precisely the same number of questions as in the general unrestricted case (arbitrary yes-no questions), for every size of the search space.

If we assume that all questions are of type: "does x satisfy the condition $a \le x \le b$?" then no search strategy can exist to find an unknown m-bit number and using $N_{\min}(2^m, 2)$ many such questions.

The Strategy. The core of the method used by Mundici and Trombetta consists in constructing the queries in such a way that, no matter what the answer, the search space and more precisely the states of the game evolve through well-defined patterns. In fact, the authors show that each state arising from 2-interval-queries questions turns out to possess a simple geometric shape that can be completely specified by eleven numbers in S. See, for example, Fig. 5.1. The top-left shape describes a possible state of the game. On the abscissa is the search space, and the shape shows for each element the number of available lies to the responder if the number is the chosen one. The two segments underneath the shape are meant to describe a 2-interval-query. And the two shapes below, still on the left, show the resulting situation, when the question asked is given by the two intervals and the answer is respectively *no* (middle shape) and *yes* (lowest shape). The three shapes on the right depict the case of a different 2-interval query. With the help of Fig. 5.1 we can describe this result using the analytic tools from the previous

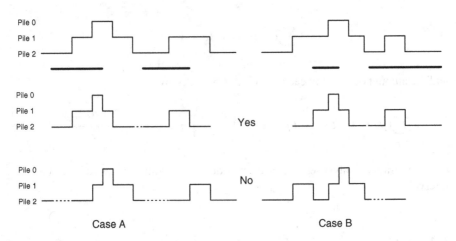

Fig. 5.1 Shapes for states in the Mundici-Trombetta analysis of the bicomparison model

section. To this aim, let $\hat{p}^1$ denote the largest pack at level 1 (representing the 1st pile). We distinguish two cases:

- *Case A: The only pack at level 2 (Pile 0) is not a neighbor of $\hat{p}^1$.*

   We can freely choose one of the other packs in level 1 to be part of the query. By including the half of the pack at level 2 which is neighbor to it, we have one of the intervals of the query. By Property 5.1, we can divide $\hat{p}^1$ so that half of the chips in level 1 are included in the query. Include in the query the half that does not have a common neighbor with another pack already in the query. This gives the second interval in the query. Notice that this query does not include any pack at the level 0 (Pile 2). But both intervals can be extended so that the query includes also half of the chips at this level.

- *Case B: The only pack at level 2 (Pile 0) and $\hat{p}^1$ are neighbors.*

   By Fact 5.1, we may divide $\hat{p}^1$ into two packs such that the pack which is a neighbor to the only one in level 2, together with the pack in level 1 (Pile 1) which is not a neighbor to it, contain half of the chips at this level. We also include in the query the half of the only pack at level 2 (Pile 0) that is a neighbor to $\hat{p}^1$. As in the previous case, the query has two intervals, but does not include any chip in level 0 (Pile 2). But the interval containing the pack at level 1 (Pile 1) which is not a neighbor of the only pack at level 0 (Pile 2) may be extended in both directions, so that the query also includes half of the chips at level 0 (Pile 2).

The analysis given above about the number of packs in the piles suggests that an analogous pattern might be used for describing the states of the game also in the case of more than two errors. It is conjectured that the basic shape for the case of e errors may be like that in Fig. 5.2. Note that each level from $0 < i < e - 1$ in this figure has exactly $2i - 1$ fragments, thus leaving open the applicability of a technique like the one described for the case $e = 2$.

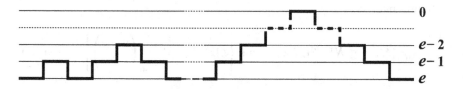

Fig. 5.2 The canonical shape of a state in the case of e lies

A Possible Generalization of Mundici-Trombetta's Approach. Let $f(e)$ denote the minimum number of intervals needed for representing a questions in a strategy for the e-lie game which uses the minimum possible number of question. Mundici and Trombetta observed that for $e = 2$ there is no strategy using only 1-interval-queries which can attain the lower bound, whilst this is possible with 2-interval-queries. Therefore $f(2) = 2$. The results of the previous section show that $f(e) \leq (e + 1)^2$, for any e. We have the following conjecture for the general case.

Conjecture 5.1. For any $e \geq 1$, it holds that $f(e) = \theta(e)$.

The exact determination of $f(e)$ is an interesting open problem together with the analogous related question regarding the size of the minimum representation of the states of the game.

5.2.2 *About Comparison Questions*

A special and probably the most basic example of the Ulam-Rényi game with multi-interval-questions is the variant where only comparison questions are allowed, that is, questions in the form "Is the secret number $x \leq a$?" for some $a \in S$. In this case we have only one interval, which is bound to be a prefix of the search space. Some of the first results on the Ulam-Rényi game were actually provided for this variant of the problem. For completeness, we are here limiting ourselves to give a brief account of some of these results.

Let $N^{(\mathrm{cmp})}(M, e)$ denote the minimum number of questions to find an unknown number x in the set $S = \{0, 1, \ldots, M - 1\}$ by using only *comparison* questions, when up to e of the answers may be mendacious.

Obviously, $N^{(\mathrm{cmp})}(M, e) \geq N(M, e)$, for all $e \geq 0$ and $M \geq 1$. Further, for $e = 0$, a moment's reflection shows that $N^{(\mathrm{cmp})}(M, 0) = N(M, 0)$, for all $M \geq 1$.

The Ulam-Rényi game with comparison questions was considered for the first time by Rivest et al. Their solution is based on embedding the search space $S = \{0, 1, 2, \ldots, M - 1\}$ into the half-open real interval $]0, 1]$, and then looking for a subset A of $]0, 1]$ such that A contains the secret number x and $|A| \leq \epsilon$, for an arbitrarily chosen $0 < \epsilon < 1$.

It turns out that

$$
N_{\min}(M, e) \leq N^{(\mathrm{cmp})}(M, e) \leq \min\left\{n \mid 2^{n-e} \geq M \sum_{j=0}^{e} \binom{n-e}{j}\right\}, \qquad (5.4)
$$

which is still valid when e is a function of M. From the above result, proceeding as in Proposition 5.2, one can easily obtain

$$
N^{(\mathrm{cmp})}(M, e) = \log_2 M + e \log_2 \log_2 M + O(e \log_2 e). \qquad (5.5)
$$

Focusing on the case $e = 1$, and $S = \{0, 1, 2, \ldots, M - 1\}$, Spencer proved the following:

- Whenever n obeys the inequality $\frac{2^n}{n+1} < M$, no winning strategy exists using n comparison questions.
- If $M \leq \frac{5}{8} \frac{2^n}{n+1}$ then there exists a winning strategy for Paul, using n comparison questions.

From this result it follows that $N^{(\mathrm{cmp})}(M, 1) \leq N(M, 1) + 1$ for all $M \geq 1$. Spencer's result was further refined by Innes, who provided a tighter upper bound, to the effect that whenever

$$
M \leq \frac{27}{128} \frac{2^n}{n + 1},
$$

there exists a winning strategy for Paul using exactly $n - 2$ comparison questions to search for an unknown number x in the set $\{0, 1, \ldots, M - 1\}$ when at most one answer is a lie.

5.3   Linearly Bounded Number of Lies

Up to this point we have always assumed that the maximum number of lies e is fixed beforehand. As we saw in the previous chapters, this resembles the classical assumption in the theory of error-correcting codes, that a *fixed* maximum number e of bits can be distorted by noise during the transmission of a message.

On the other hand, it might be argued that if the probability of an error is not too small, then it is less reasonable to assume that the number e of expected noisy bits is bounded by a constant independent of the number of actually sent bits.

In the Ulam-Rényi problem with linearly bounded numbers of errors, one assumes the existence of a fixed real value r in the open interval $]0, 1[$, known to both Paul and Carole, such that if Paul asks n questions then Carole is allowed to tell at most $\lfloor r n \rfloor$ many lies. Thus, after agreeing upon the size M of the search space and the lie fraction r, Paul announces that he is going to ask at most n questions, whence allowing Carole to fix the maximum number of lies that she is allowed to tell.

Again, we are interested in the minimum number n of sufficient questions for Paul to infallibly guess Carole's secret number, for all possible values of the parameters M and r.

The linearly bounded lie model bears an interesting relationship with the *probabilistic* model, where the responder lies at random, and an answer is mendacious with a constant probability $p < 1/2$. Here, lies are no longer malicious, and p arises as the result of a probabilistic analysis of the noisy environment.

Spencer and Winkler investigated the linearly bounded lie model for subset or membership questions, for both the fully adaptive and the fully non-adaptive model. Their main result is as follows:

Theorem 5.2. *1. For non-adaptive search over $S = \{0, 1, \ldots, M-1\}$ we have:*

(a) *If $r < 1/4$, then Paul has a winning strategy with $\Theta(\log_2 M)$ membership questions.*

(b) *If $r = 1/4$, then Paul has a winning strategy with $\Theta(M)$ membership questions.*

(c) *If $r > 1/4$, then no winning strategy exists for Paul for any $M \geq 9r/(r - 1/4)$, no matter the number of questions.*

2. *For fully adaptive search over $S = \{0, 1, \ldots, M-1\}$ we have*

(d) *If $r < 1/3$, then Paul has a winning strategy with $\Theta(\log_2 M)$ membership questions.*

(e) *If $r \geq 1/3$, then no winning strategy exists for Paul for all $M \geq 5$, no matter the number of questions.*

Dhagat et al. investigated the linearly bounded lie model when Paul is allowed to use more restrictive types of questions. They call *bit question* a query asking for the value of a bit in the binary expansion of Carole's secret number, that is, a question of the form "Is the ith bit of x equal to 1?".

Their main result is summarized in the following

Theorem 5.3. *Let $S = \{0, 1, \ldots, M-1\}$ be the search space and assume that Paul can only ask bit questions. Then the following holds:*

(a) *Paul has a non-adaptive winning strategy with n bit questions iff $M \leq 2^{\left\lfloor \frac{n}{2\lfloor rn \rfloor + 1} \right\rfloor}$.*

(b) *Paul has a fully adaptive winning strategy with n bit questions iff $M \leq 2^{\left\lfloor \frac{n - \lfloor rn \rfloor}{\lfloor rn \rfloor + 1} \right\rfloor}$.*

Proof. Let us first consider the case of a non-adaptive strategy. Assume that $M > 2^{\left\lfloor \frac{n}{2\lfloor rn \rfloor + 1} \right\rfloor}$. It follows that there are $\lceil \log M \rceil > \left\lfloor \frac{n}{2\lfloor rn \rfloor + 1} \right\rfloor$ possible bit questions. Therefore, whatever the choice of the n questions, there is a bit, say j, such that the question about j has been asked at most $2\lfloor rn \rfloor$ times. Suppose Carole answers no to all questions about a bit different from j. Then, she answers yes to exactly half of the questions about the bit j. This means that Paul collects at most $\lfloor r\,n \rfloor$ answers about the bit j saying that it is 1 and at most $\lfloor r\,n \rfloor$ saying that it is 0. Since $\lfloor r\,n \rfloor$ answers of Carole could be lies, there is no way for Paul to discriminate between the case where the secret number is 0 and the case where the secret number is 2^j. Hence, n questions are not sufficient in this case.

Suppose now that $M \leq 2^{\left\lfloor \frac{n}{2\lfloor rn \rfloor + 1} \right\rfloor}$. Then, it is not hard to see that for each $i = 1, \ldots, \lceil \log M \rceil$, Paul can now ask $2\lfloor r\,n \rfloor + 1$ questions about bit i. By taking a majority vote among such answers he can be sure about the value of the bit i and then identify the value of the secret number chosen by Carole.

We now turn to the fully adaptive case. We shall first prove the *necessity* of the condition in (b). Let $M > 2^{\left\lfloor \frac{n - \lfloor rn \rfloor}{\lfloor rn \rfloor + 1} \right\rfloor}$, and assume (*absurdum hypothesis*) that Paul has a winning strategy with n bit questions. There are $\lceil \log M \rceil$ possible bit questions. Suppose Carole keeps on answering "no" as long as there are still at least two numbers that are consistent with her answers. Note that for being sure about the value of a bit of Carole's secret number, Paul needs at least $\lfloor r\,n \rfloor + 1$ identical answers. Therefore, Carole can use the above strategy—keeping ambiguity about at least one bit of the secret number—for at least $(\lceil \log M \rceil - 1)(\lfloor r\,n \rfloor + 1) + \lfloor r\,n \rfloor > n$ questions, which proves the desired result.

We now prove the *sufficiency* of (b). Let $m = \lceil \log M \rceil$. This is the number of possible different bit questions. Because of the standing hypothesis, we have $n \geq (\lfloor rn \rfloor + 1)m + \lfloor rn \rfloor$. We shall show a strategy for Paul to ask no more than these many questions.

We start observing that while asking questions, Paul has the possibility of keeping note of the minimum number of lies told by Carole in answering questions about bit i for each $i = 1, \ldots, m$. In fact, if Carole has answered both "*yes*" and "*no*" to questions about bit i, then at least the minimum of the number of "*yes*" and "*no*" answers to these questions about bit i must be lies. Let $Y(i)$ and $N(i)$ denote the number of times Carole has responded, respectively, "*yes*" and "*no*" to a question about bit i. Then, $\min\{Y(i), N(i)\}$ is a lower bound on the number of lies told by Carole in answering questions about bit i. Moreover, as soon as $\max\{Y(i), N(i)\}$ becomes larger than $\lfloor r\,n \rfloor$, Paul can stop asking questions about the bit i, since he has enough evidence about its value. Therefore, Paul can proceed as follows: For each $i = 1, \ldots, m$, ask the question about bit i until $\max\{Y(i), N(i)\} = \lfloor rn \rfloor + 1$.

The total number of questions asked by Paul is given by

$$\sum_{i=1}^{m} \max\{Y(i), N(i)\} + \min\{Y(i), N(i)\} = m(\lfloor rn \rfloor + 1) + \sum_{i=1}^{m} \min\{Y(i), N(i)\}.$$

As observed before, $\sum_{i=1}^{m} \min\{Y(i), N(i)\}$ is a lower bound on the total number of lies told by Carole; therefore, it cannot be larger than $\lfloor rn \rfloor$, which proves the desired result about the number of questions asked by Paul.

Finally, since for each bit exactly $\lfloor rn \rfloor + 1$ identical answers have been collected by Paul, he has evidence of its value; hence, he has enough information to identify the secret number of Carole.

Theorem 5.4. *Let* $S = \{0, 1, \ldots, M - 1\}$ *be the search space in the game with linearly bounded lies where Paul is allowed to use only comparison questions. Then, the following holds:*

(a) *Paul has a non-adaptive winning strategy with n comparison questions[3] iff* $M \leq \frac{n}{2\lfloor rn \rfloor + 1} + 1.$

(b) *Paul has a fully adaptive winning strategy using only comparison questions iff* $r < 1/3$. *Moreover, for all* $r < 1/3$ *there exists a winning strategy with* n *comparison questions, where*

$$n = \left\lceil \frac{8 \log_2 M}{(1 - 3r)^2} \right\rceil. \tag{5.6}$$

Proof. We first present the proof of (b) in the more general case in which Paul is allowed to ask membership questions, i.e., questions of the type "Is $x \in S$?" for some subset $S \subset \{0, 1, \ldots, M - 1\}$. Let $r \geq 1/3$ and $M \geq 5$, and suppose (*absurdum hypothesis*) that Paul has a winning strategy of size n for some value of $n \geq 1$. We shall describe a strategy for Carole that allows her to continue the game and prevent Paul from identifying the secret number after n questions. Remember that Carole can choose the secret number as late as she wants, provided that her choice is consistent with the answers already given and with the rules of the game, i.e., at most $\lfloor rn \rfloor$ lies in total.

Recall the definition of the state of knowledge $(L_0, L_1, \ldots)$, where L_i is the set of numbers which are candidate to be the secret number assuming that Carole has lied exactly i times so far. Let $(x_0, x_1, \ldots)$ denote the type of the state, i.e., $x_i = |L_i|$ for each $i \geq 0$. Carole uses the following strategy in answering Paul's questions:

1. To the question "Is $x \in S$?", Carole replies yes if $|S \cap L_0| \geq |L_0|/2$ and no otherwise. This continues as long as $|L_0| \geq 3$.
2. Then, as long as there are at least three candidate numbers, i.e., $\sum_i |L_i| \geq 3$, Carole answers yes if and only if $|S \cap \bigcup_i L_i| \geq 2$.
3. Once there are only two numbers left as candidate ones, then Carole always answers as if the secret number was the one for which so far she has lied the most (breaking ties arbitrarily).

Let $z_0 = 0$ and, for $i = 1, 2, 3$, let

---

[3] Here, by comparison question is understood a question of the form "Is $x < a$?".

$$z_i = \begin{cases} z_{i-1} & \text{if } x_{z_{i-1}} \geq 2 \\ \min\{j > z_{i-1} | x_j > 0\} & \text{otherwise.} \end{cases}$$

Let $\phi(t) = z_1 + z_2 + \min(z_3, \lfloor rn \rfloor + 1)$. It is not hard to see that until the game ends we have $\phi(t+1) \leq \phi(t) + 1$. Moreover, because of the assumption $n \geq 5$, we have that the first answer will leave $x_0 \geq 3$, whence $\phi(0) = \phi(1) = 0$. Finally, at the end of the game, i.e., after $n' \leq n$ questions, it must be that $x_{\lfloor rn \rfloor} = 1$ and $x_i = 0$, for each $i < \lfloor rn \rfloor$, whence $\phi(n') = 3\lfloor rn \rfloor + 2$.

It follows that $n - 1 \geq 3\lfloor rn \rfloor + 2$, which is impossible since $3\lfloor rn \rfloor \geq 3\lfloor n/3 \rfloor \geq n - 2$. Since we have reached a contradiction, it follows that there cannot be any winning strategy for Paul if $r \geq 1/3$, which concludes the proof.

It remains to prove the existence of a winning strategy for Paul when $r \leq 1/3$. For the sake of the presentation we shall start with a slightly weaker result. Assume $M = 2^m$ for some m. We shall show that for any $r \leq 1/4$, Paul has a winning strategy of size

$$n = \left\lceil \frac{2m}{1 - 4r} \right\rceil.$$

Let $I_0 = \{0, 1, \ldots, M - 1\}$. Paul keeps a sequence of nested intervals, $I_0, \ldots, I_t$, such that I_t is the current candidate interval to contain the secret number of Carole and $I_0, \ldots, I_{t-1}$ are the previously trusted intervals. Paul's search proceeds in phases. In each phase, he asks a question at the midpoint of the current interval I_t. Then, according to the answer to this question, he asks another question at the rightmost point of I_t or at the leftmost point of I_t. If no inconsistency results from these two questions with respect to the current belief that the secret number is in I_t, then Paul sets the new interval I_{t+1} in accordance with the answers received. Alternatively, if the answers received in this phase are in contrast with the belief that $x \in I_t$, then Paul discards the last two questions and I_t altogether, decrementing t, i.e., keeping as the current interval of candidate solutions I_{t-1}.

Let the total number of questions asked by Paul be

$$n = \left\lceil \frac{2m}{1 - 4r} \right\rceil.$$

Let us consider the situation at the end of the game. Suppose t—nested by definition—intervals have been kept by Paul. Every time that an interval is discarded, Paul invalidates four of the questions/answers formulated so far. Of these answers at least one must be a lie. Let d be the number of times Paul discarded an interval. Then, we have $d \leq \lfloor rn \rfloor$. Moreover, since for each interval that has been kept, there have been two questions asked, we have that the total number of questions can be bounded as

$$n \leq 2t + 4d \leq 2t + 4rn,$$

from which we get that

$$t \geq \frac{n(1 - 4r)}{2}.$$

This, together with $n = \lceil \frac{2m}{1-4r} \rceil$, implies that $t \geq m$. Since every time a new interval is accepted by Paul the set of candidate solutions halves, it must be $|I_t| = 1$. Let $u = t - (m - 1)$. It follows that $u \geq 1$ counts the number of latest phases in which the current interval stayed identically equal to I_t.

We claim that the secret number is the only one in I_t.

If this were not the case, then the last u phases all contained at least one lie. Therefore, the total number of lies would be at least $u + d$. Because of the bound on the total number of lies, we have $u + d \leq rn$. Also, considering that for each newly accepted interval $I_1, \ldots, I_{m-1}$ Paul asked two questions, it follows that the total number of questions asked by Paul can be bounded as

$$n \leq 2(m - 1) + 2u + 4d$$
$$= 2m + 4(u + d) - 2(u + 1)$$
$$\leq 2m + 4(u + d) - 4$$
$$\leq 2m + 4rn - 4.$$

Finally, using the fact that $n \geq \frac{2m}{1-4r}$, we get $2m \leq (1 - 4r)n$, leading to the contradiction

$$n \leq 2m + 4rn - 4 \leq (1 - 4r)n + 4rn - 4 \leq n - 4.$$

Therefore, I_m must contain the secret number of Carole, proving that Paul's strategy is indeed winning.

In order to achieve the bound for $r \leq 1/3$, Paul's strategy must be such that each interval in the sequence $I_0, \ldots, I_t$ occurs about $\lceil \frac{2}{1-3r} \rceil$ times. In this case Paul discards mostly contradicting triples. He only discards a contradicting 4-tuple if for at least $s - 1$ consecutive times he has discarded only contradicting triples. This allows him to improve the bound to $1/3$. ∎

The bounds in (5.6) were subsequently strengthened by Pedrotti [159], who proved that[4]

$$n = \left\lceil \frac{8 \ln 2}{3} \frac{\log_2 M}{(1 - 3r)^2(1 + 3r)} \right\rceil. \tag{5.7}$$

Remarkably enough, (5.7) improves (5.6) by a factor of $\frac{3(1-3r)}{\ln 2}$.

---

[4]Here, ln denotes the natural logarithm.

5.4   Prefix-Bounded Numbers of Lies

A particular case of the linearly bounded lie model is obtained when the fractional bound on the number of lies is assumed to hold at any point of the game. The resulting model is known as the *prefix-bounded lie model*. Here, one assumes that for a given real value r in the open interval $]0, 1[$, at any point in the game, when i answers have been given, no more than $\lfloor r\,i \rfloor$ lies have been told.

It turns out that in this case the bounds on r for the existence of a winning strategy for Paul become weaker.

Theorem 5.5. *For* $r \geq 1/2$, *no winning strategy exists for Paul when the search space has size* $M \geq 3$, *no matter how many questions he asks, not even when membership questions are allowed.*

Proof. Assume $M = 3$. With the first answer Carole can guarantee that at least two numbers remain as candidate solutions. From the second question on, skipping trivialities, let us assume that each question separates the two numbers. Then, Carole always answers as if the secret number were not the one which satisfies the largest number of answers given so far. Therefore, after the first answer the two numbers falsify zero answers and there is one lie available to Carole. Henceforth, the two numbers alternate in increasing the number of answers they falsify. For every two new questions, each of them has falsified one more answer, but also one more lie is available to Carole. In conclusion, none of them ever ends up falsifying a number of answers greater than the number of lies available to Carole. Hence, Paul can never remain with only one candidate solution and win the game.

In the case of membership questions we have the following complementary results.

Theorem 5.6. *Let the search space be* $S = \{0, 1, \ldots, M - 1\}$.

For $r < 1/2$, *Paul has a winning strategy in the prefix-bounded lie model over* S *with* $\Theta(\log_2 M)$ *arbitrary yes-no questions.*

Moreover, for any $r < 1/2$, *Paul has a winning strategy in the prefix-bounded lie model over* S, *with* $O(M^{\log_2(\frac{1}{1-r})})$ *comparison questions.*

Proof. We only discuss here the strategy for the case where comparison questions have to be used. In this case Paul's strategy is simple. He uses binary search, repeating each question long enough to guarantee the reliability of the answer. Note that an answer can be considered true as soon as it has been repeated more than $\lfloor rt \rfloor$ times, where t is the number of questions asked so far.

A careful analysis shows that Paul can obtain the $\lceil \log_2 M \rceil$ reliable answers he needs to identify the secret number by asking $O((\frac{1}{1-r})^{\lceil \log_2 M \rceil}) = O(n^{\log_2 \frac{1}{1-r}}) = o(M)$ questions.

Dhagat et al. observed that the result for comparison questions holds also when only *bit questions* are used.

The bound of Theorem 5.6 was improved by Borgstrom and Kosaraju, whose results give added evidence to the conjecture that $O(\log_2 M)$ comparison questions are sufficient for successful search in the set $\{0, 1, \ldots, M-1\}$ in the prefix-bounded lie model for any value of the error fraction $r < 1/2$. They also provided an algorithm whose overall running time is $O(\log_2 M)$. This is a stronger result than simply proving that $O(\log_2 M)$ questions are sufficient, in that we are here claiming that $O(\log_2 M)$ steps are sufficient also when considering all the necessary computation supporting the search, e.g., operations like state update and question computation.

5.5 Bibliographic Notes

In [185] the Ulam-Rényi problem with comparison questions is considered for the first time. It is actually debated whether in the original formulation Ulam specifically referred to comparison searching. Although the analysis of Rivest et al. [185] is meant to give an asymptotic solution of the problem, the same technique has been successfully reused by Pedrotti [159] and Sereno [189] to provide results for finite instances. In particular, identity (5.7), which originally appeared in [159], is obtained by a refined analysis of the searching algorithm of [185]. Further results on the probabilistic model can be found in [167] and [159].

The study of fault tolerant search in the *linearly bounded lie model* and in the *prefix-bounded lie model* was originally proposed by Pelc [169] in the non-adaptive version with arbitrary yes-no questions, formulated as a problem in coding theory. Pelc [167] was also the first to consider the adaptive *prefix-bounded lie model*. He proved that search is possible if and only if $r < 1/2$ and proposed a questioner strategy of length $O(\log_2 M)$ whenever $p < 1/3$. In [167] Pelc also stated the problem of finding an $O(\log_2 M)$ strategy for the case $1/3 \leq r < 1/2$. The result we have given in Sect. 8.48.4 is due to Spencer and Winkler [199]. The proof of Theorem 5.6 is due to Aslam and Dhagat [16]. The same result for the case of bit questions was proved in [92]. The $O(\log_2 M)$ algorithm for the case of comparison questions is described in [30].

As pointed out by Yossi Azar, a winning strategy with $O(\log_2 M)$ comparison questions in the linearly bounded lie model can be obtained using the main result of [185], despite the fact that paper mainly dealt with fixed numbers of lies.

5.6 Exercises

1. Prove that Conjecture 5.1 holds in the special case $e = 1$.
2. Show that for $e = 0$ we have $N^{(\mathrm{cmp})}(M, 0) = N(M, 0)$, for all $M \geq 1$, and that the same is not true for $e = 1$.

3. Determine the minimum number of *comparison* questions necessary and sufficient in a game with $e = 1$ lie on a search space of cardinality 2^m.

4. Solve the previous exercise in the case where only 2-stage strategies are allowed.

5. Suppose that Paul decides to use the following strategy: for some fixed $t \geq 1$ he asks t comparison questions following a binary search approach and assuming that Carole's answers are correct. Let $A = [\ell, u]$ be the reservoir of candidates to be Carole's secret number, as a result of Carole's answers. Then Paul asks questions at ℓ and u respectively. If both answers confirm that the secret number is in A then Paul continues with a new set of t questions, otherwise he backtracks and starts again with the interval he had reached t questions ago.

   For the case $e = 1$, i.e., Carole can lie at most once, analyze the query complexity of such a strategy as a function of t.

6. Consider the variant of the strategy described in the previous example for which Paul does not verify the interval A after asking t questions, instead he tosses a fair coin after each question in order to decide with probability $1/2$ whether to verify the present interval of candidate solutions.

   What is the expected number of questions required by such a strategy?

Part II
Other Models

Chapter 6
Delays and Time Outs

Better to remain silent and be thought a fool
than to speak out and remove all doubt

A. Lincoln

In this chapter we study the effect of delay on the efficiency of search procedures. In the models we are going to analyze, the delay itself is a source of uncertainty for the searching procedure. A classical assumption in the theory of search is that the information obtained by the execution of a test is available right after the test has been made, that is, a "yes/no" answer is immediately received after the question has been posed, and this knowledge can be used in the formulation of successive questions. However, there are situations in which the time when the test is performed and the time when its outcome is available are decoupled. This may be due to several reasons: the execution of the test may be time-consuming, or tests and responses may be transmitted over a slow channel, etc. Regardless of the possible presence of errors, this delay is already a source of unreliability on the information available to the algorithm.

The questioner-responder game formulation of the model is as follows[1]: the two players first agree on some integer n and a search space $S = \{1, 2, \ldots, n\}$, and then the responder secretly chooses a number x in S. The questioner has to find out x by using comparison questions only, that is, questions of the form "Is $x \leq a$?" for some $a \in S$. At any time instant $i = 1, 2, \ldots$, the questioner has to ask a certain (variable) number of questions in parallel, to which the responder answers with some delay. In general, each question might be answered with its own specific delay. The problem is to determine the minimum total number of questions that are

---

[1] In the first part of this chapter we shall explicitly avoid using the names Paul and Carole for the participants in the game. In fact, we want to make such a distinction in order to clarify that here answers are reliable and we are not in the Ulam-Rényi setting.

F. Cicalese, *Fault-Tolerant Search Algorithms*, Monographs in Theoretical
Computer Science. An EATCS Series, DOI 10.1007/978-3-642-17327-1_6,
© Springer-Verlag Berlin Heidelberg 2013

necessary and sufficient to locate x. Note that some answers may be answered after they have already become obsolete.

We shall first analyze two instances of this rather general model of search with delayed—but reliable—answers. Then, we shall extend the model and analyze a variant with faulty information in which errors are not mendacious answers but rather lost answers. Finally, we shall also discuss in which sense "delayed search strategies" and broadcast of messages in networks with link latency can be considered isomorphic problems.

6.1   Search with Fixed Batches of Questions and Variable Delay in Answers

In our first problem we consider the following scenario: At the beginning of the game the questioner submits a batch of k questions in parallel to the responder. The responder chooses one question from among the k and provides an answer to it. We can assume that the k questions are put in a buffer of size k. Once an answer to a question is received, the questioner replaces the answered question with a new one. Notice that a single answer from the responder can provide a legitimate answer to *more* than one of the questions which have been put in the buffer. To see how this can happen, suppose that the two questions "Is $x \le q_i$?" and "Is $x \le q_j$?" (with $q_i \le q_j$) are both in the buffer and the responder answers "yes" to the former one. It is clear that she has also indirectly answered the latter question. Therefore, the questioner can find it time-saving to substitute both questions in the buffer with two new ones instead of waiting for the second predictable answer.

Summarizing, we can assume that in our game there are always exactly k unanswered questions in the buffer[2] at any time instant, from which the responder chooses as she wishes the one to which she provides an answer. Therefore, there exists an unpredictable though finite delay from the time the questioner formulates a question and puts it into the buffer, and the time this question is chosen and answered by the responder, although at any time instant the responder has to immediately answer the question she has chosen from the buffer.

We want to evaluate, for all $k \ge 1$ and $n \ge 1$, the least number of comparison questions necessary and sufficient to correctly guess an unknown number x chosen from the set $S = \{1, 2, \ldots, n\}$. We call this problem the (n, k)-game and we say that a winning strategy of size t exists for the (n, k)-game if t questions are sufficient to locate the secret number x for *any* possible choice of x and *any* possible sequence of delays in answering the questions. We remark that also questions which have been

---

[2]Unless the questioner does not need to formulate new questions in a specific time instant, since he can deduce the unknown number x from the last received answers, and the game ends.

formulated and whose evaluations have been stopped must be taken into account when computing the overall number of questions used by a given strategy.[3]

For any k an odd integer or $k \in \{2, 4\}$, and for all $t \geq 0$, it is possible to exactly evaluate the maximum n such that there exists a winning strategy of size t for the (n, k)-game.

The critical index defined below will play a key role in determining such a bound.

Definition 6.1. For all $k = 1, 2, 3, \ldots$ and $t = 0, 1, 2, \ldots$ the tth critical index for k is defined by

$$N_t^{[k]} = \begin{cases} t + 1 & \text{if } t \leq k, \\ N_{t-\lceil \frac{k+1}{2} \rceil}^{[k]} + N_{t-\lfloor \frac{k+1}{2} \rfloor}^{[k]} & \text{otherwise.} \end{cases} \tag{6.1}$$

The rest of this section is devoted to the proof of the following theorem.

Theorem 6.1. *Let* $\mathbf{K} = \{2b - 1 \mid b = 1, 2, 3, \ldots\} \cup \{2, 4\}$. *Fix two integers* $k \in \mathbf{K}$ *and* $t \geq 0$, *and let* n *be the size of the largest search space such that there exists a winning strategy of size* t *for the* (n, k)-game. Then

$$n = N_t^{[k]}.$$

The Upper Bound. For all fixed integers $k \geq 1$ and $t \geq 0$, we shall first prove an upper bound on the value of n such that there exists a winning strategy of size t for the (n, k)-game. We shall find it convenient to prove our result on the search space $S = \{1, 2, \ldots, n\}$ or any translation of it, that is, $\{a + 1, a + 2, \ldots, a + n\}$, with a being any integer. Also, we remark that this upper bound holds for *any* value of k, not only for those considered in the hypothesis of Theorem 6.1.

Lemma 6.1. *Fix two integers* $k \geq 1$ *and* $t \geq 0$. *For all integers* $n \geq 1$ *and* a *if there exists a winning strategy for the* (n, k)-game over the search space $\{a + 1, a + 2, \ldots, a + n\}$, then

$$n \leq N_t^{[k]}.$$

Proof. We argue by induction on t.

Induction Basis. $0 \leq t \leq k$. By definition, all the questions are asked in parallel (hence, non-adaptively). Recall that in this case, by Definition 6.1 we have $N_t^{[k]} = t + 1$. Let $n \geq t + 2$ and suppose (*absurdum hypothesis*) that there exists a *winning* strategy with t questions to search in the set $S = \{a + 1, a + 2, \ldots a + n\}$. Because

---

[3]Our analysis works also for the variant of the problem in which questions cannot be substituted before the corresponding answer has been given. Indeed, in a worst-case scenario, each time there is a useless question which is waiting for an answer, it will be the first to be considered next by the responder.

$t \le n - 2$, there must exist at least one $i \in \{1, 2, \ldots, n - 1\}$ such that the question "Is $x \le a + i$?" has not been asked.

Suppose that the secret number is $x = a + i$, and let ℓ be the maximum j such that the question "Is $x \le a + j$?" is answered "no", meaning that $x \ge a + \ell + 1$. Hence, $\ell \le i - 1$. Accordingly, let u be the minimum j such that the question "Is $x \le a + j$?" is answered "yes", meaning that $x \le a + u$.[4] We have $u \ge i + 1$. Therefore, $u \ge \ell + 2$ and for the set $T = \{y | a + \ell + 1 \le y \le a + u\}$, we have $|T| \ge 2$. Note that T is the set of the candidate solutions for the secret number x after that all the questions have been answered. Since T contains more than one element, the strategy cannot be winning. Therefore, by contradiction we get the desired result $n \le t + 1$.

Induction Hypothesis. Fix some positive integer u and let us assume that for all integers $t \le u - 1$ and a, if there exists a winning strategy of size t for the (n, k)-game over the search space $\{a + 1, a + 2, \ldots, a + n\}$, then $n \le N_t^{[k]}$.

Induction Step. Fix an integer a and let $t = u$. Let $\{\mathcal{Q}_i \equiv$ "Is $x \le q_i$?" $| i = 1, 2, \ldots, k\}$ be the set of the first k questions asked in a winning strategy of size t for the (n, k)-game over the search space $\{a + 1, a + 2, \ldots, a + n\}$. Without loss of generality, let $q_i \le q_{i+1}$ for all $i = 1, 2, \ldots, k - 1$. Suppose the adversary chooses to answer $\mathcal{Q}_s$ first, where $s = \lfloor \frac{k+1}{2} \rfloor$.

Assume first that the answer to question $\mathcal{Q}_s \equiv$ "Is $x \le q_s$?" is "yes". Then the unknown number $x \in \{a + 1, a + 2, \ldots, q_s\}$. Since the strategy is winning, the remaining questions/answers must be sufficient to locate the secret number x in the set $S' = \{a + 1, a + 2, \ldots, q_s\}$. In other words, the remaining questions must be sufficient to win the $(q_s - a, k)$-game over the set S'. Let's count how many more questions will be actually used by the questioner.

Under the standing hypothesis, $x \le q_s \le q_{s+1} \le \cdots \le q_k$. Then the (already asked) questions, "Is $x \le q_{s+1}$?", $\ldots$, "Is $x \le q_k$?" will bring no further information to the questioner. Therefore, only $s - 1$ of the already asked questions will contribute to locating x in S'. Including the $t - k$ questions which are still to be asked, all together the questioner is left with

$$(t - k) + (s - 1) = t - \left((k + 1) - \left\lfloor \frac{k + 1}{2} \right\rfloor \right) = t - \left\lceil \frac{k + 1}{2} \right\rceil$$

questions to win the $(q_s - a, k)$-game over S'.

Since the strategy is winning, by induction hypothesis we immediately have

$$q_s - a \le N_{t - \lceil \frac{k+1}{2} \rceil}^{[k]}. \tag{6.2}$$

---

[4]If no such j exists we can safely assume $u = n$.

Suppose now that the answer to the question $\mathcal{Q}_s \equiv$ "Is $x \leq q_s$?" is "no", i.e., $x \in S'' = \{q_s+1, q_s+2, \ldots, a+n\}$. Because the strategy is winning, the remaining questions/answers are sufficient to win the $(a+n-q_s, k)$-game over the set S''. In perfect symmetry with the previous case, the questions "Is $x \leq q_1$?", ..., "Is $x \leq q_{s-1}$?" will not bring any additional information to the questioner, since under the standing hypothesis we have $x > q_s \geq q_{s-1} \geq \cdots \geq q_1$. Therefore, there are $t - k$ questions yet to be asked and $k - s$ already asked questions whose answers are still effective for locating x in S''. All together there are

$$(t-k) + (k-s) = t - s = t - \left\lfloor \frac{k+1}{2} \right\rfloor,$$

questions to win the $(a+n-q_s, k)$-game over S''. Because the strategy is winning, by inductive hypothesis we have

$$a + n - q_s \leq N^{[k]}_{t - \left\lfloor \frac{k+1}{2} \right\rfloor}. \tag{6.3}$$

Summing up (6.2) and (6.3), and recalling Definition 6.1, we have

$$n = a + n - q_s + q_s - a \leq N^{[k]}_{t - \left\lfloor \frac{k+1}{2} \right\rfloor} + N^{[k]}_{t - \left\lceil \frac{k+1}{2} \right\rceil} = N^{[k]}_t,$$

which concludes the proof.

The Lower Bound: Preparatory Material. The following lemma proves that for the particular case of $t \leq k$, the upper bound provided by Lemma 6.1 is tight.

Lemma 6.2. *Fix an integer a. Then for all integers $k \geq 1$ and $t = 1, 2, \ldots, k$, there exists a winning strategy of size t for the $(N^{[k]}_t, k)$-game over the search space $S = \{a+1, a+2, \ldots, a + N^{[k]}_t\}$.*

Proof. Recall that for $t \leq k$, we have $N^{[k]}_t = t + 1$. Hence, the secret number is chosen from the set $S = \{a+1, a+2, \ldots, a+t+1\}$. Then, it is not hard to see that the t questions $\mathcal{Q}_i \equiv$ "Is $x \leq a+i$?" for $i = 1, 2, \ldots, t$ are sufficient to win the $(t+1, k)$-game over S. Indeed, these questions constitute an exhaustive search on S.

We notice the following useful fact.

Fact 6.2 *Fix integers a, n, k, with $n, k \geq 0$. Let $\mathcal{S}$ be a strategy of size t for the (n, k)-game over the search space $S = \{a+1, a+2, \ldots, a+n\}$.*

Define the map $f^S : z \in S \setminus \{a+n\} \mapsto 2a + n - z \in S$ and let $\mathcal{S}'$ be the strategy defined as follows:

1. *for any question $\mathcal{Q} \equiv$ "Is $x \leq b$?" in $\mathcal{S}$, the question $\mathcal{Q}^f \equiv$ "Is $x \leq f(b)$?" is in $\mathcal{S}'$,*

2. *if the question $\mathcal{Q}_j$ in $\mathcal{S}$ is asked immediately after the question $\mathcal{Q}_i$ has been answered "yes" (resp. "no"), then in $\mathcal{S}'$ the question $\mathcal{Q}^f_j$ is asked immediately after the question $\mathcal{Q}^f_i$ has been answered "no" (resp. "yes").*

We have that if $\mathscr{S}$ is a winning *strategy of size t then $\mathscr{S}'$ is also a winning strategy of size t for the (n, k)-game over the search space S.*

Remark 6.1. Fact 6.2 simply points out that for any winning strategy $\mathscr{S}$ there exists another equivalent (in terms of number of questions) winning strategy $\mathscr{S}'$ whose questions are symmetrical to those of the original strategy $\mathscr{S}$.

The next lemma is a key tool to obtain most of the bounds in this section. Essentially, we will show that in order to provide an (optimal) winning strategy of size t for an (n, k)-game, it is sufficient to provide a winning strategy of size t against a much less powerful adversary. More precisely, we shall consider a variant of the (n, k)-game in which the answering strategy of the responder is limited according to the following rule.

H: Let $\{\mathscr{Q}_i \equiv$ "Is $x \leq q_i$?" $\mid i = 1, \ldots, k\}$ be the set of questions in the buffer which have been asked and not answered yet at some time instant. Let $q_i \geq q_{i+1}$ for $i = 1, 2, \ldots, k - 1$. Then, the responder either answers "yes" to the question $\mathscr{Q}_1$ or answers "no" to the question $\mathscr{Q}_k$.

Hereafter, the variant of the game in which the H rule holds will be referred to as the *game with limited responder.* Conversely, the original (n, k)-game will be called the *unrestricted (n, k)-game.*

Lemma 6.3. *Fix integers a and $k \geq 1$ and $n \geq k$. Let t be the size of a winning strategy $\mathscr{S}_{(H)}$ for the (n, k)-game with limited responder over the search space $\{a + 1, a + 2, \ldots, a + n\}$. Then, from the strategy $\mathscr{S}_{(H)}$ it is possible to construct a winning strategy $\mathscr{S}$ of size $t' \leq t$ for the unrestricted (n, k)-game over the search space $\{a + 1, a + 2, \ldots, a + n\}$.*

Proof. We define a *state of the game* as the set of numbers in the search space that satisfy all the given answers together with the set of questions which have been asked and not answered yet.

The strategy $\mathscr{S}$ for the *unrestricted (n, k)-game* is defined over the states of the game produced by any possible play of the game with limited responder when the questioning strategy is $\mathscr{S}_{(H)}$. More precisely:

- The first k questions of $\mathscr{S}$ coincide with the first k questions of $\mathscr{S}_{(H)}$.
- Let σ be a state in the game with limited responder, where the questioner plays according to the strategy $\mathscr{S}_{(H)}$. Let $\{\mathscr{Q}_i \equiv$ "Is $x \leq q_i$?" $\mid i = 1, \ldots, k\}$ be the set of associated standing questions. Assume, without loss of generality, that $q_i \geq q_{i+1}$ for all $i = 1, 2, \ldots, k - 1$.

    Suppose that in the unrestricted game the responder chooses the question $\mathscr{Q}_j$ and answers "yes" to it. Let

$$\mathbf{W} = \{\mathscr{W}_i \equiv \text{"Is } x \leq w_i \text{?"} \mid i = 1, \ldots, r\}$$

be the set of questions asked by the questioner in the game with limited responder from the instant when the state is σ to the instant when the question $\mathscr{Q}_j$ is answered, assuming that the responder repeatedly answers "yes" to the rightmost question.[5] Then, the next questions in $\mathscr{S}$ to be asked by the questioner (after the "yes" answer to $\mathscr{Q}_j$) are given by the set

$$\mathbf{W}' = \{ \mathscr{W} \equiv \text{``Is } x \leq w_i ?\text{''} \in \mathbf{W} \mid w_i < q_j \}.$$

Conversely, suppose that the responder answers "no" to the question $\mathscr{Q}_j$. Let

$$\mathbf{W} = \{ \mathscr{W}_i \equiv \text{``Is } x \leq w_i ?\text{''} \mid i = 1, \ldots, r \}$$

be the set of questions asked by the questioner in the game with limited responder from the instant when the state is σ to the instant when the responder answers "no" to $\mathscr{Q}_j$, assuming that the responder repeatedly answers "no" to the leftmost question. Then, the next questions in $\mathscr{S}$ to be asked by the questioner are given by the set

$$\mathbf{W}' = \{ \mathscr{W} \equiv \text{``Is } x \leq w_i ?\text{''} \in \mathbf{W} \mid w_i > q_j \}.$$

It follows that any state which is attainable in the game when the questioner follows the strategy $\mathscr{S}$ is a state which is also attainable in the game with limited responder when the questioner uses the strategy $\mathscr{S}_{(H)}$.

Let σ be a state of the game attained when the questioner plays according to $\mathscr{S}$. Let τ be the new state after the responder has answered and the questioner has made r new questions. By definition, the state τ is also attained in the game with limited responder when the questioner uses the strategy $\mathscr{S}_{(H)}$. Moreover, in the latter case, the number of new questions made by the questioner while moving from σ to τ is at least r. This is so because the set of questions which are asked by the strategy $\mathscr{S}$ are defined to be a subset of the questions asked according to $\mathscr{S}_{(H)}$ when translating from σ to τ.

It turns out that following $\mathscr{S}$ the questioner concludes the search using at most t questions. Indeed, after any new set of questions the set of numbers satisfying all the given answers strictly decreases. Thus, the strategy $\mathscr{S}$ eventually leads to a final state, that is, a state such that only one number satisfies all the answers and, trivially, it is the secret number. Moreover, any state σ attained with d questions following $\mathscr{S}$ is also attained in the game with limited responder following the strategy $\mathscr{S}_{(H)}$ by asking $\geq d$ questions. Since $\mathscr{S}_{(H)}$ is a winning strategy of size t, any final state is attained with at most t questions. Hence, in the game with no restrictions on the responder's strategy and played by the questioner according to the strategy $\mathscr{S}$, any final state is attained with at most t questions.

---

[5]By the rightmost (resp. leftmost) question in a set $\{ \mathscr{Z}_i \equiv \text{``Is } x \leq z_i ?\text{''} \mid i = 1, \ldots, k \}$ we mean the question $\mathscr{Z}_r$ such that $z_r \geq z_i$ (resp $z_r \leq z_i$)for all $i \neq r$.

The Lower Bound: Two and Four... We now consider the particular cases $k = 2$ and $k = 4$. Note that by Definition 6.1, for the particular case $k = 2$, the tth critical index of k coincides with the $(t + 1)$th Fibonacci number, i.e., $N_t^{[2]} = t + 1$ for $t = 0, 1$, and $N_t^{[2]} = N_{t-1}^{[2]} + N_{t-2}^{[2]}$ for all $t \geq 2$. The following result proves that an optimal strategy for the $(n, 2)$-game corresponds to a Fibonacci search.

Theorem 6.3. *Fix two integers a and $t \geq 0$. Let n_* be the largest integer n such that there exists a winning strategy of size t for the $(n, 2)$-game played over the search space $\{a + 1, a + 2, \ldots, a + n\}$. Then, $n_* = N_t^{[2]}$.*

Proof. By Lemma 6.1 we have $n_* \leq N_t^{[2]}$.

In order to prove $N_t^{[2]} \leq n_*$, we shall show that for any t and a there exists a winning strategy of size t for the $(N_t^{[2]}, 2)$-game over the search space $\{a + 1, a + 2, \ldots, a + N_t^{[2]}\}$ which starts with the two questions

$$\mathcal{Q}_1 \equiv \text{``Is } x \leq a + N_{t-1}^{[k]}?\text{''} \qquad \text{and} \qquad \mathcal{Q}_2 \equiv \text{``Is } x \leq a + N_{t-2}^{[k]}?\text{''}.$$

The proof is by induction on t.

Induction Basis. $t \leq 2$. Straightforwardly by Lemma 6.2.

Induction Hypothesis. For all integers a and for each $t = 0, 1, \ldots, u - 1$, there exists a winning strategy of size t for the $(N_t^{[2]}, 2)$-game over the search space $\{a + 1, \ldots, a + N_t^{[2]}\}$, which starts with the questions "Is $x \leq a + N_{t-1}^{[2]}?$" and "Is $x \leq a + N_{t-2}^{[2]}?$".

Induction Step. Let $t = u$. Suppose that the questions $\mathcal{Q}_1$ and $\mathcal{Q}_2$, above, have been asked.

Assume for the moment that $\mathcal{Q}_1$ is the first question to be answered. We now argue by cases.

Case 1. $\mathcal{Q}_1$ is answered "yes". Then $x \in S' = \{a + 1, a + 2, \ldots, a + N_{t-1}^{[2]}\}$. By inductive hypothesis there exists a winning strategy of size $t - 1$ to locate a secret number in S' which starts with the questions "Is $x \leq a + N_{t-2}^{[2]}?$" and "Is $x \leq a + N_{t-3}^{[2]}?$". Note that the former question is exactly the question $\mathcal{Q}_2$ which has been already asked. Therefore, it suffices to ask $\mathcal{Q}_3 \equiv \text{``Is } x \leq a + N_{t-3}^{[2]}?\text{''}$ to find the secret number with an overall number of t questions (including $\mathcal{Q}_1$).

Case 2. $\mathcal{Q}_1$ is answered "no". Then $x \in S'' = \{a + N_{t-1}^{[2]} + 1, a + N_{t-1}^{[2]} + 2, \ldots, a + N_t^{[2]}\}$. Recalling Definition 6.1 we have $|S''| = N_t^{[2]} - N_{t-1}^{[2]} = N_{t-2}^{[2]}$. By induction hypothesis there exists a winning strategy of size $t - 2$ to locate the secret number x in S''. All together, including the two questions $\mathcal{Q}_1$ and $\mathcal{Q}_2$, we have proved that t questions suffice to find x in S also in this case.

There are two remaining cases arising when the question $\mathcal{Q}_2$ is answered before question $\mathcal{Q}_1$. According to whether the answer is "yes" or "no", we have $x \leq N_{t-2}^{[2]}$

or $x > N_{t-2}^{[2]}$ and the proof is perfectly symmetrical to *Case 2* and *Case 1*, respectively.

Fibonacci-like search is also optimal for the case $k = 4$, as shown by the following theorem.

Theorem 6.4. *Fix two integers a and $t = 0, 1, 2, \ldots$. Let n_* be the largest integer such that there exists a winning strategy of size t for the $(n_*, 4)$-game over the search space $S = \{a + 1, a + 2, \ldots, a + n_*\}$. Then $n_* = N_t^{[4]}$.*

Proof. By Lemma 6.1 we have $n_* \leq N_t^{[4]}$. Moreover, by Lemma 6.2 we have the desired result for any $t = 1, 2, 3, 4$.

It remains to prove $n_* \geq N_t^{[4]}$, when $t \geq 5$. We shall prove that, for any choice of integers a and $t \geq 4$, there exists a winning strategy of size t for the $(N_t^{[4]}, 4)$-game *with limited responder* over the space $S = \{a + 1, a + 2, \ldots, a + N_t^{[4]}\}$ which starts with the four questions $\mathcal{Q}_i \equiv$ "Is $x \leq a + N_{t-i}^{[4]}$?" for $i = 1, 2, 3, 4$. The desired result then follows by Lemma 6.3.

The proof is by induction on t. The induction basis ($t = 4$) is given by Lemma 6.2.

In order to prove the induction step, let $t \geq 5$ and suppose that for $i = 1, 2, 3, 4$ the question $\mathcal{Q}_i \equiv$ "Is $x \leq a + N_{t-i}^{[4]}$?" has been asked. Since we are considering the game *with limited responder*, we shall assume that the responder either answers "yes" to the question $\mathcal{Q}_1$ or answers "no" to the question $\mathcal{Q}_4$.

Case 1. The first received answer is "yes" to the question $\mathcal{Q}_1$. Then $x \in S' = \{a + 1, a + 2, \ldots, a + N_{t-1}^{[4]}\}$.

By induction hypothesis there exists a winning strategy of size $t - 1$ to find a secret number in S'. Such a strategy starts with the questions "Is $x \leq a + N_{t-2}^{[4]}$?", $\ldots$, "Is $x \leq a + N_{t-5}^{[4]}$?".

As a matter of fact, for $r = 2, 3, 4$, the question "Is $x \leq a + N_{t-r}^{[4]}$?" has been already asked. Therefore, it suffices to ask questions $\mathcal{Q}_5 \equiv$ "Is $x \leq a + N_{t-5}^{[4]}$?" in order to match the induction hypothesis and ensure finding x in S' with $t - 1$ more questions.

A fortiori, we have a winning strategy with t questions for the $(N_t^{[4]}, 4)$-game since one question had already been asked, namely the question $\mathcal{Q}_1$.

Case 2. The first received answer is "no" to the question $\mathcal{Q}_4$. Hence $x \in S'' = \{a + N_{t-4}^{[4]} + 1, \ldots, a + N_t^{[4]}\}$. By Definition 6.1 we have

$$|S''| = N_t^{[4]} - N_{t-4}^{[4]} = N_{t-2}^{[4]} + N_{t-3}^{[4]} - N_{t-4}^{[4]} = N_{t-3}^{[4]} + N_{t-5}^{[4]} \leq N_{t-3}^{[4]} + N_{t-4}^{[4]} = N_{t-1}^{[4]}.$$

Therefore, letting $a' = a + N_t^{[4]} - N_{t-1}^{[4]}$, we have

$$S'' \subseteq T = \{a' + 1, a' + 2, \ldots, a' + N_{t-1}^{[4]}\}.$$

By induction hypothesis and Fact 6.2, there exists a winning strategy of size $t - 1$ to guess the secret number x in the set T. Such a strategy starts with the questions

- "Is $x \leq a' + N_{t-1}^{[4]} - N_{t-2}^{[4]}$?",
- "Is $x \leq a' + N_{t-1}^{[4]} - N_{t-3}^{[4]}$?",
- "Is $x \leq a' + N_{t-1}^{[4]} - N_{t-4}^{[4]}$?",
- "Is $x \leq a' + N_{t-1}^{[4]} - N_{t-5}^{[4]}$?".

By Definition 6.1 we have

- $a' + N_{t-1}^{[4]} - N_{t-2}^{[4]} = a + N_t^{[4]} - N_{t-2}^{[4]} = a + N_{t-3}^{[4]}$,
- $a' + N_{t-1}^{[4]} - N_{t-3}^{[4]} = a + N_t^{[4]} - N_{t-3}^{[4]} = a + N_{t-2}^{[4]}$,
- $a' + N_{t-1}^{[4]} - N_{t-4}^{[4]} = a + N_t^{[4]} - N_{t-4}^{[4]}$,
- $a' + N_{t-1}^{[4]} - N_{t-5}^{[4]} = a + N_t^{[4]} - N_{t-5}^{[4]} = a + N_{t-1}^{[4]}$.

Thus, the first two and the fourth of the above questions exactly coincide with questions $\mathcal{Q}_3$, $\mathcal{Q}_2$ and $\mathcal{Q}_1$, respectively (which have already been asked).

Therefore, the desired result follows by induction hypothesis upon asking the question "Is $x \leq a + N_t^{[4]} - N_{t-4}^{[4]}$?".

The proof is complete.

The Lower Bound for Odd k. Here, we shall prove a converse of Lemma 6.1 for the case of k an arbitrary odd integer. The following lemma gives an explicit evaluation of the critical index which was introduced in Definition 6.1.

Lemma 6.4. *Fix an integer $b \geq 1$ and let $k = 2b - 1$. For all integers $t \geq b$, we have*

$$N_t^{[k]} = 2^h(r + b + 1),$$

where $r = t \bmod b$ and $h = \frac{t-r}{b} - 1$.

Proof. By induction on t. Let $t = b, b + 1, \ldots, 2b - 1$. Then, we have

$$r = t \bmod b = t - b \qquad \text{and} \qquad h = \frac{t - r}{b} - 1 = 0.$$

Recalling Definition 6.1, we immediately have

$$2^h(r + b + 1) = 2^0(t - b + b + 1) = t + 1 = N_t^{[k]},$$

as desired.

Now, for some fixed $u > 2b - 1$, suppose the claim to be true for all $t \leq u - 1$, with the intent of proving it for $t = u$. By Definition 6.1 we have

$$N_u^{[k]} = 2N_{u-b}^{[k]} = 2 \cdot 2^h(b + r + 1), \tag{6.4}$$

where $r = (u - b) \bmod b$ and $h = \frac{u-b-r}{b} - 1$.

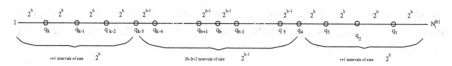

Fig. 6.1 The distribution of the first k questions in a normal strategy ($r = 3$)

Let $r_u = u \bmod b = (u - b) \bmod b = r$ and $h_u = \frac{u-r}{b} - 1 = \frac{u-b-r}{b} - 1 + 1 = h + 1$; then by (6.4) we have

$$N_u^{[k]} = 2^{h+1}(b + r + 1) = 2^{h_u}(b + r_u + 1),$$

as desired.

Definition 6.2. Fix integers $n \geq 1$ and $b \geq 1$, and let $k = 2b - 1$. For all integers a and $t = \min\{i \mid N_i^{[k]} \geq n\}$, we say that a strategy for the (n, k)-game over the search space $\{a + 1, a + 2, \ldots, a + n\}$ is *normal* if the first k questions, viz. $\mathcal{Q}_i \equiv$ "Is $x \leq q_i$?" for $i = 1, 2, \ldots, k$, are defined by

$$q_i = \begin{cases} a + N_{t-i}^{[k]} & \text{for } i = 1, 2, \ldots, b \\ a + N_t^{[k]} - N_{t-2b+i}^{[k]} & \text{for } i = b+1, b+2, \ldots, 2b-1. \end{cases} \tag{6.5}$$

Fact 6.5 *With reference to the above definition, the first k questions of a normal strategy split the space $\{a + 1, a + 2, \ldots, a + N_t^{[k]}\}$ into the $2b$ intervals, $\mathcal{I}_i = \{q_i + 1, q_i + 2, \ldots, q_{i-1}\}$ ($i = 1, 2, \ldots, 2b$), which are distributed according to a central symmetry[6]; i.e., letting $r = t \bmod b$ and $h = \frac{t-r}{b} - 1$, it holds that (see Fig. 6.1 for an example)*

$$|\mathcal{I}_i| = \begin{cases} 2^h & \text{for } i = 1, 2, \ldots, r+1 \\ 2^{h-1} & \text{for } i = r+2, r+3, \ldots, 2b-r-1, \\ 2^h & \text{for } i = 2b-r, 2b-r+1, \ldots, 2b. \end{cases}$$

Lemma 6.5. *Fix an integer $b \geq 1$. Let $k = 2b - 1$. For all integers a and $t \geq k$, there exists a normal winning strategy $\mathcal{S}_{(H)}$ of size t for the $(N_t^{[k]}, k)$-game with limited responder over the set $\{a + 1, a + 2, \ldots, a + N_t^{[k]}\}$.*

Proof. The proof is by induction on t.

Induction Basis. $t = k$. Straightforwardly by Lemma 6.2.

---

[6]For sake of definiteness, we let $q_0 = a + N_t^{[k]}$, $q_{2b} = a$.

Induction Hypothesis. For all integers a there exists a *normal* winning strategy of size $t-1$ for the $(N_{t-1}^{[k]}, k)$-game *with limited responder* over the search space $S' = \{a+1, a+2, \ldots, a+N_{t-1}^{[k]}\}$.

Induction Step. We shall show a *normal* winning strategy $\mathscr{S}_{(H)}$ for the $(N_t^{[k]}, k)$-game with limited responder over the search space $\{a+1, a+2, \ldots, a+N_t^{[k]}\}$.

Let $\{\mathcal{Q}_i \equiv \text{"Is } x \le q_i?\text{"} \mid i = 1, \ldots, k\}$ be the set of the first k questions in the strategy $\mathscr{S}_{(H)}$, where

$$
q_i = \begin{cases} a + N_{t-i}^{[k]} & i = 1, 2, \ldots, b \\ a + N_t^{[k]} - N_{t-2b+i}^{[k]} & i = b+1, b+2, \ldots, 2b-1. \end{cases}
$$

Hence, the strategy is *normal*.

By Fact 6.5 we also have that

$$
q_i = \begin{cases} q_{i-1} - 2^h & i = 2, 3, \ldots, r+1, 2b-r, 2b-r+1, 2b-1 \\ q_{i-1} - 2^{h-1} & i = r+2, r+3, \ldots, 2b-r-1, \end{cases} \tag{6.6}
$$

where

$$
r = t \bmod b \quad \text{and} \quad h = \frac{t-r}{b} - 1.
$$

Recall that under the standing hypothesis (H) the only possible answer is either "yes" to the question $\mathcal{Q}_1$ or "no" to the question $\mathcal{Q}_k$.

We first consider the case that the responder answers "yes" to the question $\mathcal{Q}_1 \equiv \text{"Is } x \le q_1?\text{"}$. Thus, $x \in S' = \{a+1, a+2, \ldots, a+N_{t-1}^{[k]}\}$.

Let $q^* = a + 2^h(r+1) - 2^{h-1} = q_{2b-r-1} - 2^{h-1}$. $\mathscr{S}_{(H)}$'s next question will be $\mathcal{Q}^{yes} \equiv \text{"Is } x \le q^*?\text{"}$.

Therefore, after the first answer has been given and a new question has been formulated, the set of standing questions is given by

$$
\mathbf{Q} = \{\mathcal{Q}_i \equiv \text{"Is } x \le q_i?\text{"} \mid i = 2, \ldots, k\} \cup \{\mathcal{Q}^{yes}\}.
$$

By the induction hypothesis there exists a *normal* winning strategy of size $t-1$ for the $(N_{t-1}^{[k]}, k)$-game with limited responder over the search space S'. Such a strategy starts with the questions

$$
\mathbf{W} = \{\mathcal{W}_i \equiv \text{"Is } x \le w_i?\text{"} \mid i = 1, 2, \ldots, k\},
$$

where

$$
w_i = \begin{cases} a + N_{t-1-i}^{[k]} & i = 1, 2, \ldots, b \\ a + N_{t-1}^{[k]} - N_{t-1-2b+i}^{[k]} & i = b+1, b+2, \ldots, 2b-1. \end{cases}
$$

By Fact 6.5 we have

$$w_i = \begin{cases} w_{i-1} - 2^{h_w} & i = 2, 3, \ldots, r_w + 1, 2b - r_w, 2b - r_w + 1, 2b - 1 \\ w_{i-1} - 2^{h_w - 1} & i = r_w + 2, r_w + 3, \ldots, 2b - r_w - 1, \end{cases} \tag{6.7}$$

where

$$r_w = t - 1 \bmod b \quad \text{and} \quad h_w = \frac{t - 1 - r_w}{b} - 1.$$

We shall prove that

$$q_i = w_{i-1} \quad i = 2, 3, \ldots, 2b - r - 1 \tag{6.8}$$

$$q_i = w_i \quad\quad i = 2b - r, 2b - r + 1, \ldots, 2b - 1 \tag{6.9}$$

$$q^* = w_{2b-r-1}, \tag{6.10}$$

that is, $\mathbf{Q} = \mathbf{W}$. Recall that by induction hypothesis $t - 1$ questions, including the ones in $\mathbf{Q}$, suffice to complete the search in the set S'. Thus, by counting also the already answered question $\mathcal{Q}_1$, it follows that t questions are sufficient to find the secret number in the $(N_t^{[k]}, k)$-game over the set S, as desired.

In order to prove $\mathbf{Q} = \mathbf{W}$, we distinguish two cases.

Case 1. $r = 0$. Then $h = t/b - 1$ and, by (6.6), we have $q_i = q_{i-1} - 2^{h-1}$ for all $i = 2, 3, \ldots, 2b - 1$. On the other hand, we have

$$r_w = (t - 1) \bmod b = (t \bmod b) - 1 \bmod b = (r - 1) \bmod b = b - 1$$

and

$$h_w = \frac{(t - 1) - (b - 1)}{b} - 1 = \frac{t}{b} - 2 = h - 1.$$

By (6.7) and $r_w = b - 1$, we have that for all $i = 2, 3, \ldots, 2b - 1$

$$w_i = w_{i-1} - 2^{h_w} = w_{i-1} - 2^{h-1}.$$

Therefore, $w_1 = a + N_{t-2}^{[k]} = q_2$ immediately implies the equalities (6.8) and (6.9). Moreover, equality (6.10) follows from

$$q^* = q_{2b-r-1} - 2^{h-1} = w_{2b-2} - 2^{h-1} = w_{2b-1}.$$

Case 2. $r \neq 0$. Therefore, we get

$$r_w = (t \bmod b) - 1 \bmod b = r - 1, \quad h_w = \frac{(t - 1) - r_w}{b} - 1 = \frac{(t - 1) - r + 1}{b} - 1 = h.$$

Thus,

(i) for $i = 2, 3, \ldots, b$, we have $q_i = a + N_{t-i}^{[k]} = a + N_{(t-1)-(i-1)}^{[k]} = w_{i-1}$,

(ii) for $i = b + 1, \ldots, 2b - r - 1$, from (6.6) and (6.7) we have

$$q_i = q_b - 2^{h-1}(i - b) = w_{b-1} - 2^{h_w-1}[(i - 1) - (b - 1)] = w_{i-1},$$

(iii) for $i = 2b - r, 2b - r + 1, \ldots, 2b - 1$, using (6.6) we have

$$
\begin{aligned}
q_i &= q_{2b-r-1} - 2^h(i - 2b + r + 1) \\
&= w_{2b-r-2} - 2^h(i - 2b + r + 1) \quad \text{(by } q_{2b-r-1} = w_{2b-r-2}) \\
&= w_{2b-r_w-3} - 2^{h_w}(i + 1 - 2b + r_w + 1) \quad \text{(by } r = r_w + 1 \text{ and } h = h_w) \\
&= w_{2b-r_w-1} - 2^{h_w} \\
&\quad -2^{h_w}(i + 1 - 2b + r_w + 1) \text{ (by } w_{2b-r_w-3} = w_{2b-r_w-1} - 2^{h_w}) \\
&= w_{2b-r_w-1} - 2^{h_w}(i - 2b + r_w + 1) \\
&= w_i,
\end{aligned}
$$

(iv) $q^* = q_{2b-r-1} - 2^{h-1} = w_{2b-r-2} - 2^{h_w-1} = w_{2b-r_w-3} - 2^{h_w-1} = w_{2b-r_w-2}$

$$= w_{2b-r-1}.$$

(i) and (ii) imply (6.8), (iii) implies (6.9) and finally (iv) implies (6.10). Hence, $\mathbf{Q} = \mathbf{W}$. This completes the proof for the case where the responder answers "yes" to question $\mathcal{Q}_1$.

Suppose now that the responder answers "no" to the question $\mathcal{Q}_k$. Then, upon asking the question $\mathcal{Q}^{no} \equiv$ "Is $x \leq q_{r+1} + 2^{h-1}$?", it turns out that the new set of questions, namely

$$\{\mathcal{Q}_i \equiv \text{"Is } x \leq q_i\text{?"} \mid i = 1, 2, \ldots, k - 1\} \cup \{\mathcal{Q}^{no}\},$$

coincides with the set of questions

$$\mathbf{Z} = \{\mathcal{Z}_i \equiv \text{"Is } x \leq z_i\text{?"} \mid i = 1, 2, \ldots, k\},$$

where

$$
z_i =
\begin{cases}
(a + N_t^{[k]} - N_{t-1}^{[k]}) + N_{t-1-i}^{[k]} & i = 1, 2, \ldots, b \\
(a + N_t^{[k]} - N_{t-1}^{[k]}) + N_{t-1}^{[k]} - N_{t-1-2b+i}^{[k]} & i = b + 1, b + 2, \ldots, 2b - 1.
\end{cases}
$$

By inductive hypothesis, these are the starting questions of a winning strategy for the $(N_{t-1}^{[k]}, k)$-game over the search space $\{a' + 1, \ldots, a' + N_{t-1}^{[k]}\}$, where $a' = a + N_t^{[k]} - N_{t-1}^{[k]}$. The proof is analogous to the one given in the analysis of the case where the responder answers "yes" to the question $\mathcal{Q}_1$. Therefore, $t-1$ questions, including the one in $\mathbf{Z}$, suffice to complete the search. Taking into account the question $\mathcal{Q}_k$, which has been already answered, again we conclude that t questions suffice to successfully complete the search in the space $\{a + 1, \ldots, a + N_t^{[k]}\}$, as desired.

Summarizing the above discussions, we have the following:

Corollary 6.1. *Fix an integer $b \geq 1$ and let $k = 2b - 1$. For all integers a and $t \geq 0$, there exists a* normal *winning strategy $\mathscr{S}$ of size t for the $(N_t^{[k]}, k)$-game over the search space $\{a + 1, a + 2, \ldots, a + N_t^{[k]}\}$.*

Proof. Straightforwardly by Lemmas 6.2, 6.5 and 6.3.

Proof of Theorem 6.1. By Lemma 6.1, Theorems 6.3 and 6.4, and Corollary 6.1. ∎

6.2 Search with Variable Batches and Delays

We now consider another variant of the general problem of searching with parallel questions and delayed answers outlined in the introduction. Here, two sequences of non-negative integers, $\mathbf{k} = k_1 k_2 \cdots k_t$ and $\mathbf{d} = d_1 d_2 \cdots d_t$, are given. The questioner has to guess the secret number x by asking comparison questions to the responder according to the following rule: At time i ($i = 1, 2, \ldots$), the questioner has to ask exactly k_i questions and the answers to these questions will be only given by the responder before time[7] $i + d_i + 1$ but after time $i + d_i$. This constitutes the $(n, \mathbf{k}, \mathbf{d})$-game, and we say that the questioner has a winning strategy of size q if q questions are sufficient to find the secret number x for any choice of $x \in S$.

For any integer t and any pair of sequences $\mathbf{k}$ and $\mathbf{d}$, we shall exactly evaluate the largest value of n such that there exists a searching strategy for the $(n, \mathbf{k}, \mathbf{d})$-game which allows us to find the secret number with at most t batches of questions. Indeed, since the number of questions that are to be asked at any time is fixed, the problem of determining the least number of questions necessary and sufficient to guess an unknown number is the same as that of determining the least integer t such that after the tth batch of questions has been asked the questioner has only to wait for the remaining answers and then is able to identify the secret number.

By a strategy (of the questioner) we understand an algorithm that produces the first k_1 questions to be asked at time 1, and then, for any $i = 2, 3, \ldots$, outputs the k_i questions to be asked at time i, having as input the answers given by the responder at times $j = 1, 2, \ldots, i - 1$, For any strategy $\mathscr{S}$, the *size* of $\mathscr{S}$ is the maximum number of questions asked by a questioner using $\mathscr{S}$ to find the secret number, where the maximum is computed over all possible choices of x.

---

[7] We require that $\sum_{i=1}^t k_i \geq n$ so that the questioner can always find x by asking n questions, namely, "Is $x \leq j$?" for $j = 1, 2, \ldots n$.

Since for any $i = 1, 2, \ldots$, the number of questions to be asked at time i is fixed in advance, we shall first consider the following problem: For any t and sequences of batch sizes $\mathbf{k}$ and delays $\mathbf{d}$, evaluate the largest value of n such that there exists a strategy $\mathscr{S}$ of size $\sum_{j=1}^{t} k_j$, which allows the questioner to successfully complete the search in t time units. We shall also say that $\mathscr{S}$ is a strategy of (time) *length* t for the $(n, \mathbf{k}, \mathbf{d})$-game.

Definition 6.3. Let $\mathbf{s} = s_1 s_2 \cdots s_t$, be any sequence of t non-negative integers. Then

- t is the *length* of $\mathbf{s}$ and is denoted by $\ell(\mathbf{s})$,
- for any $1 \le i \le j \le t$, $\mathbf{s}_{[i \ldots j]}$ denotes the subsequence $s_i \, s_{i+1} \cdots s_j$. For $j < i$, $\mathbf{s}_{[i \ldots j]} = \emptyset$,
- for any sequence $\mathbf{r} = r_1 r_2 \cdots r_m$, we denote by $\mathbf{r} \circ \mathbf{s}$ the sequence obtained by appending the sequence $\mathbf{s}$ to the sequence $\mathbf{r}$ in formulae $\mathbf{r} \circ \mathbf{s} = r_1 \cdots r_m s_1 \cdots s_t$.

Given the sequences $\mathbf{k} = k_1 \cdots k_t$ and $\mathbf{d} = d_1 \cdots d_t$, it turns out that the largest value of n such that there exists a strategy of length $t = \ell(\mathbf{k}) = \ell(\mathbf{d})$ for the $(n, \mathbf{k}, \mathbf{d})$-game is given by the formula

$$
A(\mathbf{k}, \mathbf{d}) = \begin{cases} 1 & \text{if } \mathbf{d} = \emptyset \\ A\left(\mathbf{k}_{[2 \ldots t]}, \mathbf{d}_{[2 \ldots t]}\right) + k_1 A\left(\mathbf{k}_{[d_1+2 \ldots t]}, \mathbf{d}_{[d_1+2 \ldots t]}\right) & \text{otherwise.} \end{cases} \tag{6.11}
$$

We first prove the following lower bound on the size of the largest search space, where it is possible to guess an unknown number by using t batches of questions.

Lemma 6.6. *For any integer $t \ge 0$ and for all sequences of non-negative integers $\mathbf{k}$ and $\mathbf{d}$ such that $\ell(\mathbf{k}) = \ell(\mathbf{d}) = t$, there exists a strategy of length t for the $(A(\mathbf{k}, \mathbf{d}), \mathbf{k}, \mathbf{d})$-game over the search space $S = \{1, 2, \ldots, A(\mathbf{k}, \mathbf{d})\}$ or any translation of it.*

Proof. By induction on $t = \ell(\mathbf{k}) = \ell(\mathbf{d})$. The claim is trivial for $t = 0$.

Let $t > 0$ and let the claim be true for all sequences of size $u \le t - 1$. For any sequences of batch sizes and delays $\mathbf{k}'$ and $\mathbf{d}'$ such that $\ell(\mathbf{k}') = \ell(\mathbf{d}') = u < t$, let us denote by $\mathscr{S}(\mathbf{k}', \mathbf{d}', S')$ a strategy of length u for the $(A(\mathbf{k}', \mathbf{d}'), \mathbf{k}', \mathbf{d}')$-game over some search space S', which is a translation of the set $\{1, 2, \ldots, A(\mathbf{k}', \mathbf{d}')\}$. Let $w = A\left(\mathbf{k}_{[d_1+2 \ldots t]}, \mathbf{d}_{[d_1+2 \ldots t]}\right)$ and

$$
q_i = A(\mathbf{k}, \mathbf{d}) - i \, w \qquad \text{for } i = 1, 2, \ldots, k_1,
$$

Recall that k_1 questions have to be asked at time 1. Let $\mathscr{S}$ be the strategy defined as follows:

- At time 1 the strategy $\mathscr{S}$ asks questions "Is $x \le q_i$?" for $i = 1, 2, \ldots, k_1$.
- For $j = 2, 3, \ldots, d_1 + 1$, the strategy $\mathscr{S}$ keeps on asking questions according to the strategy $\mathscr{S}(\mathbf{k}_{[2 \ldots t]}, \mathbf{d}_{[2 \ldots t]}, U)$, where $U = \{1, 2, \ldots, A(\mathbf{k}_{[2 \ldots t]}, \mathbf{d}_{[2 \ldots t]})\}$. More

precisely, the batch of questions asked by $\mathscr{S}$ at time j is the one asked by $\mathscr{S}(\mathbf{k}_{[2...t]}, \mathbf{d}_{[2...t]}, U)$ at time $j - 1$.

- For $j = d_1 + 2, d_1 + 3, \ldots$, the behavior of $\mathscr{S}$ depends on the answers given to the first k_1 questions which have become available, namely:

  - If the answer to the question "Is $x \le q_{k_1}$?" is "yes", then $\mathscr{S}$ keeps on asking questions following the strategy $\mathscr{S}(\mathbf{k}_{[2...t]}, \mathbf{d}_{[2...t]}, U)$. At time j (for each $j = d_1 + 2, d_1 + 3, \ldots$) the batch of questions asked by strategy $\mathscr{S}$ is given by the batch of questions asked at time $j - 1$ by the strategy $\mathscr{S}(\mathbf{k}_{[2...t]}, \mathbf{d}_{[2...t]}, U)$.
  - Conversely, suppose that there exists an index $i \in \{1, 2, \ldots, k_1\}$, such that the answer to the question "Is $x \le q_i$?" is "no" and the answer to the question "Is $x \le q_{i-1}$?" is "yes".[8] Then, $\mathscr{S}$ continues by following the strategy $\mathscr{S}(\mathbf{k}_{[d_1+2...t]}, \mathbf{d}_{[d_1+2...t]}, V)$, where $V = \{q_i + 1, q_i + 2, \ldots, q_{i-1}\}$. More precisely, in this case the batch of questions asked by $\mathscr{S}$ at time j will coincide with the batch of questions asked in $\mathscr{S}(\mathbf{k}_{[d_1+2...t]}, \mathbf{d}_{[d_1+2...t]}, V)$ at time $j - d_1 - 1$.

We shall now show that the strategy $\mathscr{S}$ successfully completes the search. We shall argue according to the different possible outcomes of the first k_1 questions considered in the definition of $\mathscr{S}$.

If the answer to the question "Is $x \le q_{k_1}$?" is "yes", then $\mathscr{S}$ keeps on asking questions following the strategy $\mathscr{S}(\mathbf{k}_{[2...t]}, \mathbf{d}_{[2...t]}, U)$. Since

$$q_{k_1} = A(\mathbf{k}, \mathbf{d}) - k_1 \cdot A\left(\mathbf{k}_{[d_1+2...t]}, \mathbf{d}_{[d_1+2...t]}\right) = A\left(\mathbf{k}_{[2...t]}, \mathbf{d}_{[2...t]}\right),$$

we have that $x \in \left\{1, 2, \ldots, A\left(\mathbf{k}_{[2...t]}, \mathbf{d}_{[2...t]}\right)\right\} = U$. The desired result now follows by induction hypothesis, since $\mathscr{S}(\mathbf{k}_{[2...t]}, \mathbf{d}_{[2...t]}, U)$ is a strategy of size $t - 1$ for the $\left(A\left(\mathbf{k}_{[2...t]}, \mathbf{d}_{[2...t]}\right), \mathbf{k}_{[2...t]}, \mathbf{d}_{[2...t]}\right)$-game over the set U.

Conversely, suppose that there exists an index $i \in \{1, 2, \ldots, k_1\}$, such that the answer to the question "Is $x \le q_i$?" is "no" and the answer to the question "Is $x \le q_{i-1}$?" is "yes". Therefore, $x \in \{q_i + 1, q_i + 2, \ldots q_{i-1}\} = V$, and we have that

$$|V| = q_{i-1} - q_i = A\left(\mathbf{k}_{[d_1+2...t]}, \mathbf{d}_{[d_1+2...t]}\right).$$

Recall that (induction hypothesis) $\mathscr{S}(\mathbf{k}_{[d_1+2...t]}, \mathbf{d}_{[d_1+2...t]}, V)$ is a strategy of length $t - d_1 - 1$ for the $\left(A\left(\mathbf{k}_{[d_1+2...t]}, \mathbf{d}_{[d_1+2...t]}\right), \mathbf{k}_{[d_1+2...t]}, \mathbf{d}_{[d_1+2...t]}\right)$-game over the set V. Since in this case the questions asked by $\mathscr{S}$ coincide with those asked by $\mathscr{S}(\mathbf{k}_{[d_1+2...t]}, \mathbf{d}_{[d_1+2...t]}, V)$, we have that $\mathscr{S}$ will successfully identify x within the remaining $t - d_1 - 1$ time units as desired.

---

[8]For sake of definiteness we can safely assume that $q_0 = A(\mathbf{k}, \mathbf{d})$ and there exists an implicit question "Is $x \le q_0$?" whose corresponding answer is trivially "yes".

We shall now prove an upper bound on the size of the largest search space where it is possible to locate an unknown number by using t batches of questions. We shall need the following two easy lemmas.

Lemma 6.7. *Fix an integer* $t \geq 0$ *and two sequences of integers* $\mathbf{k} = k_1 k_2 \cdots k_t$ *and* $\mathbf{d} = d_1 d_2 \cdots d_t$. *Let* $\tilde{t} = \min_{1 \leq i \leq t}\{i + d_i + 1\}$ *and* $\tilde{j} = \min\{i \mid i + d_i + 1 = \tilde{t}\}$. *Let the sequences of integers* $\mathbf{k}' = k_1' k_2' \cdots k_t'$ *and* $\mathbf{d}' = d_1' d_2' \cdots d_t'$ *be defined by*

$$
k_i' = \begin{cases} k_{\tilde{j}} & i = 1, \\ k_{i-1} & i = 2, \ldots, \tilde{j} \\ k_i & i > \tilde{j}, \end{cases}
\qquad
d_i' = \begin{cases} \tilde{t} - 2 & i = 1, \\ d_{i-1} - 1 & i = 2, \ldots, \tilde{j} \\ d_i & i > \tilde{j}. \end{cases}
$$

Then,

(i) $A(\mathbf{k}, \mathbf{d}) = A(\mathbf{k}', \mathbf{d}')$.

(ii) *For any integer* $n \geq 0$ *and for any strategy* $\mathscr{S}$ *of length* t *for the* $(n, \mathbf{k}, \mathbf{d})$*-game there exists a strategy of length* t *for the* $(n, \mathbf{k}', \mathbf{d}')$*-game.*

Proof. In order to prove the statement (i), we have

$$
A(\mathbf{k}', \mathbf{d}') = \sum_{i=1}^{\tilde{j}} k_i' A(\mathbf{k}'_{[i+d_i'+1\ldots t]}, \mathbf{d}'_{[i+d_i'+1\ldots t]}) + A(\mathbf{k}'_{[\tilde{j}+1\ldots t]}, \mathbf{d}'_{[\tilde{j}+1\ldots t]})
$$

$$
= k_1' A(\mathbf{k}'_{[\tilde{t}\ldots t]}, \mathbf{d}'_{[\tilde{t}\ldots t]}) + \sum_{i=2}^{\tilde{j}} k_i' A(\mathbf{k}'_{[i+d_i'+1\ldots t]}, \mathbf{d}'_{[i+d_i'+1\ldots t]})
$$

$$
+ A(\mathbf{k}'_{[\tilde{j}+1\ldots t]}, \mathbf{d}'_{[\tilde{j}+1\ldots t]})
$$

$$
= k_{\tilde{j}} A(\mathbf{k}_{[\tilde{j}+d_{\tilde{j}}+1\ldots t]}, \mathbf{d}_{[\tilde{j}+d_{\tilde{j}}+1\ldots t]})
$$

$$
+ \sum_{i=2}^{\tilde{j}} k_{i-1} A(\mathbf{k}_{[(i-1)+d_{i-1}+1\ldots t]}, \mathbf{d}_{[(i-1)+d_{i-1}+1\ldots t]})
$$

$$
+ A(\mathbf{k}_{[\tilde{j}+1\ldots t]}, \mathbf{d}_{[\tilde{j}+1\ldots t]})
$$

$$
= A(\mathbf{k}, \mathbf{d}).
$$

We shall now prove statement (ii). Let $\mathscr{S}$ be the strategy for the $(n, \mathbf{k}, \mathbf{d})$-game. We define a new strategy $\mathscr{S}'$ as follows. In $\mathscr{S}'$ the questions asked at time 1 are exactly those asked at time $\tilde{j}$ in the strategy $\mathscr{S}$. For $i = 2, \ldots, \tilde{j}$, the questions asked at time i in the strategy $\mathscr{S}'$ are exactly those asked at time $i - 1$ in the strategy $\mathscr{S}$. For $i > \tilde{j}$ the questions asked at time i in $\mathscr{S}$ are those asked at time i in $\mathscr{S}$. It is not hard to see that $\mathscr{S}'$ is a strategy of length t for the $(n, \mathbf{k}', \mathbf{d}')$-game. Indeed, we have only changed the time of the questions asked in that part of the game where all the questions are asked non-adaptively. The rest of the strategy, with all the causal dependencies among questions and answers, has been kept unaltered.

Lemma 6.8. *Fix an integer* $t \geq 0$ *and two sequences of integers* $\mathbf{k} = k_1 k_2 \cdots k_t$ *and* $\mathbf{d} = d_1 d_2 \cdots d_t$ *such that* $d_1 + 2 \leq i + d_i + 1$ *for each* $i = 1, 2 \ldots, t$. *Let* $F = \{i \mid 2 \leq i \leq d_1 + 1 \text{ and } i + d_i + 1 = d_1 + 2\}$. *Let the sequences of integers* $\mathbf{k}' = k_1' k_2' \cdots k_t'$ *be defined by*

$$k_i' = \begin{cases} k_1 + \sum_{j \in F} k_j & i = 1 \\ 0 & i \in F \\ k_i & otherwise. \end{cases}$$

Then,

(i) $A(\mathbf{k}, \mathbf{d}) = A(\mathbf{k}', \mathbf{d})$.

(ii) *For any integers* $n \geq 0$ *and for any strategy* $\mathscr{S}$ *of length* t *for the* $(n, \mathbf{k}, \mathbf{d})$*-game there exists a strategy* $\mathscr{S}'$ *of length* t *for the* $(n, \mathbf{k}', \mathbf{d})$*-game.*

Proof. In order to prove the statement (i), we have:

$$A(\mathbf{k}', \mathbf{d}) = A(\mathbf{k}'_{[2\ldots t]}, \mathbf{d}_{[2\ldots t]}) + k_1' A(\mathbf{k}'_{[d_1+2\ldots t]}, \mathbf{d}_{[d_1+2\ldots t]})$$

$$= \qquad\qquad \vdots$$

$$= A(\mathbf{k}'_{[d_1+2\ldots t]}, \mathbf{d}'_{[d_1+2\ldots t]}) + \sum_{\substack{i = 1 \\ i \notin F}}^{d_1+1} k_i' A(\mathbf{k}'_{[i+d_i+1\ldots t]}, \mathbf{d}_{[i+d_i+1\ldots t]})$$

$$= A(\mathbf{k}_{[d_1+2\ldots t]}, \mathbf{d}_{[d_1+2\ldots t]}) + k_1' A(\mathbf{k}'_{[d_1+2\ldots t]}, \mathbf{d}_{[d_1+2\ldots t]})$$

$$\qquad\qquad\qquad + \sum_{\substack{i = 2 \\ i \notin F}}^{d_1+1} k_i A(\mathbf{k}_{[i+d_i+1\ldots t]}, \mathbf{d}_{[i+d_i+1\ldots t]})$$

$$= A(\mathbf{k}_{[d_1+2\ldots t]}, \mathbf{d}_{[d_1+2\ldots t]}) + k_1 A(\mathbf{k}_{[d_1+2\ldots t]}, \mathbf{d}_{[d_1+2\ldots t]})$$

$$\sum_{\substack{i = 2 \\ i \in F}}^{d_1+1} k_i A(\mathbf{k}_{[i+d_i+1\ldots t]}, \mathbf{d}_{[i+d_i+1\ldots t]})$$

$$+ \sum_{\substack{i = 2 \\ i \notin F}}^{d_1+1} k_i A(\mathbf{k}_{[i+d_i+1\ldots t]}, \mathbf{d}_{[i+d_i+1\ldots t]})$$

$$= A(\mathbf{k}, \mathbf{d}).$$

With the aim of proving statement (ii), let $\mathscr{S}$ be a strategy for the $(n, \mathbf{k}, \mathbf{d})$-game. Let $\mathscr{Q}_S{}^{(i)}$ be the set of questions asked at time i in the strategy $\mathscr{S}$. The strategy $\mathscr{S}'$ is defined by stipulating that the questions $\mathscr{Q}_{S'}{}^{(i)}$ asked at time i are given by

$$\mathscr{Q}_{S'}{}^{(i)} = \begin{cases} \mathscr{Q}_S{}^{(1)} \cup \bigcup_{i \in F} \mathscr{Q}_S{}^{(i)} & i = 1 \\ \emptyset & i \in F \\ \mathscr{Q}_S{}^{(i)} & \text{otherwise.} \end{cases}$$

Therefore, the strategy $\mathscr{S}'$ coincides with strategy $\mathscr{S}$ but for the fact that the questioner asks at time 1 all the questions that in the strategy $\mathscr{S}$ were the first to be answered by the responder (and precisely at time $d_1 + 2$). Since this change does not modify the dependencies between the questions and the received answers, the new strategy $\mathscr{S}'$ behaves exactly as the strategy $\mathscr{S}$.

Lemma 6.9. *Fix an integer $t \geq 0$ and two sequences of non-negative integers $\mathbf{k}$ and $\mathbf{d}$ such that $\ell(\mathbf{k}) = \ell(\mathbf{d}) = t$. Let $\mathscr{S}(\mathbf{k}, \mathbf{d})$ be a searching strategy of length t for the $(n, \mathbf{k}, \mathbf{d})$-game over the search space $S = \{1, 2, \ldots, n\}$ (or any translation of it). Then,*

$$n \leq A(\mathbf{k}, \mathbf{d}).$$

Proof. By induction on t. The claim is trivially true for $t = 0$.

Let $t > 0$ and assume the claim true for all sequences $\mathbf{k}'$ and $\mathbf{d}'$ of length $\ell(\mathbf{k}') = \ell(\mathbf{d}') < t$.

Let $\bar{t} = \min_{1 \leq i \leq t}\{i + d_i + 1\}$ denote the time when the first batch of answers is received. Hence, the first $\sum_{j=1}^{\bar{t}-1} k_j$ questions are asked from scratch, before that any information is available from the responder's answers.

By Lemmas 6.7 and 6.8 we may safely assume that the answers received at time $\bar{t}$ are all and only those given to the k_1 questions asked at time 1.

For all $i = 1, 2, \ldots, t$, let "Is $x \leq q_i^{(1)}$?", ..., "Is $x \leq q_i^{(k_i)}$?" be the questions asked at time i. We can safely assume that $q_i^{(j)} \leq q_i^{(j')}$ for all $1 \leq j < j' \leq k_i$.

We also tacitly assume that, for all $i = 1, 2, 3 \ldots, t$, there are two additional implicit questions asked at time, i, namely, "Is $x \leq q_i^{(0)}$?" and "Is $x \leq q_i^{(k_i+1)}$?", with $q_i^{(0)} = 0$ and $q_i^{(k_i+1)} = n$, which are respectively answered "no" and "yes". These (virtual) side conditions will turn out to be useful to the analysis.

According to the answers given to the first batch of questions there exists exactly one index $j \in \{1, 2, \ldots, k_1 + 1\}$ such that

$$x \in \mathscr{I}_j = \{q_1^{(j-1)} + 1, q_1^{(j-1)} + 2, \ldots, q_1^{(j)}\}.$$

The index j is exactly identified by the fact that the question "Is $x \leq q_1^{(j)}$?" has been answered "yes" and the question "Is $x \leq q_1^{(j-1)}$?" has been answered "no".

For all $i = 2, 3, \ldots, 1 + d_1$, let $r_i^{(j)}$, be the number of questions in the ith batch (at time i) asking "Is $x \leq a$?", with $a \in \mathscr{I}_j \setminus \{q_1^{(j)}\}$. These are all and the only questions which have been already asked and are still meaningful to the overall searching strategy when the questioner realizes that $x \in \mathscr{I}_j$. By definition, we have

$$\sum_{j=1}^{k_1+1} r_i^{(j)} \leq k_i \qquad \text{for } i = 2, \ldots, d_1 + 1.$$

Let $\mathbf{r}^{(j)} = 0 \, r_2^{(j)} \, r_3^{(j)} \cdots r_{d_1+1}^{(j)}$. Since after the first answers have been already given the rest of the strategy includes only $t - 1$ batches, by inductive hypothesis we have that

$$|\mathscr{I}_j| \leq A\left(\mathbf{r}^{(j)}_{[2\ldots d_1+1]} \circ \mathbf{k}_{[d_1+2\ldots t]}, \mathbf{d}_{[2\ldots t]}\right), \tag{6.12}$$

where the right-hand side is an upper bound (by inductive hypothesis) for the size of the largest search space in which it is possible to guess an unknown number with the remaining meaningful questions, including the ones that have been already asked in the first $\bar{t} - 1 = d_1 + 1$ batches. Repeating for all $j = 1, \ldots, k_1 + 1$ and summing up, we have:

$$n = \sum_{j=1}^{k_1+1} |\mathscr{I}_j|$$

$$\leq \sum_{j=1}^{k_1+1} A\left(\mathbf{r}^{(j)}_{[2\ldots d_1+1]} \circ \mathbf{k}_{[d_1+2\ldots t]}, \mathbf{d}_{[2\ldots t]}\right)$$

$$= \sum_{j=1}^{k_1+1} \left(A\left(\mathbf{r}^{(j)}_{[3\ldots d_1+1]} \circ \mathbf{k}_{[d_1+2\ldots t]}, \mathbf{d}_{[3\ldots t]}\right) + r_2^{(j)} A\left(\mathbf{k}_{[d_2+3\ldots t]}, \mathbf{d}_{[d_2+3\ldots t]}\right)\right)$$

$$= \sum_{j=1}^{k_1+1} \left(\sum_{i=2}^{d_1+1} r_i^{(j)} A\left(\mathbf{k}_{[d_i+i+1\ldots t]}, \mathbf{d}_{[d_i+i+1\ldots t]}\right) + A\left(\mathbf{k}_{[d_1+2\ldots t]}, \mathbf{d}_{[d_1+2\ldots t]}\right)\right)$$

$$= (k_1 + 1) A\left(\mathbf{k}_{[d_1+2\ldots t]}, \mathbf{d}_{[d_1+2\ldots t]}\right) + \sum_{i=2}^{d_1+1} A\left(\mathbf{k}_{[d_i+i+1\ldots t]}, \mathbf{d}_{[d_i+i+1\ldots t]}\right) \sum_{j=1}^{k_1+1} r_i^{(j)}$$

$$\leq (k_1 + 1) A\left(\mathbf{k}_{[d_1+2\ldots t]}, \mathbf{d}_{[d_1+2\ldots t]}\right) + \sum_{i=2}^{d_1+1} k_i A\left(\mathbf{k}_{[d_i+i+1\ldots t]}, \mathbf{d}_{[d_i+i+1\ldots t]}\right)$$

$$= A\left(\mathbf{k}_{[d_1+2\ldots t]}, \mathbf{d}_{[d_1+2\ldots t]}\right) + \sum_{i=1}^{d_1+1} k_i A\left(\mathbf{k}_{[d_i+i+1\ldots t]}, \mathbf{d}_{[d_i+i+1\ldots t]}\right)$$

$$= \left[A\left(\mathbf{k}_{[d_1+2...t]}, \mathbf{d}_{[d_1+2...t]}\right) + k_{d_1+1} A\left(\mathbf{k}_{[d_{d_1+1}+d_1+2...t]}, \mathbf{d}_{[d_{d_1+1}+d_1+2...t]}\right)\right]$$

$$+ \sum_{i=1}^{d_1} k_i A\left(\mathbf{k}_{[d_i+i+1...t]}, \mathbf{d}_{[d_i+i+1...t]}\right)$$

$$= A\left(\mathbf{k}_{[d_1+1...t]}, \mathbf{d}_{[d_1+1...t]}\right) + \sum_{i=1}^{d_1} k_i A\left(\mathbf{k}_{[d_i+i+1...t]}, \mathbf{d}_{[d_i+i+1...t]}\right)$$

$$= A(\mathbf{k}, \mathbf{d}).$$

The following theorem rephrases the main results of this section in terms of the size of the optimal strategy for the $(n, \mathbf{k}, \mathbf{d})$-game.

Theorem 6.6. *Let* $\mathbf{k} = k_1 k_2 \ldots$ *and* $\mathbf{d} = d_1 d_2 \ldots$ *be two (possibly infinite, but then infinitely often nonzero) sequences of non-negative integers. For all* $n \geq 1$, *let*

$$t = \min\left\{i \mid A\left(\mathbf{k}_{[1...i]}, \mathbf{d}_{[1...i]}\right) \geq n\right\}$$

and

$$\kappa = \min\left\{j \mid 1 \leq j \leq k_t \text{ and } A\left(\mathbf{k}_{[1...t-1]} \circ j, \mathbf{d}_{[1...t]}\right) \geq n\right\}.$$

Let q *be the size of the shortest strategy to guess a number in the set* $S = \{1, 2, \ldots, n\}$ *when exactly* k_i *questions are asked at time* i *and their answers are only available before time* $i + d_i + 1$. *Then,*

$$q = \kappa + \sum_{j=1}^{t-1} k_j.$$

6.3   Lost Answers and Delays

In the search problem we shall consider in this section, errors are no longer mendacious answers, but rather lost answers.

In terms of Berlekamp's error-correcting transmission with a feedback channel, this new setting corresponds to the case where the feedback channel is only used to acknowledge the receipt (or the non-receipt) of the source bits. Any bit delivered to the receiver is taken to be correct, but some of the bits may be lost or erased during transmission. Moreover, in the model considered in this chapter, the channel might be much slower in delivering bits than is the source to produce them. Therefore, we assume that the (positive or negative) acknowledgement of the ith bit reaches the source only after the $(i + d)$th bit has been sent, where d represent the delay introduced by the channel.

Loss or erasure of an answer can be the effect of (software or hardware) devices whose task is to clear spurious bits from the channel. Altogether, we may assume that the quantity d represents the maximum time the receiver is to wait before the sent bit reaches him. After the deadline of d time units has expired, an undelivered bit is automatically destroyed (as a *time-out* bit) in order to prevent de-synchronization of the communication channel.

As a variant of the Ulam-Rényi game, the problem of searching with delays and cancellations is formally stated as follows: Paul and Carole now agree on three integers $d, c \geq 0$ and $M \geq 1$, the latter denoting as usual the cardinality of the search space $S = \{1, 2, \ldots, M\}$. Then Carole chooses a number x in S, and Paul has to identify x by only using comparison questions, e.g., "is $x \leq a$?", for some $a \in S$. For each $i = 1, 2, \ldots$, Paul must ask a question precisely at time i. This is his ith question. On the other hand, Carole's answer to the ith question is delivered to Paul during the open interval $]i + d, i + d + 1[$. Thus, in general, Paul asks his ith question when the answers to his previous d questions are still pending. Trivially, if t is the overall number of questions asked by Paul, then, for each $i = 0, 1, \ldots, d-1$, when Carole answers the $(t - i)$th question, only i questions are pending. A dual remark applies to the first d questions.

The parameter c represents an upper bound on the number of possible erasures or losses of information for Paul. In game terms, we allow Carole not to answer up to c many questions—or equivalently, up to c answers may be lost.

The problem is then to find the (minimum) number of questions sufficient for Paul to guess the secret number x.

If the total number of questions asked by Paul is t, then we say that Paul wins the (M, d, c)-game with t questions. Notice that the game actually ends at time $t + d + 1$.

Remark 6.2. The problem of coping with lost answers in the classical setting (i.e., when there is no delay between questions and answers) is trivial—for there is no better strategy than repeating all unanswered questions. Analogously, if *arbitrary* yes-no questions are permitted, then even assuming delayed answers, an optimal strategy is given by asking for the binary encoding of the secret number and repeating all unanswered questions.

The results of this section are given for a dual counterpart of the above problem. We shall be interested in determining $A_d^{(c)}(t)$ defined as the largest integer M such that Paul wins the (M, d, c)-game with t questions. We shall start looking at the case $c \in \{0, 1\}$.

Let us define the following quantity.

Definition 6.4. For any integer $t, d \geq 0$ and $c \in \{0, 1\}$, let

$$B_d^{(c)}(t) = \begin{cases} \left\lfloor \frac{t}{c+1} \right\rfloor + 1 & \text{if } t \leq d + 1 \\ B_d^{(c)}(t - 1) + B_d^{(c)}(t - d - 1) & \text{if } t \geq d + 2. \end{cases} \tag{6.13}$$

We shall prove that for all integers $t \geq 0$, $d \geq 0$ and for each $c = 0, 1$, we have

$$A_d^{(c)}(t) = B_d^{(c)}(t). \tag{6.14}$$

The following proposition provides some technical properties of $B_d^{(c)}(t)$ which will be used for obtaining (6.14). Here we limit ourselves to state such properties without proving them. The complete proofs are deferred to Lemmas 6.11, 6.12, 6.13 at the end of this section.

Proposition 6.1. *Fix two non-negative integers d and t. Then, the following inequalities hold*

1. $B_d^{(1)}(t) \leq B_d^{(0)}(t-1)$;
2. $B_d^{(1)}(t) \leq B_d^{(0)}(t+1) - B_d^{(1)}(t+1)$;
3. *if $t \geq d + 3$ and for any $j = 1, \ldots, \lfloor \frac{d}{2} \rfloor$, we have*

$$B_d^{(1)}(t-1-j) + B_d^{(1)}(t-1-(d-j)) \leq B_d^{(1)}(t-1) + B_d^{(1)}(t-d-1).$$

The Upper Bound. We are now ready to prove that $B_d^{(c)}(t)$ is an upper bound on the maximum size of the search space in which Paul can win with t questions.

Theorem 6.7. *For all integers $t \geq 0$ and $d \geq 0$ and for each $c = 0, 1$,*

$$A_d^{(c)}(t) \leq B_d^{(c)}(t).$$

Proof. We argue by induction on t.

Induction Base. $0 \leq t \leq d + 1$. In this case the whole questioning is non-adaptive. Recall that $B_d^{(c)}(t) = \lfloor \frac{t}{c+1} \rfloor + 1$. We shall show that no strategy using t questions can exist to search for an unknown number in a set of cardinality $\lfloor \frac{t}{c+1} \rfloor + 2 = B_d^{(c)}(t) + 1$; hence, $A_d^{(c)}(t) \leq B_d^{(c)}(t)$.

The argument is by contradiction. Suppose that there exists a strategy with t questions to search in the set $S = \{1, 2, \ldots \lfloor \frac{t}{c+1} \rfloor + 2\}$. Then, for at least one $i \in S$ the question "Is $x \leq i$?" has been asked at most c times. If $c = 0$, it is easy to see that all the other queries are not enough to discriminate between the case where the secret number is i and the case where the secret number is $i + 1$. Analogously, if $c = 1$ and the answer to the only occurrence of the question "Is $x \leq i$?" is cancelled, we have the same situation and the questioner cannot guess whether the secret number is i or $i + 1$. Hence, the strategy is not winning, contradicting the hypothesis. Therefore, it must be $A_d^{(c)}(t) \leq \lfloor \frac{t}{c+1} \rfloor + 1 = B_d^{(c)}(t)$, as desired.

Inductive Hypothesis. $A_d^{(c)}(i) \leq B_d^{(c)}(i)$ for all $i < t$.

Induction Step. Assume that there exists a strategy to win the $(A_d^{(c)}(t), d, c)$-game with t questions, and let "is $x \leq q_1$?" be the first question in this strategy.

Let j be the number of queries, among the pending ones, which ask "Is $x \leq a$?", for some $a \geq q_1$, and J denote the set of such j questions.

If the answer to the first question says that $x \leq q_1$ (i.e., a positive answer is received), then the answers to the questions in J will not provide any additional information since $x \leq q_1$ implies $x \leq a$ for any $a \geq q_1$, i.e., all the questions in J will be obviously answered positively.

Therefore, $t - 1 - j$ of the remaining questions (including the pending ones and the ones still to be asked) must be sufficient to identify the secret number in the set $\{1, 2, \ldots, q_1\}$. Thus, the set $\{1, 2, \ldots, q_1\}$ is not larger than the largest set which allows a successful searching strategy with $t - 1 - j$ questions, i.e., $q_1 \leq A_d^{(c)}(t - 1 - j)$.

Conversely, suppose now that the answer to the first question is "no". Then, by hypothesis, only j of the pending queries are useful, that is, exactly those in the set J. Hence, the set $\{q_1 + 1, \ldots, A_d^{(c)}(t)\}$ is not larger than the largest set which allows a successful searching strategy with $t - 1 - d + j$ questions, i.e, $A_d^{(c)}(t) - q_1 \leq A_d^{(c)}(t - 1 - d + j)$.

Finally, since for $c = 1$ the answer to the first question may also be cancelled, we have $A_d^{(1)}(t) \leq A_d^{(0)}(t - 1)$. Therefore,[9]

$$A_d^{(c)}(t) \leq \min \left\{ \max_{0 \leq j \leq \lfloor \frac{d}{2} \rfloor} \{A_d^{(c)}(t - 1 - j) + A_d^{(c)}(t - 1 - d + j)\}, A_d^{(c-1)}(t - 1) \right\}$$

$$\leq \min \left\{ \max_{0 \leq j \leq \lfloor \frac{d}{2} \rfloor} \{B_d^{(c)}(t - 1 - j) + B_d^{(c)}(t - 1 - d + j)\}, B_d^{(c-1)}(t - 1) \right\}$$

(by inductive hypothesis)

$$= \min \left\{ B_d^{(c)}(t - 1) + B_d^{(c)}(t - 1 - d), B_d^{(c-1)}(t - 1) \right\}$$

(by (3) in Proposition 6.1)

$$= \min \left\{ B_d^{(c)}(t), B_d^{(c-1)}(t - 1) \right\} = B_d^{(c)}(t).$$

The Lower Bound. We shall give an algorithm for successfully searching in a space of cardinality $B_d^{(c)}(t)$, with t questions.

Theorem 6.8. *For all integers $d \geq 0$, $t \geq 0$ and for each $c = 0, 1$, we have*

$$A_d^{(c)}(t) \geq B_d^{(c)}(t).$$

Proof. We shall show that t questions suffice to search successfully in the set $S = \{1, 2, \ldots, B_d^{(c)}(t)\}$.

---

[9]Here, we assume for sake of definiteness that $B_d^{(c)}(t) = A_d^{(-1)}(t) = \infty$ for all $t, d \geq 0$.

For $t \leq d+1$ it is enough to ask $c+1$ times for any number $1, 2, \ldots, \lfloor \frac{t}{c+1} \rfloor$. Since no more than c answers can be erased, for each $i = 1, \ldots, \lfloor \frac{t}{c+1} \rfloor$, there will be at least one answer to the question "Is $x \leq i$?". These answers provides sufficient information to identify an unknown number in the set S (recall that $B_d^{(c)}(t) = \lfloor \frac{t}{c+1} \rfloor + 1$).

Now fix $t \geq d+2$ and assume that for any $t' < t$ the claim is true, i.e., there exists a strategy of size t' to identify the unknown number in a set of cardinality $B_d^{(c)}(t')$.

We show a strategy with t queries to search in a set of size $B_d^{(c)}(t)$. Ask the first $d+1$ questions, respectively, at points $B_d^{(c)}(t-1), B_d^{(c)}(t-2), \ldots, B_d^{(c)}(t-d-1)$.

- If the answer to the first question is "no", then the unknown number belongs to the set $\{B_d^{(c)}(t-1)+1, B_d^{(c)}(t-1)+2, \ldots, B_d^{(c)}(t)\}$, which is of size $B_d^{(c)}(t) - B_d^{(c)}(t-1) = B_d^{(c)}(t-d-1)$. Then, the inductive argument shows that the remaining $t-d-1$ questions suffice to complete the search successfully.
- If the answer to the first question is "yes", then ask the $d+2$th question at point $B_d^{(c)}(t-d-2)$. Thus, we are in the same situation as we were before the answer. In fact, we are now to search in an interval of size $B_d^{(c)}(t-1)$ with $t-1$ questions. Again the desired result follows by induction.
- We have settled the case $c = 0$. The following only accounts for the case $c = 1$.
- If the answer to the first question gets cancelled, then our strategy asks the $d+2$th question at point $B_d^{(1)}(t-2) + B_d^{(0)}(t-d-2)$. In other words, we start to search the set $\{B_d^{(1)}(t-2)+1, \ldots, B_d^{(1)}(t)\}$ by using the strategy for a set of cardinality $B_d^{(0)}(t-d-1)$ with no cancellation. This accounts for the case in which the second answer is "no". If this is the case, then the unknown number is indeed in the set $\{B_d^{(1)}(t-2)+1, B_d^{(1)}(t-2)+2, \ldots, B_d^{(1)}(t)\}$, of size $B_d^{(1)}(t-d-1) + B_d^{(1)}(t-d-2) \leq B_d^{(0)}(t-d-1)$ (by (2) in Proposition 6.1), and we have the desired result by induction.

  Conversely suppose that the second answer is "yes". Then there are $t-d-2$ questions left and we know that the secret number is in the set $\{1, 2, \ldots, B_d^{(1)}(t-2)\}$. Remember that there are $d-1$ useful pending questions at points $B_d^{(1)}(t-3), \ldots, B_d^{(1)}(t-d-1)$, and the dth pending question is a useless one at point $B_d^{(0)}(t-d-2) + B_d^{(1)}(t-2)$. Our strategy consists of continuing to ask questions at points $B_d^{(0)}(t-d-3), B_d^{(0)}(t-d-4), \ldots$ until a "no" answer is received. If the "no" answer is given to one of the pending questions, say the one asked at point $B_d^{(1)}(t-2-i)$ (for some $i \in \{1, 2, \ldots, d-1\}$), then the secret number belongs to the set $\{B_d^{(1)}(t-2-i)+1, \ldots, B_d^{(1)}(t-2-i+1)\}$ of size $B_d^{(1)}(t-d-2-i)$. Since no more cancellations are allowed and, by (1) in Proposition 6.1, $B_d^{(1)}(t-d-2-i) \leq B_d^{(0)}(t-d-3-i)$, the remaining $t-d-3-i$ questions are sufficient to successfully identify the secret number.

If the "no" answer is not given to any of the first d pending queries, i.e., the secret number belongs to the set $\{1, 2, \ldots, B_d^{(1)}(t - d - 1)\}$, then because of $B_d^{(1)}(t - d - 1) \leq B_d^{(0)}(t - d - 2)$ (by (1) in Proposition 6.1), the remaining questions are sufficient to successfully identify the secret number in a set of cardinality $B_d^{(0)}(t - d - 2)$ (with no cancellation), and a fortiori we can succeed with the remaining search space of size $B_d^{(1)}(t - d - 1)$.

Theorems 6.7 and 6.8, together with Definition 6.4 gives the exact estimate of $A_d^c(t)$ for $c \in \{0, 1\}$.

Theorem 6.9. *For all $t \geq 0$, $d \geq 0$ and $c \in \{0, 1\}$, the following holds:*

$$A_d^{(c)}(t) = \begin{cases} \left\lfloor \frac{t}{c+1} \right\rfloor + 1 & \text{if } t \leq d + 1 \\ A_d^{(c)}(t - 1) + A_d^{(c)}(t - d - 1) & \text{if } t \geq d + 2. \end{cases} \tag{6.15}$$

The following corollary provides an asymptotic estimate of $A_d^{(c)}$ based on the solution of the recurrence in (6.15).

Corollary 6.2. *Let ϕ_d be the largest (positive) real root of $x^{d+1} = x^d + 1$. Then, for all $t \geq 0$, $d \geq 0$ and $c \in \{0, 1\}$, we have $A_d^{(c)}(t) \in \Theta(\phi_d^t)$, and*

$$\log_{\phi_d}(n + 1) + O(1)$$

questions are necessary and sufficient to win the (n, d, c)-game.

6.3.1 Extensions and Generalizations

It is possible to give an alternative formulation of the recurrence (6.13) that seems to be more suitable for generalizations to the case of an arbitrary (fixed) number of cancellations ($c \geq 2$).

Definition 6.5. For all integers $d, t, c \geq 0$ let

$$\tilde{B}_d^{(c)}(t) = \begin{cases} 1 & \text{for } t \leq 0 \\ \sum_{i=1}^{t+1} G_i^{(c)}(t, d) & \text{otherwise,} \end{cases} \tag{6.16}$$

where

- for $i = 1, \ldots, c + 1$,

$$G_i^{(c)}(t, d) = \min_{0 \leq j \leq i - 1} \left\{ \tilde{B}_d^{(c-j)}(t - d - i + j) - \sum_{k=1}^{j} G_{i-k}^{(c)}(t, d) \right\},$$

- for $i \geq c + 2$,

$$G_i^{(c)}(t, d) = \min_{0 \leq j \leq c} \left\{ \tilde{B}_d^{(c-j)}(t - d - i + j) - \sum_{k=1}^{j} G_{i-k}^{(c)}(t, d) \right\}.$$

For $c = 0, 1$, and for all $d, t \geq 0$, it holds that $A_d^{(c)}(t) = \tilde{B}_d^{(c)}(t)$. Moreover, we have the following:

Conjecture 6.1. If $c \leq d$ then $\tilde{B}_d^{(c)}(t) = A_d^{(c)}(t)$.

The more difficult part in proving this conjecture is to show that $\tilde{B}_d^{(c)}(t)$ is the right lower bound. For the inequality $\tilde{B}_d^{(c)}(t) \leq A_d^{(c)}(t)$ we sketch the proof in the following lemma, providing a winning strategy for the $(\tilde{B}_d^{(c)}(t), d, c)$-game with t questions. It is an open question whether the converse inequality holds.

Lemma 6.10. *For all integers $d \geq 0$, $0 \leq c \leq d$ and $t \geq 0$, we have $\tilde{B}_d^{(c)}(t) \leq A_d^{(c)}(t)$.*

Sketch of the proof. We outline a winning searching strategy for the $(\tilde{B}_d^{(c)}(t), d, c)$-game with t questions. We shall omit most of the technical details and limit ourselves to describing the main ideas. The argument will be by induction on t.

For $i = 1, 2, \ldots$, let us identify the question "Is $x \leq q_i$?" with the integer q_i. We also say that Q asks the ith question at q_i.

For $1 \leq i \leq d + 1$, we set

$$q_i = \tilde{B}_d^{(c)}(t) - \sum_{j=1}^{i} G_j^{(c)}(t, d).$$

If $t \leq d + 1$ we have

$$G_i^{(c)}(t, d) = \begin{cases} 1 & \text{for } i = 1 + (c+1)j, \ j = 0, 1, \ldots, \lfloor \frac{t}{c+1} \rfloor, \\ 0 & \text{otherwise.} \end{cases}$$

Hence, the strategy asks $c + 1$ times "Is $x \leq i$?" for each $i = 1, 2, \ldots, \lfloor \frac{t}{c+1} \rfloor$, so to be able to search successfully in the set $\{1, 2, \ldots, \lfloor \frac{t}{c+1} \rfloor + 1\}$. It is not hard to see that, in fact, in this case our strategy is optimal in the sense that $\tilde{B}_d^{(c)}(t) = \lfloor \frac{t}{c+1} \rfloor + 1 = A_d^{(c)}(t)$.

If $t > d + 1$, when the first answer is received the strategy proceeds as follows:

1. if the answer is "yes" then our strategy asks the $d + 2$nd question at point $q_{d+2} = q_{d+1} - G_{d+2}^{(c)}(t, d)$. Then we are in the same situation as before and the correctness of our strategy follows by induction;

2. if the answer is "no" then the set of possible solutions reduces to $S' = \{q_1 + 1,$ $\dots, \tilde{B}_d^{(c)}(t)\}$, and by $|S'| = G_1^{(c)}(t, d) \leq \tilde{B}_d^{(c)}(t - d - 1)$ we can complete the search with the remaining $t - d - 1$ questions, by inductive hypothesis;

3. if the first answer is not delivered, the $d + 2$th question is asked in $S'' = \{q_2 + 1,$ $\dots, \tilde{B}_d^{(c)}(t)\}$, by recursively applying the same strategy in such a set.

We have to analyze three possible cases according to how the second question is answered.

If the second answer is "no" then the set of candidates to be the secret number becomes $S'' = \{q_2 + 1, \dots, \tilde{B}_d^{(c)}(t)\}$. We have $|S''| = G_1^{(c)}(t, d) + G_2^{(c)}(t, d) \leq \tilde{B}_d^{(c-1)}(t - d - 1)$ by the definition of $G_2^{(c)}(t, d)$. Thus, by induction, we can complete the search in the set S'' with $t - d - 1$ questions. Indeed we already correctly asked the $d + 2$th question in order to accommodate such situation.

If the second answer is "yes", then, the $d + 2$th question (the one we have already asked in S'') becomes useless. However, and in analogy with what we have said in points (1) and (2) above, the pending questions allow us to complete the search if the following $i - 1$ answers are "yes" and, next, a "no" answer is received, that is, the reservoir of possible solutions reduces the interval $I_i = \{q_{i+1} + 1, \dots, q_i\}$ for some $i = 2, 3, \dots, d$. Indeed, by definition, we have $|I_i| = G_{i+1}^{(c)}(t, d) \leq \tilde{B}_d^{(c)}(t - d - (i + 1)) \leq \tilde{B}_d^{(c-1)}(t - 1 - d - (i + 1))$; hence, a fortiori, the original pending questions are effective in the present situation, now that up to $c - 1$ of the remaining questions can be lost. Then our strategy asks the $d + 3$rd question in order to cover the set $\{1, 2, \dots, q_{d+1}\}$ with the remaining $t - d - 2$ questions. This is, in fact, attainable by $\tilde{B}_d^{(c)}(t - d - 1) \leq \tilde{B}_d^{(c-1)}(t - d - 2)$.

Finally, if the second answer is lost, then we can recurse on the above reasoning to prove that the search can be completed correctly.

6.3.2   The Proof of Proposition 6.1

Lemma 6.11. *For all integers $d \geq 0$ and $t \geq 0$ we have*

$$B_d^{(1)}(t) \leq B_d^{(0)}(t - 1).$$

Proof. For $0 \leq t \leq d + 1$, we have $B_d^{(1)}(t) = \lfloor \frac{t}{2} \rfloor + 1 \leq t = B_d^{(0)}(t - 1)$. Let $t > d + 1$ and $B_d^{(1)}(i) \leq B_d^{(0)}(i - 1)$ for all $i < t$. Then,

$$B_d^{(1)}(t) = B_d^{(1)}(t-1) + B_d^{(1)}(t-d-1) \leq B_d^{(0)}(t-2) + B_d^{(0)}(t-d-2) = B_d^{(0)}(t-1).$$

Lemma 6.12. *For all integers $d \geq 0$ and $t \geq 0$ we have*

$$B_d^{(1)}(t) \leq B_d^{(0)}(t + 1) - B_d^{(1)}(t + 1).$$

Proof. The proof is by induction on t.

Induction Base. By Definition 6.4 we immediately get

$$B_d^{(0)}(t+1) - B_d^{(1)}(t+1) = (t+2) - \lfloor \frac{t+1}{2} \rfloor - 1 \geq \lfloor \frac{t+2}{2} \rfloor$$

$$= \lfloor \frac{t}{2} \rfloor + 1 = B_d^{(1)}(t),$$

for all $t = 0, 1, \ldots, d$. For $t = d+1$ we have

$$B_d^{(0)}(t+1) - B_d^{(1)}(t+1) = B_d^{(0)}(d+2) - B_d^{(1)}(d+2)$$

$$= B_d^{(0)}(d+1) + B_d^{(0)}(1) - B_d^{(1)}(d+1) - B_d^{(1)}(1)$$

$$= B_d^{(0)}(d+1) + 2 - B_d^{(1)}(d+1) - 1 \geq 1 + B_d^{(1)}(d)$$

$$\geq B_d^{(1)}(d+1) = B_d^{(1)}(t).$$

Induction Step. Now suppose that the claim is true for all $t \leq i$ and $i \geq d+1$. We shall prove that it also holds for $t = i+1$. Indeed,

$$B_d^{(0)}(t+1) - B_d^{(1)}(t+1) = B_d^{(0)}(i+2) - B_d^{(1)}(i+2) =$$

$$= B_d^{(0)}(i+1) - B_d^{(1)}(i+1)$$

$$+ B_d^{(0)}(i+1-d) - B_d^{(1)}(i+1-d)$$

(by definition, and rearranging terms)

$$\geq B_d^{(1)}(i) + B_d^{(1)}(i-d)$$

(by inductive hypothesis)

$$= B_d^{(1)}(i+1) = B_d^{(1)}(t),$$

which concludes the proof.

Lemma 6.13. *For all integers $d \geq 0$, $t \geq d+3$, and $j = 1, 2, \ldots, \lfloor \frac{d}{2} \rfloor$, we have*

$$B_d^{(1)}(t-1-j) + B_d^{(1)}(t-1-(d-j)) \leq B_d^{(1)}(t-1) + B_d^{(1)}(t-d-1).$$

Proof. Suppose the claim true for $d+3 \leq t \leq 2d+2$. Then, for $t \geq 2d+3$, we have

$$B_d^{(1)}(t-1-j) + B_d^{(1)}(t-1-(d-j)) =$$

$$= B_d^{(1)}(t-2-j) + B_d^{(1)}(t-2-d-j)$$

$$+ B_d^{(1)}(t-2-(d-j)) + B_d^{(1)}(t-2-2d+j)$$

$$\leq B_d^{(1)}(t-2) + B_d^{(1)}(t-2-d) + B_d^{(1)}(t-2-d)$$
$$+ B_d^{(1)}(t-2-2d)$$
$$= B_d^{(1)}(t-1) + B_d^{(1)}(t-d-1).$$

We shall now prove the claim for $d + 3 \leq t \leq 2d + 2$. Arguing by cases, we shall show that

$$B_d^{(1)}(t-1) - B_d^{(1)}(t-1-j) \geq B_d^{(1)}(t-1-(d-j)) - B_d^{(1)}(t-d-1). \qquad (6.17)$$

First we note that under the standing hypothesis on d, t, j we have

$$t - 1 > t - 1 - j \geq t - 1 - (d - j) > t - 1 - d.$$

Case 1. $t - 1 > t - 1 - j \geq t - 1 - (d - j) > t - 1 - d \geq d + 1$. We have $t = 2d + 2$, and the desired result follows by

$$B_d^{(1)}(2d + 1) - B_d^{(1)}(2d + 1 - j) =$$
$$= B_d^{(1)}(2d) + B_d^{(1)}(d) - B_d^{(1)}(2d + 1 - j)$$
$$= B_d^{(1)}(2d - 1) + B_d^{(1)}(d - 1) + B_d^{(1)}(d) - B_d^{(1)}(2d + 1 - j)$$
$$= \cdots (\text{after } j \text{ steps})$$
$$= B_d^{(1)}(2d + 1 - j) + \sum_{i=1}^{j} B_d^{(1)}(d + 1 - i) - B_d^{(1)}(2d + 1 - j)$$
$$= \sum_{i=1}^{j} B_d^{(1)}(d + 1 - i) + B_d^{(1)}(d + 1) - B_d^{(1)}(d + 1)$$
$$\geq \sum_{i=1}^{j} B_d^{(1)}(i) + B_d^{(1)}(d + 1) - B_d^{(1)}(d + 1)$$
$$= B_d^{(1)}(d + 1 + j) - B_d^{(1)}(d + 1).$$

Case 2. $t - 1 > t - 1 - j \geq t - 1 - (d - j) \geq d + 1 > t - 1 - d$. We write $t - 1 - (d - j) = d + 1 + k$; hence, $k < j$. Then, expanding j times the term $B_d^{(1)}(t - 1)$ as in the proof of *Case 1*, we have

$$B_d^{(1)}(t - 1) - B_d^{(1)}(t - 1 - j) = \sum_{i=1}^{j} B_d^{(1)}(t - 1 - d - i)$$
$$= \sum_{i=1}^{j-k} B_d^{(1)}(t - 1 - d - i) + \sum_{i=j-k+1}^{j} B_d^{(1)}(t - 1 - d - i)$$

$$\geq \sum_{i=1}^{k} B_d^{(1)}(t - 1 - 2d + j - i) + \lceil \frac{j - k}{2} \rceil$$

$$\geq \sum_{i=1}^{k} B_d^{(1)}(t - 1 - 2d + j - i) + \lfloor \frac{d + 1}{2} \rfloor - \lfloor \frac{d + 1 - (j - k)}{2} \rfloor$$

$$= \sum_{i=1}^{k} B_d^{(1)}(t - 1 - 2d + j - i) + B_d^{(1)}(d + 1)$$

$$- B_d^{(1)}(d + 1 - (j - k))$$

$$= \sum_{i=1}^{k} B_d^{(1)}(t - 1 - 2d + j - i) + B_d^{(1)}(t - 1 - d + j - k)$$

$$- B_d^{(1)}(t - 1 - d)$$

$$= B_d^{(1)}(t - 1 - d + j) - B_d^{(1)}(t - 1 - d).$$

Case 3. $t - 1 > t - 1 - j > d + 1 \geq t - 1 - (d - j) > t - 1 - d$. Proceeding as before, we have

$$B_d^{(1)}(t - 1) - B_d^{(1)}(t - 1 - j) = \sum_{i=1}^{j} B_d^{(1)}(t - d - 1 - i)$$

$$\geq j > \lfloor \frac{t - 1 - d + j}{2} \rfloor - \lfloor \frac{t - 1 - d}{2} \rfloor$$

$$= B_d^{(1)}(t - 1 - d + j) - B_d^{(1)}(t - 1 - d).$$

Case 4. $t - 1 > d + 1 \geq t - 1 - j \geq t - 1 - (d - j) > t - 1 - d$. Set $k = t - 1 - (d + 1)$; hence, $t - 1 - j = (d + 1) - (j - k)$. Thus, we have

$$B_d^{(1)}(t - 1) - B_d^{(1)}(t - 1 - j) =$$

$$= B_d^{(1)}(t - 1 - k) + \sum_{i=1}^{k} B_d^{(1)}(t - 1 - d - i) - B_d^{(1)}(t - 1 - j)$$

$$= \sum_{i=1}^{k} B_d^{(1)}(t - 1 - d - i) + \lfloor \frac{d + 1}{2} \rfloor - \lfloor \frac{t - 1 - j}{2} \rfloor$$

$$= \sum_{i=1}^{k} B_d^{(1)}(t - 1 - d - i) + \lfloor \frac{d + 1}{2} \rfloor - \lfloor \frac{(d + 1) - (j - k)}{2} \rfloor$$

$$\geq \sum_{i=1}^{k} B_d^{(1)}(t - 1 - d - i) + \lfloor \frac{j - k}{2} \rfloor$$

$$\geq k + \lfloor \frac{j - k}{2} \rfloor > \lfloor \frac{t - 1 - (d - j)}{2} \rfloor - \lfloor \frac{t - 1 - d}{2} \rfloor$$

$$= B_d^{(1)}(t - 1 - (d - j)) - B_d^{(1)}(t - 1 - d).$$

6.3.3   Broadcast with Latency vs. Search with Delay

We shall now analyze a correspondence between the above search problem with delays and the problem of broadcasting in the fully connected network with link latency. We shall start by formally stating what we mean by a broadcasting algorithm for a point-to-point network with link latency.

Broadcast in the Postal Model

Communication subsystems of parallel and distributed systems and high-speed networks are commonly modeled as message-passing systems in which any processor can submit to the network a *point-to-point* message destined for any other processor. The network is responsible for delivering the messages from their sources to their destinations. Networks which follow this modus operandi are called *point-to-point* networks. Models that tend to give an abstract view of these systems de-emphasize the particular organization of the processors in the system in favor of a simpler and more robust view of a fully-connected collection of processors. They typically address issues of data packetization, separation of send and receive, and communication latencies, which do not appear in traditional "telephone-like" models.

In the Postal Model, the basic unit of interprocessor communication is a *packet*. The model employs a latency parameter $\lambda \geq 1$ which measures the ratio between (a) the time it takes to deliver a message from its source to its destination, and (b) the time it takes the source of the message to send it. Since the size of packets in a system is fixed, this ratio is independent of the exact value of the setup time (b). It is thus assumed that the time it takes the source of the message to complete a submission round is one unit, and then it is free to start another round while the submitted message may still be on its way to its target.

Packet-switching networks have different characteristics than local-area networks, which are based on a broadcast channel. Using such channels, primitives of broadcasting feature almost identical performance as point-to-point messages. It is desirable to get the same speedups in the packet-switching networks. Thus, much work has been devoted to designing effective collective communication primitives in point-to-point packet-switching networks.

Broadcasting is a basic cooperative operation. It is used extensively in applications, including scientific computations, database transactions, network management protocols, and multimedia applications. The broadcast operation is as follows: Given a message M at a certain processor p of a point-to-point network $\mathcal{N}$, a broadcast algorithm on $\mathcal{N}$ is a schedule of message transmissions by its processors so that eventually M is known to all of them, and so that there are no redundant transmissions of M to the same destination. A broadcast protocol is said to be *optimal* when it is completed in the shortest possible time.

Broadcast and Comparison Search Are Isomorphic Problems

The following lemma shows in which sense the problem of searching with delayed comparison questions and the one of broadcasting in the Postal Model can be considered isomorphic problems.

Lemma 6.14. *Let $\mathcal{N}$ be a fully connected network of size n with link latency d. Then, there exists a protocol to complete a broadcast in the network $\mathcal{N}$ within t time units if and only if there exists a searching algorithm to win the $(n, d, 0)$-game with $t - d$ questions.*

Proof. We show only the direction *Broadcast* $\Rightarrow$ *Search*. The other direction can be proved in a perfectly symmetric way.

A broadcast tree is a rooted spanning tree of the network obtained obtained by establishing that a node v' is the child of the node v from which the message is communicated to v' for the first time. If the node v' receives the message for the first time concurrently from more than one node, the father is arbitrarily chosen from among the sending nodes.

Let T be a broadcast tree attaining the protocol in the hypothesis. Without loss of generality, we assume that, at any time, if there exists a node that can broadcast to an uninformed node, it actually does. Notice that any protocol can be changed in order to satisfy such an assumption without increasing the overall completion time.

We can transform T into a search tree S representing an algorithm to win the $(n, d, 0)$-game with $t - d$ questions. As a matter of fact any node z of S corresponds to a sequence of up to $d + 1$ questions: the first one is the question which is to be answered next and the remaining ones are the pending queries which have been already formulated. More precisely, the sequence of questions associated with a node in S, has generally length $d + 1$. Let $q = t - d$ be the overall number of questions to be asked; hence, the height of the search tree S is q. Then, for each $i = 0, 1, 2, \ldots, d - 1$ and any node in S at level $q - i$, the associated sequence of questions has length i, since there are exactly i more questions to be asked, all of which have been already formulated. Moreover, let the node y be a *left* (resp. *right*) child of a node z and let $[y_1, \ldots, y_{d+1}]$ be the questions in the node y and $[z_1, \ldots, z_{d+1}]$ the questions associated with z. Then $y_i = z_{i+1}$ for each $i = 1, 2, \ldots, d$. This accounts for the fact that after one answer the pending d questions are kept unaltered, and only the last pending query can be chosen.

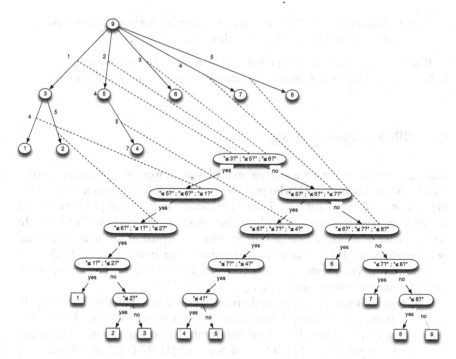

Fig. 6.2 Broadcast protocol ≡ searching strategy

Our transformation goes as follows (see also Fig. 6.2 for a pictorial representation of the case $d = 2, t = 7, n = 9$)[10]:

- Label the node in T by means of a DFS, with edges oriented from the root to the leaves.
- Associate with any link incident to the node labelled i the question "Is $x \le i$?".
- Take the first $d + 1$ links stemming from the root of T in order of increasing broadcasting time and put the corresponding questions $[q_1, \ldots, q_{d+1}]$ into the root r_S of the tree S.
- Recursively, for any node v in S define the two children of v, respectively, the left child v_ℓ and the right child v_r, as the new set of questions after the answer "yes" or "no" to the first question in v. Let "Is $x \le a$?" be the first question in v.
- If the answer is "yes" then the new question to put in v_ℓ is the one corresponding to the first edge (in order of broadcasting time) stemming in T from the node a. If no such edge exists then v_ℓ is a leaf in S corresponding to the solution $x = a$.
- If the answer is "no" then the new question to put in v_r is the one corresponding to the first link (not already considered in increasing broadcasting time) stemming

---

[10]Numbers near the edges and nodes of the broadcast tree represent time of, respectively, sending and receiving information. Numbers inside the nodes are the labels assigned by the DFS.

from the father of a in T. If no such link exists then v_r is a leaf in S corresponding to the solution $x = b$, where b is the father of a in T.

It is not hard to see that, if the number chosen is i and, in the broadcast protocol node i is reached at time j, then the number i is found within $j - d$ queries.

6.4   Bibliographic Notes

Searching with comparison questions and delayed answers was originally considered by Ambainis et al. [11], who provided the solution for the problem presented here and $c = 0$. The case $c = 1$ was considered and solved in [59]. For related research on computation with "delayed information" see also [8, 17, 18, 81]. In particular the connection between the problem presented in this chapter and the one considered in [17] was the main motivation for the material in Sect. 6.3.3.

Erasure errors had been previously considered in the non-adaptive setting in the field of error-correcting coding (see, e.g., [103, 147, 172]).

The Postal Model for the point-to-point network was introduced in [17]. In the same paper Bar-Noy and Kipnis also provided optimal broadcast protocols. Subsequently, optimal broadcast algorithms for the Postal Model were rediscovered in a more general setting by Golin and Schuster [114]. The Postal Model is a particular case of the more general *LogP* model for parallel computing. The interested reader is referred to [80, 99].

The problem in Sect. 6.1 can be seen as equivalent to the following one [137]: There are k asynchronous and concurrent processors trying to locate a unit interval containing the zero of a function f, knowing that f is monotonically increasing and takes opposite signs at the end points of the search interval.

Each processor evaluates the function f at some point y and will subsequently "move" left or right, according to whether $f(y) > 0$ or $f(y) < 0$. We assume that processors are connected by a fast channel so that if two processors are busy evaluating $f(x)$ and $f(y)$, with $x < y$, and the processor evaluating f in x ends its job before the other processor evaluates $f(y)$ and discovers that $f(x) > 0$, then this information is made *immediately* available to all processors, in particular also to the processor working on $f(y)$. As a consequence, this processor can stop its job (which has become useless) and move itself to another point z to evaluate f.

Kung [137] gave a strategy for the particular case $k = 2$. In [137] it is also claimed that the given strategy is optimal in the min-max sense, but, to the best of our knowledge, the proof has never been published.

For the particular case $k = 2$, the above problem also corresponds to that of searching with fixed constant delay $d = 1$, considered in [11]. Analogously, the problem in Sect. 6.2 can be considered a full generalization of the one solved in [11], where the special case of $\mathbf{k} = 1\,1\,1\,\cdots$ and $\mathbf{d} = d\,d\,\cdots$ is considered for all $d \geq 0$.

6.5 Exercises

1. Consider the model of search with delayed answers of Sect. 6.1. For $k = 6$ determine the minimum value of t such that there exists no winning strategy of size t if the search space has cardinality $N_t^{[k]}$.

2. With reference to the model of Sect. 6.1 show that for any even integer $k \geq 6$ there exists infinitely many values of t such that no winning strategy can exist of size t for the $(N_t^{[k]}, k)$-game.

3. Prove that if one considers the problem of searching with lost answers where there is no delay between questions and answers, then there is no better strategy than repeating all unanswered questions.

4. Consider the variant of the model of Sect. 6.3 where arbitrary subset questions can be asked, i.e., queries are not constrained to be comparison questions. Show that for any value of the delay parameter d and any value of the bound c on the number of unanswered questions, the size of an optimal strategy, when the search space has cardinality M, is $\lceil \log M \rceil + c$.

5. Verify Conjecture 6.1 for the special case $d = 3$ and $c = 2$.

6. Try to establish bounds on the size of a *non-adaptive* strategy for the problem of search with delayed answers and time-outs.

7. Show that for the case $c \in \{0, 1\}$, Definition (6.5) and (6.13) are equivalent.

Chapter 7
Group Testing

A thing may happen and be a total lie
another thing may not happen and be truer than the truth

T. O'Brien, The Things They Carried

Group testing is a search model which first appeared in the context of a biomedical application, in the last years of the Second World War. It became clear that large amounts of money were spent on testing soldiers who would eventually be found not to be infected. Finding them healthy was obviously good news, nonetheless, the large amount of "useless" testing was also considered a waste of public funds which should be avoided, since the aim of testing the troops was to find the infected individuals. It was in this context that the Research Division of the U.S. Price Administration Office proposed a new approach consisting in performing the analysis not on individual samples, but on mixtures obtained by grouping together several individual samples.

As in the above seminal application, the principle of group testing relies on the assumption that in the search space the number of individuals we are trying to discover, called from now on the *positives*, is much smaller than the total number of individuals and on the possibility of using tests whose results, if negative, imply that all the tested elements are *negatives*. A negative test on a group then can save many individual tests.

The efficiency of the approach depends on the design of the group tests. In some cases, one may want to prepare a set of groups in such a way that a single round of tests provides enough information to exactly identify all the positives. This is referred to as *non-adaptive* group testing. An alternative is approaches where tests are organized in batches and done in rounds called *stages*. In these cases, the tests to be performed in a stage depend on the output of the tests in the previous stages. The extreme case where each stage comprises exactly one test is referred to as *adaptive* group testing.

F. Cicalese, *Fault-Tolerant Search Algorithms*, Monographs in Theoretical
Computer Science. An EATCS Series, DOI 10.1007/978-3-642-17327-1_7,
© Springer-Verlag Berlin Heidelberg 2013

When optimizing group testing approaches, the main aim is the minimization of the number of tests needed for identifying the positives. In the practical applications of group testing a series of limitations have to be taken into account which motivate the study of variants of the original problem of designing the groups. For instance, although the adaptive approach usually needs a smaller number of tests, the number of stages involved is often unacceptable because of the time and cost of preparing the tests in each single stage. This is especially true when the group testing approach is applied to physical or chemical tests. In such situations, waiting for the end of a stage before performing the next stage tests might mean postponing the final results by hours or even days. On the other hand, tests sometimes cannot be automatically performed, and their parallelization is limited by the resources of the laboratory performing them. Anyway, in general, there is a preference for non-adaptive approaches, and even when adaptive group testing is used, the number of stages is seldom greater than two.

Another type of constraint that can be imposed by the application is about the structure of the tests. In some cases, a practical obstacle to the approach is that groups cannot be chosen to be arbitrarily big. There are applications where the group size is limited by physicochemical properties. For instance, in the original application for discovering patients infected with syphilis, in groups with more than eight samples a single positive sample may be so diluted that the test output is not anymore accurate. In fact, this is the main reason why the group test approach was actually not used during the Second World War for identifying syphilis-infected soldiers. However, the approach found recently its original purpose again, and is being successfully applied in tests for HIV identification. Actually, with respect to HIV tests, group testing found even more applications: exploiting the fact that the output of HIV tests is not binary, but continuous, researchers have devised a new method based on group testing for estimating the virus prevalence, or the number of contaminated people, in a population without the necessity of exactly identifying the positives. This not only saves tests, but also provides important information while keeping the identity of infected people private.

7.1 Group Testing with Subset Tests

A combinatorial group testing instance is defined by three elements: a finite set U, representing the individuals to be tested; a set $P \subseteq O$ representing the *positives*, i.e., the elements in O that we need to identify; and a family $\mathscr{Q}$ of subsets of O, which represent the tests or *queries*, we can use to identify the positive set P. The information provided by performing a test $Q \in \mathscr{Q}$ (or, equivalently, asking the query Q) is the answer to the question "Does Q contain any positive element from P?"

Assuming the number of possible stages unlimited, we denote by $N(n, p)$ the minimum number of tests necessary to identify at most p positives from among n

elements, i.e., when $|O| = n$ and $|P| \leq p$. The efficiency of a group testing strategy is measured in terms of $N(n, p)$.

A lower bound on $N(n, p)$ can be obtained with a simple information theoretic argument: With up to p positives in a search space of cardinality n, there are at least $\binom{n}{p}$ possible sets of positives. The outcome of each test is binary, i.e., it brings to the questioner up to one bit of information. We need at least $\log \binom{n}{p} \approx p \log \frac{n}{p}$ bits to represent all the possible solutions, i.e., the different possible sets of positives. Therefore, no algorithm that is able to correctly report the set of positives, however chosen, can use less than this number of questions.

Adaptively, all positive elements can be easily identified using $O(p \log n)$ tests: The strategy consists in performing binary search on O to find the first positive element, x_1. Then, we repeat binary search in $O \setminus \{x\}$, so finding the second positive, x_2. We now repeat in $O \setminus \{x_1, x_2\}$, and so on, until either we have found all the p positives or the last binary search performed does not report any positive found. For each positive this procedure uses $O(\log n)$ tests, hence a total $O(p \log n)$ tests are sufficient. In fact, it is possible to reduce the number of tests to $p \log n/p + O(p)$.

The non-adaptive case requires significantly more tests, with the best known lower bound being $\Omega(p^2 \log_p n/p)$, whilst the best known non-adaptive strategy needs $O(p^2 \log n/p)$ tests. A proof of this upper bound is presented in the next section.

We can represent a non-adaptive group testing strategy as a binary matrix, where the columns represent the elements of the search space and the rows represent the tests. More precisely, assume w.l.o.g. that the search space is $[n]$, the set of the first n integers, and $P \subseteq [n]$ denotes the set of positives. Map $[n]$ to the indices of the columns of the matrix and interpret its rows as the indicator vectors of the tests. In words, a 1 in position (i, j) indicates that the ith test contains the jth element. Now the vector of the outcomes of the tests is the Boolean sum of those columns whose index is in P, i.e., their componentwise Boolean OR. Therefore, the group testing problem can be interpreted as the task of building a Boolean matrix M with n columns and the minimum possible number of rows such that we can identify a set of up to p columns of M from their Boolean sum.

7.1.1 The (p, v, n)-SUPER-SELECTOR

Given two vectors $\mathbf{x}, \mathbf{y} \in \{0, 1\}^n$, we denote with $\mathbf{x} \oplus \mathbf{y}$ the Boolean sum of $\mathbf{x}$ and $\mathbf{y}$, i.e., their componentwise OR. Given an $m \times n$ binary matrix M and an n-bit vector $\mathbf{x}$, we denote by $M \odot \mathbf{x}$ the m-bit vector obtained by performing the Boolean sum of the columns of M corresponding to the positions of the 1's in $\mathbf{x}$. That is, if $\mathbf{x}$ has a 1 in positions, say $3, 7, 11, \ldots$, then $M \odot \mathbf{x}$ is obtained by performing the $\oplus$ of the 3rd, 7th, 11th, $\ldots$, column of M. Given a set $S \subseteq [n]$, we use $M(S)$ to denote the submatrix induced by the columns with index in S. Also we use $\mathbf{a}_S$ to indicate the Boolean sum of the columns of $M(S)$. Given two n-bit vectors $\mathbf{x}, \mathbf{y}$ we say that x is *covered* by **y** if $x_i \leq y_i$, for each $i = 1, \ldots, n$. Note that if **x** is not covered by **y** then it means that **x** has a 1 in a position in which **y** has a 0.

Definition 7.1. Fix integers n, p, k, with $n \geq p \geq k$. A (p, k, n)-selector is an $m \times n$ binary matrix such that for any subset S of $p \leq n$ columns, the submatrix $M(S)$ induced by S contains at least k rows of the identity matrix I_p.[1] The parameter m is the *size* of the selector.

Definition 7.2. Fix integers n, p, with $p \leq n$ and an integer vector, $\mathbf{v} = (v_1, \ldots, v_p)$, such that $v_i \leq i$, for each $i = 1, \ldots, p$. We say that an $m \times n$ binary matrix M is a $(p, \mathbf{v}, n)$-SUPER-SELECTOR if M is a (i, v_i, n)-selector for each $i = 1, \ldots, p$. We call m the size of the SUPER-SELECTOR.

The following theorem, whose proof will be given in Sect. 7.1.3, provides a bound on the size of $(p, \mathbf{v}, n)$-SUPER-SELECTOR.

Theorem 7.1. *A* $(p, \mathbf{v}, n)$-SUPER-SELECTOR *of size*

$$m = O(\max_{j=1,\ldots,p} k_j \log(n/j)), \qquad where \; k_j = \min\left\{ \frac{3pej}{(j - v_j + 1)}, \frac{ej^2}{\log_2 e} \right\}$$
$$(7.1)$$

can be constructed in time polynomial in n and exponential in k.

The "identification" capabilities of a SUPER-SELECTOR are as follows.

Lemma 7.1. *Let* M *be a* $(p, \mathbf{v}, n)$-SUPER-SELECTOR, $\mathbf{v} = (v_1, \ldots, v_p)$. *Let* S *be any set of* $x < v_p$ *columns of* M. *Let* $\mathbf{a}_S$ *denote the Boolean sum of the columns in* S. *Then, from* $\mathbf{a}_S$ *it is possible to identify at least* v_{x+y} *of the columns in* S, *where* y *is the number of columns of* M *which are not in* S *but are covered by* $\mathbf{a}_S$. *Moreover,* $y < \min\{j \mid x < v_j\} - x$.

Proof. Let $T = \{\mathbf{b} \mid \mathbf{b} \notin S \text{ and } \mathbf{b} \oplus \mathbf{a}_S = \mathbf{a}_S\}$, i.e., T is the set of columns not in S but covered by $\mathbf{a}_S$. Then, $y = |T|$. We first prove the last statement.

Claim. $y < \min\{j \mid v_j > x\} - x$. Let j^* be a value of j achieving the minimum. The claim is a consequence of M being a (j^*, v_{j^*}, n)-selector. To see this, assume, by contradiction, that $|T| \geq j^* - x$. Let $T' \subseteq T$ and $|T' \cup S| = j^*$. Then, there are at least $v_{j^*} > |S|$ columns in $T' \cup S$ with a 1 in a row where all the other columns have a 0. Thus, there is at least one column of T' which has a 1 where all the column of S have a 0. This contradicts the fact that all the columns of T (and hence of T') are covered by $\mathbf{a}_S$.

Since $x + y < j^* \leq p$, and M is an $(x + y, v_{x+y}, n)$-selector, among the columns of $S \cup T$ there are at least v_{x+y} which have a 1 where all the others have

---

[1]the Boolean matrix with p rows and p columns, where only the entries (i, i) for $i = 1, \ldots, p$ are 1 and all the other entries are 0.

a 0. Let W be such a set of columns. By an argument analogous to the one used in the claim we have that $W \subseteq S$ and we can identify them. ∎

Remark 7.1. Notice that if $v_i > v_{i-1}$, for each $i = 2, \ldots, p$, then we have a situation that, at first look, might appear surprising: the larger the number of spurious elements, i.e., columns not in S but covered by $\mathbf{a}_S$, the more information we get on S, i.e., the more columns of S are identified.

Remark 7.2. The same argument used in the proof above shows that Lemma 7.1 also holds when $\mathbf{a}_S$ is the componentwise *arithmetic* sum of the columns in S.

Corollary 7.1. *There exists a non-adaptive group testing strategy to identify up to p positives in a search space of size n which uses $O(p^2 \log n / p)$ tests.*

Proof. By Lemma 7.1 a $(p+1, \mathbf{v}, n)$-SUPER-SELECTOR, with $\mathbf{v} = (1, 2, \ldots, p+1)$ encodes a non-adaptive group testing strategy which identifies up to p positives in a space of cardinality n. The desired bound on the size of such a super-selector follows directly from Theorem 7.1. ∎

7.1.2 Approximate Group Testing

In approximate group testing one is interested in strategies with the minimum number of tests, such that a subset P' is reported satisfying $|P' \setminus P| \leq e_0$ and $|P \setminus P'| \leq e_1$, where P is the set of positives and e_0 and e_1 are parameters bounding the maximum number of false positives and false negatives which are tolerated.

Let M be an appropriate $(p + e_0, \mathbf{v}, n)$-SUPER-SELECTOR, with the components of vector $\mathbf{v}$ defined by $v_i = i - \min\{e_0, e_1\} + 1$. We can use M to attain approximate identification in the above sense. Proceeding as before, map $[n]$ to the indices of the columns of the super-selector and interpret the rows of the super-selector as the indicator vectors of the tests. Now the vector of the outcomes of the tests is the Boolean sum $\mathbf{a}_P$ of those columns whose index is in P. Let P' be the set of the indices of the columns covered by $\mathbf{a}_P$. We have $P \subseteq P'$ and by Lemma 7.1 also $|P'| \leq |P| + e_0$. Moreover, from Lemma 7.1 we also know that a set of positives $P'' \subseteq P$ can be exactly identified, with $|P''| \geq |P| - e_1$. Therefore, any set P^* with $P'' \subseteq P^* \subseteq P'$ satisfies the bounds on the false positives and false negatives.

If we assume that e_0 and e_1 are bounded as some fixed fraction of p, then the strategy provided by the above super-selector is asymptotically best possible since it uses $O(p \log \frac{n}{p})$ tests, which matches the following extension of the information theoretic lower bound provided by Cheraghchi for the case of approximate group testing.

Theorem 7.2. *At least $p \log \frac{n}{p} - p - e_0 - O(e_1 \log \frac{n-p-e_0}{e_1})$ tests are necessary to report a set P', such that $|P' \setminus P| \leq e_0$ and $|P \setminus P'| \leq e_1$.*

Another nice feature of the above solution is that it guarantees the exact identification of at least $p' - \min\{e_0, e_1\} + 1$ positives, where $p' \leq p$ is the actual number of positive elements.

7.1.3　Bounds on the Size of a $(p, \mathbf{v}, n)$-SUPER-SELECTOR

In this section we prove the bound on the size of a $(p, \mathbf{v}, n)$-SUPER-SELECTOR as announced in Theorem 7.1.

The proof relies on the probabilistic method for showing the existence of a matrix of the size desired. The method of conditional probabilities can then be used for derandomizing the randomized construction implied by the probabilistic proof.

We use the following two lemmas to prove the existence of two distinct matrices, each satisfying one of the bounds in the min-expression of (7.1). Then, the desired super-selector can be obtained by the juxtaposition of these two matrices, one on top of the other.

Lemma 7.2. *There exists a* $(p, \mathbf{v}, n)$-SUPER-SELECTOR *of size*

$$m = O\left(\max_{j=1,\ldots,p} \frac{3pej}{(j - v_j + 1)} \log(n/j)\right).$$

Proof. Generate the $m \times n$ binary matrix M by choosing each entry randomly and independently, with $Pr(M[i, j] = 0) = (p - 1)/p = x$. Fix an integer $j \leq p$. Fix $S \in \binom{[n]}{j}$, where $\binom{[n]}{j}$ denotes the family of all subsets of j elements of $[n]$. For any subset R of $j - v_j + 1$ rows of I_j let $E_{R,S}$ be the event that the submatrix $M(S)$ does not contain *any* of the $(j - v_j + 1)$ rows of R. We have

$$Pr(E_{R,S}) = \left(1 - (j - v_j + 1)x^{j-1}(1 - x)\right)^m \tag{7.2}$$

Let $R_1, \ldots, R_t$, $t = \binom{j}{j-v_j+1}$ be all possible subsets of exactly $j - v_j + 1$ rows of the matrix I_j, and let N_S be the event that, for some index $i \in \{1, \ldots, t\}$, the sub-matrix $M(S)$ does not contain *any* of the rows of the subset R_i. By the union bound we have

$$Pr(N_S) = Pr\left(\bigvee_{i=1}^{t} E_{R_i,S}\right) \leq \binom{j}{j-v_j+1}\left(1 - (j - v_j + 1)x^{j-1}(1 - x)\right)^m \tag{7.3}$$

One can see that N_S coincides with the event that the sub-matrix $M(S)$ contains strictly less than v_j rows of I_j. To see this, it is enough to observe that if $M(S)$ contains less than v_j rows of I_j it means that there is some i such that $M(S)$ does not contain any of the rows in R_i.

Let Y_M denote the event that the matrix M is a $(p, \mathbf{v}, n)$-SUPER-SELECTOR. We can use again the union bound to estimate the probability of the negated event $\overline{Y_M}$. If M is not a $(p, \mathbf{v}, n)$-SUPER-SELECTOR then there exists an integer $j \in [p]$ such that for some $S \in \binom{[n]}{j}$ the event N_S happens. Therefore,

$$Pr(\overline{Y_M}) = Pr\left(\bigvee_{j=1}^{p} \bigvee_{S \in \binom{[n]}{j}} N_S \right),$$

whence we obtain:

$$Pr(Y_M) \geq 1 - \sum_{j=1}^{p} \binom{n}{j}\binom{j}{j - v_j + 1}\left(1 - (j - v_j + 1)\, x^{j-1}(1-x)\right)^m. \quad (7.4)$$

Any value of m such that the above probability is positive implies the existence of a super-selector of size m. If no such super-selector existed then the probability would be 0.

Since we are interested in the minimum such m, we can conclude that there exists a $(p, \mathbf{v}, n)$-SUPER-SELECTOR of size $m^* = \mathrm{argmin}_{m \geq 1} Pr(Y_M) > 0$. The rest of the proof will consist in showing that m^* satisfies the bound claimed.

Let us focus on the value c_j such that the j-th summand in (7.4) satisfies the following inequality

$$\binom{n}{j}\binom{j}{j - v_j + 1}\left(1 - (j - v_j + 1)\, x^{j-1}(1-x)\right)^{c_j\, j\, \log n/j} \leq 1/p \quad (7.5)$$

We shall use the following two inequalities

$$\left(1 - (j - v_j + 1)\, x^{j-1}(1-x)\right)^{c_j\, j\, \log(n/j)} \leq \left(\frac{n}{j}\right)^{-\frac{(j - v_j + 1)c_j\, j}{ep}} \quad (7.6)$$

$$\binom{n}{j}\binom{j}{j - v_j + 1} \leq n^j\, 2^{\frac{j}{2}} e^{\frac{3j}{2}} j^{-j} \quad (7.7)$$

By (7.6)–(7.7), we have that the left-hand-side of (7.5) can be upper bounded by

$$n^{j - \frac{c_j(j - v_j + 1)j}{pe}}\, 2^{\frac{j}{2}} e^{\frac{3j}{2}} j^{-\left(j - \frac{c_j(j - v_j + 1)j}{pe}\right)} = n^{j - \frac{c_j(j - v_j + 1)j}{pe}}\, 2^{\frac{j}{2}} e^{\frac{3j}{2}} j^{-j + \frac{c_j(j - v_j + 1)j}{pe}}. \quad (7.8)$$

Therefore, if we take $c_j = \frac{3pe}{(j-v_j+1)}$ we have that (7.8) can be further upper-bounded with $n^{-2j} e^{2j} j^{2j}$ which is not larger than $1/p$ for all $n \geq 20$ and $n > p \geq j > 0$. Therefore, by taking

$$m = \max_{j=1,\dots,p} c_j \log(n/j) = \max_{j=1,\dots,p} \frac{3pej}{(j-v_j+1)} \log \frac{n}{j} \qquad (7.9)$$

we can have each of the summands in (7.4) smaller than $1/p$, hence guaranteeing $Pr(Y_M) > 0$. By definition $m^* \leq m$ which concludes the proof. ∎

The same analysis as above, tailored for the (p,k,n)-selector gives the following slightly sharper bounds.

Lemma 7.3. *For each $0 \leq k < p < n$, there exists a (p,k,n)-selector of size*

$$m = \left(\log_2 \frac{e}{e-1+\frac{k}{p}} \right)^{-1} p \log \frac{n}{p} (1+o(1)) \leq \frac{2p^2}{p-k+1} \log \frac{n}{p} (1+o(1)).$$

$$(7.10)$$

Moreover, there exists a (p,p,n)-selector of size $m = \frac{ep^2}{\log_2 e} \log(n/p)\, (1+o(1))$.

We can now combine the last two lemmas to obtain the upper bound on the size of a SUPER-SELECTOR in Theorem 7.1.

Theorem 7.3. *There exists a $(p,\mathbf{v},n)$-SUPER-SELECTOR of size*

$$m = O(\max_{j=1,\dots,p} k_j \log(n/j)), \qquad \text{where } k_j = \min \left\{ \frac{3pej}{(j-v_j+1)}, \frac{ej^2}{\log_2 e} \right\}$$

Proof. Fix $k = \max \left\{ j \mid \frac{3pej}{(j-v_j+1)} > \frac{ej^2}{\log_2 j} \right\}$. Let M_1 be a minimum size (k,k,n)-selector. In particular this is a $(k, < 1,2,\dots,k >, n)$-SUPER-SELECTOR hence *a fortiori* it is also a $(k,(v_1,\dots,v_k),n)$-SUPER-SELECTOR.

Let M_2 be a minimum size $(p,(0,\dots,0,v_{k+1},\dots,v_p),n)$-SUPER-SELECTOR.

Let M be the binary matrix obtained by pasting together, one on top of the other, M_1 and M_2. It is not hard to see that M is a $(p,\mathbf{v},n)$-SUPER-SELECTOR. By Lemmas 7.3 and 7.2, M satisfies the desired bound. The proof is complete. ∎

Remark 7.3. Note that, if there exists a constant α such that $v_j \leq \alpha j$ for each $\sqrt{p} < j \leq p$, then the size of the SUPER-SELECTOR is $O(p \log \frac{n}{p})$, matching the information theoretic lower bound. Particular cases are given by instances where for each j, we have $v_j = f_j(j)$ for some function f_j such that $f_j(j) = o(j)$.

More generally, we have the following almost matching lower bound on the size of a $(p,\mathbf{v},n)$-SUPER-SELECTOR, which follows from a bound on the size of (p,k,n)-selectors, whose proof is beyond the scope of this chapter and hence is omitted here.

Theorem 7.4. *The size of a* $(p, \mathbf{v}, n)$-SUPER-SELECTOR *has to be*

$$\Omega \left(\max_{j=1,\dots,p} \frac{j^2}{j - v_j + 1} \frac{\log(n/j)}{\log\left(j/(j - v_j + 1)\right) + O(1)} \right).$$

Proof. By definition, a $(p, \mathbf{v}, n)$-SUPER-SELECTOR is simultaneously a (v_j, j, n)-selector, for each $j = 1, \dots, p$. Therefore, obviously, the size of the SUPER-SELECTOR is at least as large as the size of the largest (v_j, j, n)-selector it includes, over all $j = 1, \dots, p$. The desired result now directly follows from a bound by Chlebus et al. on the minimum size of selectors [46, Theorem 2], which states that any (v_j, j, n)-selector has size $\Omega \left(\frac{j^2}{j-v_j+1} \frac{\log(n/j)}{\log(j/(j-v_j+1)) + O(1)} \right)$.

Deterministic Construction. By using the method of the conditional expectations the above result can be derandomized, to obtain a deterministic construction of the $(p, \mathbf{v}, n)$-SUPER-SELECTOR of Theorem 7.3. The resulting procedure is polynomial in n but exponential in the second parameter p as recorded in the following proposition which together with Theorem 7.3 completes the proof of Theorem 7.1.

Proposition 7.1. *There exists a deterministic* $O\left(p^3 n^{p+1} \log n\right)$ *construction of the* $(p, \mathbf{v}, n)$-SUPER-SELECTOR *given by Theorem 7.3.*

7.2 Interval Group Testing

In Interval Group Testing the search space is linearly sorted, and the only tests allowed are those whose elements define an interval of the search space.

An instance of the problem is given by three non-negative integers n, p, s. The search space, $\mathcal{O}$, is the set of the first n positive integers $[n] = \{1, 2, \dots, n\}$. The set of positives P is any arbitrary subset of $\mathcal{O}$, of size at most p. The tests (or queries) allowed are the intervals $[i, j] = \{i, i + 1, \dots, j\}$, for each $1 \leq i \leq j \leq n$. More precisely, each such interval represents the binary test asking "Is $P \cap \{i, i + 1, \dots, j\} \neq \emptyset$?", for some $1 \leq i \leq j \leq n$.

We assume that tests are arranged in s *stages*: in each stage a certain number of tests is performed non-adaptively, while tests of a given stage can be determined based on the outcomes of the tests in all previous stages.

We will be interested in bounds for the number $N(n, p, s, e)$, the worst-case number of tests that are necessary (and sufficient) to successfully identify all positives in a search space of cardinality n, under the hypothesis that the number of positives is at most p and s-stage algorithms are used and up to e tests may report an incorrect answer. For the case where non-adaptive search is used ($s = 1$) it is possible to precisely estimate $N(n, p, 1, e)$, for any value of the other parameters. Then, we will focus on the case where the maximum number of stages is two, which is the most common case in practical uses of this approach (see Sect. 7.3). We will

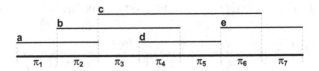

Fig. 7.1 A query scheme with five queries dividing the search space into seven pieces

provide several bounds on $N(n, p, 2, e)$. A tighter estimate will be given for the special situation $e = 1$.

Given an interval $\pi = [i, j]$, we denote its size by $|\pi|$, i.e., $|\pi| = j - i + 1$. By definition each query asks about the intersection of a given interval with the set of positive elements. Therefore, we identify a query with the interval it specifies. We say that a query $Q \equiv [i, j]$ covers an element $k \in [n]$ if and only if $k \in [i, j]$.

A query $Q \equiv [i, j]$ has two boundaries: the left boundary is $(i - 1, i)$, and the right boundary is $(j, j + 1)$. For the sake of definiteness, we assume that, for any $a \in [n]$, the query $[1, a]$ has left boundary $(0, 1)$, and the query $[a, n]$ has right boundary $(n, n + 1)$. A multiset of queries $\mathcal{Q}$ defines a set of boundaries $\mathcal{B}(\mathcal{Q}) = \{(i_1, i_1 + 1), (i_2, i_2 + 1), \ldots\}$, where $0 \leq i_k < i_{k+1} \leq n$. Every interval $[i_k + 1, i_{k+1}]$ is called a *piece*. Because every query has two distinct boundaries, but two queries may share some boundaries, we have $|\mathcal{B}(\mathcal{Q})| \leq 2|\mathcal{Q}|$.

Let π be a piece defined by the set $\mathcal{Q}$ of queries. We define the *roof* of π, denoted by $\mathcal{R}(\pi)$, the subset

$$\mathcal{R}(\pi) = \{Q \in \mathcal{Q} : \pi \subseteq Q\}.$$

The definition of the roof of a piece can be extended to a set of pieces $\mathcal{P}$ as

$$\mathcal{R}(\mathcal{P}) = \bigcup_{\pi \in \mathcal{P}} \mathcal{R}(\pi).$$

Sets of Queries and YES-Sets

Let $\mathcal{Q}$ be a set of interval queries. It should be clear that not all combinations of positive and negative answers are possible. For instance, let us consider the situation depicted in Fig. 7.1. Assume $p = 1$, i.e., at most one positive element is in P. Then, it cannot happen that the answer to each question is yes: trivially, the queries a, d, and e are disjoint, and answering yes to all of them would mean that the only positive element would be at the same time in one of the pieces π_1 and π_2; and in one of the pieces π_4 and π_5; and in one of the pieces π_6 and π_7.

The point here is that there are sets of answers, like this one, which will never be received when $p = 1$. The same happens for the case of at most two positives. If more than two positives are allowed, this pattern could be observed if the pieces

π_2, π_4 and π_7 contain at least one positive. Another forbidden combination is the one where only the query b has a positive answer: since all pieces covered by this query are also covered by the queries a, c, or d, a positive in the interval b would automatically force another positive answer.

A set $\mathscr{Y} \subseteq \mathscr{Q}$ of queries such that answering yes to the queries in $\mathscr{Y}$ and no to all others corresponds to valid scenarios is called a YES-set for $\mathscr{Q}$. Formally speaking, a YES-set can be defined as follows:

Definition 7.3. Let $\mathscr{Q}$ be a multiset of queries, and let $\mathscr{Y} \subseteq \mathscr{Q}$. If there is a set of pieces $\mathscr{P}$ such that $|\mathscr{P}| \leq p$ and $\bigcup_{\pi \in P} \mathscr{R}(\pi) = \mathscr{Y}$, then $\mathscr{Y}$ is a YES-*set* for $\mathscr{Q}$ in the case for p positives.

A YES-set is called *specific* if the intersection of all its queries corresponds to a single piece, and the piece has at most one positive; otherwise, it is called *unspecific*. More formally, a YES-set $\mathscr{Y} \subset \mathscr{Q}$ is specific if and only if there is a piece π of $\mathscr{Q}$, with $|\pi \cap P| \leq 1$, such that $\bigcap_{Q \in \mathscr{Y}} Q = \pi$.

7.2.1 Non-adaptive Fault-Tolerant Interval Group Testing

In adaptive group testing, there is a basic difference between the last stage and all the other stages: while the first stage may focus on reducing the search space, the last stage must point out the positives. In other words, the last stage is non-adaptive per se. As a result, studying non-adaptive group testing is a prerequisite to studying any multi-stage adaptive strategy. Therefore, the results in this section will be the basis for the analysis of the more practical two-batch case.

The following two theorems completely characterize one-stage e-fault-tolerant interval group testing.

Theorem 7.5. *For all $n \geq 1$ and $e \geq 0$, it holds that $N(n, 1, 1, e) = \left\lceil \frac{(2e+1)(n+1)}{2} \right\rceil$.*

Proof. The lower bound directly follows from the following claim.

Claim. Every strategy that correctly identifies the (only) positive or reports $P = \emptyset$ uses a set of questions such that there are at least $2e+1$ question boundaries $(i, i+1)$ for each $i = 0, 1, \ldots, n$.

By contradiction, let us consider a strategy such that for some $i \in [n]$ there are $b \leq 2e$ questions with a boundary $(i, i + 1)$. Let $\mathscr{Q}$ be the set of such questions and $\mathscr{Q}_1$ the set of all questions in $\mathscr{Q}$ which contain i. Assume, without loss of generality, that $|\mathscr{Q}_1| \geq |\mathscr{Q} \setminus \mathscr{Q}_1|$.

Let the adversary answer

- no to all the questions having empty intersection with $\{i, i + 1\}$,
- yes to all questions including both i and $i + 1$,
- yes to exactly $\lceil |\frac{\mathscr{Q}}{2}| \rceil$ questions in $\mathscr{Q}_1$ and no to the remaining ones in $\mathscr{Q}_1$,
- yes to all the questions in $\mathscr{Q} \setminus \mathscr{Q}_1$.

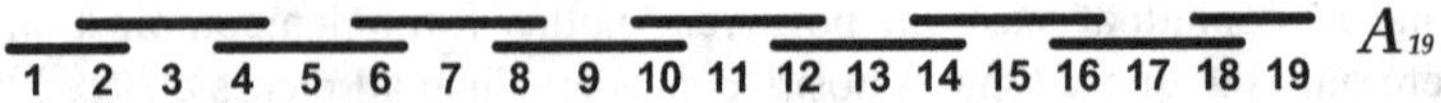

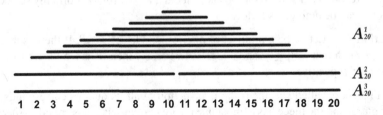

A_{19}

1 2 3 4 5 6 7 8 9 10 11 12 13 14 15 16 17 18 19

Fig. 7.2 An example of the query pattern in the optimal algorithm of Theorem 7.5 for the case of a search space with an odd number of elements. Here the search space has cardinality 19. The *horizontal bars* indicate the interval queries

A_{20}^1

A_{20}^2
A_{20}^3

1 2 3 4 5 6 7 8 9 10 11 12 13 14 15 16 17 18 19 20

Fig. 7.3 An example of the query pattern in the optimal algorithm of Theorem 7.5 for the case of a search space with an even odd number of elements. Here the search space has cardinality 20. The *horizontal bars* indicate the interval queries

A moment's reflection shows that, due to the possibility of having up to e erroneous answers, the above set of answers is consistent with both cases when $P = \{i\}$ and $P = \{i+1\}$.[2] Hence, the given strategy cannot correctly discriminate among the above possibilities. The claim is proved.

Therefore, any strategy that is able to correctly identify P must use in total at least $(2e + 1)(n + 1)$ boundaries. Then, the desired result follows by observing that each question can cover at most two boundaries.

We now turn to the upper bound. Direct inspection shows that for $n \leq 3$ there exists an easy strategy with the desired number of questions.

For each $k \geq 2$, let $\mathscr{A}_{2k+1} = \{[1,2],[2,4],[4,6],\ldots,[2k-2,2k],[2k,2k+1]\}$ and $\mathscr{A}_{2k}^1 = \{[2,2k-1],[3,2k-2],\ldots,[k,k+1]\}$, $\mathscr{A}_{2k}^2 = \{[1,k],[k+1,2k]\}$, and $\mathscr{A}_{2k}^3 = \{[1,k]\}$.

Then, for $n \geq 4$, the following strategy attains the desired bound.

If n is odd, the strategy consists of asking $2e + 1$ times the questions in $\mathscr{A}_n$. Figure 7.2 shows the groups of questions found in this algorithm. These amount to $(2e + 1)\lceil(n + 1)/2\rceil = \lceil(2e + 1)(n + 1)/2\rceil$ questions which clearly cover $2e + 1$ times each boundary $(i, i + 1)$ for each $i = 0, 1, \ldots, n$.

If n is even, let $k = n/2$. Now, the strategy consists of asking $2e + 1$ times the questions in $\mathscr{A}_n^1$, plus $e + 1$ times the questions in $\mathscr{A}_n^2$, plus e times the questions in $\mathscr{A}_n^3$. Figure 7.3 shows the groups of questions found in this algorithm. In total, in this case, the strategy uses $(2e + 1)(k - 1) + 2(e + 1) + e = (2e + 1)k + e + 1 = \lceil(2e + 1)(2k + 1)/2\rceil = \lceil(2e + 1)(n + 1)/2\rceil$, as desired.

For the case of more positives we have the following generalization.

---

[2]In particular, for the case $i = 0$ (respectively, $i = n$) the ambiguity is whether P contains no elements or the positive is the element 1 (resp. n).

Theorem 7.6. *For all integers $n \geq 1$, $p \geq 2$, $e \geq 0$, it holds that*

$$N(n, p, 1, e) = (2e + 1)n.$$

Proof. The upper bound is trivially obtained by a strategy made of $(2e + 1)$ copies of the singleton questions $\{1\}, \{2\}, \ldots, \{n\}$.

The lower bound is obtained proceeding in a way analogous to the argument used in the previous theorem. Here, we argue that every strategy that correctly identifies P must ask, for each $i = 1, 2, \ldots, n - 1$, at least $2e + 1$ questions with boundary $(i, i + 1)$ and including i, and at least $2e + 1$ questions with boundary $(i, i + 1)$ and including $i + 1$. Moreover, it must ask at least $2e + 1$ questions with boundary $(0, 1)$ and $2e + 1$ questions with boundary $(n, n + 1)$. Otherwise, assume that there exists $i \in \{1, 2, \ldots, n - 1\}$ such that one of the above $4e + 2$ boundaries $(i, i + 1)$ is missing.

Proceeding as in the proof of the previous theorem, it is possible to define an answering strategy for the adversary that balances the answers on the two sides of the boundary so that with the information provided by the answers and given the possible number of lies, it is not possible to discriminate between the cases $P = \{i\}$ and $P = \{i, i + 1\}$, or between the cases $P = \{i + 1\}$ and $P = \{i, i + 1\}$.

Alternatively, if some of the above boundaries $(0, 1)$ (resp. $(n, n+1)$) are missing, the adversary can answer in such a way that it is not possible to discriminate between the cases $P = \emptyset$ and $P = \{1\}$ (resp. $P = \{n\}$).

7.2.2 Two-Stage Fault-Tolerant Interval Group Testing

In the previous section, we proved that the number of queries necessary and sufficient to detect more than one positive in a set of n elements in the presence of at most e lies is $(2e + 1)n$. This result shows that group testing does not bring any advantage when tests are constrained to be intervals of the search space and have to be asked non-adaptively. In fact, in this case, the optimal strategy implies exhaustively testing each single element in order to be sure it is a positive. The study of non-adaptive interval group testing is still useful for understanding the multi-stage case, which we are going to focus on in the following sections: as explained above, the last stage in an adaptive strategy is always a non-adaptive strategy.

An Averaging Argument for Lower Bound on Two-Stage Interval Group Testing

Suppose we want to find up to p positives in a search space $\mathcal{O} = [n]$ in two stages. Let $\mathcal{Q}$ be the multiset of interval queries used in the first stage, and suppose that $\mathcal{Q}$ divides the search space into l pieces. There can be many different YES-sets for $\mathcal{Q}$, and positives are differently spread over the pieces in each YES-set. The analysis of the number of queries needed to uniquely identify the positives in a second stage for each YES-set gives us the opportunity to look for the YES-sets that force the greatest number of queries in total. These YES-sets correspond to the worst scenario faced when using the query scheme $\mathcal{Q}$, and the minimum (over all $\mathcal{Q}$) of the number of queries forced by such YES-sets corresponds exactly to $N(n, p, 2, e)$.

Let $\mathcal{Y}$ be a YES-set for a query scheme. We define the *weight* of $\mathcal{Y}$ as the number of queries needed to discover the positives in the search space after observing $\mathcal{Y}$. It is difficult to characterize the heaviest YES-sets for a general query scheme. And actually we do not need to know what this YES-set looks like. All we need is the weight of this YES-set, or at least bounds for the number of queries.

Consider a multiset of YES-sets, and let η be the average weight of the YES-sets in this multiset. Because η is less than or equal to the maximum weight in the multiset, it is also a lower bound for the weight of the heaviest YES-set in the multiset. Obviously, the heavier the YES-sets in this multiset are, the closer the lower bound is to the real weight of the heaviest YES-set.

Along this line of reasoning, we can use an averaging argument to provide lower bounds for two-stage interval group testing strategies based on bounds for the non-adaptive case. In particular, the approach is based on averaging the weight of a multiset of YES-sets, without the necessity of relying on the knowledge about the weight of the individual YES-sets. Instead of analyzing all the possible YES-sets we can concentrate on the individual pieces, and rely on estimating the number of queries needed in specific YES-set to look for positives inside the pieces in the second stage.

More formally, suppose that the number of queries needed to reveal the positives inside a piece π_j when observing the YES-set $\mathcal{Y}_i$ is given by $w(\mathcal{Y}_i, \pi_j) |\pi_j|$, where $w(\mathcal{Y}_i, \pi_j)$, the piece *weight*, is a function of the YES-set and the piece, and $|\pi_j|$ is the size of the piece. If the total number of pieces in the query scheme is l, we may express the weight of the YES-set $\mathcal{Y}_i$ as

$$w(\mathcal{Y}_i) = \sum_{j=1}^{l} w(\mathcal{Y}_i, \pi_j) |\pi_j|.$$

This means that the average weight in a multiset of k YES-sets is given by

$$\eta = \frac{\sum_{i=1}^{k} \sum_{j=1}^{l} w(\mathcal{Y}_i, \pi_j) |\pi_j|}{k} = \frac{\sum_{j=1}^{l} \left(|\pi_j| \sum_{i=1}^{k} w(\mathcal{Y}_i, \pi_j) \right)}{k}$$

Suppose now that we know neither the piece sizes nor their individual weights, but we know that, for each piece, the sum of weights over all YES-sets is not smaller than a number r, that is, for each $j = 1, \dots, l$

$$\sum_{i=1}^{k} w(\mathcal{Y}_i, \pi_j) \geq r.$$

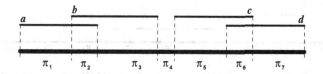

Fig. 7.4 A pattern of four queries for exemplifying the averaging argument on YES-sets

Thus, we have that

$$
\eta = \frac{\sum_{j=1}^{l}\left(|\pi_j|\sum_{i=1}^{k} w(\mathcal{Y}_i, \pi_j)\right)}{k}
$$

$$
\geq \frac{\sum_{j=1}^{l}\left(|\pi_j|\, r\right)}{k}
$$

$$
= n\frac{r}{k}.
$$

We have proved the following lemma which we are going to use for finding lower bounds in fault-tolerant interval group testing.

Lemma 7.4. *Consider a multiset of k—not necessarily distinct—YES-sets, and for each $i = 1, 2, \ldots, k$ and $j = 1, 2, \ldots, \ell$, let $w(\mathcal{Y}_i, \pi_j)$ be the weight of the jth piece in the YES vector associated to the ith YES-sets. If there exists an $r > 0$ such that for all $j = 1, 2, \ldots, \ell$, it holds that $\sum_{i=1}^{k} w(\mathcal{Y}_i, \pi_j) \geq r$, then an adversary can force at least $\frac{r}{k}n$ queries in the second stage.*

The Averaging Argument in Use

We exemplify the use of the average argument by giving a lower bound for the number of queries used by an algorithm able to find up to two positives using the queries shown in Fig. 7.4 in the first stage. We analyze two YES-sets: $\mathcal{Y}_1 = \{a, b\}$ and $\mathcal{Y}_2 = \{c, d\}$. By Theorems 7.5 and 7.6, in an error-free scenario, the number of queries necessary to identify p positives in a search space of size n is not smaller than $\frac{1}{2}n$, if $p = 1$, and not smaller than n, if $p \geq 2$.

We start analyzing $\mathcal{Y}_1$. Notice that when this YES-set is observed we can have three situations: (1) both positives are in the piece π_2; (2) the two positives are separated in two of the pieces π_1, π_2 and π_3; (3) one positive is in piece π_2 and the other is in the uncovered piece π_4. Since each piece that may contain a positive has to be analyzed in the second stage with a strategy able to find the positives in any possible case, the piece π_2 has to be analyzed with a strategy able to find up to two positives; the pieces π_1, π_3 and π_4 have to be analyzed with a strategy able

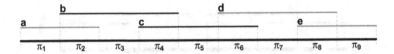

Fig. 7.5 A multiset of queries with two positive answers (to the queries b and c) and three negative answers (to the queries a, d, and e). The *stronger horizontal line* represents the search space, while the *thinner lines* represent the interval queries. Queries in *black* have positive answers, whereas the ones in *grey* have a negative answer. The projections of the borders in the search space are indicated by *dashed lines* and the consequent pieces are labeled $\pi_1, \dots, \pi_9$

to find up to one positive; and all other pieces may be ignored in the second stage. This means that this YES-set forces at least: $\frac{1}{2} |\pi_1|$ queries in piece π_1, $|\pi_2|$ queries in piece π_2, $\frac{1}{2} |\pi_3|$ queries in piece π_3 and $\frac{1}{2} |\pi_4|$ queries in piece π_4 in the second stage. Moreover, the weight given from $\mathcal{Y}_1$ to each piece is given by

$$w(\mathcal{Y}_1, \pi_1) = \frac{1}{2}, w(\mathcal{Y}_1, \pi_2) = 1, w(\mathcal{Y}_1, \pi_3) = \frac{1}{2}, w(\mathcal{Y}_1, \pi_4) = \frac{1}{2}, w(\mathcal{Y}_1, \pi_5) = 0,$$

$$w(\mathcal{Y}_1, \pi_6) = 0, w(\mathcal{Y}_1, \pi_7) = 0.$$

Notice that a similar analysis for the YES-set $\mathcal{Y}_2$ gives also the weights

$$w(\mathcal{Y}_2, \pi_1) = 0, w(\mathcal{Y}_2, \pi_2) = 0, w(\mathcal{Y}_2, \pi_3) = 0, w(\mathcal{Y}_2, \pi_4) = \frac{1}{2},$$

$$w(\mathcal{Y}_2, \pi_5) = \frac{1}{2}, w(\mathcal{Y}_2, \pi_6) = 1, w(\mathcal{Y}_2, \pi_7) = \frac{1}{2}.$$

As a result, for each piece π_i, it holds that $w(\mathcal{Y}_1, \pi_i) + w(\mathcal{Y}_2, \pi_i) \geq \frac{1}{2}$. Using the notation of Lemma 7.4, we have $k = 2$ and $r = 0.5$; therefore, there is at least one YES-set that can force at least $\frac{r}{k} n = \frac{n}{4}$ queries in the second stage, given a lower bound of $4 + \frac{n}{4}$ queries for algorithms using this pattern of queries.

In this example we analyzed only one set of queries. Later, we will use similar arguments applied to general query multisets.

YES-sets and Errors

When errors are allowed, YES-sets may represent several different scenarios. As an example, we consider the set of queries in Fig. 7.5, and estimate the consequences in terms of pieces which can contain the positives and the questions which are still necessary, according to the number of possible errors allowed when at most one positive is present.

In an error-free case, the only piece containing the positive is clearly π_4. However, if one error is allowed, then the answer to either b or c can be wrong.[3] If we assume that the answer to b is wrong, then the positive should be in π_5. This is so because at most one error is allowed, hence, the only possible situation is that the positive is in a piece for which only question c is answered positively. Dually, if we assume that the answer to c is wrong, then the positive must be in π_3.

Let us assume that the YES-set represents the set of answers to the first stage of questions in a two-stage game with at most one error. Since the second stage must identify the positive, it must be able to accommodate all three above possible scenarios: (1) There must be enough queries covering π_4 in the case that no errors happened in the first stage, hence, at least $\frac{3}{2}|\pi_4|$; (2) there must be enough queries covering π_3 (resp. π_5) to accommodate the case in which one error happened in the first stage affecting the answer to c (resp. b), namely at least $\frac{1}{2}|\pi_3|$ (resp. $\frac{1}{2}|\pi_5|$).

In conclusion, remembering the averaging argument presented in the previous section, with this YES-set the pieces π_3 and π_5 get weight $\frac{1}{2}$, the piece π_4 gets weight $\frac{3}{2}$, and all other pieces get weight 0.

The situation becomes more involved and the pieces get more weight when more errors are allowed. When two errors are allowed, some new scenarios are possible, and other pieces enter the game. For instance, now both the answer for b and the answer for d can be wrong, and it becomes possible that the positive is in piece π_6. The same happens with queries a and c, and the piece π_2. The hypothesis that only one error occurred cannot be discarded, so pieces π_3 and π_5 must be searched with at least a 1-error-tolerant algorithm. Also the hypothesis that no error occurred cannot be ignored, and piece π_4 must be analyzed with an even heavier 2-error-tolerant algorithm. Using Theorem 7.5, in total, at least

$$\frac{5}{2}|\pi_4| + \frac{3}{2}(|\pi_3| + |\pi_5|) + \frac{1}{2}(|\pi_2| + |\pi_6|)$$

queries are necessary in the second stage.

When errors are allowed, the number of possible YES-sets increases, and the simple definition given in Definition 7.3 does not cover all valid sets of answers to a multiset of queries. As a result, the definition of YES-sets becomes slightly more complex, as does their analysis.

Definition 7.4. Let $\mathscr{Q}$ be a multiset of queries, and let $\mathscr{Y} \subseteq \mathscr{Q}$. If there exists a set of pieces $\mathscr{P}$ such that $|\mathscr{P}| \leq p$ and $|(\mathscr{R}(\mathscr{P}) \cup \mathscr{Y}) \setminus (\mathscr{R}(\mathscr{P}) \cap \mathscr{Y})| \leq e$, then $\mathscr{Y}$ is a YES-*set* for $\mathscr{Q}$ in the case of p positives and e lies.

In other words, for error-tolerant interval group testing algorithms, a YES-set is the set of positively answered questions in a valid scenario, which may differ from the roof of a set of pieces by at most e answers.

---

[3]Notice that these are the only answers that may be wrong in the case of at most one positive. In fact, if another answer was wrong we would have a yes answer to two disjoint interval queries, which is impossible under the assumption of having at most one positive.

Definition 7.4 suggests a simple way to construct YES-sets for instances with up to p positives and up to e errors allowed. We choose a set of pieces $\mathscr{P}$, with $|\mathscr{P}| \leq p$, and let $\mathscr{Y} = \mathscr{R}(\mathscr{P})$. A YES-set built in this way is called *consistent* (with the set of pieces $\mathscr{P}$). We may also use the allowed lies when creating YES-sets by adding (and/or removing) up to e elements to (from) $\mathscr{Y}$. Sets created in this way are called *inconsistent*. Notice that the consistency refers to the construction process, namely to the choice of adding or removing yes answers from the ones which will be given in the case of a consistent YES-set. Therefore, the same YES-set (as a family of intervals) might be consistent with respect to a given $\mathscr{P}$ and inconsistent if we assume a different placement of the positives. If two consistent YES-sets $\mathscr{A}$ and $\mathscr{B}$ differ in at most e elements, then $\mathscr{B}$ can be constructed by consistently creating $\mathscr{A}$, and further transforming $\mathscr{A}$ into $\mathscr{B}$.

Bounds for Two-Stage Algorithms with One Positive

The aim of this section is to prove asymptotically tight upper and lower bounds on the query number of two-stage interval group testing algorithms when up to one of the answers is a lie. We shall first analyze the case where P contains *at most one positive*.

Let $\pi_1, \ldots, \pi_\ell$ be the pieces determined by the intervals of a set of interval questions $\mathscr{Q}$. Given a YES-set $\mathscr{Y}$, we define the *weight* it assigns to the piece π_i according to the following scheme:

- A piece π gets weight $1/2$ if it can contain a positive but, if this was the case there could not be an error in the next stage, because, due to the other yes' in the YES-set, an error must have already happened. This is so, because there is a yes which indicates that the positive is in some other piece different from π.
- A piece π gets weight $3/2$ if it can contain a positive and there might be still an error in the next stage. This is so, because all the other yes' in the YES-set do not contrast with the hypothesis that the positive is in the piece π.

Here, "can" means that this possibility is consistent with the YES-set.

Recall that $w(\mathscr{Y})$ denotes the weighted sum of the lengths of the pieces created by the interval questions, weighted according to the weights associated with $\mathscr{Y}$. In formulas, if $w(\mathscr{Y}, \pi_j)$ is the weight given to the piece π_j, we have $w(\mathscr{Y}) = \sum_j w(\mathscr{Y}, \pi_j) |\pi_j|$.

Assume now that $\mathscr{Q}$ is the set of interval questions asked in the first stage of a two-stage group testing algorithm that finds more than one positive. Using Theorems 7.5 and 7.6 it follows that if $\mathscr{Y}$ is the set of intervals in $\mathscr{Q}$ that answer YES, the number of queries to be asked in the second stage in order to find all the positives is *at least* $w(\mathscr{Y})$. Indeed, each piece π_j that may contain a positive, in the second stage, will induce an independent interval group testing problem with universe of size $|\pi_j|$ and such that $w(\mathscr{Y}, \pi_j) |\pi_j|$ is the correct lower bound for the number of queries necessary according to Theorems 7.5 and 7.6 in the case of one error.

We will use the averaging argument to show that for each possible first stage of interval questions, $\mathcal{Q}$, there exists a YES-set $\mathcal{Y}$ such that $w(\mathcal{Y}) \geq n/|\mathcal{Q}|$. From this we will obtain a lower bound of $\Omega(\sqrt{n})$ on $N(n,1,2,1)$.

In the following, when it is necessary to distinguish among different query-sets, we will explicitly specify the query-set we refer to by a subscript to the notation for the roof of a piece and the weight of a piece or a YES-set.

Proposition 7.2. *Let $\mathcal{Q}$ be a set of interval questions producing a partition of the search space in which there are pieces a and b such that $\mathscr{R}_{\mathcal{Q}}(a) = \mathscr{R}_{\mathcal{Q}}(b)$. Then, there exists a set of interval questions $\mathcal{Q}'$ of the same cardinality as $\mathcal{Q}$ such that the following two conditions hold: (i) for each two pieces a' and b' in the partition produced by $\mathcal{Q}'$ it holds that $\mathscr{R}_{\mathcal{Q}'}(a') \neq \mathscr{R}_{\mathcal{Q}'}(b')$; (ii) for each YES-set $\mathcal{Y}'$ for $\mathcal{Q}'$ there exists a YES-set $\mathcal{Y}$ for $\mathcal{Q}$ such that $w_{\mathcal{Q}'}(\mathcal{Y}') = w_{\mathcal{Q}}(\mathcal{Y})$.*

Proof. Let c be any piece between a and b on the line in the partition generated by the intervals in $\mathcal{Q}$. Intervals in $\mathscr{R}_{\mathcal{Q}}(c) - \mathscr{R}_{\mathcal{Q}}(a) = \mathscr{R}_{\mathcal{Q}}(c) - \mathscr{R}_{\mathcal{Q}}(b)$ are entirely between a and b. We can produce a new set of interval questions $\mathcal{Q}_1$ by changing some of the intervals in $\mathcal{Q}$ as follows: For all c in between a and b we move the intervals in $\mathscr{R}_{\mathcal{Q}}(c) - \mathscr{R}_{\mathcal{Q}}(a) = \mathscr{R}_{\mathcal{Q}}(c) - \mathscr{R}_{\mathcal{Q}}(b)$ towards b. Then, b shrinks to zero whereas a is finally extended by the length of b. Let us denote by a' this elongated version of a in the partition generated by $\mathcal{Q}_1$. Note that $\mathcal{Q}_1$ does not contain the piece b.

We now note that every YES-set Y_1 for $\mathcal{Q}_1$ is obviously also a YES-set for $\mathcal{Q}$. Moreover since $\mathscr{R}_{\mathcal{Q}}(a) = \mathscr{R}_{\mathcal{Q}}(b)$ in $\mathcal{Q}$ the pieces b and a are weighted the same and in particular the same as the piece a' in $\mathcal{Q}_1$. Since a and b are not in the partition of $\mathcal{Q}_1$ but they are replaced by a' whose length equals the sum of the lengths of a and b we get $w_{\mathcal{Q}}(\mathcal{Y}) = w_{\mathcal{Q}_1}(\mathcal{Y})$.

If for each two pieces a' and b' cut by $\mathcal{Q}_1$ it holds that $\mathscr{R}_{\mathcal{Q}_1}(a') \neq \mathscr{R}_{\mathcal{Q}_1}(b')$, then setting $\mathcal{Q}' = \mathcal{Q}_1$ the proof is completed. Otherwise we can iteratively apply the same procedure to the newly generated set of interval questions, until the desired condition is fulfilled. Since at each new step the number of pieces gets smaller the procedure must terminate and will produce the desired $\mathcal{Q}'$ (see Fig. 7.6). $\blacksquare$

After these preliminaries we can prove the lower bound. Let $\mathcal{Q}$ be the set of questions asked in the first stage by a two-stage interval group testing algorithm. Let $q = |\mathcal{Q}|$. By Proposition 7.2 we can assume that for each two pieces π_1 and π_2 determined by $\mathcal{Q}$ it holds that $\mathscr{R}(\pi_1) \neq \mathscr{R}(\pi_2)$. We also have that the total number ℓ of pieces is at most $2q$, since the number of pieces covered by query intervals is at most $2q - 1$ (by a simple inductive argument), and by Proposition 7.2 at most one piece, π_o, is outside all query intervals ($\mathscr{R}(\pi_o) = \emptyset$).

Lemma 7.5.

$$N(n,1,2,1) \geq \sqrt{5n}.$$

Proof. With reference to the averaging argument and Lemma 7.4, we show that we can achieve on each piece a total weight not smaller than $r = 5/2$ with not more

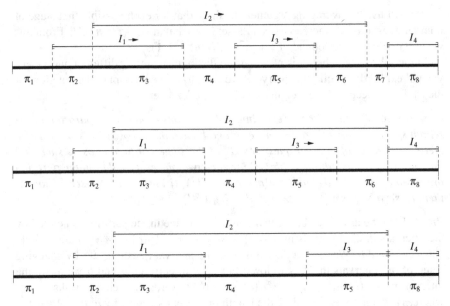

Fig. 7.6 An application of Proposition 7.2. Since in the *upper partition* we have $\mathscr{R}(\pi_1) = \mathscr{R}(\pi_7)$ we move rightward the intervals I_1, I_2, I_3 which are completely between π_1 and π_7. Note that the lengths of the pieces $\pi_2, \ldots, \pi_6$ and their $\mathscr{R}(\cdot)$ do not change. The *second* and *third pictures* show the case $\mathscr{R}(\pi_4) = \mathscr{R}(\pi_6)$ handled by sliding I_3 to the right

than $2q$ YES-*sets*, where q is the number of queries in the first stage. By Lemma 7.4, this implies that in the second stage at least $\frac{5n}{4q}$ queries have to be asked. Therefore, in total for both stages, the number of questions needed is at least

$$\min\left(q + \frac{5n}{4q}\right) = \sqrt{5n}.$$

In order to achieve $r = 2.5$, we create a *specific* YES-set for each piece which is created by the q queries in the first stage. Recall that there are at most $2q$ distinct pieces. This already guarantees weight $3/2$ on each piece.

Now let us consider two adjacent pieces, sharing boundary $(i, i + 1)$ of some query (or queries). One of the following three cases can apply according to whether $(i, i + 1)$ is the boundary of exactly one query, of exactly two queries, or of at least three queries.

Case 1. $(i, i + 1)$ is the boundary of exactly one query. This query is the only one separating the two adjacent pieces. The YES-set created as consistent for the piece containing i is also an inconsistent YES-set for the case where the positive is in the piece containing $i + 1$. Therefore, it gives weight $1/2$ to the piece containing $i + 1$, since there is the chance that the query having the boundary $(i, i + 1)$ was an error.

Therefore, by symmetry, each piece in a pair of neighbors separated by a single boundary automatically gets an extra weight $\frac{1}{2}$ from the specific YES-set created for its neighbour.

Case 2. $(i, i + 1)$ is the boundary of exactly two queries. Therefore, the YES-set created for one of them indicates precisely the piece containing the positive between the ones flanking the boundary $(i, i + 1)$. In such a case, we do not get the extra weight of $\frac{1}{2}$ for the neighbor. However, when such a case happens, there must be less than $2q$ pieces defined by the q queries of the first stage. This is so because there are two boundaries without a piece in between. Therefore, we can create an *unspecific* YES-set involving both pieces, separated by the double boundary. More precisely, the unspecific YES-set is the one that answers yes to all queries including both pieces and answers the two questions with boundaries $(i, i + 1)$ inconsistently, i.e., one indicating the piece containing i and one indicating the piece containing $i + 1$. This YES-set provides the desired extra weight $\frac{1}{2}$ to both the adjacent pieces containing i and $i + 1$, respectively.

Case 3. $(i, i + 1)$ is the boundary of more than two queries. Using the same argument as in the previous case, we can conclude that the number of pieces decreases by at least two. Then we may use two new specific YES-sets, one for each piece in the pair. Hence, each one of the pieces involved gets an extra weight of $\frac{3}{2}$ without the necessity of exceeding the total of $2q$ YES-sets.

In conclusion, by repeated application of the above cases, we are able to extend the multiset of YES-sets consistent with the single pieces in such a way that each piece gets at least extra weight $\frac{1}{2}$ from some additional unspecific YES-sets. As a result, all the pieces receive total weight at least 2.5 with a multiset of at most $2q$ YES-sets, as desired.

The lower bound in the previous lemma is almost matched by the following result.

Lemma 7.6.

$$N(n, 1, 2, 1) \leq \sqrt{5.5n}.$$

Proof. We show a two-stage algorithm that is able to find a positive in a set of n elements using at most $\sqrt{5.5n}$ queries. In the first stage we use q queries divided into two groups, A and B, as shown in Fig. 7.7. Let q_A and $0 < r < 1$ be two parameters such that $(q_A - 1)(1 + r) + 2 = q$ and whose value will be defined by the analysis. The two groups of questions are defined as follows.

Group A consists of q_A queries which split the search space into $2(q_A - 1)$ pieces of the same size, which we denote by $\pi_1, \ldots, \pi_{2q_A - 2}$. In particular, the queries in this group are $\pi_1 \cup \pi_2$, $\pi_{2q_A - 2}$ and $\pi_{2i} \cup \pi_{2i+1} \cup \pi_{2i+2}$ for each $i = 1, \ldots, q_A - 2$. We will refer to the queries in this group as A-queries. Notice that as a result of the queries in this group, the search space is partitioned into pieces in such a way that pieces covered by one query alternate with pieces covered by two queries.

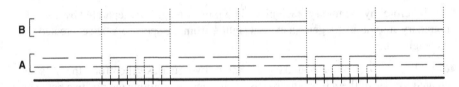

Fig. 7.7 Query multiset used in the first stage of a two-stage strategy. The *thicker line* represents the set of objects, whereas all the others represent the a- and b-queries. In this example we have $q_A = 25$ and $r = 1/8$

Group B consists of $r(q_A - 1) + 1$ queries distributed along the same alternating pattern as the queries in group A, but each of which covers $1/r$ of the pieces $\pi_1, \ldots, \pi_{2q_A-2}$, defined by the A-queries. Queries in this group will be also referred to as B-queries.

In the following, we use the term piece to refer to one of the $2q_A - 2$ intervals in which the search space is divided by the A-queries. We will instead use the term macro-pieces to refer to the $2r(q_A - 1)$ parts into which the B-queries divide the search space. Notice that in total in the first stage we have $q = (1 + r)q_A + 1 - r$ many queries.

We shall split the analysis of the answers to the first stage of queries into several cases. In order to simplify the description we shall refer to an A-query (resp. B-query) which has been answered yes as an A-yes (resp. B-yes). Let us first observe that, because of the full coverage of the search space by both A-queries and B-queries, it follows that if there is a positive there should be at least one A-yes and at least one B-yes, unless an error has occurred.

Let a be an A-query. We shall refer to the piece covered by a and not covered by any other A-query, as a's *private piece*. Instead we shall refer to the remaining pieces of a as a's *shared pieces*.

Case 1. All queries in the first stage are answered no. Then the only possibility is that no positive is present. This is so, because every piece is covered by at least two queries, therefore, if a positive was present in some piece then at least two of the answers would be errors, which is not allowed.

Therefore, if no yes answer is provided, no more questions are necessary in the second stage.

Case 2. There are no A-yes but at least one B-yes. First we notice that all the B-yes' must intersect. In fact, if there were two disjoint B-yes, one of them must be an error and the other a correct answer. Since one B-yes is not an error, it means that there is a positive, hence there should be also a yes answer to some A-query. Since all A-query answered no, then also one of these answers is an error. Then, there would have been in total at least two errors, which is not allowed.

As a consequence, in such a situation, in the second stage it is enough to use the 0-fault tolerant strategy for one positive (see Theorem 7.5) in the interval covered by the intersecting B-yes. Such an interval has size $\frac{n}{2r(q_A-1)}$, and half of its pieces are covered by two A-queries and half of its pieces are covered by exactly one A-query. Only these latter pieces are possible candidates to contain the positive, because if a piece shared by two A-queries contained the positive, then both no answers to these A-queries would be errors which is not possible. This means that $(\frac{n}{4r(q_A-1)} + 1)/2$ additional queries are sufficient in the second stage.

Case 3. There is exactly one A-yes. Let a denote this A-query. Clearly, if there is a positive element, it can only belong to one of the pieces covered by a. For, otherwise, if the positive was in a piece covered by another A-query, call it b, and not by a, both the answer to b and to a would be errors, contradicting the assumption of at most one error. Moreover, if the positive is in one of a's shared pieces, then there was an error already.

Therefore, in the second stage, it is enough to use a 1-fault tolerant strategy in a's private piece and a 0-fault tolerant strategy in both a's shared pieces. By Theorem 7.5, it follows that this requires at most $\frac{5}{2}\frac{n}{2(q_A-1)}$ queries in the second stage.

Case 4. There are exactly two A-yes. Let a and b denote these A-queries. It is not hard to see that, if there is a positive, it can only be in the piece in the intersection of a and b (in case they intersect at all), or in one of the private pieces of a and b. In this latter case, it is also easy to see that there was an error. Notice that any other piece is either covered by only one of a and b, but also by some other A-query which answered no; or it is covered by neither a nor b. In both cases, the presence of a positive in such a piece would mean that there were two errors in the answers.

Therefore, in the second stage, it is enough to use a 1-fault tolerant strategy in the piece shared by a and b (if it exists) and a 0-fault tolerant strategy in the private pieces of a and b. Like in the previous case, by using Theorem 7.5, we have that also in this case we need at most $\frac{5}{2}\frac{n}{2(q_A-1)}$ queries in the second stage.

Case 5. There are exactly three A-yes'. Let a, b, c denote these A-queries. We first observe that in this case at least two of these A-queries must be non-intersecting, hence there must be at least one error in the answers.

Moreover, a positive element, if present, could only belong to a piece shared by two of these queries, for otherwise at least two of them would constitute an error.

It follows that it is enough to use a 0-fault tolerant strategy in each of the (at most two) pieces shared by two of the queries a, b, and c. Hence, in this case it is enough to ask $\frac{n}{2(q_A-1)}$ queries in the second stage.

The above cases cover all the possible situations since there cannot be more than three A-yes'. In fact, if this was the case, each piece covered by one of these queries would be not covered by at least two others. Hence, since the positive should belong to one of them, there would be, in any case, at least two errors in the answers, which is impossible by assumption.

Putting together the above cases, we have that the maximum number of queries asked in the two stages together is given by the following expression (where we are ignoring lower-order terms):

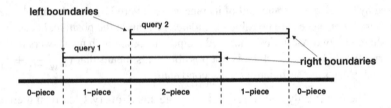

Fig. 7.8 A set of two interval queries which partition the search space into 0-, 1- and 2-pieces. The thicker line represents the search space

$$q_A(1 + r) + \max\left(\frac{5n}{4\,q_A}, \frac{n}{8\,r q_A} \right).$$

This is minimized when $r = 0.1$ and $q = \sqrt{50n/44}$, which yields a total number of $\sqrt{5.5n}$ queries. The proof is complete.

More Positives

For the analysis of the cases where more than one positive is present, it is useful to introduce some additional notation related to the structure of the pieces in which the search space is partitioned by the first stage of tests.

A boundary B of a piece π is said to be *turned to* the piece if there is a query Q such that $\pi \subset Q$ and B is also a boundary of Q. A piece is called a *2-piece* if both its boundaries are turned to it. A piece that has only one of its boundaries turned to it is called a *1-piece*. If none of the boundaries is turned to the piece, it is called a *0-piece*. Figure 7.8 illustrates the definitions given so far.

Recall the definition of the roof of a set of pieces. Consider two pieces π_i and π_j. If $\mathscr{R}(\pi_i) \subset \mathscr{R}(\pi_j)$ then the piece π_i is called a *satellite* of piece π_j. There are two simple facts about satellite pieces which will be useful.

Fact 7.7 *Every 1-piece is a satellite of some 2-piece. Every 0-piece b contained in some query interval is a satellite of two 2-pieces, namely the ones next to both sides of b. If a 0-piece d outside all query intervals exists, then d is a satellite of every 2-piece.*

Proof. Consider any 1-piece π. Clearly, π is contained in some query interval I. Suppose that π is not associated with any query interval at its right end, the other case is symmetric. Let π' be the next piece to the right of π, such that π' is associated with some query interval at its right end. Such a piece π' exists, since for instance I ends somewhere. By the choice of π', the left end of π' must be the left end of some query interval, too, hence π' is a 2-piece. Moreover, no query interval includes π but not π', in other words, $\mathscr{R}(b) \subset \mathscr{R}(a)$. This proves the assertion for 1-pieces. The argument for 0-pieces contained in query intervals is analogous. The last assertion is trivial, due to $\mathscr{R}(d) = \emptyset$.

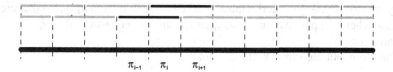

Fig. 7.9 Queries in the first stage of the algorithm used in the proof of Theorem 7.9.

In the following we use c_i to denote the number of i-pieces.

Fact 7.8 *Consider a stage in which q queries are asked. Let c_i be the number of i-pieces. Then, we have that $c_1 + 2c_2 \le 2q$, and in particular $c_2 \le q$. Furthermore, $c_2 \ge 1$.*

Proof. For the first statement, it is enough to observe that every i-piece is by definition associated with at least i query intervals, but each query interval is associated with at most two pieces. The second is a direct consequence of the first. For the third statement, simply observe that a 2-piece is, for example, the rightmost piece in the query interval with the leftmost right end.

Theorem 7.9.

$$N(n, 2, 2, 1) \le 4\sqrt{n} + 1.$$

Proof. Consider an algorithm where the first stage consists of q queries dividing the search space into $q - 1$ pieces of the same size $\frac{n}{q-1}$. The set of queries in the first stage is:

$$\mathcal{Q} = \{\pi_1, \pi_1 \cup \pi_2, \pi_2 \cup \pi_3, \ldots, \pi_{q-2} \cup \pi_{q-1}, \pi_{q-1}\}.$$

Notice that each piece in this stage is covered by two queries (Fig. 7.9).

We can analyze the different possible answering strategies like in the proof of Lemma 7.6. It is not hard to realize that the worst scenario is when two yes answers are received to two overlapping queries. In order to compute the total number of queries necessary in such a case, let $a = \pi_{i-1} \cup \pi_i$ and $b = \pi_i \cup \pi_{i+1}$ be the queries which are answered yes.

It is possible that the two positives are both in the piece π_i and in this case no error was present in the answers. Therefore, by Theorem 7.6, at least $\frac{3n}{q-1}$ queries should be asked to search for the positives in π_i in the second stage.

Alternatively, the answers are consistent with the case where the positives are one in π_i and one in π_{i+1} and the no answered to the question $\pi_{i+1} \cup \pi_{i+2}$ was an error. Therefore, at least $\frac{n}{2(q-1)}$ additional queries are to be asked for searching for the possible positive in π_{i+1}. This is because, in this case, an error has already occurred and we can use a 0-error tolerant strategy for one positive as by Theorem 7.5.

Symmetrically, $\frac{n}{2(q-1)}$ queries must be asked for searching in π_{i-1}, to take care of the case where the positives are in π_{i-1} and π_i and the no answered to $\pi_{i-2} \cup \pi_{i-1}$ was an error.

Therefore, our algorithm will use in total

$$\min_q \left(q + \frac{4n}{q-1} \right) = 4\sqrt{n} + 1.$$

This completes the proof of the upper bound.

The above upper bound can also be extended to the case of more positives. We have the following result regarding the case of at least three positives.

Theorem 7.10. *For $p \geq 3$,*

$$N(n, p, 2, 1) \leq 2\sqrt{6(p-2)n} + 1.$$

Proof. Like in the previous theorem we consider the strategy that in the first stage asks the set of q queries given by

$$\mathscr{Q} = \{\pi_1, \pi_1 \cup \pi_2, \pi_2 \cup \pi_3, \dots, \pi_{q-2} \cup \pi_{q-1}, \pi_{q-1}\},$$

as shown in Fig. 7.9.

It is not hard to see that the worst case for such a first stage is when the adversary chooses $p - 2$ disjoint pairs of consecutive questions and answers yes only to these queries.

Let $(\pi_{i-1} \cup \pi_i, \pi_i \cup \pi_{i+1})$ be one such pair. Again, it is possible that π_i contains two positives even if there were no errors in the first stage. However, it is also possible that π_{i-1} (resp. π_{i+1}) contains two positives, if in the first stage there was one error. Therefore, in the second stage we need to use $\frac{3n}{q-1}$ queries in π_i, like in the proof of the previous theorem. However, now we also have to ask $\frac{3n}{(2q-1)}$ queries in each one of the pieces π_{i-1} and π_{i+1}, since we must take into account the case that any such pieces contain two positives and there was an error in the first stage.

Therefore, each pair of positive answers induces a total of $\frac{6n}{q-1}$ queries in the second stage.

In total, we need at least $\frac{6n(p-2)}{q-1}$ queries in the second stage. Optimizing with respect to q, the total number of queries in the two stages is

$$\min_q \left(q + \frac{6n(p-2)}{q-1} \right) = 2\sqrt{6n(p-2)} + 1,$$

providing the upper bound.

Before giving a lower bound for the number of queries needed to successfully find at most two positives while tolerating at most one error, we define three types of YES-sets:

Type 0: Choose p pieces $\pi_1, \dots, \pi_p$ and define the YES-set as $\cup_{i=1}^{p} \mathscr{R}(\pi_i)$. In this case, since each piece can contain one positive, each piece gets weight $\frac{3}{2}$.

Type 1: Choose $p-1$ pieces $\pi_1, \dots, \pi_{p-1}$ and define the YES-set as $\cup_{i=1}^{p-1} \mathscr{R}(\pi_i)$. Notice that in this case, since we have $p-1$ base pieces, each can contain two positives, and therefore gets weight 3. Moreover, for each 2-piece each corresponding satellite piece gets also a weight of $\frac{3}{2}$.

Type 2: Choose $p-2$ pieces $\pi_1, \dots, \pi_{p-2}$ and define the YES-set as $\cup_{i=1}^{p-2} \mathscr{R}(\pi_i)$. Notice that in this case both the base pieces and the satellites get a weight of 3.

Lemma 7.7.

$$N(n, 2, 2, 1) \geq 2\sqrt{3n}.$$

Proof. Let q be the number of queries asked in the first stage by a two-stage interval group testing algorithm for finding up to two positives. We will show that it is always possible to get weight at least 3 in each piece using at most q YES-sets. We start with a simple case where there is only one 2-piece. In this case we build two YES-sets of type 1, both having the 2-piece as base piece. Notice that this already gives weight 3 to this 2-piece. Since all other pieces are satellites of this 2-piece, all of them also get automatically a weight of 3, and we are done.

When there is more than one 2-piece, we create for each 2-piece a YES-set of type 1. As each 0-piece is a satellite of at least two 2-pieces, it also gets a weight of at least 3. The 1-pieces get at least weight $\frac{3}{2}$, since each of them is a satellite of a 2-piece. The extra $\frac{3}{2}$ weight for each 1-piece is obtained by creating some additional type 0 YES-sets. For this, we partition the 1-pieces in pairs, and create one YES-set of type 0 for each pair, using the 1-pieces as base pieces.

Using $c_1 + 2c_2 \leq 2q$, where c_i is the number of i pieces (see Fact 7.8), we have that $\frac{c_1}{2} + c_2 \leq q$ if c_1 is even, and $\frac{(c_1-1)}{2} + c_2 \leq t_1 - 1$ if c_1 is odd. In both cases, the number of YES-sets is not greater than q. Therefore, by Lemma 7.4, we need at least $\frac{3n}{q}$ queries in the second stage, which gives a lower bound of

$$\min_{q} \left(q + \frac{3n}{q} \right) = 2\sqrt{3n}.$$

The following easy lemma will be used in the lower bound for the case $p \geq 3$.

Lemma 7.8. *Let x, y be positive integers with $x \geq 2y$ and x even. In x cells arranged in a cycle, we can place pebbles from x sets, each with y pebbles, so that every cell gets y pebbles and every pair of neighboring cells get pebbles from $2y$ distinct sets. If $x > 2y$ is odd, at most $x + 1$ sets are needed to achieve the same.*

Proof. Let us first consider the case where x is even and $x \geq 2y$. For $i = 1, \dots, x$, let C_i denote the ith cell and B_i denote the ith set of y pebbles.

We start with the set B_1, and place its y pebbles in every other cell, i.e., $C_1, C_3, \ldots, C_{2y-1}$. Since $x \geq 2y$, no neighboring cells receive pebbles from this set—in particular we do not complete the circle. We proceed similarly with the set B_2 but we start one cell later, i.e., with C_2, so that the gaps are filled. Thus, a consecutive set of cells, namely $C_1, \ldots, C_{2y}$ has one pebble. It is obvious now that we can fill the cells with pebbles from further pairs of sets in the same way and achieve perfect balance. Since every pair of neighboring cells got $2y$ pebbles and no two from the same set, the requirements are fulfilled.

If x is odd, we proceed as above, but using $x - 1$ sets of pebbles. At the end of this procedure, there will be a consecutive block of y cells which has got only $y - 1$ pebbles. We can now add the missing pebble to each of these cells using two further sets, again without putting pebbles from one set in neighboring cells.

Theorem 7.11. *For $p \geq 3$,*

$$N(n, p, 2, 1) \geq 2\sqrt{3n(p-1)} + O(p),$$

provided that the number of queries in the first stage is at least $2\frac{(p-1)^2}{p-2}$.

Proof. Let q be the number of queries asked in the first stage. Again, we rely on the averaging argument and Lemma 7.4. We show that it is possible to achieve weight at least $3(p-1)$ with no more than $q + \frac{p}{2} + 1$ YES-sets. For doing that, we analyze three different cases:

Case 1. $c_2 \leq p - 2$. We create q YES-sets of type 2, with all the c_2 2-pieces as base pieces. Since all 1-pieces are satellites of some 2-piece, the YES-sets give a weight at least $3q$ to all the pieces. Since, by assumption, $q = \omega(p)$, as desired we have guaranteed weight at least $3(p-1)$ to each piece with no more than $q + \frac{p}{2} + 1$ YES-sets.

Case 2. $c_2 \geq p - 1$ and $q(p-2) \geq c_2(p-1)$. We create q YES-sets of type 2, using $(p-2)$ many 2-pieces as base pieces for them. This is done in such a way that every 2-piece appears at least $p - 1$ times, using the inequality $q(p-2) \geq c_2(p-1)$. A simple construction is obtained by putting the c_2 many 2-pieces in a circle and constructing each q YES-set by going along the circle and picking up $(p-2)$ consecutive 2-pieces. The inequality says that we need to scan the whole circle at least $p - 1$ times, i.e., each 2-piece appears in at least $p - 1$ YES-sets. As a result, the desired weight is reached.

Case 3. $c_2 \geq p - 1$ and $q(p-2) < c_2(p-1)$. We create at most $c_2 + 1$ type 1 YES-sets with $p - 1$ many 2-pieces as base pieces in such a way that each 2-piece appears exactly $p - 1$ times. By using the previous lemma, since under the standing hypothesis we have $c_2 > 2(p-1)$, we can guarantee that each pair of consecutive 2-pieces (in their natural order on the line closed to a circle) appear in $p - 1$ YES-sets.

We have that with at most $c_2 + 1$ YES-sets we provide weight $3(p-1)$ for each 2-piece.

Let us now focus on the 0-pieces. Consider the cyclic ordering of the 2-pieces, which consists of their natural order on the line closed to a cycle. Each 0-piece inside some interval query is also between two (consecutive) 2-pieces and is a satellite of both of them. Moreover, without loss of generality, we can assume that if there is a 0-piece outside all query intervals, it lies between the first and the last 2-piece in the cyclic order, and it is a satellite of them.

As a result, since each 0-piece gets weight $\frac{3}{2}$ from each 2-piece in the pair surrounding it, we have that with the at most $c_2 + 1$ YES-sets defined so far, we also ensure weight at least $3(p-1)$ in every 0-piece. Moreover, the 1-pieces already have a weight of at least $\frac{3}{2}(p-1)$, since each one of them is a satellite of some 2-piece. It remains to show how to provide an additional weight of $3(p-1)/2$ for each 1-piece.

We consider two sub-cases according to whether $c_1 \geq p - 1$.

If $c_1 \geq p - 1$, we create $\frac{c_1}{2}$ YES-sets of type 1, each of them with $p - 1$ many 1-pieces as base pieces. Notice that this can be done in such a way that every piece appears at least $\frac{p-1}{2}$ times. Therefore, each 1-piece get the desired $3(p-1)/2$ weight and the total number of YES-sets in this case is $\frac{c_1}{2} + c_2 + 1 \leq q + 1$ YES-sets.

Alternatively, if $c_1 < p - 1$ we can build $\frac{p-1}{2}$ YES-sets of type 2, each with all 1-pieces as base pieces. Since $c_2 \leq q$, we have that the total number of YES-sets used, in this case, is upper bounded by $q + \frac{p}{2} + 1$.

Putting together all the above cases, we conclude that we can reach weight $3(p-1)$ on each piece using at most $q + \frac{p}{2} + 1$ YES-sets. Therefore, the minimum number of queries needed in the worst case is

$$\min_q \left(q + \frac{3(p-1)}{q + \frac{p}{2} + 1} n \right) = 2\sqrt{3n(p-1)} + O(p).$$

More Errors

The analytical tools shown so far for the case where at most one error can occur can be also employed for obtaining more general bounds on the size of two-stage fault-tolerant interval group testing strategies. We shall limit ourselves to provide some such results by only sketching the idea of the proofs, referring to the analogous result in the previous section. The complete proofs are left as an exercise to the reader.

Table 7.1 summarizes the lower and upper bounds on fault-tolerant interval group testing, which we presented here. The rightmost column shows the ratios between the lower and upper bound given here. This ratio also provides an estimate on the approximation that the known algorithm can offer. Exercise 6 provides hints on how to try and shrink such gaps.

Theorem 7.12.

$$N(n, 2, 2, e) \geq 2\sqrt{(2e+1)n}.$$

Table 7.1 Upper and lower bounds for instances of the interval group testing problem

Parameters	Lower Bound	Upper Bound	Upper Bound / Lower Bound
$p = 1, \ s = 1, \ e \geq 1$	$\left\lceil \frac{(2e+1)(n+1)}{2} \right\rceil$	$\left\lceil \frac{(2e+1)(n+1)}{2} \right\rceil$	1
$p \geq 2, \ s = 1, \ e \geq 1$	$(2e+1)n$	$(2e+1)n$	1
$p = 1, \ s = 2, \ e = 1$	$\sqrt{5n}$	$\sqrt{5.5n}$	$\sqrt{1.1}$
$p = 2, \ s = 2, \ e = 1$	$2\sqrt{3n}$	$4\sqrt{n}$	$\sqrt{\frac{4}{3}}$
$p \geq 3, \ s = 2, \ e = 1$	$2\sqrt{3(p-1)n}$	$2\sqrt{6(p-2)n}+1$	$\sqrt{2\frac{p-2}{p-1}}$
$p = 2, \ s = 2, \ e \geq 1$	$2\sqrt{(2e+1)n}$	$2\sqrt{(e+1)(2e+1)n}$	$\sqrt{e+1}$
$p \geq 3, \ s = 2, \ e \geq 1$	$2\sqrt{(2e+1)(p-1)n}$	$2\sqrt{(e+1)(2e+1)(p-1)n}$	$\sqrt{e+1}$

The instances are presented on the leftmost column, while the ratio upper/lower bound for each instance is presented in the rightmost columns

Proof. The analysis of YES-sets made in Theorem 7.7 can be repeated. Here pieces containing a single positive get weight at least $\frac{2e+1}{2}$ in the corresponding YES-set, while pieces containing more than one positive get weight at least $2e + 1$. As a result, we can achieve weight at least $2e + 1$ in each piece with at most q YES-sets, giving a lower bound of

$$\min_q \left(q + \frac{(2e+1)}{q}n \right) = 2\sqrt{(2e+1)n}.$$

Theorem 7.13. *For $p \geq 3$,*

$$N(n, p, 2, e) \geq 2\sqrt{(2e+1)(p-1)n} + O(p),$$

provided that the number of queries in the first stage is at least $2\frac{(p-1)^2}{p-2}$.

Proof. We can employ the same reasoning as in the corresponding 1-error version (Theorem 7.10). Let q be the number of queries in the first stage of the algorithm. We can then show that at least weight $(2e+1)(p-1)$ for each piece can be obtained using no more than $q + \frac{p}{2} + 1$ YES-sets. Therefore the minimum number of queries needed in the worst case is

$$\min_q \left(q + \frac{(2e+1)(p-1)}{q + \frac{p}{2} + 1}n \right) = 2\sqrt{(2e+1)(p-1)n} + O(p).$$

Theorem 7.14. *For $p \geq 2$,*

$$N(n, p, 2, e) \leq 2\sqrt{(2e+1)(e+1)(p-1)n}.$$

Proof. For this upper bound, we partition the search space into q pieces and create for each of them $(e + 1)$ queries covering only the corresponding piece. This means that we ask $q(e + 1)$ queries in the first stage. Notice that with these questions every error can be easily identified in the first stage. Therefore, it is not hard to show that the worst case occurs when all queries covering $(p - 1)$ pieces answer Yes. In this case, each one of these $p - 1$ positive pieces has to be analyzed in the second stage with an e-error tolerant strategy. Since each piece has size $\frac{n}{q}$, the total of queries is given by:

$$\min_q \left(q(e + 1) + (p - 1)(2e + 1)\frac{n}{q} \right) = 2\sqrt{(e + 1)(2e + 1)(p - 1)n}.$$

7.3 Some Typical Applications of Group Testing in Computational Biology

In a genome research project, even simple tasks, like comparing two genomes, may involve thousands of tests. Therefore, it is not surprising that group testing approaches are used for improving the efficiency of tasks like DNA library screening, physical mapping, gene detection, assembly finishing, and many others. In biology, typically, non-adaptive group testing procedures are preferred. The groups are in most cases called *pools* and the model is referred to as *pooling design*.

Library Screening. Libraries are sets of clones, which are copies of parts of a DNA molecule. Very small chemically modified DNA molecules called *probes* may bind to clones, helping biologists to identify them. Library screening concerns the problem of verifying which clones in a library hybridize with at least one probe in a given set. For this purpose, one can model the problem as pooling clones so that it is possible to identify up to p positives using the minimum number of tests in a non-adaptive approach. A positive in this case is a clone (or pool) which hybridizes with a probe. Probes are small DNA molecules which are chemically labeled, so that biologists can easily test for their presence.

Protein–Protein Interaction. Because many functions in organisms are controlled through complex networks of interactions between different kinds of proteins, an efficient way of identifying pairs of interacting proteins is of great interest to biologists. A group testing approach using complete bipartite graphs for testing protein–protein interaction is as follows.

Let $K_{A,B}$ be a complete bipartite graph where each vertex represents a protein, and each edge an interaction. The proteins on partition A are called *baits*, and the ones on partition B are called *preys*. An edge is called positive if the two proteins it connects interact; otherwise, it is called negative. Let $C \subseteq A$ and $D \subseteq B$. We say that the test (C, D) is positive if there is a positive edge (c, d), with $c \in C$ and $d \in D$.

Finding the Borders of Assembly Gaps. A genome can be seen as a set of *chromosomes*, which are very long strings from the small alphabet $\Sigma = \{A, C, G, T\}$. Due to technological limitations, biologists have access only to small substrings of the chromosomes, and need to put these small pieces together in order to obtain the whole genome. When the amount of sequence data obtained in a genome sequencing project is not sufficient to uncover the whole genome sequence, the result is a set of large strings corresponding to the uncovered parts of the chromosomes. Therefore, after a series of sequencing experiments, the chromosomes may be divided into two kinds of substrings: the parts uncovered by the sequencing data, called *contigs*, and the parts for which no sequence information is available, called *gaps*. By definition, contigs and gaps alternate in the chromosomes: contigs are flanked by at most two gaps, which are flanked by at most two contigs.

If a gap is small enough, the extremities of its flanking contigs can be used as starting points for a reaction called *polymerase chain reaction*, or simply PCR, which uses the original DNA molecule of the chromosomes to create many copies of the gap. These copies can be used to obtain the missing gap sequence, which is called *closing the gap*.

The problem is that, since we do not know the strings corresponding to the chromosomes, we cannot tell which pair of contigs flanks a gap. If we try to perform a PCR using the extremities of a wrong pair of contigs, we will never get a gap sequence. A partially known genome with c contigs has $2c$ extremities. Doing a PCR for each of the $\binom{2c}{2} - c$ possible pairs of contig extremities is infeasible. Fortunately, when doing a PCR using many contig extremities, we get some result only if at least two of the extremities flank a gap. This variant, where many extremities are used together in a single PCR, is called *multiplex PCR*, and this is everything we need for a group testing approach.

Let G be a complete graph where the vertices are contig extremities. The edges corresponding to the pairs of gap flanking sequences form a hidden matching in G. Each unsuccessful PCR using many extremities reveals a set of vertices that contain no edges from the matching, whereas successful PCRs give hints about the location of the matching edges. By grouping the primers carefully it is then possible to identify the correct pairs with significantly less testing than in the exhaustive procedure.

Testing with Inhibitors. In real applications, samples can be damaged or contaminated, and force the tests including them to always produce a negative result, even in the presence of positives. Samples that influence test outcomes are called *inhibitors* here. In 1997, Farach et al. [104] introduced a variant of the group testing model where the search space contains three kinds of objects: positives, negatives, and inhibitors. They introduced a new parameter r, which represents an upper bound for the number of inhibitors in the search space; and devised a randomized algorithm able to identify the positives with $O((r+p) \log n)$ queries on average, assuming that $r + p \ll n$. De Bonis and Vaccaro [85] were able to devise an adaptive deterministic algorithm using $O((r^2 + p) \log n)$ queries. This algorithm could be extended to a three-stage algorithm that uses $O((r^2 + p^2) \log n)$ tests.

De Bonis [86] considers both the model variant where p is the exact number of positives and the variant where this parameter is an upper bound for the amount of positives. She showed that any algorithm with any number of stages that finds up to p positives in the presence of at most r inhibitors is lower bounded by the length of a superimposed code of size n, which is $\Omega(\frac{r^2}{p \log r} \log n)$.

Interval Group Testing for Identifying Exon–Intron Boundaries. An important motivation for the study of interval group testing comes from its application to the problem of determining exon–intron boundaries within a gene. In a very simplified model, a gene is a collection of disjoint substrings within a long string representing the DNA molecule. These substrings, called *exons*, are separated by substrings called *introns*. The boundary point between an exon and an intron is called a *splice site*, because introns are spliced out between transcription and translation. Determining the splice sites is an important task, e.g., when searching for mutations associated with a gene responsible for a disease.

An experimental protocol for determining exons boundaries can be designed using group testing. This consists of selecting two positions in the cDNA, a copy of the original genomic DNA from which introns have been spliced out, and determining whether they are apart the same distance as they were in the original genomic DNA string. If these distances do not coincide then at least one intron (and hence a splice site) must be present in the genomic DNA between the two selected positions. Non-adaptive strategies are desirable in this context in order to avoid long waiting periods necessary to prepare each experiment. However, as shown in the previous sections, a totally non-adaptive algorithm needs unreasonably many queries. Thus, the necessity arises to trade more stages for fewer queries, while still keeping the number of stages small.

7.4 Bibliographic Notes

The exact place of birth of group testing was the Price Administration of the US Government, Research Division, Price Statistics Branch. Robert Dorfman published the first report on the subject; and David Rosenblatt, who worked in the same research group, claims to have suggested the method's basic principle. A brief history of group testing, including briefs of Dorfman and Rosenblatt explaining their viewpoints about the origin of the approach, can be found in [94]. By any means, what called the attention of the research group to the subject was the number of identical clinical tests performed in order to identify a few cases of syphilis among US troops.

The lower bound on the size of non-adaptive group testing strategies was given by Dyachckov and Rykov in [100]. An alternative and purely combinatorial proof was given by Ruszinkó in [188]. Explicit construction of group testing strategies with $O(p^2 \log n/p)$ queries have been provided by Porat and Rothschild in [177] and by Indyk et al. in [127], where the construction also allows fast decoding.

Selectors were introduced in [87] by De Bonis et al. and used to provide two-stage group testing strategy achieving the information-theoretic lower bound. Improved constructions of two-stage group testing procedures are by Cheng and Du [44] and Cicalese and Vaccaro in [75]. In the latter the authors introduced superselectors and show how to use them to subsume many analogous combinatorial structures used in group testing and related areas.

Group testing variants where one is interested in identifying some approximate version of the set of positives P, here referred to as approximate group testing, was considered by Cheraghchi [47], in the context of error-resilient group testing, by Gilbert et al. [112], in the context of sparse signal recovery, and by Alon and Hod [10], in the context of monotone encoding. Cheraghchi [47] provided the lower bound in Theorem 7.2. In the same paper, the author considers the case when some tests might be erroneous and only focuses on the case of zero false negatives. Alon and Hod [10] consider the case of zero false positives and obtain $O(p \log(n/p))$ tests procedures, which are in fact optimal for this case. Gilbert et al. [112] allow both false positives and false negatives but their procedures use $O(p \log^2 n)$ tests.

In [212], interval group testing is proposed for a new experimental protocol that searches for the exon boundaries. The advantages of this group testing-based splice site detection approach over sequence-based methods using, for example, Hidden Markov Models, are that the former method works without expensive sequencing of genomic DNA and it gives the results directly from experiments, without relying on inference rules. The work [212] and the book [173] report on the experimental evaluation on real data, of the algorithm ExonPCR, which finds exon–intron boundaries within a gene. The authors of [212] only give a simple asymptotic analysis of their $\Theta(\log n)$-stage algorithm. They leave open the question about whether there exist algorithms able to cope with the technical limitations of the experiments, and particularly with errors. In [64] the first rigorous algorithmic study of the problem was presented, and for the case $s \leq 2$ a precise evaluation of $N(n, p, s)$ was given. In [62] a sharper asymptotic estimation of $N(n, p, s)$ is found, which is optimal up to the constant of the main term in the case of large s. The necessity of dealing with errors in the tests had been already stated in the seminal papers [173,212] and reaffirmed in the subsequent ones. The first non-trivial results on this variant of the problem appeared in [63].

Besides the splice site detection problem, group testing with interval tests also arises in a variety of domains, e.g., detecting holes in a gas pipe [79, 94], finding faulty links in an electrical or communication network, and data gathering in sensor networks [123–125].

7.5 Exercises

1. Design an adaptive group testing procedure for identifying up to p positives in a search space of cardinality n using at most $p \log \frac{n}{p} + 2p + 1$ tests.
2. Let A be a binary $n \times m$ matrix with g and w being non-negative integers such that:

   (i) each column of A contains at least w ones;
   (ii) for every pair of columns there are at most g rows where both columns have a one.

   Show that for any $d \leq \frac{w-1}{g}$ the matrix A is a $(d+1, d+1, n)$-selector.

3. Show that there exists no adaptive group testing strategy of size 7 for identifying up to two positives in a search space of cardinality 8 when up to one answer can be answered mendaciously.

4. Show that if there exists a $(d + 1, d + 1, n)$-selector of size m then there exists a non-adaptive group testing strategy of size m to identify up to d defectives in a search space of cardinality n.

5. Show that any (p, k, n)-selector is a $(p - 1, k - 1, n)$-selector.

6. Consider the two-stage interval group testing with $p = 3$ positives and at most one error. Show that for this particular case it holds that $N(n, 3, 2, 1) = 2\sqrt{6n} + O(1)$.

7. One possibility to improve the lower bound in Lemma 7.5 is to consider an additional empty YES-set. Analyze which are the pieces whose weights get increased by the presence of such an additional YES-set.

8. Provide a sufficient condition analogous to the one in Exercise 2 under which a binary matrix is a (p, k, n)-selector.

Chapter 8
Resilient Search

A truth that's told with bad intent
Beats all the lies you can invent

W. Blake, Auguries of Innocence

In this chapter we analyze a model of fault-tolerant search in which reiterating a question cannot help the search algorithm because the errors are due to permanent memory faults. A *memory fault* occurs if the correct value stored in a memory location changes because of some failure. The change can occur at any moment in a dynamic and unpredictable fashion. More failures can also occur simultaneously. Clearly, if a memory fault affects the result of a query, after this fault has occurred any instance of the query will produce the same faulty result. This is in sharp contrast with the situation in the *liar* model considered in other parts of this book, since in that case errors are assumed to be the result of transient faults, due to, e.g., ALU failures or transmission noise.

Informally, one says that an algorithm is *resilient to memory faults* if, despite the fact that errors may affect the values stored in some memory locations before and during its execution, the algorithm will provide the correct output with respect to the set of uncorrupted values.

8.1 The Definition of the Problem and a Lower Bound

An instance of the problem is given by (1) a list $X = x_1, \ldots, x_n$ of n keys (initially) sorted in increasing order, i.e., $x_i < x_j$ for each $i < j$; (2) a key x.

A *resilient searching algorithm* is asked to answer whether there exists an index i^* such that $x_{i^*} = x$, and in the positive case to report such an index.

F. Cicalese, *Fault-Tolerant Search Algorithms*, Monographs in Theoretical
Computer Science. An EATCS Series, DOI 10.1007/978-3-642-17327-1_8,
© Springer-Verlag Berlin Heidelberg 2013

The operations allowed to the algorithm are comparisons of two types: (a) comparisons among elements in the list, i.e., "$x_i \leq x_j$?"; (b) comparisons among the key x and an element of the list, i.e., "$x \leq x_i$?", for any i, j.

The first type of comparison might appear strange, since we said that the list is sorted in increasing order. In fact, we assume that during the execution of the algorithm up to δ memory faults can occur which might change the value of some keys, thereby affecting the initial sorted order. Thus, questions of type (a) might be useful for the algorithm to check whether in certain positions the list has been altered by faults.

We require that the algorithm works as follows:

1. if there is some correct key equal to x, then the algorithm reports that the key we are searching for is in the list and answers with an index i such that $x_i = x$ (this might also be an occurrence of x due to some memory fault);
2. if there is no key (correct or faulty) equal to x, then the algorithm reports the absence of x;
3. if the only occurrences of x are due to memory faults, then the algorithm may or may not report the index of one of these faulty occurrences.

We assume that a resilient algorithm may count on $O(1)$ fully reliable memory locations, i.e., those cannot be affected by corruptions. It has to be remarked that this is a minimal necessary assumption. In fact, in the absence of some reliable memory, no resilient computation can be possible.

We are now going to present a simple lower bound on the number of comparisons of any resilient search algorithm. A way to read this theorem is that any resilient search algorithm which is asymptotically optimal in a non-faulty environment cannot tolerate more than $O(\log n)$ memory faults.

Theorem 8.1. *Every comparison-based resilient searching algorithm which tolerates up to δ memory faults performs at least $\Omega(\log n + \delta)$ comparisons on a sequence of length $n \geq \delta$.*

Proof. Any algorithm, even in the absence of any memory fault, needs at least $\log n$ comparisons. Therefore, it is enough to prove that any algorithm requires $\Omega(\delta)$ comparisons when $\delta = \omega(\log n)$.

Assume that an algorithm $\mathbb{A}$ makes only $N < \delta/2$ comparisons.

Let Q be the set of elements mentioned at least once in the comparisons performed by the algorithm $\mathbb{A}$.

Suppose that each comparison of the type $x_i \leq x_j$ is answered yes if and only if $i \leq j$ and each comparison of the type $x \leq x_i$ is answered yes.

Let $Y = X \setminus Q$ be the set of elements in the sequence X which are not mentioned in any comparison performed by $\mathbb{A}$. Since each comparison involves at most two elements of X and there are fewer than $\delta/2$ comparisons, clearly $Y \neq \emptyset$.

It follows that the algorithm $\mathbb{A}$ does not have enough information to discriminate between the following two possible solutions, which are both compatible with the result of the comparisons and the parameters of the problem:

1. the item x is smaller than any element in X and in particular it is not in the list X;
2. the item x is in the list X, and it is one of the elements in Y. In particular, if Y only contains elements bigger than any element in Q, then all the elements in Q have been affected by faults and were originally smaller than x.

8.2 Randomized Resilient Search

We first present a randomized algorithm, RANDSEARCH, which performs resilient search over a list of n elements in expected time $O(\log n + \delta)$, i.e., it can tolerate up to $O(\log n)$ faults while still being able to complete the search in $O(\log n)$ time. In particular, RANDSEARCH attains the lower bound of Theorem 8.1.

```
Algorithm RANDSEARCH(I[1...n], ℓ, r, c, C, δ)
    If r − ℓ > Cδ
        Choose h uniformly at random in {ℓ + (r − ℓ)(1 − c)/2, ..., ℓ + (r − ℓ)(1 + c)/2}
        If I[h] = x then return h
        else if I[h] < x then RANDSEARCH(I[1...n], ℓ, h − 1, c, C, δ)
            else RANDSEARCH(I[1...n], h + 1, r, c, C, δ)
    else
        For i = ℓ − 2δ, ... r + 2δ
            If I[i] = x then return i
            If i ≤ ℓ and I[i] < x then ℓ-witness + = 1
            If i ≥ r and I[i] > x then r-witness + = 1
        End For

        If ℓ-witness > δ and r-witness > δ then return NO
        Else RANDSEARCH(I[1...n], 1, n, c, C, δ)
```

RANDSEARCH uses two (constant) parameters $0 < c < 1$ and $C > 1$ such that $c \times C > 1$. Informally, the algorithm performs a sort of binary search using as the splitting element one chosen at random from the central subsequence of $I[\ell \ldots r]$ of length $(r - \ell)c$. This way the search is restricted to smaller and smaller sub-lists. This process continues as long as the size of such sub-list $I[\ell \ldots r]$ is "big" compared to the number of possible faults. Here, big means larger than $C \times \delta$ for the given parameter C.

As soon as the sub-list becomes "small", i.e., not larger than $C \times \delta$, the algorithm uses exhaustive search to check whether it contains the key searched for. If such an exhaustive search succeeds then the position in the sub-list where the key is found is returned. On the other hand, while performing exhaustive search the algorithm also checks for witnesses flanking the sub-list. This means that 2δ elements are compared to the given key on both the left and the right of the sub-list to be searched exhaustively. If at least $\delta + 1$ elements are found which are smaller than x in

$I[\ell - 2\delta, \ldots, \ell]$ it means that if x was in the original list, it would be in a position $h \geq \ell$, since at most δ of the witnesses can be faulty. Analogously, if at least $\delta + 1$ elements are found which are bigger than x in $I[r, \ldots, r + 2\delta]$ it means that if x was in the original list, it would be in a position $h \leq r$, since at most δ of the witnesses can be faulty. Therefore, if both cases occur and x is not found in $I[\ell, \ldots, r]$, it means that x was not originally in I.

The following result completes the above argument about the correctness of RANDSEARCH and proves that it achieves the bound of Theorem 8.1

Theorem 8.2. *The algorithm* RANDSEARCH *correctly searches a list of size n in the presence of up to δ memory faults; the expected number of comparisons it performs is $O(\log n + \delta)$.*

Proof. As regards the correctness of the algorithm, it is obvious that whenever RANDSEARCH reports the presence of the key x in I, it does it correctly. Alternatively, the observation preceding the statement of the theorem also shows that RANDSEARCH only reports the absence of the key x if such a key was not in the original list (before any fault occurred). In fact, the algorithm reports NO only when there are enough reliable witnesses to identify the segment of the list $I[\ell + 1 \ldots r - 1]$ in which x could lie—this is the effect of having more than δ tests indicating that x cannot be in $I[1 \ldots \ell]$ and more than δ tests indicating that x cannot be in $I[r \ldots n]$—and after exhaustively checking that x is not in $I[\ell + 1 \ldots r - 1]$. Note that it might be that there is a faulty x somewhere else in the list; nonetheless, the output of the algorithm is correct with respect to the correct section of the input, in accordance with the requirements of the model.

We are now ready to prove the bound on the (expected) time complexity of RANDSEARCH. We need to analyze the number of times the algorithm executes a random choice. Also, we need to give a bound on the number of times the algorithm starts over from scratch.

We shall define an iteration of the algorithm as the set of operations between two consecutive times when the algorithm starts executing random choices over the initial list $I[1 \ldots n]$. We shall prove that the algorithm spends at most $O(\log n + \delta)$ time within the same iteration. The desired result will then follow from proving that the expected number of iterations of RANDSEARCH is bounded by a constant.

Let us fix an iteration of the algorithm. Let $h_1, \ldots, h_t$ be the randomly generated indices within such an iteration, i.e., RANDSEARCH performs comparisons between x and $I[h_i]$, for $i = 1, \ldots, t$, before the algorithm restricts the list of possible candidate positions for x to be at most $C\delta$. For each $i = 1, \ldots, t$, let ℓ_i and r_i be the leftmost and rightmost indices of the sub-list to which the algorithm has restricted the search before choosing h_i. At the beginning, we have $\ell_1 = \ell$ and $r_1 = r$. After the index h_i has been chosen, either $I[h_i] = x$, or the search is restricted to one of the sub-lists $I[\ell_i \ldots h_i - 1]$ or $I[h_i + 1 \ldots r_i]$. Since $\ell_i + (r_i - \ell_i)(1 - c)/2 \leq h_i \leq \ell_i + (r_i - \ell_i)(1 + c)/2$, the new sub-list will be at most $(1 + c)/2$ times as big as the previous one. Since every step reduces the size of the sub-list by a constant factor, $2/(1 + c)$, it follows that $t = O(\log n)$. After the tth step, we have $r_t - \ell_t \leq C\delta$, and the algorithm exhaustively searches in the reduced sub-list. Therefore, this adds at most $O(\delta)$ time to the overall time complexity to complete an iteration. We have shown that each iteration is completed in time $O(\log n + \delta)$.

It remains to show that RANDSEARCH finishes after at most a constant number of iterations. To see this, let us consider the size of the sub-list before randomly choosing the last index h_t. We have $r_t - \ell_t > C\delta$. Recall that h_t is chosen from the set $\{\ell_t + (r_t - \ell_t)(1 - c)/2, \ldots, \ell_t + (r_t - \ell_t)(1 + c)/2\}$, which is of size $(r_t - \ell_t)c \geq \delta Cc$. Since there are at most δ faulty elements, the probability that h_t is the position of a faulty one is at most $1/Cc$.

In general, h_i is chosen from a set of cardinality $(r_i - \ell_i)c$. For each $i = 1, \ldots, t - 1$, we have that $(r_i - \ell_i) \geq 2(r_{i+1} - \ell_{i+1})/(1 + c)$. And using the fact that $(r_t - \ell_t) > \delta C$, we have that h_i is chosen from a set of cardinality $(r_i - \ell_i)c \geq \left(\frac{2}{1+c}\right)^{t-i} \delta Cc$. In particular, the probability that h_i is the position of a faulty element is at most $\left(\frac{1+c}{2}\right)^{t-i} \frac{1}{Cc}$.

Therefore, the probability that none of $I[h_1], \ldots, I[h_t]$ is faulty is not smaller than

$$\prod_{i=1}^{t}\left(1 - \left(\frac{1+c}{2}\right)^{t-i}\frac{1}{Cc}\right) \geq \left(1 - \frac{1}{Cc}\right)^{\sum_{i=1}^{t}\left(\frac{1+c}{2}\right)^{i}} \geq \left(1 - \frac{1}{Cc}\right)^{\frac{2}{1-c}} > 0,$$

where the first inequality follows from $(1 - ab) \geq (1 - x)^b$, for each $a, b \in [0, 1]$, and the second inequality follows from $\sum_{i=1}^{t}\left(\frac{1+c}{2}\right)^{i} \leq \sum_{i=1}^{\infty}\left(\frac{1+c}{2}\right)^{i} = \frac{1}{1 - \frac{1+c}{2}} = \frac{2}{1-c}$.

8.3 Optimal Deterministic Resilient Search

We are now going to show how the bound of Theorem 8.1 can be actually matched deterministically.

Let us call the originally sorted sequence $I[0 \ldots n - 1]$. The basic idea is as follows: we start performing binary search over a subsequence of equally spaced non-adjacent elements of I. The binary search is meant to identify a contiguous subsequence I' of I which is a candidate for containing an element with the key we are searching for—if such an element is present at all. Once such a contiguous subsequence is selected, a verification procedure is run which is meant to guarantee that the binary search was not fooled by some error. If the verification phase is passed, then the subsequence I' is exhaustively searched for x. If the verification phase is not passed the algorithm backtracks and continues over a different subsequence with another attempt of binary search.

For the ease of the presentation let us assume that $n = m \times (5\delta + 1)$ for some integer m. We partition the sequence I into m blocks of $5\delta + 1$ consecutive elements each. For $i = 0, \ldots, m - 1$, the block B_i contains the elements $I[(5\delta + 1)(i - 1) \ldots (5\delta + 1)i - 1]$. Moreover, we subdivide B_i into three segments. The leftmost 2δ elements are denoted by LV_i. The rightmost 2δ elements are denoted by RV_i.

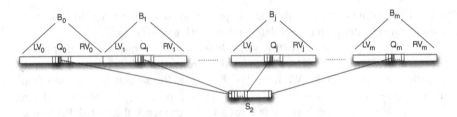

Fig. 8.1 The data structure for the deterministic optimal resilient search algorithm: The partition of the sequence into blocks B_j's and sub-blocks LV_j's, RV_j's and Q_j's, and the sequence S_k ($k = 2$) on which the binary search is performed

Finally, the remaining central $\delta + 1$ elements are denoted by Q_i. The subsequences LV_i, RV_i, and Q_i are respectively called the ith *left verification segment*, the ith *right verification segment*, and the ith *query segment*. The reason for such names will be soon clear. We assume that the elements in the above segments are indexed from 0. Then, in particular, the ith query segment's first element is $Q_i[0]$ and its last element is $Q_i[\delta]$.

For $i = 0, \ldots, \delta$ we define the subsequence S_i, whose jth element coincides with the ith element in the query segment Q_j, i.e, $S_i[j] = Q_j[i] = I[(5\delta + 1)j + 2\delta + i]$. See Fig. 8.1 for a pictorial example.

A value $k \in \{0, \ldots, \delta\}$, counting the errors detected at any point during the execution of the algorithm, is stored in *safe* memory. According to the value of k, binary search is performed on the sequence S_k. More precisely, in safe memory are stored also the search key x and two pointers ℓ and r indicating the indices in the subsequence S_k such that, according to the comparisons performed so far, $S_k[\ell] \leq x \leq S_k[r]$.

Also, we may assume that initially $\ell = -1$ and $r = m$, and that reliably $I[j] = -\infty$ for any $j < 0$ and $I[j] = \infty$ for any $j \geq n$.

Notice that since distinct elements of S_k belong to distinct blocks, we can also think of the pointers ℓ and r as pointing to two blocks.

Initially, we have $k = 0$, so we start performing binary search on the sequence S_0, with $\ell = -1$ and $r = m$. At each step we set $q = \lfloor (\ell + r)/2 \rfloor$ and compare x with $S_k[q]$. If x is greater than $S_k[q]$, the pointer ℓ is set to q. In addition, the pointer r is decremented by 1, and $S_k[r]$ is compared to x. If x is smaller than $S_k[r]$ then we continue with binary search by selecting a new index q and proceed as before. Otherwise, it means that $x \geq S_k[r]$ and, since by the previous comparisons we have $x \leq S_k[r + 1]$, then x belongs to one of the two blocks B_r or B_{r+1}. When such a situation occurs, as in this case or because ℓ and r are such that $\ell = r - 1$, we execute the verification procedure, which is meant to verify that the two adjacent blocks have been correctly identified, or, alternatively, that in the comparisons performed in S_k at least the output of one comparison was erroneous because of some fault.

8.3.1   The Verification Procedure

In the verification phase, we compare elements from LV_i and RV_{i+1} with x in order to check that the blocks B_i and B_{i+1} are correctly identified to contain x. To this aim, we start with two counters, c_ℓ and c_r, stored in reliable memory and initially containing the value 1. Also, we set $v_\ell = 2(\delta - k)$ and $v_r = 2k$. While $0 < \min\{c_\ell, c_r\} < \delta - k + 1$ we perform the following two comparisons: first we compare x to the element $LV_i[v_\ell]$. According to whether this element is smaller than x or not, we increase or decrease c_ℓ. Then, we compare x to the element $RV_{i+1}[v_r]$. According to whether this element is greater than x or not, we increase or decrease c_r. Every decrease of one of the counters is also followed by an increase of k, since it indicates that at least one corruption has been detected.

If we exit from this loop because $\min\{c_\ell, c_r\} = \delta - k + 1$, we declare the verification to have succeeded. Otherwise, if we exit because $\min\{c_\ell, c_r\} = 0$, we declare the verification to have failed.

In other words, we use c_ℓ, c_r for measuring our trust in the fact that x is in the blocks B_i, B_{i+1}. Every comparison which increases such counters is a comparison whose result confirms that x is in the blocks identified so far. Each comparison which fails indicates that at least one corruption has occurred.

If the verification succeeds, we proceed with an exhaustive search for x in the blocks B_i, B_{i+1}. We return an element whose value is x if we find one, and otherwise we return false, meaning that no reliable element is equal to x.

If the verification fails, we perform a backtracking of the binary search by resetting the same situation we had before the last two iterations of binary search. For this purpose we have to remember for each iteration of the binary search (1) the direction in which the interval of candidate blocks was restricted and (2) whether the computation of q needed a rounding. By (1) we mean whether we set ℓ to q and decreased r or set r to q and increased ℓ. By (2) we mean whether the floor involved in the computation of q satisfied $\lfloor (\ell + r)/2 \rfloor < (\ell + r)/2$.

The information necessary for the backtracking is stored in two binary vectors, D (for direction) and R (for rounding), kept in reliable memory. For each $i = 1, \ldots,$ we set the ith bit of D to 1 if at the ith iteration of the binary search we set $\ell = q$ and $r = r - 1$. Also, we set the ith bit of R to 1 iff at the ith iteration we had $q = \lfloor (\ell + r)/2 \rfloor < (\ell + r)/2$.

Notice that the choice of updating both ℓ and r at each iteration guarantees that the last faulty comparison in a sequence of iterations of the binary search leading to a verification phase is actually verified within the next two iterations of the binary search. To see this, let us write ℓ_t, q_t, r_t to denote the value of ℓ, q, r at the tth iteration of binary search. Let t be the iteration when the last faulty comparison occurs before the verification phase. Imagine that originally we had $S_k[q_t] < x$, but because of a fault, the corrupted value satisfies $\tilde{S}_k[q_t] \geq x$. Then, the algorithm enters the $(t + 1)$th iteration with $\ell_{t+1} = \ell_t + 1$ and $r_{t+1} = q_t$. In the absence of further faults, we also have $S_k[\ell_{t+1}] < S_k[q_t] < x$; hence, we continue with binary search in the interval $S_k[\ell_{t+1} \ldots r_{t+1}]$. Then,

$q_{t+1} = (\ell_{t+1} + r_{t+1})/2 < S_k[q_t] < x$, which implies that we proceed with $\ell_{t+2} = q_{t+1}$ and $r_{t+2} = r_{t+1} - 1 = q_t - 1$. Assuming that $S_k[r_{t+1}]$ is not corrupted, we have that the comparison between $S_k[r_{t+2}]$ and x leads to a verification in the blocks $B_{r_{t+2}}, B_{r_{t+2}+1}$. Under the standing assumptions, such a verification will fail and will be followed by a backtracking to the situation at time t, which is the last time a corrupted element was used by the algorithm. Therefore, because of the updates on both sides, the last corruption affecting binary search is actually verified at most two iterations later. This also explains the double backtracking.

In order to show that the above algorithm is correct and has the desired complexity, we first show that the value of k exactly counts the number of corruptions identified. Notice that, whenever the verification fails, at least one corruption has been found; hence, k has increased and the next iteration of binary search proceeds on a different S_k sequence.

Lemma 8.1. *Every time one of the counters c_ℓ, c_r is decreased, a corruption has been detected. In addition, every corruption detected influences exactly one decrease operation of the counters.*

Proof. We shall argue only with respect to c_ℓ. An analogous argument works for c_r as well. Let B_i and B_{i+1} be the blocks on which the verification takes place. The decrease of c_ℓ follows a comparison between an element y of LV_i and x such that $y > x$. Let $y_1, \ldots, y_r$ be the list of elements in LV_i which are compared to x in the verification phase. Let t be the number of indices i such that y_i is found to be not larger than x. We call these the *true* comparisons. Let f be the number of indices i such that y_i is found to be larger than x. We call these the *false* comparisons. Clearly, at any point after a false comparison we have $f \le t + 1$. This is because as soon as the number of false comparisons overcomes the number of true comparisons, we have $c_\ell = 0$ and the verification phase ends with a failure.

Therefore, we can pair distinctly each element y_i involved in a false comparison with an element y_j involved in a successive true comparison. We can pair the last false comparison with the element in Q_i which during the binary search was found to be not larger than x. Now, every such pair implies a corruption, since the element from the false comparison was originally smaller than the paired element from the true comparison (recall that our pairing is such that the false comparison element has an index smaller than that of the true comparison element, and LV_i was originally sorted in increasing order). However, we have that the false comparison element is now larger than x, which is not smaller than the true comparison element. The proof of the first statement is complete.

The second statement of the lemma says that no corruption is counted more than once. For this it is enough to show that every two verification phases on the same blocks will be based on comparisons performed on disjoint sets of elements. First we observe that every time a verification phase is executed on the blocks B_i, B_{i+1}, a different element y of Q_i has been compared with x and resulted in $y \le x$. This is because we use a different sequence S_k after each verification phase that fails. Moreover, we can show that each element of LV_i is involved in at most one verification phase. In fact, two different verification phases on B_i, B_{i+1} would start with two different values of k, say $k_1 < k_2$. Suppose that in the first one of these two verification phases the elements $LV_i[2(\delta - k_1) \ldots 2(\delta - k_1) + r]$ were analyzed. From the argument in the proof of the first statement of this lemma, it follows that at least $(r + 1)/2$ corruptions were detected, i.e., one for each decrease of c_ℓ. Hence, $k_2 \geq k_1 + (r + 1)/2$, and in the second verification phase we will perform comparisons with elements of $LV_i[2(\delta - k_2) \ldots 2\delta]$. Since $2(\delta - k_2) \geq 2\delta - 2k_1 + r + 1$, it follows that the sublist of LV_i on which the second verification phase acts is disjoint from the sublist on which we perform comparisons in the first verification phase. As desired, new decrease operations will follow from comparisons on elements never considered before, and hence from newly detected corruptions.

Theorem 8.3. *The algorithm correctly reports the presence or absence of x if at most δ values are corrupted and it finishes in time $O(\log n + \delta)$.*

Proof. By Lemma 8.1 if $\alpha \leq \delta$ faults were detected, there will eventually be a verification phase which ends with a success, i.e., $\min\{c_\ell, c_r\} = \delta - \alpha + 1$. Then, the algorithm proceeds by exhaustively searching for x in the blocks B_i, B_{i+1}. We have to prove two things. If there is a non-corrupted element equal to x then it belongs to B_i, B_{i+1}. Moreover, if the exhaustive search does not find any element with key x in B_i, B_{i+1}, then no uncorrupted element exists with value x.

We observe that because of the verification phase, we know that at least $\delta - \alpha + 1$ elements of LV_i were found which are not larger than x and at least $\delta - \alpha + 1$ elements of RV_{i+1} were found which are not smaller than x. Since apart from the detected α faults there could be at most $\delta - \alpha$ additional faults, it means that at least one uncorrupted element of LV_i and one uncorrupted element from RV_{i+1} were considered; hence, any uncorrupted x should belong to the blocks B_i, B_{i+1}. Therefore, if the exhaustive search will not find any element in B_i, B_{i+1} of value x, no such element could have originally been in the list, since, by the last argument, it would be in B_i, B_{i+1}. It follows that the output of the algorithm correctly reports the presence or absence of uncorrupted x in the list.

Finally, we have to argue about the complexity of the algorithm. Clearly, the cost of the verification phases is $O(\delta)$. For this, it is enough to observe that the cost of each verification phase is linearly proportional to the number of corruptions detected, which in total cannot exceed δ. Moreover, we charge the two backtracking operations in the binary search to the verification phase which determined them. Therefore, considering both the verification phases and the binary search, the overall complexity of the algorithm is $O(\log n + \delta)$, as desired.

8.4 Bibliographic Notes

The faulty memory RAM and the model of resiliency described in this chapter were introduced by Finocchi and Italiano in [107]. In this seminal paper the authors provided the $\Omega(\log n + \delta)$ lower bound for the problem of searching in a sorted array.

The matching randomized upper bound was given in [108]. Finally, the optimal deterministic algorithm for resilient search, here presented in Sect. 8.3, appeared in [35]. In the paper [107], Finocchi and Italiano presented lower bounds also for the problem of resilient sorting, for which matching (hence, optimal) algorithms were given in [108]. Resilient search trees supporting insertions, deletions and search operations in $O(\log n + \delta^2)$ amortized time were introduced in [109]. Jørgensen et al. [129] proposed priority queues supporting insert and delete-min operations in $O(\log n + \delta)$ amortized time. Finally, in [35], a resilient deterministic dynamic dictionary was provided which supports searches in $O(\log n + \delta)$ worst-case time, updates in $O(\log n + \delta)$ amortized time, and range queries in $O(\log n + \delta + t)$ time, where t is the size of the output. In addition, in [35], a lower bound was proved to the effect that every resilient dictionary (satisfying some reasonable constraints) must require $\Omega(\log n + \delta)$ worst-case time for search operations.

Very recently, Kopelowitz and Talmon [136] gave a linear-time deterministic algorithm for the selection problem in the faulty memory RAM model. Interestingly, the running time does not depend on the number of faults. Moreover, the algorithm does not need to know δ explicitly. The authors also provide the first in-place randomized resilient sorting algorithm with expected running time $O(n \log n + \alpha\delta)$, where α is the number of faults that occurred during the execution of the algorithm.

8.5   Exercises

1. A trivially δ-resilient algorithm can be obtained by storing replicas of each element and then implementing a memory access to any x via computing the majority of the values found in the replicas of x.
   State exactly how to implement such trivially δ-resilient algorithms for the problems of searching and sorting. Prove the correctness of the statement and estimate the overheads of such an approach in terms of space and time requirements

2. Consider the problem of resilient search. Assume that at most one memory fault is expected during the whole process and design an algorithm which uses not more than $2\lceil \log n \rceil$ operations.

3. Modify RANDSEARCH to provide an algorithm for finding the minimum element in a set of n elements with expected time $O(n + \delta)$.

4. Design an algorithm that receives in input an n-element array $X[1 \ldots n]$ of distinct values (not necessarily sorted) and an index j. The algorithm, by using $O(n)$ comparisons among the elements of X, should returns an element y of the array, different from $X[j]$, and such that if X was sorted y would be not more than α positions away from the position occupied by $X[j]$, where α is the number of memory faults in the whole procedure.
   In other words, denote by $\tilde{X}$ the sorted version of X. Let $\tilde{j}$ be such that $X[j]$ is in position $\tilde{j}$, in $\tilde{X}$. Then, the algorithm should output any one of the values in $\tilde{X}[\tilde{j} - \alpha \ldots \tilde{j} - 1] \cup \tilde{X}[\tilde{j} + 1 \ldots \alpha \tilde{j} + \alpha]$.

Chapter 9
A Model for Learning

I guess sometimes you have to lie to find the truth

S. Westerfeld

Learning can be thought of as the activity which allows the learner to formulate the hypothesis likely to agree with previous observations. New observations might induce the learner to revise previous hypotheses, and thus to modify/improve the current state of knowledge in order to combine the new and the old observations. Observations are usually examples and counterexamples provided "randomly" to the learner. Alternatively, the learner may have the possibility to ask for the correct classification of an example chosen from a given pool. In many concrete applications the learning process is affected by noise. In this chapter we shall discuss several examples of learning in noisy environments, showing their relations to both Ulam-Rényi games and computational learning theories.

9.1 Computational Learning

We shall briefly describe the components of the basic model introduced by Valiant as a criterion of correctness for learning concepts from examples and emphasizing the importance of polynomial learning algorithms. Much of the study in the field of computational learning can be understood as variations on this theme. A *concept* is understood to be a Boolean function over some universe X. Examples are points in X, which is usually taken to be some set of binary vectors.

An unknown target concept is to be learnt. A particular class C of possible target concepts is chosen and the learnability of C is investigated in terms of the number of examples needed by an algorithm to formulate a hypothesis $h \in C$ which approximates a chosen target concept $c \in C$ with a small probability of error.

F. Cicalese, *Fault-Tolerant Search Algorithms*, Monographs in Theoretical
Computer Science. An EATCS Series, DOI 10.1007/978-3-642-17327-1_9,
© Springer-Verlag Berlin Heidelberg 2013

More precisely, we say that the algorithm A PAC-identifies concepts from C in terms of a class of hypothesis H ($C \subseteq H$) with respect to a class of distribution $\mathscr{D}$ if for every concept $c \in C$, for each distribution $D \in \mathscr{D}$, and for all positive numbers δ and ϵ, when the examples are taken according to the distribution D, the algorithm halts with a concept $h \in H$ such that with probability at least $1 - \delta$ the probability that an example drawn according to D is misclassified by h is smaller than ϵ. PAC stands for *probably* (except for δ) *approximately* (except for ϵ) *correct*.

If one requires the probability of error to be zero, than we have *exact learning*. For example, in an *online prediction model,* the learning algorithm indefinitely repeats a cycle of (1) requesting an example, (2) predicting its classification according to the target concept (i.e., whether $c(x) = 0$ or $c(x) = 1$), and (3) receiving the correct classification.

In the *absolute mistake bound* model of prediction, the worst-case number of mistakes in prediction over any sequence of examples must be bounded by a polynomial in the length of examples and the size of the target concept. A polynomial-time algorithm in the absolute mistake bound model can be transformed into a PAC-learning algorithm for the same class of concepts. However, if one-way functions exist then there are PAC-learnable concept classes that are not predictable in the absolute mistake bound by a polynomial-time algorithm.

9.2   Predicting from Expert Advice

Let us consider the following simple problem. A learning algorithm is given the task each day of predicting whether or not it will rain. In order to make this prediction, the algorithm is given as input the advice of M "experts". Each day, each expert predicts "yes" or "no", and the learning algorithm must use this information to make its own prediction (the algorithm is given no other information besides the yes/no bits produced by the experts). After making its prediction, the algorithm, at the end of the day, is then told whether or not, in fact, it rained. Suppose we make no assumption about the quality or independence of the experts so that we cannot hope to achieve any absolute level of quality in our predictions. In that case, a natural goal is to perform nearly as well as the best expert. We shall call the sequence of events in which the algorithm (1) receives the prediction of the experts, (2) makes its own prediction, and then (3) is told the correct answer a *trial.* We shall show that under the additional assumption that the maximum number of mistakes made by the best expert is bounded by $e \geq 0$ and such a bound is known to the learning algorithm, the problem can be recast as a particular variant of the Ulam-Rényi problem.

First of all, let us note that the above problem can be seen as a particular case of exact learning. The concept to be learnt is the Boolean function corresponding to the best expert. The class of possible target functions is represented by the set of experts. It is also assumed that there exists some source of noise which is, however, bounded to affect at most e of the given examples.

We map the learning problem with M experts and bound e on the maximum number of mistakes made by the best expert into the Ulam-Rényi problem over the search space $S = \{0, 1, \ldots, M - 1\}$ with e lies. Intuitively, we may think of the learning problem as that of finding from among the M different experts the best one, and despite the fact that such an expert can give us up to e wrong predictions, we cannot recognize her until all the others have wrongly predicted more than e times. Recall that in the Ulam-Rényi game we cannot claim to know the secret number until the moment when all the other numbers happen to falsify more than e of the questions received. The difference with respect to a classical instance of searching is that, here, we cannot directly determine the tests/questions. On the other hand, this is not important as long as we are penalized with a mistake only for a wrong prediction. So the number of questions in a searching strategy here becomes the number of wrong predictions.

Alternatively, one can turn the problem of prediction in the presence of mistake-bounded experts into a gambling variant of the Ulam-Rényi problem.

The situation is as follows: Carole chooses a number $x \in S = \{0, 1, \ldots, M - 1\}$. Then, Carole and Paul start the first round of the gambling-game. At any round Carole shows Paul a set $T \subseteq S$, meaning that $x \in T$. Paul has to decide whether to bet (one dollar) or not on Carole's claim. Once Paul has decided whether to bet on the claim "$x \in T$" or on the opposite one "$x \notin T$", Carole tells Paul if he has to pay or not. The aim of Paul is to find out the secret number and to save as much money as he can. Carole, on the other hand, tries to make Paul lose money, also by lying in some rounds. It is agreed that Carole does not lie more than e times.

The problem is to find out how many dollars Paul has to lose before finding the secret number and, if possible, to devise a strategy for Paul which allows him to lose no more than the above lower bound.

It turns out that this problem has exactly the same result as the original one. Indeed, the best Paul can do in any round is to bet or not according to whether the state resulting from a "yes" answer has a smaller nth volume with respect to the state resulting from a "no" answer. Here, $n + 1$ represents the least number of questions necessary for Paul to find out x starting in the present state, according to the Volume Bound. On the other hand, Carole's aim is to prevent Paul from guessing x and also to make him lose money. Therefore, she has to use balanced questions and then always say that Paul's bet is wrong. The necessity to use balanced questions depends on Paul's strategy. If an unbalanced question is used, when Paul loses money, he also gains more information. On the other hand, at any step Paul gains some information, so Carole has to make Paul lose money in every round, for otherwise she is giving him information for free. Finally, instances of the classical game (e.g., the case $M = 2^{78}$, $e = 2$) forcing even splitting of the volume at any step immediately yield worst cases in the predictive model where $N(M, e)$ dollars are to be lost by Paul.[1]

Thus, we show that there exists a learning strategy making at most $N(M, e)$ mistakes when advised by M experts, one of whom makes at most e mistakes.

---

[1] $N(M, e)$ is the minimum number of questions that Paul has to ask in order to infallibly determine Carole's number in a binary Ulam-Rényi game with e lies over a search space of cardinality M.

Moreover, it is possible to devise situations (choices of M and e and the set of trials) where $N(M, e)$ errors are the minimum possible.

9.3   Learning in Noisy Environments

9.3.1   Rényi's Probabilistic Example

We start our excursion from Ulam-Rényi games to computational learning theories with a probabilistic variant of the Ulam-Rényi problem, considered by Rényi.

Arbitrarily fix an integer $M \geq 2$, together with a real number $0 < \alpha < 1$. Let $S = \{0, 1, 2, \ldots, M - 1\}$ be the search space and $T_1, T_2, \ldots, T_k$ be randomly selected subsets of S. Let x be a fixed unknown element of S. Suppose that we know the answer to each question "does x belong to T_j?", and that each answer is correct with probability β, with $1/2 < \beta \leq 1$ a fixed but otherwise arbitrary real number.

Problem: How large must the integer k be so that we can identify x with probability $\geq \alpha$?

Intuitively speaking, the entropy

$$H(\beta) = \beta \log_2 \frac{1}{\beta} + (1 - \beta) \log_2 \frac{1}{1 - \beta}$$

measures our uncertainty: the information content of each answer is $\leq 1 - H(\beta)$. Since the amount of information needed to detect x is $\log_2 M$, we may reasonably conjecture that k answers to the above random questions will suffice to determine x only if $k(1 - H(\beta)) \geq \log_2 M$, i.e.,

$$k \geq \frac{\log_2 M}{1 - H(\beta)}. \tag{9.1}$$

This heuristic argument indeed provides a lower bound which is not too far from the solution of the above problem. Rényi's precise estimate [183] shows that the number k of answers is almost independent of α and has the same rate of growth as $\log M$. Thus, no matter what the desired "accuracy parameter" α is, the number k surprisingly agrees with the naive estimate given by (9.1).

9.3.2   Learning with Negative Reinforcement

The worst-case variant of Rényi's probabilistic example has a distinctly algorithmic nature, and yields a first, albeit rudimentary, quantification of the effects of (negative) reinforcement, as follows.

Carole chooses a number $x^* \in S = \{0, 1, \ldots, M - 1\}$. During the tth round of the game, $t = 1, 2, \ldots$, a subset $T_t \subseteq S$ is randomly[2] chosen and submitted to Paul, who must now guess whether $x^* \in T_t$ or $x^* \in \overline{T_t} = S \setminus T_t$. Thus, Paul's guess is just a subset $T^* \in \{T_t, \overline{T_t}\}$. Then, Carole *declares* what the correct guess should have been, thereby *confirming* or *refuting* Paul's guess T^*. In the latter case, Paul must pay a one dollar fee to (his supervisor) Carole.

It is agreed that Carole can mendaciously or erroneously refute Paul's correct guess for up to e rounds, while still cashing Paul's dollar. On the other hand, *whenever Carole confirms Paul's guess, she is always sincere, and no fee is paid by Paul*.

Paul's aim is to learn the secret number x^* as cheaply as possible. Thus, we are not concerned with the actual length of the game. Unless we tighten our notion of "random" set, much as Rényi did in his example, it is in principle possible that Paul learns the secret number very cheaply, but after a large number of rounds—an altogether common situation.

Recalling the definition of character given in Chap. 2, in Theorem 9.1 and Proposition 9.1 below we shall prove the following two results:

- For all M and e there is a betting strategy $\mathscr{B}$ enabling Paul to infallibly learn x^*, paying a (tuition) fee that even in the worst possible case never exceeds $\mathrm{ch}(M, \underbrace{0, \ldots, 0}_{e \text{ times}})$ dollars (see Definition 2.6).

- On the other hand, for certain values of M and e, $\mathrm{ch}(M, 0, \ldots, 0) - 3$ dollars may turn out to be insufficient for Paul to learn x^*, whatever strategy he may choose.

For the proof we need a minor adaptation of the notions of state and strategy, as follows: As the result of Carole's confirmations and refutations, Paul, starting from the initial state $(M, 0, \ldots, 0)$, will find himself in a *state* $\sigma = (A_0, \ldots, A_e)$, where for every $i = 0, \ldots, e$, $A_i \subseteq S$, and for each $y \in S$

> $y \in A_i$ iff y agrees with all of Carole's confirmations, and fails to agree with exactly i refutations.[3]

By a *betting strategy* we mean a function $\mathscr{B}$ assigning to each pair (σ, T), with σ a non-final[4] state and $T \subseteq S$, a set $T^* = \mathscr{B}(\sigma, T) \in \{T, \overline{T}\}$.

Theorem 9.1. *Fix integers $e \geq 0$ and $M \geq 2$. Let $q = \mathrm{ch}(M, 0, \ldots, 0)$. Then, in the present gambling game with e lies over the search space $S = \{0, \ldots, M - 1\}$, there is a betting strategy $\mathscr{B}$ with the following property.*

Whatever Carole's secret number $x^* \in S$, for any random sequence (in the above sense) $T_1, T_2, \ldots \subseteq S$, and for any sequence of declarations, say with $\lambda \in$

---

[2]Here, by "randomly" we mean that every subset T of S occurs as T_t for infinitely many t. Thus, no probabilistic notion is used.

[3]Thus, $y \notin \cup A_i$ iff either y falsifies a confirmation, or else y falsifies $> e$ refutations.

[4]The definition of final state is unchanged.

$\{0, \ldots, e\}$ *false refutations, Paul following $\mathscr{B}$ always learns x^* by paying a total fee not exceeding $q - e + \lambda$ dollars.*

Proof. We prepare some notations and record some easy facts. For any set $U \subseteq S$ with its complementary set $\overline{U} = S \setminus U$, assuming Paul to be in a non-final state $\sigma = (A_0, \ldots, A_e)$, we let

$$\sigma^{no(U)} = (A'_0, \ldots, A'_e)$$

denote Paul's new state of knowledge in case Carole happens to refute his bet "$x^* \in U$." Since Carole is sincere when she confirms Paul's bet, this refutation does not have the same effect as Carole confirming the opposite bet "$x^* \in \overline{U}$." In more detail, by analogy with (2.1) we can write

$$\begin{cases} A'_0 = A_0 \cap \overline{U} \\ A'_j = (A_j \cap \overline{U}) \cup (A_{j-1} \cap U) \quad (j = 1, \ldots, e). \end{cases} \tag{9.2}$$

For every $n > 0$ we then have the conservation law of Theorem 2.2:

$$V_n(\sigma) = V_{n-1}(\sigma^{no(U)}) + V_{n-1}(\sigma^{no(\overline{U})}).$$

By definition of character, it follows that for every state σ with $\mathrm{ch}(\sigma) > 0$, there exists $U^* \in \{U, \overline{U}\}$ such that $\mathrm{ch}(\sigma^{no(U^*)}) < \mathrm{ch}(\sigma)$.

Supposing now σ to be a non-final state and $T \subseteq S$, we are ready to define $\mathscr{B}(\sigma, T)$. Since $\mathrm{ch}(\sigma) > 0$, there is a $T^* \in \{T, \overline{T}\}$ such that $\mathrm{ch}(\sigma^{no(T^*)}) < \mathrm{ch}(\sigma)$. Strategy $\mathscr{B}$ prescribes that Paul should bet on T^*.[5] Thus, we can write

$$T^* = \mathscr{B}(\sigma, T) \quad \text{and} \quad \mathrm{ch}(\sigma^{no(T^*)}) < \mathrm{ch}(\sigma). \tag{9.3}$$

To conclude the proof, assume for some random sequence $T_0, T_1, \ldots$, for some $x^* \in S$, for some sequence of Carole's declarations, say with λ false refutations ($\lambda \in \{0, \ldots, e\}$), Paul, following $\mathscr{B}$, learns x^* at a price exceeding $q - e + \lambda$ dollars (absurdum hypothesis.)

Notwithstanding its extreme generality, our present notion of randomness still ensures that Paul sooner or later does learn x^*. Therefore, our absurdum hypothesis states that Paul learns x^* after paying

$$q - e + \lambda + \delta$$

---

[5] If $\overline{T^*}$ also has the property that $\mathrm{ch}(\sigma^{no(\overline{T^*})}) < \mathrm{ch}(\sigma)$, Paul must choose between T^* and $\overline{T^*}$ following some predetermined criterion. A deeper analysis shows that—except in such a trivial case as $e = 0$ and M is a power of two—a careful choice of Paul's priority criterion does result in his saving further.

dollars, for some integer $\delta > 0$. Upon learning x^*, Paul enters a final state σ_{end} of the form

$$\sigma_{end} = (\underbrace{\emptyset, \ldots, \emptyset}_{\lambda \text{ times}}, \{x^*\}, \underbrace{0, \ldots, 0}_{e-\lambda \text{ times}}).$$

As an immediate consequence of the definition of volume (Definition 2.5), one gets

$$V_{e-\lambda}(\sigma_{end}) = 2^{e-\lambda}.$$

Since every confirmation leads Paul from a state ρ to a state ρ' with $\mathrm{ch}(\rho') \leq \mathrm{ch}(\rho)$, it follows that every state $\tau \neq \sigma_{end}$ that Paul has experienced during this game before entering σ_{end} is not final and also satisfies the inequality

$$\mathrm{ch}(\tau) > e - \lambda. \tag{9.4}$$

Now, the number $q - e + \lambda + \delta$ of Carole's refutations coincides with the tuition fee paid by Paul. These refutations lead Paul from his initial state of character q to a final non-zero state σ_{end}. Further, by (9.3), Carole's first $q - e + \lambda + \delta - 1$ refutations have led Paul to a state τ such that $\mathrm{ch}(\tau) \leq e - \lambda - \delta + 1 \leq e - \lambda$, thus contradicting (9.4)

Corollary 9.1. *For each $e = 0, 1, 2, \ldots$, and all suitably large M, Paul's tuition fee to learn Carole's secret number $x^* \in \{0, \ldots, M - 1\}$ with e false refutations never exceeds $\log_2 M + e \log_2 \log_2 M + e$ dollars, provided he follows the above betting strategy $\mathcal{B}$.* ∎

Proof. Setting $q = \log M + e \log \log M + e$, we have for all large M:

$$M \sum_{i=0}^{e} \binom{q}{i} \leq M \binom{q+e}{e} \leq \frac{M}{e!}(q+e)^e$$

$$= \frac{M}{e!}(\log M + e \log \log M + 2e)^e \leq M(2 \log M)^e = 2^q.$$

Thus, the character of the initial state $(M, 0, 0, \ldots, 0)$ is $\leq q$. As shown by the proof of Theorem 9.1, q dollars are sufficient for Paul to learn the secret number.

Exercises 1 and 2 discusses the actual extent to which the above strategy $\mathcal{B}$ is "best possible". Here, we limit ourselves to state the following instructive special case.

Proposition 9.1. *Let $e = 2$ and $M = 2^{78}$. Then, no matter what Paul's betting strategy $\mathcal{G}$ is, it turns out that $87 = ch(M, 0, 0) - 3$ dollars will not enable him to infallibly learn Carole's secret number. In more detail, depending on $\mathcal{G}$ there exist*

- *an integer $\lambda \in \{0, 1, 2\}$*
- *a sequence $T_1, \ldots, T_{88+\lambda}$ of subsets of S*

- *a sequence of* $88 + \lambda$ *declarations*
- *an element* $x^* \in S = \{0, \ldots, M - 1\}$

with the following properties:

- *all declarations are refutations;*
- *Paul learns* x^* *precisely after* $88 + \lambda$ *rounds, thus paying* $88 + \lambda$ *dollars;*
- *the number of Carole's false refutations is* λ.

As a final remark, we notice that—at the expense of overburdening the notation—Proposition 9.1 can be generalized to any fixed e and infinitely many M whenever the nth volume of the initial state $(M, 0, \ldots, 0)$ is just a little below the value 2^n, n being the character of $(M, 0, \ldots, 0)$.

9.3.3   Supervised Learning for Online Prediction

We shall give a simple example of supervised learning and show its essential equivalence with the example of the previous section (Theorem 9.2 below).

A learning algorithm called Cassandra has the following task: under the supervision of a team of expert meteorologists, after a certain, hopefully short, training stage, Cassandra must become an expert meteorologist.

On each day $t = 0, 1, 2, \ldots$, Cassandra is expected to predict whether or not the $(t+1)$th day will be rainy. Each member i of a supervising team $S = \{0, 1, \ldots, M - 1\}$ of meteorologists tells Cassandra his individual prediction about day $t+1$. The bit $b_{it} \in \{0, 1\} = \{\text{sunny}, \text{rainy}\}$ records such a *prediction*. At the end of the $(t + 1)$th day, Cassandra is told by Jupiter whether her own prediction b_t was right. These daily $M + 1$ input bits of information must be efficiently recorded and used by Cassandra to improve her predicting capabilities.

When all supervisors are unable to forecast reliably, Cassandra will hardly become an expert meteorologist. If *precisely one of the M experts is infallible*, in order to become an infallible meteorologist, Cassandra must only identify the infallible expert. For this purpose, since the predictions made on day t by the M experts partition them into two subsets, at the end of the $(t + 1)$th day Cassandra shall simply discard the subset of experts that made a wrong prediction. Initially, she is just training: her predictions may be considered as mere guesses on who the infallible expert is. A moment's reflection shows that, after no more than $\lceil \log_2 M \rceil$ wrong guesses, Cassandra will always detect the infallible expert. In concrete situations one can safely assume that, sooner or later, all experts but one will have made at least one mistake. Then, Cassandra's training terminates, and she acquires the desired predicting capabilities.

As a generalization, let us fix an integer $e \geq 0$ and assume that precisely one of the M experts, denoted by i_*, is *e-fallible*, in the sense that, during the potentially infinite sequence of days $t = 0, 1, 2, \ldots$, expert i_* (and only this expert) is guaranteed to make at most e wrong predictions.

Problem: What is the minimum number of wrong guesses *sufficient* for Cassandra to identify i_*, and eventually acquire infallible predicting capabilities?[6]

To solve the problem we shall first give the appropriate notions of state and strategy.

As the result of Jupiter's declarations, Cassandra, starting from the initial state $(M, 0, \ldots, 0)$, will be in a *state* $\sigma = (A_0, \ldots, A_e)$, where for every $j = 0, \ldots, e$, $A_j \subseteq S$ is the set of experts given by

expert y is a member of A_j iff y agrees with all of Jupiter's declarations, with exactly j exceptions.[7]

By a *predicting strategy* we mean a function $\tilde{\mathscr{P}}$ assigning to each pair (σ, T), with σ a non-final state and $T \subseteq S$, a set $T^* = \tilde{\mathscr{P}}(\sigma, T) \in \{T, \overline{T}\}$.

We are now in a position to answer the above problem.

Theorem 9.2. *Fix integers* $e \geq 0$, $M \geq 2$, *and* $g \geq 0$. *Let the search space* S *be given by* $S = \{0, 1, \ldots, M - 1\}$. *Then, the following conditions are equivalent:*

(i) *Given that up to e of Carole's refutations may be mendacious, Paul has a betting strategy $\tilde{\mathscr{B}}$ to find Carole's secret number $x^* \in S$, paying $\leq g$ dollars.*

(ii) *Cassandra has a predicting strategy $\tilde{\mathscr{P}}$ which, under the supervision of a team of M experts containing precisely one e-fallible member i_*, successfully identifies i_* after $\leq g$ wrong predictions.*

Proof. For the proof we first settle the following.

Claim 1. Paul has a betting strategy $\tilde{\mathscr{B}}$ as in (i) if and only if Paul has a strategy $\mathscr{B}$ to find Carole's secret number $x^* \in \{0, 1, \ldots, M - 1\}$, paying $\leq g$ dollars, under the special hypothesis that all of Carole's declarations are refutations.

The nontrivial direction is from $\mathscr{B}$ to $\tilde{\mathscr{B}}$. Let Σ be the (finite) set of all possible states in the present game over S with e lies. Let $\Sigma_{\mathscr{B}} \subseteq \Sigma$ be the set of all possible states that Paul can reach in a game played according to strategy $\mathscr{B}$, starting from the initial state $(S, \emptyset, \ldots, \emptyset)$ for any possible sequence of sets $T_0, \ldots, T_u$, under the standing hypothesis that all of Carole's declarations are refutations.

For any state $\tau \in \Sigma_{\mathscr{B}}$ let $||\tau||$ denote the (worst-case) maximum fee paid by Paul to learn Carole's secret number, under the assumption that Paul follows strategy $\mathscr{B}$ starting from state τ and all of Carole's declarations are refutations. By hypothesis, $||\rho|| \leq g$ for all $\rho \in \Sigma_{\mathscr{B}}$.

---

[6] Again, we are tacitly assuming that sooner or later all experts but one will have made more than e errors in their predictions. Further, we are not concerned with the duration of the learning process, but only with its cost, as measured by the number of Cassandra's wrong predictions.

[7] Thus, $y \notin \cup_j A_j$ iff y fails to agree with $> e$ of Jupiter's declarations. Note the difference between the present notion of state and the one given in Sect. 9.3.2.

For each state $\sigma \in \Sigma$ among all states $\tau \in \Sigma_{\mathscr{B}}$ such that $\sigma \leq \tau$ let $\tilde{\sigma}$ be the one having minimal $||\tilde{\sigma}||$.[8] The existence of $\tilde{\sigma}$ is easily settled, since σ is a substate of the initial state.

Let the betting strategy $\tilde{\mathscr{B}} : \Sigma \times \text{powerset}(S) \to \text{powerset}(S)$ be defined by

$$\tilde{\mathscr{B}}(\sigma, T) = \mathscr{B}(\tilde{\sigma}, T), \tag{9.5}$$

for all $\sigma \in \Sigma$ and $T \subseteq S$.

Then, $\tilde{\mathscr{B}}$ satisfies the requirements of our claim. For otherwise (absurdum hypothesis) there exists a sequence $T_1, \ldots, T_u \subseteq S$ and corresponding declarations $d_1, \ldots, d_u$, containing at least g refutations, leading Paul to a non-final state after u rounds and after having already paid g dollars. Let $T_1^*, \ldots, T_u^*$ record Paul's bets following strategy $\tilde{\mathscr{B}}$. Let $t_1 < \ldots < t_g$ list g rounds where Paul's bet was refuted.[9] For each $\iota = 1, \ldots, g$ denote by $\sigma_{t_\iota-1}$ and σ_{t_ι} Paul's states before and after his ιth refuted bet. The following verifications are easy:

(a) $\sigma_{t_\iota} \leq \sigma_{t_\iota-1} \leq \tilde{\sigma}_{t_\iota-1}$ and $\sigma_{t_\iota} \leq \tilde{\sigma}_{t_\iota}$.
(b) Suppose Paul is in state $\tilde{\sigma}_{t_\iota-1}$ and, *following strategy $\mathscr{B}$*, bets on $T_{t_\iota}^* = \mathscr{B}(\tilde{\sigma}_{t_\iota-1}, T_\iota)$. Call τ_{t_ι} his state after receiving Carole's refutation. Then, by definition of $\tilde{\mathscr{B}}$, we have the inequality $\sigma_{t_\iota} \leq \tau_{t_\iota}$.
(c) $||\tilde{\sigma}_{t_\iota}|| \leq ||\tau_{t_\iota}|| \leq ||\tilde{\sigma}_{t_\iota-1}|| - 1$.
(d) Whenever $\iota < \omega$, $\sigma_{t_\omega-1} \leq \sigma_{t_\iota}$.
(e) Whenever $\iota < \omega$, $||\tilde{\sigma}_{t_\omega-1}|| \leq ||\tilde{\sigma}_{t_\iota}||$.

We are then left with a decreasing sequence

$$g \geq ||\tilde{\sigma}_{t_1-1}|| > ||\tilde{\sigma}_{t_1}|| \geq ||\tilde{\sigma}_{t_2-1}|| > ||\tilde{\sigma}_{t_2}|| \geq \ldots \geq ||\tilde{\sigma}_{t_g-1}|| > ||\tilde{\sigma}_{t_g}|| \geq 1$$

(because $\sigma_{t_g} \leq \tilde{\sigma}_{t_g}$ is a non-final state). This is impossible and our first claim is proved.

Claim 2. Cassandra has a predicting strategy $\tilde{\mathscr{P}}$ as in (ii) if and only if she has a predicting strategy $\mathscr{P}$ which identifies such an i_* after $\leq g$ wrong predictions, under the additional hypothesis that all her predictions are wrong.

The proof of this claim proceeds exactly as the proof of the previous claim. Note that the information provided by Jupiter's confirmations of Cassandra's predictions is smaller than the information provided by Carole's confirmations of Paul's bets. However, the proof of inequalities (a)-(e) is not affected by such a distinction: as a matter of fact, any state σ' resulting from a state σ after a confirmation, whether in the first model or in the second model, is always a substate of σ.

---

[8]If there are several candidates we let $\tilde{\sigma}$ be the first one, according to some fixed lexicographic order.

[9]For definiteness, one may take the last g, or the first g, such rounds.

Having thus settled both claims, we conclude the proof as follows: For the $(i) \rightarrow$ (ii) direction, we can safely identify the set of expert meteorologists with the search space $S = \{0, \ldots, M - 1\}$ in the gambling game of Sect. 9.3.2. For each day (= round) $t = 0, 1, \ldots$, let

$$T_t = \{y \in S \mid \text{expert } y \text{ predicts rain for day } t + 1\}.$$

By our claims we can safely assume that both Paul and Cassandra always receive refutations to their bets and predictions. From Paul's betting strategy $\mathscr{B}$ one can define Cassandra's predicting strategy $\mathscr{P}$ as follows: Cassandra, being in state σ over input T_t, will output prediction $\mathscr{P}(\sigma, T_t)$ by just mimicking Paul's betting strategy; in symbols,

$$\mathscr{P}(\sigma, T_t) = \mathscr{B}(\sigma, T_t) = T_t^* \in \{T_t, \overline{T_t}\}.$$

Jupiter's refutation has precisely the same effect as Carole's refutation. Notice that the asymmetry between Carole's and Jupiter's confirmations has no longer any effect, for the trivial reason that there are no confirmations at all. In fact, Paul and Cassandra will experience the same sequence of states. Cassandra will identify i_* after $\leq g$ wrong guesses following $\mathscr{P}$, because Paul using $\mathscr{B}$ infallibly learns Carole's secret number paying $\leq g$ dollars.

Similarly, for the $(ii) \rightarrow (i)$ direction, we can safely assume that both Cassandra and Paul only receive refutations. Letting $\mathscr{B} = \mathscr{P}$ we then have the desired conclusion.

Using the betting strategy $\tilde{\mathscr{B}}$ of Theorem 9.1 we have the following.

Corollary 9.2. *In the present instance of supervised learning with a team of M experts containing a unique e-fallible element, there is a predicting strategy $\tilde{\mathscr{P}}$ allowing Cassandra to learn the art of giving infallible $\{\text{sunny}, \text{rainy}\}$ predictions after a maximum of $\text{ch}(M, 0, \ldots, 0)$ wrong predictions.*

As in the case of Paul's betting strategy $\tilde{\mathscr{B}}$, a more detailed analysis shows that, in fact, $\text{ch}(M, 0, \ldots, 0) - 1$ wrong predictions suffice in most nontrivial cases. Corollary 9.1 gives a useful estimate of the rate of growth of q.

Thus, under the supervision of a team of M experts containing one e-fallible member i_*, a Turing machine P implementing strategy $\tilde{\mathscr{P}}$ can acquire infallible predicting capabilities, by trial, error and emulation, after a two-stage training, during which at most $q = \text{ch}(M, 0, \ldots, 0)$ wrong predictions are made. During the first stage, P looks for the e-fallible expert i_* using $\tilde{\mathscr{P}}$. As soon as i_* is detected, P becomes e'-fallible, where $e' = e - \lambda$ and λ is the number of wrong predictions made by i_* so far. The current number of P's wrong predictions is $\leq q - e + \lambda$. The first stage is over. Afterwards, P will just emulate i_*, making a maximum of e' wrong predictions: once the last mistake is made, the second stage also terminates, and P becomes infallible (together with its supervisor i_*).

Other Learning Models. We can now try to link our examples to other learning models in the literature, we reformulate the above prediction problem as follows.

For a suitably large fixed integer n, let us assume that the core of meteorological data about today's weather—that is sufficient to predict whether tomorrow will be a sunny or a rainy day—is completely described by some n-bit integer $\mathbf{x}$. Let $W = \{0, 1\}^n$ be the set of all these exhaustive descriptions. Any $\mathbf{x}_t \in W$ containing all relevant meteorological data on day t infallibly determines the weather forecast

$$f_*(\mathbf{x}_t) \in \{\text{sunny}, \text{rainy}\} = \{0, 1\}$$

for day $t + 1$ ($t = 1, 2, \ldots$), where $f_*: W \to \{\text{sunny}, \text{rainy}\}$ is a Boolean function transforming the set $\mathbf{x} \in W$ of today's meteorological data into an infallible prediction of tomorrow's weather.

We assume the existence of a team $S = \{0, \ldots, M-1\}$ of expert meteorologists. Each $i \in S$ is equipped with a Boolean function $f_i: W \to \{\text{sunny}, \text{rainy}\}$ transforming today's meteorological data into expert i's forecast for tomorrow. Precisely one expert, say i_*, is equipped with a function f_{i_*} that coincides with f_*, up to a maximum number e of input-output discrepancies. In other words, $e \geq |\{\mathbf{x} \in W \mid f_*(\mathbf{x}) \neq f_{i_*}(\mathbf{x})\}|$.

We must devise an algorithm A which, under the supervision of the experts in S, learns f_* by detecting and emulating i_*. On each day t, A receives in its input (a Boolean formula of $\lceil \log_2 M \rceil$ variables, representing) the set of those experts whose forecast for day $t + 1$ is "rainy". A now makes its own forecast $b_t \in \{\text{sunny}, \text{rainy}\}$, and at the end of day $t + 1$, A is told whether b_t or $1 - b_t$ was the correct forecast.

For each day $t = 1, 2, \ldots$, expert $i \in S$, and data $\mathbf{x}_t \in W$, let $\mathbf{f}_i^t$ denote the t-tuple of forecasts $\mathbf{f}_i^t = (f_i(\mathbf{x}_1), f_i(\mathbf{x}_2), \ldots, f_i(\mathbf{x}_t)) \in \{0, 1\}^t$. We say that a function $g: W \mapsto \{0, 1\}$ belongs to the e-*neighborhood* E_i of expert i iff for all $t = 1, 2, 3, \ldots$, the t-tuple of bits $(g(\mathbf{x}_1), g(\mathbf{x}_2), \ldots, g(\mathbf{x}_t))$ differs from $\mathbf{f}_i^t$ for at most e *distinct* $\mathbf{x}$'s. In other words, g and f_i coincide all over their common domain W, at up to e many exceptional points.

The existence of a unique e-fallible expert in the team S means that there exists precisely one $i_* \in S$ such that f_* belongs to the e-neighborhood E_{i_*} of i_*. The results of Sect. 9.3.3 yield a tight upper bound for the following.

Problem: Assuming that the target Boolean function f_* belongs to the e-neighborhood E_{i_*} of a unique expert $i_* \in S$, assuming no two days have exactly the same weather condition $\mathbf{x} \in W$, find an algorithm to learn f_* with the minimum number of wrong predictions.

In the final notes to this chapter, the reader will find more evidence and pointers to why and to what extent Cassandra's predicting strategy $\tilde{\mathscr{P}}$ of Corollary 9.2 can be thought of as a device to "computationally learn" a function f_* in the "hypothesis space" $\mathscr{H} = \bigcup_{i \in S} E_i$.

9.4 Bibliographic Notes

The seminal paper for computation learning is Valiant's [203]. The absolute mistake bound is defined in [142]. The description and the result given here are mainly based on [65] and [40], where a different mapping of advised prediction to the Ulam-Rényi game was presented. For a pleasant introductory reading on learning algorithms see also [28]. Rényi's probabilistic model can be found in [183].

The problem of predicting from expert advice, together with its many variants, is investigated by various authors, under various denominations, including "sequential compound decision problem" [25, 186], "universal prediction" [105], "universal coding" [193] and others. Littlestone and Warmuth [143], De Santis et al. [91] and Vovk [208] were among the first to consider this problem within the computational learning community (see also [39]).

Our supervised prediction model above is reminiscent of Littlestone's Mistake Bound Model ([142]; also see [12]). Here, too, one is interested in understanding a natural phenomenon described by some unknown function f. While f may be very complex, our ability to represent f suffers from all sorts of limitations, in time, space, interest, and expressive power. Considering f as our learning target, we may assume that input-output pairs

$$(\mathbf{x}_1, f(\mathbf{x}_1)), (\mathbf{x}_2, f(\mathbf{x}_2)), \ldots, (\mathbf{x}_t, f(\mathbf{x}_t))$$

are provided to us as experimental data about f. Our task is to form a tentative hypothesis h_t about f so that the following two conflicting desiderata are fulfilled: (i) matching experimental data and (ii) having a simple description. To fix ideas, let us assume that each $\mathbf{x}_i$ is an n-bit number, and that f is an n-ary Boolean function. We are interested in the actual representation of our tentative hypotheses about f as strings of symbols (say, as Boolean formulas). This yields a convenient tool to measure the complexity of the target concept to be learned, and is a prerequisite for the efficient learnability of f, a main issue in the theory of computational learning.

Very much as in the prediction problem of the previous section, in Littlestone's Mistake Bound Model, learning is understood as the result of trial and error. The learning process occurs in several rounds $t = 1, 2, 3, \ldots$: During each round an input value $\mathbf{x}_t \in \{0, 1\}^n$ is presented to the learning algorithm A. Depending on what A already knows about f from the past rounds, A must predict the value of $f(\mathbf{x}_t)$, and is penalized whenever its prediction is wrong.

Algorithmic learning with erroneous input data is also considered in the literature. For the particular case where the target function f to be learned is Boolean, Valiant [204] investigates *malicious errors* within the following setup: For some real number $0 \leq \beta \leq 1$, a coin flip with success probability β determines whether or not a pair $(\mathbf{x}, y)$ is erroneous. If no error occurs, then it is understood that $y = f(\mathbf{x})$. On the other hand, the occurrence of an error may indifferently produce both the cases $y = f(\mathbf{x})$ and $y = 1 - f(\mathbf{x})$.

Another interesting setup for learning with errors, called *classification noise*, is described by Angluin and Laird [14]. As in Valiant's model, a coin flip with success probability β decides which examples are to be affected by error. In contrast to Valiant's model, here an erroneous example always has the form $(\mathbf{x}, 1 - f(\mathbf{x}))$. This sort of error turns out to be more benign than Valiant's malicious errors.

We close with the following quotation by Blum [28]: "Perhaps one of the key lessons of this work in comparison to work of a more statistical nature is that one can remove all statistical assumptions about the data and still achieve extremely tight bounds (see Freund [110])."

9.5   Exercises

1. Prove Proposition 9.1.
2. Consider the betting game in Sect. 9.3.2. Show that for any integer $e \geq 1$ there exist infinitely many integers M such that $ch(M, 0, \ldots, 0) - e - 1 = \min\{n \mid M \sum_{j=0}^{e} \binom{n}{j} \leq 2^n\} - e - 1$ dollars will not enable Paul to infallibly learn Carole's secret number.
3. Consider a variant of the Ulam-Rényi game in which the goals of the players are swapped. Carole's strategy is to answer each question in order to make the game finish as early as possible. Conversely, Paul's aim is to have the game last as long as possible. For a search space of size M, how long can such a game last at most (in terms of number of questions asked by Paul) if the rules of the game allow Carole to lie up to e times?
4. Analyze the relationships between the game of Exercise 3 and the betting game in Sect. 9.3.2.
5. Let $U = \{1, \ldots, N\}$, and $T_1, \ldots, T_k$ be k randomly chosen subsets of U. Provide a lower bound on k such that for any fixed $x, y \in U$ there exists a j such that $x \in T_j$ and $y \notin T_j$.
6. Let $x_1 < x_2 < \cdots < x_n$, be n integers. Let $p > 1/2$ and $\epsilon > 0$. Given x, the goal is to determine the index i such that $x_i \leq x < x_i + 1$, or certify that either $x < x_1$ or $x > x_n$.
   A query consists of comparing x with some x_j. With probability $1 - p$ such a comparison will give an incorrect result.
   Consider a strategy that initially assigns probability $1/n$ to each candidate x_j. Then, in each round, the index j of the element to compare to x is chosen according to the current distribution. After each comparison the probabilities are updated according to the answer received.
   Show that such a strategy succeeds with probability $1 - \epsilon$ while using $O\left((1 - \epsilon)\frac{\log n}{1 - H(p)}\right)$ questions.

Bibliography

1. R. Ahlswede, L. Bäumer, N. Cai, H. Aydinian, V. Blinovsky, C. Deppe, H. Mashurian, *General Theory of Information Transfer and Combinatorics*. Lecture Notes in Computer Science, vol. 4123 (Springer, Berlin, 2006)
2. R. Ahlswede, F. Cicalese, C. Deppe, Searching with lies under error cost constraints. Discrete Appl. Math. **156**(9), 1444–1460 (2008)
3. R. Ahlswede, F. Cicalese, C. Deppe, U. Vaccaro, Two batch search with lie cost. *IEEE Trans. Inf. Theory* **55**(4), 1433–1439 (2009)
4. R. Ahlswede, I. Wegener, *Search Problems* (Wiley, Chichester, 1987)
5. M. Aigner, Searching with Lies. J. Comb. Theory Ser. A, **74**, 43–56 (1995)
6. M. Aigner, *Combinatorial Search* (Wiley, New York, 1988)
7. F. Albers, P. Damaschke, Delayed correction—binary search with errors made very simple but efficient. In Proc. CATS'98 Aust. Comput. Sci. Commun. **20**(3), 97–105 (1998)
8. S. Albers, M. Charikar, M. Mitzenmacher, Delayed information and action in on-line algorithms, in *Proceedings of 39th IEEE Symposium on Foundation of Computer Science (FOCS)* (1998), pp. 71–81
9. N. Alon, R. Beigel, S. Kasif, S. Rudich, B. Sudakov, Learning a hidden matching. SIAM J. Comput. 33(2), 487–501 (2004)
10. N. Alon, R. Hod, Optimal monotone encodings. IEEE Trans. Inf. Theory **55**(3), 1343–1353 (2009)
11. A. Ambainis, S.A. Bloch, D.L. Schweizer, Delayed binary search, or playing Twenty Questions with a procrastinator, in *Proceedings of 10th AMC SIAM Symposium on Discrete Algorithms (SODA)* (1999), pp. 844–845
12. D. Angluin, Queries and concept learning. Mach. Learn. **2**, 319–342 (1988)
13. D. Angluin, Computational learning theory: survey and selected bibliography, in *Proceedings of 24th ACM Symposium on the Theory of Computing (STOC)* (1992), pp. 351–369
14. D. Angluin, P. Laird, Learning from noisy examples. Mach. Learn. **2**, 343–370 (1988)
15. D. Angluin, P. Laird, Identifying k-CNF formulas from noisy example. DCS 478, Yale University, 1986
16. J. Aslam, A. Dhagat, Searching in the presence of linearly bounded errors, in *Proceedings of 23rd ACM Symposium on the Theory of Computing (STOC)* (1991), pp. 486–493
17. A. Bar-Noy, S. Kipnis, Designing broadcast algorithms in the postal model for message-passing systems. *Math. Syst. Theory* **27**, 431–452 (1994)
18. A. Bar-Noy, S. Kipnis, B. Shieber, An optimal algorithm for computing census functions in message-passing systems. *Parallel Process. Lett.* **3**(1), 19–23 (1993)

F. Cicalese, *Fault-Tolerant Search Algorithms*, Monographs in Theoretical Computer Science. An EATCS Series, DOI 10.1007/978-3-642-17327-1,
© Springer-Verlag Berlin Heidelberg 2013

19. L.A. Bassalygo, Nonbinary error-correcting codes with one-time error-free feedback. Probl. Inf. Transm. **41**(2), 125–129 (2005) [Translated from Problemy Peredachi Informatsii **2**, 63–67 (2005)]

20. L.A. Bassalygo, V.A. Zinoviev, V.K. Leontiev, N.I. Feldman, Nonexistence of perfect codes for some composite alphabets. Problemy Peredachi Informatsii **11**, 3–13 (1975) (in Russian) [English Translation: Probl. Inf. Transm. **11**, 181–189 (1975)]

21. J.M. Berger, A note on error detecting codes for asymmetric channels. Inf. Control **4**, 68–73 (1961)

22. E.R. Berlekamp, Block coding for the binary symmetric channel with noiseless, delayless feedback, in *Error-Correcting Codes*, ed. by H.B. Mann (Wiley, New York, 1968), pp. 61–68

23. E.R. Berlekamp, *Algebraic Coding Theory* (McGraw-Hill, New York, 1968)

24. D. Bertsekas, R. Gallager, *Data Networks*, 2nd edn. (Prentice Hall, Englewood Cliffs, 1992)

25. D. Blackwell, An analog of the minimax theorem for vector payoff. *Pac. J. Math.* **6**, 1–8 (1956)

26. M. Blaum, *Codes for Detecting and Correcting Unidirectional Errors* (IEEE Computer Society, Los Alamitos, 1993)

27. A. Blikle, Three-valued predicates for software specification and validation. Fundam. Inf. **14**, 387–410 (1991)

28. A. Blum, On-line algorithms in machine learning, in *Survey Talk given at Dagstuhl Workshop on On-line algorithms*, June 1996

29. A.D. Booth, *Inf. Control* **1**, 159–164 (1958)

30. R.S. Borgstrom, S. Rao Kosaraju, Comparison-based search in the presence of errors, in *Proceedings of 25th ACM Symposium on the Theory of Computing (STOC)* (1993), pp. 130–136

31. B. Bose, On systematic SEC-MUED codes, In *Digest of Papers, 11th Annual International Symposium on Fault-Tolerant Computer* (1981), pp. 265–267

32. B. Bose, T.R.N. Rao, Theory of Unidirectional error correcting/detecting codes. IEEE Trans. Comput. **C-31**(6), 520–530 (1982)

33. B. Bose, D.K. Pradhan, Optimal Unidirectional error detecting/correcting codes. IEEE Trans. Comput. **C-31**(6), 564–568 (1982)

34. R.C. Bose, S.S. Shrikhande, E.T. Parker, Further results in the construction of mutually orthogonal Latin squares and the falsity of a conjecture of Euler. Can. J. Math. **12**, 189–203 (1960)

35. G.S. Brodal, R. Fagerberg, I. Finocchi, F. Grandoni, G.F. Italiano, A.G. Jørgensen, G. Moruz, T. Mølhave, Optimal resilient dynamic dictionaries, in *Proceedings of the 15th European Symposium on Algorithms (ESA 2007)*. Lecture Notes in Computer Science, vol. 4698 (2007), pp. 347–358

36. A.E. Brouwer, T. Verhoeff, An updated table of minimum-distance bounds for binary linear codes. IEEE Trans. Inf. Theory **39**, 662–677 (1993)

37. A.E. Brouwer, J.B. Shearer, N.J.A. Sloane, W.D. Smith, A new table of constant weight codes. IEEE Trans. Inf. Theory **36**, 1334–1380 (1990)

38. P. Burcsi, F. Cicalese, G. Fici, Z. Lipták, Algorithms for jumbled pattern matching in strings. Int. J. Found. Comput. Sci. **23**(2), 357–374 (2012)

39. N. Cesa-Bianchi, Y. Freund, D.P. Helmbold, D. Haussler, R. Schapire, M.K. Warmuth, How to use expert advice. J. ACM **44**(3), 427–485 (1997)

40. N. Cesa-Bianchi, Y. Freund, D. Helmbold, M.K. Warmuth, On-line prediction and conversion strategies. Mach. Learn. **25**, 71–110 (1996)

41. C.C. Chang, Algebraic analysis of many valued logics. Trans. Am. Math. Soc. **88**, 467–490 (1958)

42. C.C. Chang, A new proof of the completeness of Lukasiewicz's axioms. Trans. Am. Math. Soc. **93**, 74–80 (1959)

43. W.Y.C. Chen, J.S. Oliveira, Implication algebras and the Metropolis-Rota axioms for cubic lattices. J. Algebra **171**, 383–396 (1995)

44. Y. Cheng, D.Z. Du, New constructions of one- and two-stage pooling designs. J. Comput. Biol. **15**(2), 195–205 (2008)

45. Y. Cheng, D.Z. Du, G. Lin, On the upper bounds of the minimum number of rows of disjunct matrices. Optim. Lett. **3**, 297–302 (2009)

46. B.S. Chlebus, D.R. Kowalski, Almost optimal explicit selectors, in *Proceedings of FCT 2005.* Lecture Notes in Computer Science, vol. 3623 (2005), pp. 270–280

47. M. Cheraghchi, Noise-resilient group testing: limitations and constructions, in *Proceedings of FCT 2009.* Lecture Notes in Computer Science, vol. 5699 (2009), pp. 62–73

48. M. Chrobak, L. Gasieniec, W. Rytter, Fast broadcasting and gossiping in radio networks. in *Proceedings of FOCS 2000* (2000), pp. 575–581

49. F. Cicalese, The multi-interval Ulam-Rényi game, in *Proceedings of FUN with Algorithms 2012.* Lecture Notes in Computer Science, vol. 7288 (2012), pp. 69–80

50. F. Cicalese, D. Mundici, Optimal binary search with two unreliable tests and minimum adaptiveness, in *Proceedings of the 7th European Symposium on Algorithms, ESA 1999.* Lecture Notes in Computer Science, vol. 1643 (1999), pp. 257–266

51. F. Cicalese, D. Mundici, Recent developments of feedback coding and its relations with many-valued logic, in *Proof, Computation and Agency - Logic at the Crossroads*, ed. by J. van Benthem et al. Synthese Library, vol. 352, part 3 (Springer, Berlin, 2011), pp. 115-131

52. F. Cicalese, U. Vaccaro, An improved heuristic for Ulam-Rényi Game. Inf. Process.Lett. **73**(3–4), 119–124 (2000)

53. F. Cicalese, D. Mundici, U. Vaccaro, Least adaptive optimal search with unreliable tests, in *Proceeding of SWAT 2000.* Lecture Notes in Computer Science, vol. 1851 (2000), pp. 547–562

54. F. Cicalese, D. Mundici, Perfect 2-fault tolerant search with minimum adaptiveness. Adv. Appl. Math. **25**, 65–101 (2000)

55. F. Cicalese, D. Mundici, Optimal coding with one asymmetric error: below the sphere packing bound, in *Proceedings of COCOON 2000.* Lecture Notes in Computer Science, vol. 1858 (2000), pp. 159–169

56. F. Cicalese, C. Deppe, D. Mundici, q-ary Ulam-Rényi game with weighted constrained lies, in *Proceedings of COCOON 2004.* Lecture Notes in Computer Science, vol. 3106 (2004), pp. 82–91

57. F. Cicalese, q-ary searching with lies, in *Proceedings of the 6th Italian Conference on Theoretical Computer Science (ICTCS '98)*, Prato (1998), pp. 228–240

58. F. Cicalese, U. Vaccaro, Optimal strategies against a liar. Theor. Comput. Sci., **230**, 167–193 (2000)

59. F. Cicalese, U. Vaccaro, Coping with delays and time-outs in binary search procedures, in *Proceedings of ISAAC 2000.* Lecture Notes in Computer Science, vol. 1969 (2000), pp. 96–107

60. F. Cicalese, D. Mundici, U. Vaccaro, Perfect, minimally adaptive, error-correcting searching strategies, in *Proceedings of IEEE ISIT 2000* (2000), p. 377

61. F. Cicalese, D. Mundici, U. Vaccaro, Least adaptive optimal search with unreliable tests. Theor. Comput. Sci. **270**(1–2), 877–893 (2001)

62. F. Cicalese, P. Damaschke, L. Tansini, S. Werth, Overlaps help: improved bounds for group testing with interval queries. Discrete Appl. Math. **155**(3), 288–299 (2007)

63. F. Cicalese, J. Quitzau, 2-Stage fault tolerant interval group testing, in *Proceedings of ISAAC 2007.* Lecture Notes in Computer Science, vol. 4835 (2007), pp. 858–868

64. F. Cicalese, P. Damaschke, U. Vaccaro, Optimal group testing algorithms with interval queries and their application to splice site detection. Int. J. Bioinform. Res. Appl. **1**(4), 363–388 (2005)

65. F. Cicalese, D. Mundici, Learning and the art of fault-tolerant guesswork, in *Adaptivity and Learning - An Interdisciplinary Debate*, ed. by R. Khün, R. Menzel, W. Menzel, U. Ratsch, M.M. Richter, I.O. Stamatescu (Springer, Berlin, 2003), pp. 115–140

66. F. Cicalese, D. Mundici, U. Vaccaro, Rota-Metropolis cubic logic and Ulam-Rényi games, in *Algebraic Combinatorics and Computer Science—A Tribute to Giancarlo Rota*, ed. by H. Crapo, D. Senato (Springer, Milano, 2001), pp. 197–244

67. F. Cicalese, T. Jacobs, E. Laber, C. Valentim, The binary identification problems for weighted trees. Theor. Comput. Sci. **459**, 100–112 (2012)

68. F. Cicalese, P.L. Erdős, Z. Lipták, A linear algorithm for string reconstruction in the reverse complement equivalence model. J. Discrete Algorithms **14**, 37–54 (2012)

69. F. Cicalese, E. Laber, The competitive evaluation complexity of monotone Boolean functions. *J. ACM* **58**(3) (2011) [Article no. 9]

70. F. Cicalese, T. Jacobs, E. Laber, M. Molinaro, On the complexity of searching in trees and partially ordered structures. Theor. Comput. Sci. **412**, 6879–6896 (2011)

71. P. Burcsi, F. Cicalese, G. Fici, Z. Lipták, On approximate jumbled pattern matching in strings. Theory Comput. Syst. **50**, 35–51 (2012)

72. F. Cicalese, M. Milanič, Graphs of separability at most two. Discrete Appl. Math. **160**, 685–696 (2012)

73. F. Cicalese, T. Gagie, E. Laber, M. Milanič, Competitive Boolean function evaluation. Beyond monotonicity and the symmetric case. Discrete Appl. Math. **159**, 1070–1078 (2011)

74. F. Cicalese, M. Milanič, Competitive evaluation of threshold functions in the priced information model. Ann. Oper. Res. **188**(1), 111–132 (2011)

75. F. Cicalese, U. Vaccaro, Superselectors: efficient constructions and applications, in *Proceedings of the 18th Annual European Symposium on Algorithms (ESA 2010)*. Lecture Notes in Computer Science, vol. 6346 (Springer, Berlin, 2010), pp. 207–218

76. R. Cignoli, I.M.L. D'Ottaviano, D. Mundici, *Algebraic Foundations of Many-Valued Reasoning*. Trends in Logic, Studia Logica Library, vol. 7 (Kluwer, Dordrecht, 2000)

77. A.E.F. Clementi, A. Monti, R. Silvestri, Selective families, superimposed codes, and broadcasting on unknown radio networks, in *Proceedings of Symposium on Discrete Algorithms (SODA'01)* (2001), pp. 709–718

78. S.D. Constantin, T.R.N. Rao, On the theory of binary asymmetric error correcting codes. Inf. Control **40**, 20–26 (1979)

79. Z.A. Cox Jr., X. Sun, Y. Qiu, Optimal and heuristic search for a hidden object in one dimension. IEEE Int. Conf. Syst. Man Cybern. Hum. Inf. Technol. **2**, 1252–1256 (1994)

80. D.E. Culler, R.M. Karp, D.A. Patterson, A. Sahay, E. Santos, K.E. Schauser, R. Subramonian, T. von Eicken, LogP: a practical model of parallel computation, in *Communications of the ACM*, November 1996

81. D. Culler, R. Karp, D. Patterson, A. Sahay, K.E. Schauser, E. Santos, R. Subramonian, T. von Eicken, LogP: toward a realistic model of parallel computation, in *ACM SIGPLAN Symposium on Principles and Practice of Parallel Programming* (1993), pp. 1–12

82. J. Czyzowicz, K. B. Lakshmanan, A. Pelc, Searching with a forbidden lie pattern in responses. Inf. Process. Lett. **37**, 127–132 (1991)

83. J. Czyzowicz, D. Mundici, A. Pelc, Ulam's searching game with lies. J. Comb. Theory Ser. A **52**, 62–76 (1989)

84. J. Czyzowicz, K.B. Lakshmanan, A. Pelc, Searching with local constraints on error patterns. Eur. J. Comb. **15**, 217–222 (1994)

85. A. De Bonis, U. Vaccaro, Improved algorithms for group testing with inhibitors. Inf. Process. Lett. **66**, 57–64 (1998)

86. A. De Bonis, New combinatorial structures with applications to efficient group testing with inhibitors. J. Comb. Optim. **15**, 77–94 (2008)

87. A. De Bonis, L. Gasieniec, U. Vaccaro, Optimal two-stage algorithms for group testing problems. SIAM J. Comput. **34**(5), 1253–1270 (2005)

88. P. Delsarte, Bounds for unrestricted codes, by linear programming. Philips Res. Rep. **27**, 272–289 (1972)

89. C. Deppe, Solution of Ulam's searching game with three lies or an optimal adaptive strategy for binary three-error-correcting-codes. Technical Report No. 98–036, University of Bielefeld, Fakultät für Mathematik

90. C. Deppe, Coding with feedback and searching with lies, in *Entropy, Search, Complexity*, vol. 16, ed. by I. Csiszár, Gy.O.H. Katona, G. Tardos. Bolyai Society Mathematical Studies (János Bolyai Mathematical Society and Springer, 2007), pp. 27–70

91. A. De Santis, G. Markowsky, M. Wegman, Learning probabilistic prediction functions, in *Proceedings of 29th IEEE Symposium on Foundation of Computer Science (FOCS)* (1988), pp. 110–119

92. A. Dhagat, P. Gács, P. Winkler, On playing "Twenty Questions" with a liar, in *Proceedings of 3rd Annual ACM SIAM Symposium on Discrete Algorithms (SODA 92)* (1992), pp. 16–22

93. R.L. Dobrushin, Information transmission in a channel with feedback. Theory Probab. Appl. **34**, 367–383 (1958) [Reprinted in: *Key Papers in the Development of Information Theory*, ed. by D. Slepian (IEEE, New York, 1974)]

94. D.Z. Du, F.K. Hwang, *Combinatorial Group Testing and its Applications*. Series on Applied Mathematics, vol. 12, 2nd edn. (World Scientific, Singapore, 2000)

95. D.Z. Du, F.K. Hwang, *Pooling Design and Nonadaptive Group Testing* (World Scientific, Singapore, 2006)

96. A.I. Dumey, Comput. Autom. **5**(12), 6–9 (1956)

97. I. Dumitriu, J. Spencer, The liar game over an arbitrary channel. Combinatorica **25**, 537–559 (2005)

98. I. Dumitriu, J. Spencer, The two-batch liar game over an arbitrary channel. SIAM J. Discrete Math. **19**, 1056–1064 (2006)

99. A.C. Dusseau, D.E. Culler, K.E. Schauser, R. Martin, Fast Parallel Sorting under LogP: Experience with the CM-5, In *IEEE Transaction on Parallel and Distributed Systems*, August 1996

100. A.G. D'yachkov, V.V. Rykov, Bounds of the length of disjunct codes. Probl. Control Inf. Theory **11**, 7–13 (1982)

101. A.G. D'yachkov, V.V. Rykov, A.M. Rashad, Superimposed distance codes. Probl. Control Inf. Theory **18**, 237–250 (1989)

102. P. Elias, *IBM F. Res. Dev.* **3**, 346–353 (1958)

103. M.A. Epstein, Algebraic decoding for a binary erasure channel. IRE Natl. Conv. Rec. **6**(4), 56–69 (1958)

104. M. Farach, S. Kannan, E. Knill, S. Muthukrishnan, Group testing problems with sequences in experimental molecular biology, in *Proceedings of the Compression and Complexity of Sequences 1997*, ed. by B. Carpentieri, A. De Santis, U. Vaccaro, J. Storer (1997), pp. 357–367

105. M. Feder, N. Merhav, M. Gutman, Universal prediction of individual sequences. IEEE Trans. Inf. Theory **38**, 1258–1270 (1992)

106. U. Feige, D. Peleg, P. Raghavan, E. Upfal, Computing with unreliable information, in *Proceedings of ACM Symposium on Theory of Computing (STOC)* (1990), pp. 128–137

107. I. Finocchi, G.F. Italiano, Sorting and searching in faulty memories. Algorithmica **52**, 309–332 (2008)

108. I. Finocchi, F. Grandoni, G.F. Italiano, Optimal resilient sorting and searching in the presence of dynamic memory faults, in *Proceedings of ICALP'06*. Lecture Notes in Computer Science, vol. 4051 (2006), pp. 286–298

109. I. Finocchi, F. Grandoni, G.F. Italiano, Resilient search trees, in *Proceedings of the ACM-SIAM Symposium on Discrete Algorithm (SODA'07)* (2007), pp. 547–555

110. Y. Freund, Predicting a binary sequence almost as well as the optimal biased coin, in *Proceedings of the 9th Annual Conference on Computational Learning Theory* (1996), pp. 89–98

111. C.V. Freiman, Optimal error detection codes for completely asymmetric binary channel. Inf. Control **5**, 64–71 (1962)

112. A.C. Gilbert, M.A. Iwen, M.J. Strauss, Group testing and sparse signal recovery, in *Proceedings of the 42nd Asilomar Conference on Signals, Systems, and Computers* (2008), pp. 1059–1063

113. M.J.E. Golay, Notes on digital coding. Proc. IEEE **37**, 657 (1949)

114. M. Golin, A. Schuster, Optimal point-to-point broadcast algorithms via lopsided trees. Discrete Appl. Math. **93**, 233–263 (1999)

115. W. Guzicki, Ulam's searching game with two lies. J. Comb. Theory Ser. A **54**, 1–19 (1990)

116. R.W. Hamming, Error detecting and error correcting codes. Bell Syst. Tech. J. **29**, 147–160 (1950)

117. R. Hähnle, W. Kernig, Verification of switch level design with many-valued logic, in *Proceedings of LPAR'93*. Lecture Notes in Artificial Intelligence, vol. 698 (1993), pp. 158–169

118. R. Hassin, M. Henig, Monotonicity and efficient computation of optimal dichotomous search. Discrete Appl. Math. **46**, 221–234 (1993)

119. R. Hill, Searching with lies, in *Surveys in Combinatorics*, ed. by P. Rowlinson (Cambridge University Press, Cambridge, 1995), pp. 41–70

120. R. Hill, J. Karim, E.R. Berlekamp, The solution of a problem of Ulam on searching with lies, in *Proceedings of IEEE ISIT 1998*, Cambridge (1998), p. 244

121. R. Hill, J.P. Karim, Searching with lies: the Ulam problem. Discrete Math. **106/107**, 273–283 (1992)

122. K. Hinderer, M. Stieglitz, On polychotomous search problems. Eur. J. Oper. Res. **73**, 279–294 (1994)

123. Y.-W. Hong, A. Scaglione, On multiple access for distributed dependent sources: a content-based group testing approach, in *Proceedings of the IEEE Information Theory Workshop, 2004 (ITW 2004)* (2004), pp. 298–303

124. Y.-W. Hong, A. Scaglione, Group testing for sensor networks: the value of asking the right questions, in *Conference Record of the Thirty-Eighth Asilomar Conference on Signals, Systems and Computers (COSSAC 2004)*, vol. 2 (2004), pp. 1297–1301

125. Y.-W. Hong, A. Scaglione, Generalized group testing for retrieving distributed information, in *Proceedings of the IEEE International Conference on Acoustics, Speech, and Signal Processing (ICASSP 2005)*, vol. 3 (2005), pp. 681–684

126. D.A. Huffman, Method for the construction of minimum redundancy codes. Proc. IRE **40**, 1098–1101 (1952)

127. P. Indyk, H.Q. Ngo, A. Rudra, Efficiently decodable non-adaptive group testing, in *Proceedings of 21st Annual Symposium on Discrete Algorithms (SODA)* (2010), pp. 1126–1142

128. D. Innes, Searching with a lie using only comparison questions (unpublished manuscript)

129. A.G. Jørgensen, G. Moruz, T. Mølhave, Priority queues resilient to memory faults, in *Proceedings of the 10th Workshop on Algorithms and Data Structures (WADS'07)*. Lecture Notes in Computer Science, vol. 4619 (2007), pp. 127–138

130. R. Karp, ISIT'98 plenary lecture report: variations on the theme of "Twenty Questions". IEEE Inf. Theory Soc. Newslett. **49**(1), 1–5 (1999)

131. G. Katona, Combinatorial search problems, in *A Survey of Combinatorial Theory* (North-Holland, Amsterdam, 1966), pp. 285–308

132. M. Kearns, M. Li, Learning in presence of malicious errors, in *Proceedings of 20th ACM Symposium on Theory of Computing (STOC)* (1988), pp. 267–280

133. C. Kenyon, A. Yao, On evaluating Boolean function with unreliable tests, Int. J. Found. Comput. Sci. **1**(1), 1–10 (1990)

134. E. Knill, Lower bounds for identifying subset members with subset queries, in *Proceedings of 6th ACM SIAM Symposium on Discrete Algorithms (SODA)* (1995), pp. 369–377

135. D. Knuth, *Searching and Sorting, The Art of Computer Programming*, vol. 3 (Addison-Wesley, Reading, 1998)

136. T. Kopelowitz, N. Talmon, Selection in the presence of memory faults, with applications to in-place resilient sorting. ArXiv (2012)

137. H.T. Kung, Synchronized and asynchronous parallel algorithms for multiprocessors, in *Algorithms and Complexity: New Directions and Recent Results*, ed. by J.F. Traub (Academic, London, 1979), pp. 153–200

138. E.L. Lawer, S. Sarkissian, An algorithm for "Ulam's Game" and its application to error correcting codes. Inf. Process. Lett. **56**, 89–93 (1995)

139. Y. Li, M.T. Thai, Z. Liu, W. Wu, Protein-protein interaction and group testing in bipartite graphs. Intl. J. Bioinform. Res. Appl. **1**(6), 414–419 (2005)

140. N. Linial, M. Sacks, Every poset has a central element. J. Comb. Theory Ser. A **40**, 195–210 (1985)

141. N. Linial, M. Sacks, Searching ordered structures. J. Algorithms **6**, 86–103 (1985)
142. N. Littlestone, Learning quickly when irrelevant attributes abound: a new linear-threshold algorithm. Mach. Learn. **2**, 285–318 (1988)
143. N. Littlestone, M.K. Warmuth, The weighted majority algorithm. Inf. Comput. **108**(2), 212–261 (1994)
144. J. Lukasiewicz, O Logice Trówartosciowej. *Ruch Filozoficzny* **5**, 170–171 (1920) [English Translation: J. Lukasiewicz, On three-valued logic, in *Selected Works* (North-Holland, Amsterdam, 1970), pp. 87–88]
145. F.J. MacWilliams, N.J.A. Sloane, *The Theory of Error-Correcting Codes* (North-Holland, Amsterdam, 1977)
146. A. Malinowski, k-ary searching with a lie. Ars Comb. **37**, 301–308 (1994)
147. J.J. Metzner, Improvements in block-retransmission schemes. IEEE Trans. Commun. **27**(2), 525–532 (1979)
148. R.J. McEliece, E.R. Rodemich, H.C. Rumsey, L.R. Welch, New upper bounds on the rate of a code via the Delsarte-MacWilliams inequalities. IEEE Trans. Inf. Theory **23**, 157–166 (1977)
149. E.F. Moore, C.E. Shannon, Reliable circuits using less reliable relays, part I. J. Franklin Inst. **262**, 191–208 (1956)
150. E.F. Moore, C.E. Shannon, Reliable circuits using less reliable relays, part II. J. Franklin Inst. **262**, 281–297 (1956)
151. D. Mundici, Ulam's game, Łukasiewicz logic and AF C^*-algebras. Fundam. Inf. **18**, 151–161 (1993)
152. D. Mundici, The C^*-algebras of three-valued logic, in *Proceedings of Logic Colloquium 1988, Padova*, ed. by R. Ferro, C. Bonotti, S. Valentini, A. Zanardo. *Studies in Logic and the Foundations of Mathematics* (North-Holland, Amsterdam, 1989), pp. 61–77
153. D. Mundici, The logic of Ulam's game with lies, in *Knowledge, Belief and Strategic Interaction*, ed. by C. Bicchieri, M.L. Dalla Chiara, Cambridge Studies in Probability, Induction, and Decision Theory (Cambridge University Press, 1992), pp. 275–284
154. D. Mundici, Fault-tolerance and Rota-Metropolis cubic logic, in *Paraconsistency, the Logical Way to the Inconsistented*, ed. by W.A. Carnielli, M.E. Coniglio, I.M.L. D'Ottaviano. Lecture Notes in Pure and Applied Mathematics, vol. 228 (Marcel Dekker, New York, 2002), pp. 397–410
155. D. Mundici, A. Trombetta, Optimal comparison strategies in Ulam's searching game with two errors. Theor. Comput. Sci. **182**, 217–232 (1997)
156. S. Muthukrishnan, On optimal strategies for searching in presence of errors, in *Proceedings of 5th ACM-SIAM Symposium on Discrete Algorithms (SODA'94)* (1994), pp. 680–689
157. A. Negro, M. Sereno, Ulam's Searching game with three lies. Adv. Appl. Math. **13**, 404–428 (1992)
158. M.B. Or, A. Hassidim, The Bayesian learner is optimal for noisy binary search (and pretty good for quantum as well), in *Proceedings of 49th Annual IEEE Symposium on Foundations of Computer Science (FOCS'08)* (2008), pp. 221–230
159. A. Pedrotti, Reliable RAM computation in the presence of noise. Ph.D. thesis, Scuola Normale Superiore, Pisa, 1998
160. A. Pelc, Searching games with errors—fifty years of coping with liars. Theor. Comput. Sci. **270**(1–2), 71–109 (2002)
161. A. Pelc, Detecting errors in searching games. J. Comb. Theory Ser. A **51**, 43–54 (1989)
162. A. Pelc, Solution of Ulam's problem on searching with a lie. J. Comb. Theory Ser. A **44**, 129–142 (1987)
163. A. Pelc, Lie patterns in search procedures. Theor. Comput. Sci. **47**, 61–69 (1986)
164. A. Pelc, Weakly adaptive comparison searching. Theor. Comput. Sci. **66**, 105–111 (1989)
165. A. Pelc, Detecting a counterfeit coin with unreliable weighing. Ars Comb. **27**, 185–202 (1989)
166. A. Pelc, Searching with permanently faulty tests. Ars Comb. **38**, 65–76 (1994)
167. A. Pelc, Searching with known error probability. Theor. Comput. Sci. **63**, 185–202 (1989)
168. A. Pelc, Prefix search with a lie. J. Comb. Theory Ser. A **48**, 165–173 (1988)
169. A. Pelc, Coding with bounded error fraction. Ars Comb. **24**, 17–22 (1987)

170. W.W. Peterson, IBM J. Res. Dev. **1**, 130–146 (1957)
171. W.W. Peterson, Encoding and error-correction procedures for Bose-Chaudhuri codes. IEEE Trans. Inf. Theory **6**, 459–470 (1960)
172. W.W. Peterson, E.J. Weldon, *Error-Correcting Codes* (MIT, Cambridge, 1971)
173. P.A. Pevzner, *Computational Molecular Biology: An Algorithmic Approach* (MIT, Cambridge, 2000)
174. C. Picard, *Theory of Questionnaires* (Gauthier-Villars, Paris, 1965)
175. J.R. Pierce, Optical channels: practical limits with photon counting. IEEE Trans. Comm. **COM-26**, 1819–1821 (1978)
176. N. Pippenger, On networks of noisy gates, in *Proceedings of 26th IEEE Symposium on Foundation of Computer Science (FOCS)* (1985), pp. 30–38
177. E. Porat, A. Rothschild, Explicit non-adaptive combinatorial group testing schemes. IEEE Trans. Inf. Theory **57**(12), 7982–7989 (2011)
178. E. Post, Introduction to a general theory of elementary propositions. Am. J. Math. **43**, 163–185 (1921)
179. Y. Tohma, Coding Techniques in Fault-tolerant, self-checking, and fail-safe circuits, in *Fault-Tolerant Computing, Theory and techniques*, ed. by D.K. Pradhan (Prentice-Hall, Englewood, 1986), pp. 336–411
180. B. Ravikumar, K. B. Lakshmanan, Coping with known patterns of lies in a search game. Theor. Comput. Sci. **33**, 85–94 (1984)
181. I.S. Reed, G. Solomon, Polynomial codes over certain finite fields. SIAM J. Appl. Math. **8**, 300–304 (1960)
182. A. Rényi, *Napló az információelméletről* (Gondolat, Budapest, 1976) [English translation: *A Diary on Information Theory* (Wiley, New York, 1984)]
183. A. Rényi, On a problem of information theory. MTA Mat. Kut. Int. Kozl. **6B**, 505–516 (1961)
184. A. Rényi, *Lecture Notes on the Theory of Search*. University of North Carolina at Chapel Hill, Institute of Statistics Mimeo Series No. 600.7 (1969)
185. R.L. Rivest, A.R. Meyer, D.J. Kleitman, K. Winklmann, J. Spencer, Coping with errors in binary search procedures. J. Comput. Syst. Sci. **20**, 396–404 (1980)
186. H. Robbins, Asymptotically subminimax solutions of compound statistical decision problems, in *Proceedings of 2nd Berkeley Symposium on Mathematical Statistics and Probability* (1951), pp. 131–148
187. G.-C. Rota, N. Metropolis, Combinatorial structure of the faces of the n-cube. SIAM J. Appl. Math. **35**, 689–694 (1978)
188. M. Ruszinkó, On the upper bound of the size of the r-cover-free families. J. Comb. Theory Ser. A **66**, 302–310 (1994)
189. M. Sereno, Binary search with errors and variable cost queries. Inf. Process. Lett. **68**(5), 261–270 (1998)
190. C.E. Shannon, A mathematical theory of communication. Bell Syst. Tech. J. **27**, 379–423, 623–658 (1948) [Reprinted in: *A Mathematical Theory of Communication*, ed. by C.E. Shannon, W. Weaver (University of Illinois Press, Urbana, 1963)]
191. C.E. Shannon, Communication in the presence of noise. Proc. IEEE **37**, 10–21 (1949)
192. C.E. Shannon, Zero-capacity of noisy channels. IEEE Trans. Inf. Theory **2**, 8–19 (1956)
193. J. Shtarkov, Universal sequential coding of single measures. Probl. Inf. Transm. **23**(3), 3–17 (1987)
194. R.C. Singleton, Maximum distance q-nary codes. IEEE Trans. Inf. Theory **10**, 116–118 (1964)
195. B. Sklar, *Digital Communications: Fundamentals and Applications* (Prentice-Hall, Englewood, 2001)
196. J. Spencer, Balancing games. J. Comb. Theory Ser. B **23**, 68–74 (1977)
197. J. Spencer, Guess a number with lying. Math. Mag. **57**, 105–108 (1984)
198. J. Spencer, Ulam's searching game with a fixed number of lies. Theor. Comput. Sci. **95**, 307–321 (1992)
199. J. Spencer, P. Winkler, Three thresholds for a liar. Comb. Probab. Comput. **1**, 81–93 (1992)

200. T.M. Thompson, *From Error-Correcting Codes through Sphere Packings to Simple Groups*. Carus Mathematical Monograph, vol. 21 (Mathematical Association of America, Washington, 1983)
201. A. Tietäväinen, On the nonexistence of perfect codes over finite fields. SIAM J. Appl. Math. **24**, 88–96 (1973) ·
202. S.M. Ulam, *Adventures of a Mathematician* (Scribner's, New York, 1976)
203. L.G. Valiant, A theory of the learnable. Commun. ACM **27**, 1134–1142 (1984)
204. L. Valiant, Learning disjunctions of conjunctions, in *Proceedings of 9th IJCAI* (1985), pp. 560–566
205. J.H. van Lint, *Introduction to Coding Theory* (Springer, Berlin, 1982)
206. J.H. van Lint, R.M. Wilson, *A Course in Combinatorics* (Cambridge University Press, Cambridge, 1992)
207. J. von Neumann, Probabilistic logics and the synthesis of reliable organisms from unreliable components, in *Automata Studies*, ed. by C. Shannon, J. McCarthy (Princeton University Press, Princeton, 1956), pp. 43–98
208. V. Vovk, Aggregating strategies, in *Proceedings of 3rd Annual Workshop on Computational Learning Theory* (1990), pp. 371–383
209. S.B. Wicker, V.K. Bhargava (ed.), *Reed-Solomon Codes and Their Applications* (Wiley, London, 1999)
210. S. Winograd, F.D. Cowan, *Reliable Computation in the Presence of Noise* (MIT, Cambridge, 1963)
211. W. Wu, Y. Li, C.H. Huang, D.Z. Du, Molecular biology and pooling design, in *Data Mining in Biomedicine*, vol. 7. Springer Optimization and Its Applications (Springer, Berlin, 2008), pp. 133–139
212. G. Xu, S.H. Sze, C.P. Liu, P.A. Pevzner, N. Arnheim, Gene hunting without sequencing genomic clones: finding exon boundaries in cDNAs. Genomics **47**(2), 171–179 (1998)
213. A.M. Yaglom, I.M. Yaglom, *Verojatnost' i Informacija* (Nakua, Moscow, 1957) [French Translation: *Probabilité et Information* (Dunod, Paris, 1969)]
214. S.A. Zenios, L.M. Wein, Pooled testing for HIV prevalence estimation: exploiting the dilution effect. Stat. Med. **17**, 1446–1467 (1998)
215. V.A. Zinoviev, V.K. Leontiev, The non-existence of perfect codes over Galois fields. Probl. Contr. Inf. Theory **2**, 123–132 (1973)
216. V.A. Zinoviev, G.L. Katsman, Universal code families. Inf. Theory Coding Theory **29**(2), 95–100 (1993)

Printed in the United States
By Bookmasters